TO PROVE A VILLAIN:

Shakespeare's Villains

Charles W. Reick

Dedicated to
Debbie Berry,
Wife, best friend and muse.
Without her, this book could not have
existed.

Special thanks to
Linda Schwartz
whose thoughtful editing and
suggestions greatly enhanced the
quality of this work.

Foreword

This book, more than ten years in the making, is not the work of a scholar, but of a fanboy. That is not to say it is without scholarship; it is founded on pretty solid research rooted in Shakespeare criticism. It relies on the close reading of the texts and attempts to look at the relevance of the texts to the concerns of Shakespeare's time and ours. It was written to exult rather than dissect the Bard and to help those folk who want to dip into the experience of his world and works instead of diving immediately into the deep end. It is designed for those who want to approach Shakespeare as a hobby, not a career.

To that end, I have chosen to self-publish. I want the book to be accessible and self-publishing seems the best way to do this. I have been frankly appalled by the increasing cost of book, particularly in the age of digital publishing. I am using Amazon because it allows me some degree on control over the price of the book and my goal, being comfortably retired, is to encourage the book to be read, not to pad a publisher's coffers or my own. Since this is my first attempt at self-publication, I am sure the final product will lack the polish of a professional edited and published book, but I hope that the readers will pardon the faults provide feedback to improve the second edition.

CONTENTS

INTRODUCTION

New Wine, Old Bottles

Some Shakespeare scholars might suggest, considering the forest of pages and oceans of ink devoted to the study of England's greatest dramatist, that there is nothing new to be said. Perhaps they are correct. Surely any aspiring commentator perusing the shelves of any local college library must be intimated when confronted with row after row of books, old and new, dealing with the Bard and his works. Add to these the numerous scholarly journals devoted to Shakespearean study and the countless dissertations dissecting his every play and poem, and it becomes apparent to all but the most arrogant of writers that there can indeed be nothing new to say. Lacking that level of arrogance, I will not promise anything new. I would, however, like to suggest that even if there is nothing new to say, there are ways to compound and express what has already been said in imaginative and interesting ways.

Directors of the stage and screen have been taking this approach to Shakespeare for centuries, interpreting (and editing and rewriting) the plays in new and interesting ways while remaining more or less faithful, if not literally true, to the original text. A recent example is the surprisingly popular *William Shakespeare's Romeo + Juliet* (1996), directed by Baz Luhrmann and featuring Leonardo DiCaprio and Clair Danes as the star-crossed lovers. In the film, Luhrmann recreates Shakespeare's Verona as a late 20th century, American, Venice Beach type of urbanscape. In his created world called Verona Beach, "a collage of modern and classic images, drawn from religion, theater, folklore, technology and pop art," Luhrmann lays his scene. The film's opening visual is a floating television emitting white noise. The channel changes and a 'talking head" newscaster appears on the screen to speak the lines of Shakespeare's prologue. The effect is to set the film firmly in a recognizably modern world where the language, customs and codes of Elizabethan England still hold sway. The opening image also informs the viewer that the film will be overtly media conscious; allusions to genre, style and technique abound. An MTV style montage of images introduces the principal players interspaced with religious icons and scenes of street violence and media coverage. The shots are underlined by a bombastic choral score that will remind viewers of the satanic theme of the *Omen* series and a sonorous voiceover of the first octave of the prologue.

The story proper opens with a brawl as it does in the play. The "Montague boys" are young Caucasian gang thugs dressed in open tropical shirts. They drive through the street of Verona Beach to the sound of Alternative Rock band *One Inch Punch,* yelling out at passing cars. Loud, disrespectful and abusive, they cover their cowardice with bravado. At a gas station, they encounter the Capulets, their more subdued and threatening rivals. The Capulets, recalling *West Side Story,* are clearly Hispanic in ethnicity and ready for a brawl at the slightest insult. They are led by black-clad Tybalt, brilliantly played by John Leguizamo, who also sports a bright red vest imprinted with an image of Jesus, extending the religious imagery of the opening montage. Words are exchanged and gunfire erupts. According to the Production Notes on the film's official web-page, the weaponry of the gang-bangers mimics the elaborately decorated weapons the Elizabethan nobles carried as extensions of their character and families. The guns of the gangs display beautiful idiosyncratic adornments ranging from florid family crests to images of the Madonna. The gunfight is choreographed to highlight Tybalt's cat-like grace and ferocity. To the brass and string soundtrack reminiscent of dozens of "spaghetti" westerns, Tybalt twirls, leaps and fires, part bullfighter, part Flamenco dancer. The duel culminates in an exploding gasoline pump and Captain Prince, the Verona Beach Chief of Police, interrupting a standoff between Tybalt and Benvolio.

This opening brawl, with its MTV style editing and its imbedded referencing of various film traditions and genres, is certainly attention getting and quite capable of drawing its intended adolescent audience into the film. Soon following the brawl, the audience is introduced to the solitary Romeo played by teen heartthrob Leonardo DiCaprio as a semi-sullen and alienated James Dean style rebel without a cause. His quiet manner and subdued wardrobe set him apart from the "Montague Boys" and it is noteworthy that he shares not a single scene with his parents. When he speaks his lines, DiCaprio reminds me of a typical high school student who is forced to read Shakespeare aloud in class. There is an adolescent awkwardness that fails to do justice to the beauty of Shakespeare's words, but which does in a manner communicate to his youthful audience. The cadence of his speech is the same as one might hear repeated in the mall on a Friday night, coming in spats with exaggerated emphasis. DiCaprio's Romeo is one of them. The audience recognizes him and identifies with him.

Claire /Danes and Leonardo DiCaprio in Baz Luhrmann's *William Shakespeare's Romeo + Juliet* (1996)

Juliet is another matter. Played by Claire Danes, Juliet speaks her lines with a grace worthy of Shakespeare. Additionally, she can speak volumes with an expression or gesture. As a result, Juliet is less immediately assessable to a young audience. Instead, Luhrmann allows Juliet's environment to define her. The audience is introduced to Juliet in her bedroom. Set designer Catherine Martin and costume designer Kym Barrett provide an entrée to Juliet in images more telling than Shakespeare's words. With its large carved mahogany bed, the room is full of stuffed animals and dolls set alongside pastel-colored saints, lighted angels, and an altar to the Virgin – "the inexplicable treasures of a little girl. [W]hen people see the sets," Martin comments, "they think of a rich girl's bedroom with religious iconography in a place where religion is still important."[1] These trappings set against the assured and competent delivery of Juliet's lines by Danes portrays a little girl transitioning to womanhood. She has the self-presence of a young woman, but has not yet cast off her childhood. Remember, she still has a nurse!

Juliet is rarely seen alone. Her bedroom is her only refuge, but it is a realm constantly invaded by her mother and her nurse. The Capulet mansion is paroled by security guards and monitored by security cameras. Unlike Romeo whom we repeatedly see against the background of his peers, the Montague and Capulet youth gangs, Juliet appears to have no peer group relationships. It is telling to note her bedroom has no telephone or television. She seems completely cut off from the outside world, insulated in a cocoon of protective isolation. In spite of this, Danes' Juliet exudes innocence and at the same time a wise beyond her years quality that allows the audience to believe this character is capable of doing the things the part demands. Of the two principals, Juliet is the more active. External forces buffet Romeo. He attends the "old accustom'd feast" of the Capulets at the urging of his friends He is provoked into killing Tybalt. He is driven from Verona by the law. He is ultimately undone by a trick of fate and circumstance. He is, indeed, fortune's fool. Juliet, on the other hand, makes her own decisions. It is she who proposes marriage. She who defies her father. She who holds Father Lawrence at bay with a loaded gun and a determined look. And it is she who tempts death by drinking Lawrence's potion. Commenting on Juliet for the production notes, Claire Danes has this to say:

> Juliet is a remarkable part because she is so determined and mature, but at the same time, she has an innocence to her, a youth and a freshness. She is very thoughtful, smart and passionate. She is an incredibly modern character. She makes her own decisions and takes fate into her own hands which, for a woman, was unheard of in Shakespeare's time.[2]

Considering Danes was only 16 years old when she made the film, we will forgive her forgetting Shakespeare's monarch, Queen Elizabeth I.

Luhrmann uses every opportunity to have the visuals illuminate the plot and language. The Capulet feast where Romeo and Juliet meet and fall in love is a garish grotesque affair that serves as the backdrop and a stark contrast for the quiet intensity of the young lovers. Gloria Capulet, Juliet's mother, is dressed as an aging Cleopatra playing against her husband's debauched and sweating Antony, a visual allusion to Shakespeare's later tragedy of love. In contrast, Juliet is dressed as a winged fairy and Romeo as a knight in armor. The lovers glimpse each other through the water of a tropical fish tank and time stops. The soundtrack fades to a soft, romantic ballad and as Daniel Rosenthal says in *Shakespeare on Screen* (2000), "love at first sight has never seemed more convincing."[3]

Costume designer Kym Barrett has said in the film's production notes that the use of such details and visual particulars help to define both the characters and Shakespeare's language.

> The language, for most people, is a little daunting at first. In most movies, what people say conveys the facts, but in this it will take the audience some time to get into listening to the language and relaxing into the rhythm of it. What I tried to do with the costumes was to help smooth the way. The first information they may get is through what they see. The language will reinforce what they see and, sooner or later, the audience,

> hopefully, won't be able to tell which came first. At one point during the story -- and for everyone, it'll be a different place -- the language and the visual information will become interchangeable. They won't actually have to think what a rose by any other name' means; it will just be clear. That will be the liberation for the audience. It's like the moment when you're learning a new language and, one night, you dream in that language and understand it. It's that click of consciousness.[4]

Probably the scene with the greatest emotional impact is, of course, the death scene in "Capels' monument." The confrontation with Paris is replaced by a police chase through the streets of Verona Beach leading to the vault where Juliet's body has been laid. Romeo enters the death chamber where Juliet is surrounded by "2000 flickering candles, a host of Juliet's porcelain saints and angels and the gilded glow of ornate candelabras. There are hundreds of white flowers fill[ing] the church...White floral crosses with brightly-colored plastic centers, bordered by a thin halo of blue neon, line the aisle."[5] The slick marble floors look like still pools of water, harkening back to the displaced balcony scene that had taken place in Capulet's pool. Unfortunately, DiCaprio is unable to rise to the pathos of the scene. He delivers his lines in the same dull recitation that dominates most of his performance, but Luhrmann saves the scene by introducing a plot twist not usually seen in performance. Juliet awakens just before Romeo drinks the poison. As she reaches out to him, he downs the lethal potion. Her hand touches his arm and, startled, he sees her alive with his dying eyes. Juliet, realizing what Romeo has done, takes up his gun and shoots herself in the head. The heightened emotion coming from the irony a tragedy nearly averted compensates for DiCaprio's weak performance as does Danes hopeless grief and resignation so effectively communicated in her face.

Although the script is severely edited in the film, all the words spoken are those penned by Shakespeare. The plot is unaltered in any important way. What Luhrmann has done is up-date the setting, dress and accessories of the play to allow a youthful audience access to the beauty of Shakespeare's language and story. That is, he has compounded and expressed what has already been said hundreds of times in the classroom, on the stage and on the screen in a new and interesting way. The $147 million worldwide box office is testimony to the entertainment value of the film, but where exactly is its appeal; in its substance or in its style? Did the audience flock to see Shakespeare presented in a new or interesting way or to see a Leonardo DiCaprio action film hyped on MTV and during episodes of *Friends* and *The X-files*? Commenting on the films youthful audience, Bernard Weinraub wrote, "It's doubtful...that it is Shakespeare's themes or language that is luring teenagers to movie houses. There are several Shakespeare films in release – Al Pacino's *Looking for Richard* and *Twelfth Night* with Helena Bonham Carter – and neither has done very well."[6] Not surprisingly, president of marketing for Fox Filmed Entertainment, Bob Harper said "The reason we made this movie is we felt there was an audience for this story that hadn't heard it on their own terms yet."[7] Janet Mastin at the *New York Times* took a middle ground when reviewing the film on its opening weekend, calling it "a witty and sometimes successful experiment, an attempt to reinvent Romeo and Juliet in the hyperkinetic vocabulary of postmodern kitsch." In the same article, she describes it as "a classic play thrown in the path of a subway train." Mastin asked, "where is the audience?"[8] She found out when teens stormed the theaters and the film generated $11.6 million during its opening weekend. I would ask, did the audience get its money's worth? Did the teens leave the Cineplex hungry to rush the libraries is search of more Shakespeare or did they simply peruse the lobby cards for the next action-adventure flick to fill a Friday evening? In the final analysis, is *William Shakespeare's Romeo + Juliet* a cleaver and faithful rendering of Shakespeare's treatise on fate and failed love or is it simply a spectacle that in the end is full of sound and fury, signifying nothing?

Being an optimist, I believe the Luhrmann film and in fact all the Shakespeare films of the past two decades serve as an invitation to the rich world of Shakespeare and his ideas. We are fortunate in that we have access to a large portion of Shakespeare's canon on film for viewing and reviewing. We can study his language and his thoughts at our leisure. We can ponder how contemporary actors and directors interpret and recreate the world's greatest dramas. These films invite discussion. What, however, seems lacking in spite of the volumes of scholarly books that line the library shelves are a sufficient number of resources for the everyman who feels encouraged to engage with Shakespeare by today's filmic treatments.   My goal in this volume is to provide such a resource by focusing on Shakespeare's villains. Why villains? Because they are fun and fascinating. Because they represent some of Shakespeare's most vividly drawn characters. Because they invite discussion of themes such as the nature of justice and of evil that are as relevant today as they were in Shakespeare's day.

In evidence that villains can be fun, I offer Edward Lionheart, the central protagonist of the 1973 black comedy/thriller/horror film, *Theater of Blood*.

Box art from Midnight Movies release of United Artist's *Theater of Blood* (1973).

Lionheart, brilliantly played by Vincent Price in what has been said to be his favorite role, is systematically murdering nine of London's leading theater critics who deprived him of a best actor's award he believed he had earned starring in a nine play Shakespeare season. Using the "tragic flaws" of the critics against them, Lionheart with the assistance of his daughter and his meth-drinking groundlings/derelicts orchestrates each murder as a set piece from one of the plays. The film's opening title sequence is interspaced with short violent cuts from silent Shakespeare films setting the scene for what is to follow. The story begins with George Maxwell, theater critic and local housing association chairman, being called to assist the police in rousting a pack of squatters from an abandoned building. Maxwell's wife warns him against going, citing a dream she had where Maxwell was torn apart by a pack of wild lions. His horoscope also warns that March will be a bad month for him. The date is March 15th. He proudly announces that he must go because the circumstances "need someone with real authority." Only the dullest of moviegoers would miss the allusions.

Arriving at the abandoned building, Maxwell is met by two constables and a rabble of filthy derelicts. His attempts to roust the vagabonds only incites them and they turn on the critic with broken bottles and other makeshift weapons. As he is ripped and torn, Maxwell looks to the constables who watch impassively and as he staggers to them, the taller of the two speaks from the third act of Shakespeare's *Julius Caesar*.

> *O pardon me, thou bleeding piece of flesh*
> *That I am so meek and gentle with these butchers.*
>
> (JC, III, 1, 154-55) *

Lionheart then reveals himself to the dying Maxwell and launches into the famous Antony speech from *Julius Caesar* which he begins in the tenement and ends in an abandoned theater which serves as Lionheart's center of operations.

The second victim, Hector Snipe, is lured to the theater with a promise to interview Lionheart who all believe to be dead by suicide following his loss of the Critics' Circle Award for best actor two years prior to the events of the film. As Snipe enters the theater, Lionheart intones

> *Look, Hector, how the sun begins to set,*
> *How ugly night comes breathing at his heels;*
> *Even with the vail and darkening of the sun,*
> *To close the day up, Hector's life is done.*
>
> (T&C, V, 7, 5-9)

This quote is a little more difficult for the average audience as it is drawn from the fifth act of Shakespeare's *Troilus and Cressida*, a tragic-comedy about the Trojan War. Lionheart presents himself before Snipe, costumed as the Greek champion Achilles, and then proceeds to berate him for his unfair review of Lionheart in his production of *Troilus and Cressida*. Calling for his derelicts to restrain the now panicked Snipe, Lionheart again quotes from *Troilus and Cressida*

> *The dragon wing of night o'erspreads the earth,*
> *And strickler-like, the armies separate.*
> *My half-supp'd sword that frankly would have fed,*
> *Pleased with this dainty bait, thus goes to bed.*
>
> (T&C, V, 7, 17-20)

and on the final word, thrusts a spear through Hector Snipe.

The scene shifts to the graveside ceremony for the murdered George Maxwell. As the service ends, the mourners, including the remaining members of the critics' circle move away from the grave and reveal Lionheart, heavily disguised as a gravedigger, sitting on a headstone. He murmurs a few lines from Hamlet, and then a horse galloping down the cemetery pathway, dragging the mutilated body of Hector Snipe, interrupts the graveside scene.

Up to this point, the film has taken a relatively serious tone, with Price delivering his lines in a respectful, if hammy, manner consistent with his character. Vincent Price was the perfect actor for this part. He was a theatrically trained actor who was at odds with the method acing of the last-half of the 20th century. Gaining popularity in the 50's and 60's as a successor to Boris Karloff and Bela Lugosi in the horror film genre, Price was never able to break out into more serious film roles. Critically, he was always accused of over-acting, a by-product of his theatrical training with its booming delivery and exaggerated gestures. Nevertheless, his popularity continued well into the 80"s. He often expressed an interest in performing Shakespeare. Early in his career, he had an opportunity to play George, Duke of Clarence in the non-Shakespearean *Tower of London* (1939) with Basil Rathbone playing Richard III. Twenty-three years later, in the 1962 remake of *Tower of London*, Price graduated to the role of Richard. In *Theater of Blood*, Price has the gratifying experience of speaking lines from many of Shakespeare great and not so great dramas and to do them on his own terms, showing off both his acting skills and his wry sense of self-parody.

Following the graveside scene, the film takes a silly turn with the third murder descending into black comedy. Smuggled into the bedroom of critic Horace Sprout in a huge crate, Lionheart emerges in full surgical garb, sedates Sprout and his wife, and then surgically removes the critic's head. There are no clever Shakespearean lines delivered (perhaps because there are no outstanding lines in *Cymbeline,* the play here referenced in the murder). In the morning, the wife awakens to find the decapitated body of her husband in bed beside her, mimicking the scene in *Cymbeline* when Imogen awakens next to the headless body of Cloten.

By now, it is becoming clear to the police, headed by Inspector Boot (Milo O'Shea who played Friar Lawrence in Franco Zeffirelli's 1968 film, *Romeo and Juliet*) that the remaining Critics' Circle members are at risk and he places each under police protection. Unfortunately, this decision comes too late to help the fourth victim, Trevor Dickman, the Circle's lecher. Lured to the abandoned theater, Dickman plays Antonia to Lionheart's Shylock from *The Merchant of Venice*. In probably the best Shakespearean performance of the film, Price presents a chilling Shylock, mixing lines from Act I, scene 3 with others from Act IV, scene 1 fluidly and with real malevolence. In the end, he has the temerity to re-write the source work and in this performance, Antonia losses his pound of flesh.

Lionheart/Shylock (Vincent Price) prepares to get his pound of flesh in United Artist's *Theater of Blood* (1973).

In spite of the police guards, the murders continue apace. The next to go is Oliver Larding who, while attending a wine tasting at Geo. Clarence & Son (a London wine merchant), is drowned in a vat of malmsey on the order of Lionheart's Richard III. His demise is followed by the murder of Maisie Psaltery, smothered by her husband, critic Solomon Psaltery, after Lionheart persuades him that Maisie has been unfaithful. After the police arrive and Psaltery is led away, the ever insightful Inspector Boot, obviously unfamiliar with *Othello*, wonders, "How does this fit into Lionheart's scheme? After all, Mrs. Psaltery is dead, not her husband." It is left to Peregrine Devlin, the leader of the Critics' Circle, to answer, "He's as good as dead, isn't he? At his age, he'll never leave prison alive. No, Lionheart has destroyed him just as certainly as if he had murdered him." Meanwhile, the only female member of the Circle, Chloe Moon is driven to her hairdresser by her police guard. Inside, she is greeted by Lionheart who is disguised as a hairdresser so flamboyantly gay that he is uncomfortable to watch today. Once Moon is connected to the hair curlers, Lionheart reveals himself and restrains the unfortunate critic in the chair and quoting from *Henry VI, Part I*, throws a switch channeling current to the hair curlers and burning Moon to death is an updating of the fiery death of Joan of Arc.

What follows is the film's most infamous scene taken from Shakespeare's most infamous play, *Titus Andronicus*. Meredith Merridew is played by comedic character actor, Robert Morley as another flagrantly homosexual, complete with lavender suit and a pair of poodles. When he arrives at his home under full police guard, he is greeted by Lionheart, this time disguised as a French chef from the TV show, *This is Your Dish*. The pretense is that the chef prepares a dish for the selected guest and in this performance a pie has been prepared for Merridew. As the critic savors the dish, he inquiries about the whereabouts of his poodles, his "babies," and Lionheart recites

> *Why, there they are, but baked in this pie,*
> *Whereof their mother daintily hath fed.*
> *Eating the flesh that she herself hath bred,*
>
> (TA, V, 3, 60-62)

While the implication of the words settles on Merridew, Lionheart uncovers a silver dish revealing the heads of the poodles set upon a pair of pastries. The shocked critic is quickly subdued and then force feed the remainder of the poodle pie through a funnel, choking to death on the baked flesh of his "babies."

To complete his revenge, only one critic remains, Lionheart's arch nemesis, Peregrine Devlin. Lionheart's daughter, Edwina serves as a lure to enable Devlin's abduction. Awakening from a blow to the head, Devlin finds himself strapped to a chair in Lionheart's lair. Lionheart is surrounded by his rabble, sporting grotesque masks of the now deceased members of the Critics' Circle. Lionheart sitting regally on the stage demands that Devlin relive the award ceremony and this time present the prize the "correct" nominee. When Devlin predictably refuses, a pair of daggers mounted on tracks is slowly rolled toward his eyes, threatening Devlin with the fate of Gloucester in *King Lear*. Edwina at her father's direction takes on the role of presenter and awards Lionheart his coveted prize. The triumph is short-lived as police sirens surround the theater. Lionheart taking torches in his hands sets fire to theater shouting, "Burn, burn, come fire, consume this petty world and in its ashes, let my memories lie." Panic breaks out among Lionheart's followers and in the ensuing melee, Edwina is clubbed by one of the rabble. In a poignant death scene drawn from *King Lear*, Edwina dying in her father's arms asks "How does my royal lord? How fares Your Majesty?" Lionheart replies in Lear's word,

> *You do me wrong to take me out o' the grave,*
> *Thou art a soul in bliss; but I am bound*
> *Upon a wheel of fire, that mine own eyes*
> *Do scold like molten lead.*
>
> (KL, IV, 7, 44-47)

As the police rush in to release Devlin, Lionheart takes up his daughter in his arms and climbs to the roof of the burning building. Turning to the crowd below, he cries

> Had our your tongues and eyes, I'd use them so
> That heaven's vault should crack. She's gone forever.
> I know when one is dead and one is living;
> She's dead as earth.
>
> (KL, V, 3, 24-27)

Flames shoot up from the theater below, the roof collapses and Lionheart falls to his death where he lived.

Theater of Blood, although dated by its 1970's styles, still holds up because of a witty and intelligent script and Vincent Price's outstanding performance. It is great fun with its mix of thrills, black humor, and classical references to the works of Shakespeare. The film offers up an introduction to Shakespeare to the uninitiated by presenting quotes and scenes from Shakespeare's great and not so great dramas. Script writer Anthony Greville-Bell and director Douglas Hickox not only go for the low hanging fruit of *Julius Caesar*, *Othello*, and *Richard III*, but also include provocative scene from less known works including *Troilus and Cressida*, *Henry VI, Part I*, and the much maligned *Titus Andronicus*. Working in the Elizabethan tradition of the revenge tragedy, the villainous Lionheart at once recalls the two dimensional cartoon villain of Christopher Marlowe's *The Jew of Malta* and still manages to invoke the complex pathos of Shakespeare's *King Lear*. The film invites thoughts about the meaning of justice and evil. Lionheart, the villain of the piece, although a maniacal, supremely egotistical killer, is the most likable character of the story. The police are laughable louts and the critics are riddled with vices, callousness and inflated self-importance. We feel little sorrow over their gruesome fates, but for Lionheart, as he holds his dying daughter in his arms, we feel a real sympathy. We in the audience are conflicted because Lionheart is without doubt the villain of the piece. There is no reasonable justification for the excesses of his revenge. He has become a sadistic killing machine, but we are nevertheless drawn to him by his cunning and inventiveness. We feel his rage and his pain as he is ridiculed by the critics and we feel his grief for the death of his daughter. In the end, are we willing to give Lionheart a pass, declaring him innocent by reason of insanity?

Like Edward Lionheart, Shakespeare's villains tend to invoke a degree of interest and sympathy unlike the villains of any of Shakespeare's predecessors or contemporaries. Harold Bloom, the noted Shakespeare scholar, has credited Shakespeare with "inventing the human." By this he means that Shakespeare has created characters that reflect human nature with a range of virtues and vices, filled with ambiguities and contradictions. Shakespeare moved his characters beyond the allegories and types that peopled the drama of his predecessors in the theater and breathed life into them, creating what Percy Shelley called "forms more real than living men." [9]   Shakespeare's characters were based on "types", the foils, doubles, vices, fools, and strangers. These "types" were immediately recognizable to his audience, but Shakespeare would infuse these characters with a life beyond the play. In a single line or two, he could suggest an entire backstory for a character. Often their motives are obscure and their actions are as inexplicable as those of the weird neighbor who lives down the block. His characters are neither paragons of virtue nor pits of depravity. Even the heroic Henry V displays Machiavellian motives for his war in France and the fiendish Aaron in *Titus Andronicus* is willing to sacrifice himself to insure the safety of his son.   On the other hand, Shakespeare often omits key scenes or withholds important information thereby inviting the performers and audience to fill in the blanks based on their individual biases and backgrounds. The "real" motive for Iago's attack on Othello remains a source of discussion and interpretation as does the cause and impact of the Macbeths' childlessness on their actions.

For Professor Bloom, Hamlet and Falstaff represent Shakespeare's supreme creations; for me, it is his villains.   In Hamlet and Falstaff we have creatures fashioned whole from the dust and animated by the divine breath of the Bard. In the villains we can see evolution; characters crawling up from primal ooze of the cartoonish Aaron in *Titus Andronicus* to the emotional complexity of Shylock in *The Merchant of Venice* to what Samuel Coleridge called the "motiveless malignity" of *Othello*'s Iago.   Shakespeare's villains are active characters, the engines that drive many of Shakespeare's narratives. Tamora works her revenge on Titus Andronicus and his family. Richard III systematically eliminates all obstacles that stand between him and the throne of England. Shylock demands his pound of flesh.   Iago manipulates reality to drive Othello mad.   Muriel C. Bradbrook noted that Elizabethan villains were "hardly ever interesting. Their business was to complicate the action and produce the tragic situation."[10] Charles Norton Coe wrote that Elizabethan villains "were accepted with or without motivation. They were accepted as types because they were black like Aaron, deformed like Richard III, Italian like Iago or illegitimate like Edmund." Coe goes on to say that "nineteenth century critics [mistakenly in his opinion] overlook...convention[s] and extend sympathy to villains like Shylock."[11] It is precisely the genius of Shakespeare, I believe, that he works with the conventions of his theatrical tradition and builds on then to humanize his characters. One needs only to compare Christopher Marlowe's Barabas, *The Jew of Malta* with

Shakespeare's Shylock to see what the convention looked like and compare that with what Shakespeare was able to do with the convention.

Jews were frequently the evil or comic villains of Elizabethan drama. Portrayed as Machiavellian or greedy or both, they were not generally complex characters. Christopher Marlowe, created such a character in his play *The Jew of Malta*, written in 1589 -- nearly a decade before Shakespeare's *The Merchant of Venice*. Both Barabas in *The Jew of Malta* and Shylock are money-lenders and they both have daughters who leave home, but there the similarity ends. Barabas is an over-the-top villain who steals, cheats, and murders until he finally meets a gruesome end. Shakespeare's characterization of Shylock broke with theatrical tradition. Shylock is a complex man whose actions can be understood and who can elicit understanding from his audience.

Christopher Marlowe's, *The Jew of Malta*, is thought to have been performed as early as 1590, although the first recorded performance was in February of 1592. Published in 1633, the title page describes the play as the "Famous Tragedy of the Rich Jew of Malta," leaving one to wonder, in the absence of a tragic hero, why it would be titled a tragedy. The play opens with the spirit of Machiavelli, an arch-villain for the English, who serves up a prologue that introduces the central theme of the drama: hypocrisy. He says

> *Admir'd I am of those that hate me most.*
> *Though some speak openly against my books,*
> *Yet will they read me, and thereby attain*
> *To Peter's throne....*
>
> *(JM, Prologue: 10-13)* **

calling attention to the hypocrites who openly attack his writings but covertly employee his methods. He then introduces the protagonist of the play:

> *...a Jew*
> *Who smiles to see how full his bags are cramm'd;*
> *Which money was not got without my means,*
> *I crave but this, -- grace him as he deserves,*
> *And let him not be entertain'd the worse*
> *Because he favours me.*
>
> *(JM, Prologue: 30-35)*

The prologue frames the chief conflict of the story as a battle between covert Christian Machiavellians and the overtly Machiavellian Jew. Marlowe himself was outspokenly critical of religion in general, so the callous and hypocritical Christians in this play do not come off particularly well. The fact that they are Catholic makes his position acceptable to his audience. Neither does the Jew not garner any respect on the basis of his religion, but he does seem to enjoy, in spite of his monstrous deeds, the favor of the playwright because he is an outsider and an over-reacher using whatever means necessary to make his way in the world. There is no hypocrisy in the Jew; he is openly and gleefully villainous. For Marlowe, who's other protagonists from Tamburlaine to Doctor Faustus were men set apart by their talents; the Jew is a kind of admirable super-villain, awe-inspiring in his strength of will. The fact that the Jew may have been thought of by Marlowe in some manner a hero by defying a deck stacked against him and that this hero fails to achieve his goals in the end, may suggest why the playwright titled the drama a tragedy.

The first act finds the Jew, Barabas, sitting in his counting house surrounded by heaping bags of gold. To further advance the stereotype, Barabas would most likely be wearing a large false nose, bright red wig and a long, coarse gabardine (a cloak-like garment) that was the traditional "costume" of the Jew on the Elizabethan stage.[12] As he revels in his wealth, he is interrupted by three fellow Jews who inform him that the Turks have arrived in Malta and that all the Jews in the city are called to the Senate House. We learn that Malta has for ten years failed to pay the tribute owed to the Turks and the Jews speculate that they have come to collect or wage war. At this, Barabas first shows the depths of his villainy in an aside to the audience.

> ..let 'em combat, conquer, and kill all.
> So they spare me, my daughter, and my wealth.
> (JM, I, 1, 55-56)

The scene shifts to the Senate House where the speculation of the Jews is confirmed. The Turks have demanded payment of the ten year tribute in full. Should Malta fail to comply within a month, the city will be placed under siege. Ferneze, the governor of Malta, elects to raise the tribute by seizing one half of the total wealth of the city's Jews, explaining that Malta is subjected to the Turks as a heavenly punishment for their tolerance of Jews in their community. Outraged, Barabas protests and for doing so is stripped of all his wealth and possessions. When the governor attempts to further justify the seizure by blaming the Jew's "inherent sin", Barabas cries out at the hypocrisy:

> What, bring you Scripture to confirm your wrong?

Preach me not out of my possessions.

(JM, I, 2, 14-15)

The house of Barabas has been seized and converted to a nunnery, but within it he has secreted gold and jewels. To gain access to his hidden hoard, he has his daughter, Abigail, enter the nunnery as a novice and she is able to smuggle the treasures out to her father. With his restored resources, Barabas sets out to have his revenge. First, as most Elizabethan villain-revengers do, he acquires an accomplice, Ithamore, a Moorish slave to aid him in his venture. We find they share a penchant for villainy. Barabas says

> *...I walk abroad a-nights,*
> *And kill sick people moaning under walls.*
> *Sometimes I go about and poison wells;*
> *...I studies physics, and began*
> *To practice first upon the Italians;*
> *There I enriched the priests with burial,*
> *And, after that, was I an engineer,*
> *And in the wars 'twixt France and Germany*
> *Slew friend and enemy with my stratagems:*
> *Then after that was I a usurer,*
> *And with extorting, cozening, forfeiting,*
> *And tricks belonging to unto broker,*
> *I fill'd the gaols with bankrupts in a year,*
> *And with young orphans planted hospitals;*
> *(JM, II, 3, 179-181, 186-187, 191-198)*

Up to this point, Barabas has been portrayed as a perhaps unpleasant fellow, but one more sinned against than sinning. Now he is revealed for the villain that he is. Ithamore, when asked by Barabas how he has spent his time, responds

> *In setting Christian villages on fire,*
> *Chaining of eunuchs, binding galley slaves.*
> *One time I was an hostler in an inn,*
> *And in the night time secretly would I steal*
> *To travelers chambers and cut their throats.*
> *(JM, II, 3, 208-212)*

So here we have a convenient juncture of two serial killers, one a Jew, the other a Moor, who are bound together by bloodlust and a shared hatred of Christians.

With the help of Ithamore, Barabas manipulates the Governor's son, Lodowick, and his friend, Mathias, into fighting over the affections of Abigail. An unforeseen consequence of his plan is that Abigail falls in love with Mathias and is appalled when the friends kill one another in a duel arranged by her father. In a fit of remorse, Abigail runs away to become a Christian nun. In retribution, Barabas then goes on to poison her along with the whole of the nunnery. In a deathbed confession to Friar Barnadine, Abigail denounces her father and reveals his role in the deaths of Lodowick and Mathias. Straightaway, Barnadine accompanied by another friar, Jacomo, confronts Barabas with his crime. The Jew, in true Machiavellian fashion, dissembles and swears to convert to Christianity and donate all his wealth to the Church. Catching Barnadine alone, Barabas and Ithamore strangle the friar and then frame Jacomo for the murder.

Back-grounding these actions, Malta with the backing of Spain, decides to reject the Turks demand for tribute and Malta comes under siege. Ithamore falls in love with a prostitute and conspires with her criminal friend to blackmail and expose Barabas. Barabas, in what was probably a broadly comedic scene, disguises himself as a French musician and enters the den of the courtesan to uncover their plans and then poison them. Before the poison works its effect, the prostitute betrays Barabas and Ithamore to the governor, and when confronted with their crimes, Ithamore confesses all and dies along with his co-conspirators. Anticipating his arrest, Barabas has prepared and now drinks a draught "of poppy and cold mandrake juice" that simulates death. Taken for dead and cast outside the city, Barabas is left alone to continue his nefarious plans.

> *I'll be reveng'd on this accursed town;*
> *For by my means [the Turks] will enter in.*
> *I'll help to slay their children and their wives,*
> *To fire the churches, pull their houses down*
> *Take my goods too, and seize upon my lands.*
>
> *(JM, V, 1, 62-66)*

Barabas makes contact with the Turks and leads them through a forgotten drainage ditch into the city that quickly falls to the invaders. As a reward, the Turks appoint Barabas as governor of Malta, but soon the Jew begins to have doubts.

> *I am now Governor of Malta; true, --*
> *But Malta hates me, and in hating me,*
> *My life's in danger...*
>
> *(JM, V, 2, 30-32)*

To correct this situation, he switches sides and contracts with the former governor to overthrow the Turks and restore the former governor to his position in exchange for "friendship" and great sums of money. After devising a trap for the Turks' galley slaves and soldiers in which they will all be demolished by gunpowder, he then secures a trap for the Turkish prince and his men, hoping to boil them alive in a hidden cauldron. Just at the right moment, however, the former governor emerges to thwart the plan and cause Barabas to fall into his own trap. The Jew dies cursing the Christians and the Turks, but not before the Turkish army has indeed been demolished according to his plans, thus delivering the Turkish prince into the hands of the Christians.

With this extended synopsis, I have tried to show that Marlowe uses the stereotypes common to the stage Jew and the characteristics consistent with the stage villain on the Elizabethan stage. Because he adheres to the stereotypes and conventions, Marlowe's Barabas, while perhaps fun, has far more in common with Jason Voorhees in the *Friday 13th* series than with Edward Lionheart in *Theater of Blood*. Barabas is a monster driven by greed, a desire for revenge, and just down-right meanness. He doesn't even make any attempt to justify himself except for exhibiting a strong sense of self-preservation. As a Jewish stereotype he is obsessed with acquiring and maintaining wealth by any means. He is a professed "physic" or poisoner, a skill associated with Jews and Italians and abhorred by the English. As a villainous "type", he is a solid Machiavellian, manipulating others including his own daughter, to achieve his ends. He reveals in and boasts of his evil deeds. He acquires and discards accomplices as the need arises. He kills even his own daughter without remorse because she may pose a threat to him. True, he was treated unfairly but his evils pre-dated his injury and his response to the seizure of his property is even more out of proportion than is the disproportional response of the mad Edward Lionheart to the slight of his critics. Barabas is not overtly mad, so when we ask "Why does he behave so badly?" we can only reply, "Because he is a villain."

In contrast to the two dimensional cartoon of Barabas, Shakespeare provides us with a three dimensional, more truly human character in his Jewish villain, Shylock. *The Merchant of Venice* is a tragedy wrapped in a comedy. It exists in two worlds: the comic and romantic world of Belmont and the harsh and tragic world of Venice. Antonio, the titular merchant, and Shylock, the Jew, are part of the later. Venice is painted as a brooding center of religious intolerance where anti-Semitism is far more pervasive than in the city of Malta. It would appear that the Jews of Venice endure daily smaller indignities while the Jews of Malta suffer one large indignity. This situation is exemplified by the relationship between Antonio and Shylock. Shylock tells the audience in an aside of Antonio.

I hate him for he is a Christian;
But more for that in low simplicity
He lends out money gratis and brings down
The rate of usance here with us in Venice.

(MOV, I, 3, 42-45)

Later, when Antonio comes to Shylock asking for a loan on behalf of his young friend Bassanio, Shylock says

Signior Antonio, many a time and oft
In the Rialto you have rated me
About my moneys and my usances:
Still have I borne it with a patient shrug;
For sufferance is the badge of all our tribe.
You call me misbeliever, cut-throat dog,
And spit upon my Jewish gabardine,
And all for use of that which is mine own.

(MOV, I, 3, 106-113)

To this, Antonio replies:

I am as like to call thee so again,
To spit on thee again, to spurn thee too.

(MOV, I, 3, 130-131)

Their hatred of one another is both global, based on their mutual religious animosity, and particular, based on Antonio's undermining of Shylock's source of income, i.e., charging interests on loans. Nevertheless, Shylock agrees to lend the money sans interest for "friendship" (where have we heard that before?) and then for "merry sport" adds this condition to the loan.

If you repay me not on such a day
In such a place, such sum or sums as are
Expressed in the condition, let the forfeit
Be nominated for an equal pound
Of your fair flesh, to be cut off and taken
In what part of your body pleaseth me.

(MOV, I, 3, 146-151)

So far, Shylock sounds very similar to Barabas. Keep in mind, Shylock would have appeared on stage dressed in the same costume as Barabas, (false nose, red wig, gabardine cloak). He speaks clearly of his hatred for Christians in general and Antonio in particular. He professes to offer Antonio the loan for "friendship" than "for sport" to tack on the absurd condition requiring a forfeiture of flesh if Antonio fails to repay the loan as specified. I find myself asking, is Shylock serious? In the case of Barabas, I would have no doubt, because from the first he is presented as a villain. Shylock, though, does not present as instantly villainous as Barabas. He is a hard businessman for sure; he by his own admission hates Christians in general and Antonio in particular. But is his hatred sufficient to drive him to court-sanctioned murder? Barabas is a killer, past, present and future; Shylock has no such history. Barabas is a stereotypical Machiavellian; Shylock is quite direct. Is Shylock really a potential murderer? It doesn't feel that way to me, at least not in this first scene. So if murder is not his intent, why strike such a "merry" deal? Marjorie Garber in *Shakespeare After All* suggests in a discussion of the doubling of Shylock and Antonio that Shylock may have something other than Antonio's heart in mind when he suggests the forfeiture. "Nearest the heart," the bond says. But the original iteration is not so specific: the flesh is "to be cut off and taken / In what part of your body pleaseth me." ... I do not suggest that he wants to castrate Antonio, but that he wants, symbolically, to circumcise him [one's mind boggles at a one-pound foreskin]. To make him a "Jew."[13]

As interesting as this proposal is, I find it hard to defend with internal evidence. As we all know, what is spoken prior to a contract is not always memorialized in the contract. It appears that the terms of the forfeiture were more concisely defined after the initial discussion and before the trial scene in Act IV. In fact, it seems that Antonio himself defines the terms. Shylock tells Antonio at the end of the scene, "... meet me forthwith at the notary's; / **Give him directions for this merry bond**;" [emphasis added]. So it appears that Antonio himself is responsible for the specificity of the forfeiture. Did Antonio think the forfeiture clause was a sick joke on the part of Shylock and decide to one-up him? Or did Antonio intuit Shylock's intention as Garber did and decide he would rather be dead than circumcised? Or, perhaps, did Antonio believe that to make the bond so absurd as to permit murder would protect him in court? Shakespeare provides no answer. My main point here is to call attention to the fact that Shylock, like real people in our lives, raises questions. With Barabas, all we can ask is "What's he going to do next?' With Shylock, we are encouraged to ask "Why is he doing what he is doing?" This adds the depth of characterization that in Harold Bloom's words "invents the human."

Also adding to the humanity of the character of Shylock is his relationship to his daughter, Jessica, and his late wife. Barabas also had a daughter, Abigail. He exhibited no fatherly concern or warmth toward his child. He used her as a tool and when she displeased him, he discarded her. Shylock is also cold toward his daughter. In his case, however, he treats her as a precious possession to be locked away and protected. Unlike Abigail, Jessica is valued. She first appears in Act II, scene iii where the audience immediately learns she considers her home "hell," that she is "ashamed to be my father's child" and plans to run away with a Christian suitor. Only one scene is shared by Shylock and Jessica, Act II, scene v. Shylock instructs his daughter to secure his house while he is out and to ignore the merriment on the street outside. For her part, Jessica speaks only two short lines, perfunctory responses to Shylock's call and question. Jessica's apparent existence is to be shut up in Shylock's "sober house," to guard his treasures, and to be his obedient and sober daughter, not exactly a fairy tale lifestyle. Immediately after her father has left, Jessica is about heaving bags of gold and jewels out of her bedroom window and climbing down from her casement to the waiting arms of her Christian lover.

Can we plum the relationship between Shylock and Jessica from this simple scene or should we just shrug shoulders and say "it is what it is" in the same way we explain Barabas by saying "he is a villain"? I would suggest this relationship demonstrates Shakespeare's unique skill at inviting rather than inventing a back-story. The audience is invited to take scraps and weave a whole cloth. If we simply want to accept the stereotype, we can simply say that Shylock, being a Jew, is simply too obsessed with wealth to take interest in his daughter beyond her value as one of his possessions. Shylock maintains a joyless, sober house that his daughter describes as tedious and "hell." And when his daughter elopes with his wealth and goes on a debauched spending spree with her new husband, Shylock articulates only a concern for his lost wealth, wishing his daughter dead and in her grave. All of these would support the audience expectations of the Jew. Only two scrapes of cloth undercut this simple interpretation of the character. First, when Shylock vents his rage at his daughter, he says

> I would my daughter were dead at my foot, and the jewels
> in her ear! Would she were hearsed at my foot, and the
> ducats in her coffin!
>
> (MOV, III, 1, 87-90)

In his rant, Shylock demonstrates a relative indifference to his wealth by leaving it in the imagined coffin. He is focused here, as later in the case of

Antonio, on revenge. That he is outraged at the loss of jewels and ducats is apparent, but Jessica's betrayal is a blow beyond his ability to express. He does not simply wish for the return of his possessions; he wishes his only daughter dead first and foremost, jewels and ducats be damned. This scene foreshadows the trial scene from Act IV where Shylock will be offered and will refuse three times the value of forfeited ducats to exact his revenge on Antonio. Both Jessica and Antonio have irreparably injured Shylock's dignity and he values that beyond possessions; this refutes the stereotype of the money-worshipping Jew and gathers him in to the dark collective of generally human values.

The second scrape appears in a single powerful line uttered by Shylock when he learns that his daughter has traded a turquoise ring for a monkey. He says to Tubal, his friend,

> I had it of Leah when I was a bachelor:
> I would not have given it for a wilderness of monkeys.
> (MOV, III, 2, 121-123)

Here Shakespeare provides us with a complete back-story waiting to be written. Leah is presumably Shylock's deceased wife. The ring is given prominence among all his possessions, implying a value exceeding its material worth. Can we, in these two lines, envision another Shylock? A man in love with a woman? A man, perhaps, robbed of his joy of life by the death of his wife? In his grief, has he cut himself off from all affections? A man left only with a smoldering rage for his God and his happier neighbors? If we write this kind of story, Shylock becomes a rather bitter, sad and entirely human character. In this context we can understand his hatred of Antonio as a scapegoat for the entire Christian community and its anti-Semitism, for his daughter's betrayal of her father and heritage, and for the God who robbed him of his wife. Is there internal evidence to support such a back-story? No. But what other story can we offer? Perhaps none. But the story of the turquoise ring and the monkey certainly has poignancy inconsistent with the rest of the scene and allows us to round out and explain the character of Shylock.

We first hear of Shylock's response to the elopement second hand. Two of Antonio's cronies, Salarino and Salanio, joke

> I never heard a passion so confused,
> So strange, outrageous, and so variable,
> As the dog Jew did utter in the streets;
> "My daughter! O my ducats! O my daughter!
> Fled with a Christian! O my Christian ducats!

Justice! The law! My ducats, and my daughter!

(MOV, II, 8, 12-17)

Shylock is clearly distraught, having been robbed of his possessions: his daughter and his ducats and I think it is interesting that Shylock's street scene is reported and not shown. It would most assuredly have been played for absurd comedy, with the frenzied Jew bounding about the stage, ranting and pulling at his hair as a crowd of boys follows him with taunts. Why would Shakespeare let such a scene pass unseen in this comedy? Because it would undercut the seriousness of Shylock. Shakespeare clearly does not want Shylock perceived as a clown, as a figure of fun. He wants the audience to see the Jew as a unique individual, not as a "type" that the audience has come to anticipate. He wants to give the audience something new.

When we next see Shylock, some time has elapsed. He encounters Salarino and Salanio and they can't resist baiting him. Shylock responds with cold, subdued rage. He is now more fully in control of himself. He rages at his daughter, but in the absence of the object of his anger, he redirects it to Antonio, sinisterly repeating "Let him look to his bond." When the amazed Salarino asks "if he forfeit, thou wilt not take his flesh; what's that good for?" Shylock responds with his most famous and revealing speech.

To bait fish withal. If it will feed nothing else, it will feed my revenge. He hath disgrac'd me and hind'red me half a million; laugh'd at my losses, mock'd at my gains, scorned my nation, thwarted my bargains, cooled my friends, heated mine enemies. And what's his reason? I am a Jew. Hath not a Jew eyes? Hath not a Jew hands, organs, dimensions, senses, affections, passions, fed with the same food, hurt with the same weapons, subject to the same diseases, healed by the same means, warmed and cooled by the same winter and summer, as a Christian is? If you prick us, do we not bleed? If you tickle us, do we not laugh? If you poison us, do we not die? And if you wrong us, shall we not revenge? If we are like you in the rest, we will resemble you in that. If a Jew wrong a Christian, what is his humility? Revenge. If a Christian wrong a Jew, what should his sufferance be by Christian example? Why, revenge. The villainy you teach me I will execute; and it shall go hard but I will better the instruction.

(MOV, III, 1, 53-73)

In this magnificent speech, Shakespeare truly invents the human Shylock. Some critics have suggested that these lines were originally delivered for comic effect. Perhaps it is my 21st century sensibilities that can't accept this, but I cannot (or will not) believe that Shakespeare was not attempting to build sympathy for the presumed villain of the play. Shylock's appeal to the common humanity of both Jews and Christians is both moving and reasonable, but it is also bracketed by an enraged defense of his need for revenge. For me, the speech is less Shakespeare's personal plea for religious tolerance as some 20th century apologists have proposed, than his theatrical device for provoking sympathy for his villain. By highlighting Shylock's shared human capacity for good and evil, he calls attention to how the Christians of Venice have molded his revengeful determination by example and action. In his list of qualities from *"Hath not a Jew eyes?"* to *"If you poison us, do we not die?"* Shylock enumerates common anatomical and physiological aspects shared by all humans. The only common cognitive-emotional characteristic he can come up with is *"... if you wrong us, shall we not revenge"*? More than 100 years before Jean Jacques Rousseau crystallized the nature versus nurture discussion, Shylock is framing it on the streets of Venice. Arguing that he is not revengeful by nature (it was the common Elizabethan belief that Jews were), Shylock say *"The villainy **you teach me** I will execute; and it shall go hard but I will better the instruction."* Villainy, he says, is a learned response and by adding *"and it shall go hard"* he implies that the villainy does not come easily to him. He has to steel himself to execute his revenge against his all his Christian neighbors represented by his scapegoat, Antonio.

I believe it is part of Shakespeare's brilliance that by humanizing Shylock and his other villains that he enables contemplation of deeper matters. *The Merchant of Venice* with its stereotypical, albeit humanized version, of the Jew raises questions about religious intolerance in general and anti-Semitism is particular. Is the Merchant of Venice anti-Semitic; was Shakespeare an anti-Semite? I think we are forced to say yes. It should be remembered that the 16th century was the time of the Inquisition when Jews were constantly under threat. The Catholic Church was unabashedly anti-Semitic. Spain expelled all Jews in 1492; Portugal followed suit in 1487. England had acted even earlier by expelling all Jews in 1290 under the reign of Edward I. By the time of Shakespeare there were very few Jews left in England, so the playwright and his contemporaries only had documents and stereotypes to work from. It is possible Shakespeare may have never even met a Jew. So the anti-Semitism of Shakespeare and his fellow Englishmen was largely academic. Most, like Marlowe were willing to accept the stereotype without question to generate a laugh or a shiver or to advance a plot. Only Shakespeare rises above this to question the validity of the stereotype and the consequence of religious intolerance.

The Merchant of Venice is also one of Shakespeare's most legalistic plays: it centers its action on bonds and trials. It raises questions about justice and the quality of mercy. Does Antonio receive justice at the hand of the Duke? Does Shylock? What is justice? Antonio has entered into a bond with the Jew willingly and has agreed to the absurd penalty for forfeiture. What if the terms of the forfeiture were less absurd? For example, what if the penalty for forfeiture had required Antonio to raise funds for and build a new synagogue for the Jews of Venice? Would the Duke have been any more likely to support Shylock's bond? Would we applaud Portia/Balthazar devising a stratagem to nullify that bond? What if the penalty had been a turquoise ring worn by the Merchant? Now is the bond valid?

Is the deck stacked against the Jew from the start because he is a Jew prosecuting a Christian, and a well-connected one at that? I don't think we can say that because, when it appears that Shylock has won the case and he approaches Antonio with knife in hand, it is not the Duke who interrupts him. It seems the Duke is willing to allow Shylock the agreed upon pound of flesh and it is only a legal technicality that saves the Merchant. The audience breathes a sigh of relief and cheers Portia's resourcefulness, but why do we feel comfortable with the law and the bond being contravened by a cleaver lawyer's trick? Simply because we are taught to believe that humanity and moderation should be applied to the law. Shylock's bond is inhuman and immoderate, demanding a penalty for forfeiture far in excess of the value of the forfeited goods. But his rigid demand is for the letter of the law, and it is the letter of the law that is turned against him. The bond does not allow him a single drop of blood to accompany his pound of flesh. Because he cannot possibly claim his agreed upon prize without violating the precise terms of the bond, Shylock's bond is voided. But the matter doesn't end here. Portia now turns the law of Venice against the Jew:

> It is enacted in the laws of Venice,
> If it is proved against an alien
> That by direct or indirect attempts
> He seek the life of and citizen,
> The party 'gainst the which he doth contrive
> Shall seize one half his goods; the other half
> Comes to the privy coffer of the state;
> And the offender's life lies in the mercy
> Of the Duke...

(MOV, IV, 1, 348-356)

The Duke exercises mercy and grants Shylock his life, then Antonio exercises mercy by allowing Shylock to keep the half of his wealth assigned to Antonio.   Antonio does place conditions on his mercy: 1) upon the death of Shylock, all of his wealth will go to his daughter and her Christian husband and 2) that "[Shylock] presently become a Christian." Modern audiences will recoil in horror at this second condition.   The idea of forced religious conversion is repellent to 21st century sensibilities. But, in the context of the play, the audience should ask, is Antonio being vindictive or merciful?   In Antonio's mind, the conversion of Shylock will ensure the divine salvation of his soul and if the demand is made for such a reason, than Antonio is being truly merciful. On the other hand, if Shylock converts to Christianity, he will be a man alone, rejected by his fellow Jews and never accepted by the Christian community. Furthermore, he will no longer be able to practice his trade, usury, since that occupation is prohibited to Christians. In this case, Antonio's mercy has in fact sentenced Shylock to a life of virtual solitary confinement. He will be forced to drift like a sad ghost through the community of Venice, invisible to his kinsmen and the object of derision to everyone else. In this context, one has to wonder if the Duke and Antonio have been merciful at all.

Shylock represents one of Shakespeare's most complex and interesting characters, both a villain and a victim. He reflects the Elizabethan stereotype of the malicious Jew and subverts the stereotype by creating a uniquely human character. He induces a discussion of the origin of evil and invites the audience to examine their own preconceptions and prejudices. He is both a figure of terror and a figure of pity. Like all of Shakespeare's great villains, he cannot be dismissed as a cartoon.

Villainy, like virtue, is of course in the eye of the beholder. I suspect many who read the following chapters will readily agree with some of my villainous subjects and strongly disagree with others. Few I suspect would dispute the villainy of Iago or Macbeth, but some will probably be surprised to find Hamlet or Brutus in their company. Many, given the feminist sensibility of our age, will surely take exception to my inclusion of Juliet and Desdemona in the same chapter discussing Lady Macbeth and Lear's vicious daughters. In the 21st century, we are trained to consider and assign value to that which motivates an action rather than view the action in isolation, but I will raise the question if good motives in fact mitigate or excuse an evil act. Because Macbeth's murder of Duncan is motivated by his ambition to be king is he more villainous than Brutus who murders Caesar because he fears Caesar's ambitions? In both case, the victims are dead at the point of a knife wielded by men they trusted. Is commission of an evil act (and what exactly is evil) both necessary and sufficient to label the actor a villain? If a man with the power of precognition had murdered Adolph Hitler as an innocent child, would he not have been considered a villain by his contemporaries, even if his motive was to prevent the evil he was convinced the murdered child would commit? Is the willful commission of a wrongful, but not necessarily evil act, e.g., defying a king or a father, which triggers a calamitous series of unintended events sufficient to label the actor villainous? Can the virtuous end can justify the villainous means, and can a villainous end also condemn otherwise excusable or explainable means?

Shakespeare's villains and bad actors (figuratively, not literally) challenge us to consider these conditions and more. In the time of Shakespeare the concept of evil was dominated by religious definition. The Elizabethan world view envisioned an eternal struggle between God and the Devil for the soul of man and evil was simply any act against God and the Christian view of world order. This battle was dramatized throughout the Middle Ages by the morality plays where evil was shown as an external force, frequently portrayed as the Vice figure, applied to man to lead him into conflict with God's will. It is Shakespeare genius that he begins to portray his characters as consciously aware of that the battle between good and evil was internal and personal. However, although the battle was individualized, the triumph of evil extended beyond the downfall of the protagonist to engulf those around him. Now, not only the individual soul was at stake, but also the wellbeing of the community.

Instead of laying the blame for evil at the doorstep of the Devil, Shakespeare and his contemporaries began to assign blame to the weakness and/or malevolence of the individual. Intentionality began to be factored in to consideration of evil actions, but Shakespeare's audience was more concerned with what the villain did than why they did it.[14] It wasn't until the early post-Freudian 20th century that audiences would begin to attach the notion of intentional malevolence to acts designated as evil. While it could be argued that an evil act can't be involuntary, evil doesn't have to be the explicit objective of the one who commits it. Consider for example the proverbial drunk driver who kills a child on the street. She does not intend to kill a child when she gets behind the wheel, but she voluntarily chooses to drive, a wrongful (some would say evil) act. Her decision to drive becomes the proximate cause of the child's death. So, are we considering a tragic accident, an evil action or something between the two? Is the driver a tragic figure or a villain? Does she deserve pity or punishment? Similar dilemmas will arise again and again as we consider Shakespeare's villains.

To explore Shakespeare's villains, I have divided them into several broad categories based on what drives their villainy. The first category is the 'revenger," probably the most common villainous character in Elizabethan/Jacobian drama. They may be driven by the grievous acts perpetrated against them, e.g. the murder of loved ones, or by petty slights, real or imaged. They may begin the play as a villain and the audience will be encouraged to follow along as they enact their nefarious plans, or they may be initially virtuous men and women who are drug down into villainy by the obsessive pursuit of revenge.

The second category, only slightly less popular in Elizabethan/Jacobian drama, is the "usurper." The best known of Shakespeare's villains fall into this grouping: Macbeth and Richard III. These are men generally driven by their ambition to upset the natural order of things in their pursuit of power, but sometimes they may also be driven by their perceived need to right the wrongs committed by an incompetent or malicious ruler. Richard, Duke of York in the Henry VI plays and Henry Bolingbroke (later Henry IV) in *Richard II*, while not without personal ambition, are primarily driven to usurp the throne because the ruling king is not up to the job.

The third category is closely connected to that of the second in that it is political in nature. "Traitors," like usurpers also upset the natural order, but they are not motivated by personal ambition to rule. Instead, the traitors they either fear for what their government may become or resent what their government has become.

The fourth category, I suspect will be the most controversial. "Shakespeare's Bad Girls" I have divided into three sub-groupings: Shrews, Defiant Daughters, and Bitches and Witches. The last sub-group is the least controversial and includes truly evil women like Lear's two elder daughters and Lady Macbeth. The first sub-group includes Shakespeare's unruly women, most prominently, Katherina in *The Taming of the Shrew*. Like the usurpers and traitors, they also seek to disrupt the natural order and their weapons are a sharp tongue instead of a sharp sword. With micro instead of macro consequences, they are not villains in the sense that Goneril and Regan are villains; however, their rebellions are in opposition to God's natural order, are willingly committed in pursuit of personal power (some will say independence), and result in discord. In other words, their actions are little different from those of Richard III other than in the magnitude of the consequences. Similarly, the defiant daughters are rebels within their own homes. They offend the natural order by defying or deceiving their fathers; and like the shrews, they willingly commit their act of defiance, but do so deceptively instead of boldly as is the case with the shrews. The shrews generally accept that their actions will have consequence and they are willing to accept those consequence, but the defiant daughters fail to foresee the consequence of their actions and they are invariably more disastrous than their small indiscretions would warrant.

The final category is a catch all of miscreants from liars and lechers like Angelo in *Measure for Measure* to psychotics like Jack Cade, the madcap leader of a rebellion in 2 *Henry VI*. It also includes the nameless and often pathetic murderers who are sprinkled through Shakespeare's play. No more than tools are their powerful lords, these often overlooked characters are given unusually distinct personalities by Shakespeare to highlight the impact of poverty and oppression on villainy in the masses. Finally, we will consider Shakespeare's literal monster: Caliban. A creature perhaps more sinned against than sinning, Caliban is at once comedic and pathetic. He plots the overthrow and murder of his master, Prospero, but this is in response to his dispossession of his land and his enslavement. His situation is analyzed in the context of the experience of Native Americans and other colonized peoples, and invites the question of who is more monstrous: Prospero or Caliban.

Notes

*   This and all subsequent quotes and line numbers from Shakespeare are taken from *The Riverside Shakespeare*, G. B. Evans, ed. (Boston: Houghton Mifflin Co., 1974).

**   This and all subsequent quotes and line numbers from Marlowe are taken from *The Complete Plays*, J. B. Steane, ed. (Baltimore: Penguin, 1969).

---

1.   *Production Notes*, http://www.romeoandjuliet.com/players/pn3.html .
2.   *Production Notes*, http://www.romeoandjuliet.com/players/pn2.html .
3.   Daniel Rosenthal. *Shakespeare on Screen* (London: Octopus Publishing Group, 2000), 131.
4.   *Production Notes*, http://www.romeoandjuliet.com/players/pn3.html .
5.   *Production Notes*, http://www.romeoandjuliet.com/players/pn5.html .
6.   Bernard Weinraub. "Audiences In Love With the Doomed Lovers." *New York Times*, (Nov 1, 1996). http://query.nytimes.com/gst/fullpage.html?res=9805E0DE1238F936A3 5752C1A960958260&sec=&spon=&pagewanted=1.
7.   Ibid.
8.   Janet Maslin. *Soft! What Light? It's Flash, Romeo."* *New York Times*, (Nov 1, 1996). http://www.nytimes.com/1996/11/01/movies/soft-what-light-it-s-flash-romeo.html

9. Harold Bloom. *Shakespeare: The Invention of the Human* (New York: Penguin 1998).
10. Muriel C. Bradbrook. *Themes and Conventions of Elizabethan Tragedy* (London: Cambridge University Press 1935) 50–51.
11. Charles Norton Coe. *Demi-Devil: The Character of Shakespeare's Villains* (New York: Bookman Associates 1963) 19.
12. Marjorie Garber. *Shakespeare After All* (New York: Anchor Books 2004) 308.
13. Ibid: 309.
14. Barnet, Sylvan. "Coleridge on Shakespeare's Villains." *Shakespeare Quarterly* 7:1(1956), 16.

THE REVENGERS

Many of Shakespeare's villains (and heroes) are focused on exacting revenge. Study of Elizabethan and Jacobean drama shows us this was not unique to Shakespeare. Dozens of so-called revenge tragedies paraded across the English stage and were, according to contemporaneous records and reports, the real crowd-pleasers of the day. Clearly the English were concerned about the issues of justice and revenge. From the time of Henry VII, personal vendettas and private revenge had been outlawed in England. The exercise of justice became the exclusive prerogative of the State. This legal prohibition was supported by the Church which either ignored Mosaic laws legitimizing blood revenge or by contrasting them to the new teaching of Christ and Paul. The Old Testament attempted to moderate revenge by awarding the injured party "...life for life, eye for an eye, tooth for tooth, hand for hand, foot for foot...."[1] But in the New Testament, Christ taught at his sermon on the Mount, "Ye have heard that it hath been said, An eye for an eye, and a tooth for a tooth: But I say unto you, That ye resist not evil: but whosoever shall smite thee on thy right cheek, turn to him the other also."[2] and Paul wrote in his letter to the Romans, "Avenge not yourselves, but rather give place unto wrath: for it is written, Vengeance is mine; I will repay, saith the Lord."[3] Additionally, the philosophers of the age generally railed against private revenge. Most famous among them is Sir Francis Bacon who in 1625 penned his well circulated essay "*On Revenge.*"

> *REVENGE is a kind of wild justice; which the more man's nature runs to, the more ought law to weed it out. For as for the first wrong, it doth but offend the law; but the revenge of that wrong pulleth the law out of office. Certainly, in taking revenge, a man is but even with his enemy; but in passing it over, he is superior; for it is a prince's part to pardon. And Salomon, I am sure, saith, It is the glory of a man to pass by an offence.*

But that said, Bacon equivocates

> The most tolerable sort of revenge is for those wrongs for which there is no law or remedy; but then let a man take heed the revenge be such as there is no law to punish; else a man's enemy is still beforehand, and it is two for one.[4]

36

It is precisely this situation that frames many of the popular revenge tragedies of the day.

The common theater-going audiences, as evidenced by the popularity of the revenge tragedies, were probably more ambiguous in their feelings about personal revenge. Fredson Bowers in *Elizabethan Revenge Tragedy* cautions us not to impose modern conceptions of ethical thinking on the age of Elizabethan. We are reminded that Elizabethans attended gruesome public executions for entertainment and would be drawn more to the revenge tragedy for the characteristic violence and bloodshed rather than to ponder the morality of revenge. [5]   This is probably true, but because the audience in general may have been in the theatre to quench their bloodlust and need for excitement, I would argue that the playwrights, particularly Shakespeare, were concerned to a greater or lesser degree with the moral questions raised by the drama. Bear in mind that Shylock was a would-be revenger, but as I have tried to show Shakespeare goes to great length to evoke sympathy for his villain and raise questions about the exercise of justice. Had he been indifferent to these moral issues, Shakespeare could just have reverted to type and drawn Shylock as a Barabas-like cartoon. While such complexities may have soared over the heads of the groundlings, they are placed in the play as seedlings intended to encourage reflection and perhaps discussion.

The Elizabethan revenge tragedy did not spring spontaneously from English soil, but from a fusion of the Classical dramas of Lucius Annaeus Seneca with the popular Italian novels of the 15th and 16th centuries. Seneca, an influential Roman senator and philosopher lived during the first half of the first century, serving under the rule of Tiberius, Caligula and Nero. He wrote tragic dramas based on the myths of the Greeks and focused his creative energy on elaborating three central themes: 1) the Stoic virtues of simplicity, moderation and humility; 2) the inconstancy of fortune; and 3) the horrors of great crimes. Seneca's works were translated into English between 1559 and 1581 and became models for the evolving English theater. Professor Bower notes

> Classical tragedy had gained an enormous prestige in England, because of the great value set on classical learning, of which tragedy was supposed to be the highest expression; and knowing little of Greek, the Elizabethans came to regard Seneca as the most tragic, the most perfect of ancient writers.[6]

His major contributions included the five act structure adopted by Shakespeare and his contemporaries, the high, rhetorical and bombastic language best imitated by Marlowe, supernatural characters such as ghosts who serve as prologues to the action, and the vivid portrayal of horrific and bloody acts. The elements became defining elements in what would become the formula for the revenge tragedies that would appear of the Elizabethan stage.

The second influence is the influx of Italian novels and plays into England. These works provided story sources and models for villainous characters based on the stereotypical depiction of Italians. In Elizabethan England, the attitude toward Italians (and Spaniards) was one of deep distrust. Travel guides written by Englishmen, most notably Thomas Nashe and Thomas Palmer, did a great deal to mold the dominant stereotypes. That the Italians were "Papists" was particularly disconcerting, but they were also considered "hot blooded" and prone to violence. They were viewed as revengers par excellence: patient, secretive, deceptive and brutal. These "villains" were almost always associated, implicitly or explicitly, with Niccolo Machiavelli, the Florentine philosopher and author of *The Prince*, whose "end justifies the means" approach to politics appalled the English.

The first great Elizabethan revenge tragedy that set the pattern for all that followed was *The Spanish Tragedy* written sometime between 1587 and 1589 by Thomas Kyd. In the Senecan tradition, the tragedy opens with a prologue dialogue between the ghost of Andrea and the allegorical figure of Revenge. We learn that Andrea has been killed by Balthazar, a prince of Portugal, in fair combat (hardy a strong motive for revenge). His former lover, Bel-Imperia, daughter of the King's brother, intents to exact revenge for his death by inducing her current lover, Horatio, son of Hieronimo, Knight Marshall of Spain, to kill Balthazar. Balthazar is conveniently smitten with Bel-Imperia, but inconveniently his suit is supported by her brother, Lorenzo. Balthazar discovers that Bel-Imperia is, in fact in love with Horatio and in a jealous pique joins with Lorenzo to murder his rival. Bel-Imperia is then sequestered by her brother pending a forced marriage to Balthazar. The whole serpentine path leads up to the real revenger of the piece, Hieronimo, father of the slain Horatio.

Though sequestered, Bel-Imperia manages to get a letter, written in her own blood no less, identifying Balthazar and her brother as Horatio's murderers. Hieronimo, unable to conceive of a motive for such an act, demurs and attempts to contact Bel-Imperia directly only to find his path blocked by her brother. Fearing Hieronimo has uncovered his guilt, Lorenzo in the fashion of the typical Machiavel contrives to eliminate his murderous accomplices, Serberine and Pedringano. Pedringano, at the end, realizes he has been betrayed and arranges for a letter corroborating Bel-Imperia's accusations to be delivered to Hieronimo. Now that his suspicions are confirmed, he decides to go to the King and demand justice. Unfortunately, by the time he reaches the court, he is near mad from grief and rage. His rant and antics are taken as madness by the King and his suit for justice goes unheard. In the very next scene, Hieronimo enters alone and carrying a book, a copy of Seneca we learn from the quotes. He has by now regained his composure and has resolved, deprived of a normal way to justice, that he will exact his revenge "by a secret, yet a certain means." By so choosing to follow the vengeful path by Machiavellian means, he signals the audience that he has crossed the bridge from victim to villain and the audience's sympathy for his plight will slowly degrade over the remainder of the play.

In the fourth and final act (the five act structure had not yet gained popularity), Bel-Imperia and Hieronimo are finally able to join forces and combine their efforts to execute their revenge. Together they contrive to put on a play for the royal court and they recruit Balthazar and Lorenzo to assume roles in the performance. During the performance, Hieronimo stabs Lorenzo, Bel-Imperia stabs Balthazar then herself, Hieronimo reveals the dead body of his son, Horatio, explains to those present what brought all this about, then attempts to flee the chamber to hang himself. The King has him restrained and under the threat of torture demands Hieronimo further explain himself. Hieronimo declines to speak and to assure his silence, bites out his tongue and spits it at the royals. Undeterred by this madness, the King provides Hieronimo with a pen so he can write out an explanation. When given a knife to sharpen the pen, Hieronimo rather predictably turns the knife on the King's brother, Lorenzo's father, killing him and then with the same knife killing himself. The play ends with six bloody bodies (and one tongue) lying on the stage as the ghost of Andrea and Revenge retake the stage to gloat over their victory.

The Spanish Tragedy was one of the most popular plays of the Elizabethan theater and established the formula by which or against which all subsequent revenge tragedies would develop. Fredson Bower outlined the key elements of the formula in his definitive work, *Elizabethan Revenge Tragedy*, and they are as follows:

1. The fundamental motive for the action is revenge.
2. The revenge extends not only to a specific offender, but also to his/her kindred.
3. The revenger and the object of the revenge are both aided by accomplices who commit suicide or are otherwise killed during the course of the action.
4. A ghost appears on stage and in some manner figures into the action.
5. There is a justifiable delay in exacting revenge because of a lack of evidence, lack of opportunity, or a failure on the part of the State's legal machinery.
6. Madness is important as a dramatic device.

7. Machiavellian intrigue is used by and against the revenger.
8. Actions are bloody and numerous.
9. Revenge is accomplished in some horrific fashion, accompanied by intense violence and a high body count.[7]

Unlike the revenge tragedies that follow, there is no known primary source for the story of Hieronimo. It appears the story emerged from the imagination of Kyd, but that is not to say there is no evidence of borrowing from both Seneca and the Italian novels of the day. The Senecan contributions in *The Spanish Tragedy* include the centrality of revenge in the drama, the malignant presence of a ghostly prologue, the bloodshed and onstage horrors, and long, descriptive bombastic speeches. From the Italian novel, Kyd crafts the Machiavellian villain, Lorenzo, who displays the characteristic indifference to the suffering of others, the willingness to employ deceitful means to attain his ends, and the tendency to use and discard accomplices. The successful fusion of the influences by Kyd in *The Spanish Tragedy* ignited a genre that held the stage through the Golden Age of the English theater and directly inspired the first tragedy of a young playwright, William Shakespeare.

A WILDERNESS OF TIGERS: *TITUS ANDRONICUS*: AARON THE MOOR

William Shakespeare wrote The Most Lamentable Roman Tragedy of Titus Andronicus sometime between 1589 and 1594. The first recorded performance was in January of 1594, but there is evidence that the play had been on the stage for several years prior to that. It is important in that it represent Shakespeare's first attempt at tragedy. By the time of *Titus Andronicus*, he had already produced one to two comedies (*The Comedy of Errors* and probably *Love's Labor Lost*) and two to three histories (the *Henry VI* series). There is evidence to suggest that the tragedy was a Spielberg-like success that enjoyed frequent revivals until the closing of the theaters in 1642. It saw three printings, 1594, 1600 and 1611, that are testimony to its sustained popularity and Ben Jonson referred to it in *Bartholomew Fair* (1615) "as an enduring favorite of a public with low tastes."[8] Jonson was not the last of the public with "high tastes" to lay scorn on *Titus Andronicus*. Of all Shakespeare's plays, *Titus Andronicus* is the most maligned. In 1678, Edward Ravenscroft revised and adapted the tragedy, calling it "a heap of rubbish" that presumably his version improved upon. [9] T. S. Elliot called *Titus Andronicus* "one of the stupidest and most uninspired plays ever written."[10] Critics from Samuel Johnson (1765) to Samuel Coleridge (1812) to Brian Vickers (2002) were so embarrassed by this play, one that they considered so far below the dignity and talent of the great Bard; they tried unsuccessfully to prove Shakespeare was not its author.

Personally, I love *Titus Andronicus*. It is for me a tragedy that resonates with the popular cinema of the late 20th century. Its emphasis on gratuitous violence and visual horrors presages the movies of Sam Peckenpah, George Romero, Wes Graven, and Ron Zombie. I picture *Titus Andronicus* as penned by a young, talented playwright who has seen the successes of *The Spanish Tragedy* and *The Jew of Malta* and decides to give the audience what it wants and then some. What he produced is a Senecan style revenge tragedy more gruesome that Kyd's and a Machiavellian villain more evil than Marlowe's. He pours outrage on outrage, piling up a body count that leaves few of the principals standing at play's end, and he peoples the play with so many villains one has difficulty deciding who to cheer for.

The probable source of this tragedy is a prose history entitled *The History of Titus Andronicus, The Renowned Roman General*. The only known copy of this narrative is a booklet dated from the mid-eighteenth century and believed to be a reprint from an early work dating to the late 16th century. The story is placed in the declining years of the Roman Empire under siege by the Goth barbarians from the North. By the time of the story, Rome was largely Christianized, but the world of *Titus Andronicus* is significantly pagan. Breaking with the Senecan tradition, Shakespeare does not open the play with a prologue, but with a dynastic conflict instead. The Emperor has died and his two sons, Saturninus, the elder, and Bassianus are vying for control of Rome. The Tribunes, represented by Marcus Andronicus, Titus' brother, plan to offer Titus the crown. It is into this fray that Titus returns after a successful 10-year war against the Goths in which he has lost 21 of his 25 sons. In tow he brings the captured Tamora, Queen of the Goths, her three sons, and her Moorish (meaning black, not Muslim) slave, Aaron. His first act is to inter the body of his most recently lost son in the family vault, then at the behest of his remaining sons, he agrees to the sacrifice of Tamora's eldest son to appease the ghosts of their lost brothers. Tamora cries out a heart piercing plea for the life of her son and Titus rejects it out of hand. From that point on, she is his mortal enemy, bent on revenge. Titus is offered the empery by the tribunes, but he rejects it and then approves Saturninus as the new emperor. Saturninus offers to take Lavinia, Titus's only daughter who is already betrothed to Bassianus, as his bride and queen. Lavinia refuses and flees the scene with her brothers and Bassianus. One brother, Mutius, remains behind to guard their retreat and in a rage at his daughter's "betrayal," he slays his own son for daring to block his way. Saturninus rebukes Titus and his "lawless sons," then announces he will take Tamora as his queen, reversing her situation and placing her in a position to exact her revenge. Titus begs forgiveness of Saturninus and Tamora supports the old general's suit, explaining in an aside her Machiavellian rationale and her vengeful purpose.

> *My lord, be ruled by me, be won at last,*
> *Dissemble all your griefs and discontents*
> *You are newly planted in your throne--*
> *Lest then the people, and patricians too,*
> *Upon a just survey, take Titus' part,*
> *The party 'gainst the which he doth contrive*
> *And so supplant you for ingratitude...*
> *...then let me alone.*
> *I'll find a day to massacre them all,*
> *And race their faction and their family,*
> *The cruel father and his traitorous sons,*
> *To whom I sued for my dear son's life;*

And make them know what 'tis to let a queen
Kneel in the street and beg for grace in vain.

(TA, I, 1, 443-448, 450-456)

All of this transpires in the very first scene of the first act, hinting that what follows will be densely filled with action. It is notable that it is Titus who is set up in the traditional role of the villain by his initial actions and Tamora who would appear to be the wronged revenger. Titus has casually and callously allowed the ritual slaughter of Tamora's first born and then, in a fit of rage, kills his own son for crossing him. He is rigid, proud, and tradition bound; clearly brave, patriotic and without political ambition. In some ways he looks forward to the character of King Lear, who for his foolish pride, places himself and his kingdom at risk. So Titus, being rigidly tradition bound, foolishly promotes the clearly craven Saturninus to emperor and sacrifices the son of Tamora, buying her eternal enmity. In his pride, he disregards his daughter's betrothal to Bassianus by acquiescing to Saturninus demand for her as his bride. When his daughter refuses the "honor" and flees the scene protected by her brothers, Titus kills one of them, and then refuses to even allow him burial in the family vault. Titus hardly finishes the scene as sympathetic or heroic and can be best defined by his own description, "Titus, unkind and careless of thine own" (*TA*, I, 1, 86).

The other principal in the first scene is the wronged mother and former queen of the Goths, Tamora. Initially, in this first packed scene, she is presented in a sympathetic light: a sad, defeated and presumably widowed queen, paraded through the streets of Rome as a humbled emblem of the conquered Goths. She is forced to beg the Roman conqueror for the life of her eldest son in terms that should have moved the hardest of parents, but that fails to move Titus. Her son is slain and then suddenly and unlooked for, her fortunes are reversed: she is set free along with her remaining sons and elevated to Empress of Rome. Now is placed in her hands the means to revenge her slaughtered son and she would seem perfectly justified in doing so, but she chooses a Machiavellian route to achieve her revenge, partly from practical considerations and partly to signal the audience that she will not be the virtuous revenger suggested by her introduction.

Tamora is the most complex of the characters in the relatively uncomplicated cast and serves as the principal foil of Titus and the ultimate enemy of Roman order. She is an outsider who is ironically elevated to a position of power on the inside of society, while at the same time, Titus is removed from the inner circle of Roman power and reduced to the role of outsider in his own country. Tamora is also a woman, making her doubly strange in this world of men. Leslie A. Fiedler in *The Stranger in Shakespeare* notes that women, "Certainly in his first plays... [are] portrayed as utter strangers: creatures so totally alien to men as threaten destruction rather than offer the hope of salvation."[11] She is a mother, and the defender and avenger of her children; Titus, the father, kills his own.   She challenges the morality and value of the rigid Roman patriarchy, represented by Titus, that places an egotistical weakling on the throne, casually murders the sons of others, and is "unkind and careless of [his/their] own."

The play's third principal of the play is introduced in the second scene: the arch villain in this world of villains, Aaron the Moor. Aaron is Shakespeare's earliest villain and the prototype for most of the villains that follow. Like the play itself, Aaron has been much maligned by the critics most enthralled by Shakespeare's characterizations. Charles Norton Coe in *Demi-Devils: The Character of Shakespeare's Villains* articulates the general consensus that Aaron is simply "unrealistic," too over-the-top in his evil to be believed. Since he is both slave and lover to Tamora, his role in her revenge is, I believe, understandable. What critics object to is the pure delight he takes in orchestrating and executing the evils set loose on the Andronici. First, he arranges for the murder of Bassianus and the rape and mutilation of Lavinia. He then frames two of Tutus' sons for the murder. Promising their release, Aaron convinces Titus to cut off his own hand in exchange for the lives of his sons, then returns only the heads of the two sons along with the offered hand.

Aaron's speeches throughout recall Marlowe's Barabas. While lying in wait for Bassianus and Lavinia, he says

> *Vengeance is in my heart, death in my hand,*
> *Blood and revenge are hammering in my head,*
> *(TA, II, 3, 38-39)*

And after taking Titus' hand, he chortles to himself,

> *...O, how this villainy*
> *Doth fat me with the very thought of it!*
> *Let fools do good, and fair men call for grace*
> *Aaron will have his soul black like his face.*
> *(TA, III, 1, 202-205)*

And when in Act V, he gleefully confesses his crimes against the Andronici, he delivers his most famous and Marlovian speech when asked "Art thou not sorry for these heinous deeds"?

> *Ay, that I had not done a thousand more,*
> *Even now I curse the day—and yet I think,*

Few come within the compass of my curse —
Wherein I did not some notorious ill:
As kill a man or else devise his death,
Ravish a maid or plot the way to do it,
Accuse some innocent and forswear myself,
Set deadly enmity between two friends,
Make poor men's cattle break their necks,
Set fire on barns and haystacks in the night,
And bid the owners quench them with their tears.
Oft have I digged up dead men from their graves
And then set them upright at their dear friends' door,
Even when their sorrows almost was forgot
And on their skins, as on the bark of trees,
Have with my knife carved in Roman letters.
"let not your sorrow die, though I am dead."
But I have done a thousand dreadful things
As willingly as one would kill a fly,
And nothing grieves me heartily indeed,
But that I cannot do ten thousand more.

$$(TA, V, 1, 124\text{-}144)$$

What a wonderfully wicked speech!

Aaron, while clearly owing a debt to Marlowe, also owes his character, as does Shylock, to Shakespeare's fascination with the strangers and outsiders in Elizabethan English. By Shakespeare's time, a substantial body of folklore had grown up about the more exotic members of mankind who would occasionally appear on the English landscape. Stereotypes abounded about the Jews and about blacks and Shakespeare would use, but also question and challenge these stereotypes in his dramas. Earlier, we discussed how he worked with and challenged the stereotypical Jew in his characterization of Shylock. In *Titus Andronicus*, he turns to blacks in his creation of Aaron. Like Jews, blacks in Elizabethan England were something of a rarity, and the impressions and stereotypes the English held were largely drawn from travelogues like Richard Hakaluyt's *Principal Navigations* and Africanus' *A Geographical Historie of Africa*. In these works, Moors were described as unpredictable and devious.[12] Generally, blacks were viewed as more like animals than men, intellectually weak but with a naturally cruel shrewdness. They were also credited with "some unusual power of attraction over white women."[13] As he will do in his later plays, Shakespeare's black stranger adheres to most of the preconceived stereotypes. Aaron is certainly devious and cruel, but is certainly not intellectually weak.

But most importantly, Aaron has his true origin in the older tradition of the medieval devil. By the end of the 16th century when Shakespeare was starting his career, a substantial body of folklore had also been established concerning the Prince of Darkness. In folkloric tradition the Devil could assume nearly any form, but according to Jeffrey Burton Russell in *The Prince of Darkness*, the "Devil is usually black [like Aaron], symbolizing the absence of light and goodness." He usually "comes from the north [like the Goths], domain of darkness and punishing cold" and he favors places consecrated to Pagan gods [like Rome]. He is also associated with wild hunts and it is noteworthy that the murder of Bassianus, the rape of Lavinia, and the framing of Titus' sons all occur during a great hunt in the forest of Rome.[14] Like the Devil, Aaron uses the lust and malice of others to achieve his evil ends and uses trickery and lies to undo the just. And lest we miss these subtler suggestions, Aaron is explicitly called "devil," no less than five times, "Cimmerian" (dweller in darkness), "hellish dog," "black dog," "incarnate devil," "accursed devil," "inhuman dog," "irreligious Moor".

Fiedler refers to Tamora as "the witch-mother from across the Alps," but does not follow up on this important insight.[15] I believe this comment offers a key to really understanding the connection between Tamora and Aaron. If we accept Tamora as a legitimate witch, the diabolic Aaron can be seen as her familiar. The medieval conception of women shared much with the corresponding medieval conception of Jews. In both cases, a perennial attribution of secret, bountiful, malicious "power," is made. Linked to theological traditions of Eve and Lilith, women were perceived as embodiments of inexhaustible negativity. Though not quite quasi-literal incarnations of the Devil as were Jews, women are, rather, their ontological "first cousins" who, like the Jews, emerged from the "left" or sinister side of being. The *Malleus Maleficarum* (The Hammer of Witches), published by the Catholic inquisition in 1485-86 taught "All wickedness is but little to the wickedness of a woman. ... What else is woman but a foe to friendship, an unescapable [sp] punishment, a necessary evil, a natural temptation, a desirable calamity, domestic danger, a delectable detriment, an evil nature, painted with fair colours [sp]. ... Women are by nature instruments of Satan -- they are by nature carnal, a structural defect rooted in the original creation."[16] It is apparent that witchcraft was very real to the people of 16th century. The European witch-craze of 1550 to 1650 was in full swing in Germany, France and Switzerland where thousands of witches were burned at the stake; and in England, where the craze was less intense, Elizabeth I and her Parliament found it necessary to pass the Witchcraft Act of 1563 that imposed the death sentence for any dealings with evil spirits for any purpose or witchcraft resulting in a death.

Tamora, the barbarous, exotic and pagan Queen of the Goths, coming as she does from the hotbed of witchcraft in the north and accompanied by a black man who is both her slave and her lover would immediately suggest diabolic tendencies. Her almost preternatural attractiveness is evidenced by her immediate seduction of Saturninus and her ability to manipulate him to her ends. In fact, all of the men in her immediate sphere: Saturninus, Aaron, and her two remaining sons, Chiron and Demetrius become extensions of her will. Tamora and her devilish familiar enjoy a symbiotic relationship necessary to the goals of both. The *Malleus Maleficarum* explicitly states that in order achieve an effect of magic, the devil must intimately cooperate with the witch and the witch with the devil. Tamora's goal is to destroy the Andronici; Aaron's goal is evil and disorder. But just as Aaron will serve Tamora's goal, Tamora will also serve Aaron's. Speaking of Tamora, Aaron says,

> *This siren, that will charm Rome's Saturnine*
> *And see his shipwrack and his commonweal's.*
> > (TA, II, 1, 23-24)

The witch's medieval folklore and some medieval theologians suggested that the witch cannot harm someone directly, but only through the agency of others. Tamora is never directly guilty of injuring the Andronici, although she clearly wills their every injury. Aaron plots her revenge, but is responsible for only one of the fourteen stage deaths, and that death has nothing to do with revenge on the Andronici. Lavinia is raped and mauled, and her husband Bassianus is murdered by Tamora's thuggish sons, but they take their direction from their mother as they drag Lavinia away.

> *...away with her, and use her as you will;*
> *The worse to her, the better loved of me.*
> > (TA, II, 3, 166-167)

Aaron frames Titus' two sons, Martius and Quintus, but it is the State that executes them. Tamora is really the font of all evil, and all that surround her, simply tools to achieve her nefarious ends. As tool and devil-familiar of Tamora, Aaron specifically serves her appetite for revenge and for sexual gratification. In return, he has the freedom and means to spread evil and ferment chaos, the raison d'être of devils. When viewed from this perspective, the "unrealistic, motiveless malignity" of Aaron suddenly can be explained and his character takes on significance far deeper than normally credited to him.

There are two key turning points in the progress of *Titus Andronicus*. The first comes in Act III, scene i when Titus has lost his hand and his two sons, when Lucius his remaining son has been banished, and his daughter Lavinia has been raped and mutilated. It is at this point that Titus realizes the importance of family above State and of love above rigid honor. In soaring Senecan rhetoric, Titus cries out his grief, then having "not another tear to shed," Titus resolves to seek out "Revenge's Cave." He orders his banished son Lucius to the Goths and there to raise an army to storm Rome and unseat the Emperor.

The second turning point comes in Act IV, scene 2 when the alliance between Tamora and Aaron falls apart. Aaron has begotten a son on the empress. To hide her infidelity from Saturninus, Tamora sends the child to Aaron with instructions that the child must be killed. Aaron refuses, saying of the child,

> ...this [the child] is myself,
> The vigor and the picture of my youth:
> This before all the world do I prefer;
> This mauger all the world will I keep safe.
>
> (TA, IV, 2, 107-110)

Aaron's protective attitude toward his child is juxtaposed against Titus' relative indifference to his own. It is this significant humanizing "hath not a Jew eyes" moment of the play that raises Aaron above the cartoonish Barabas and shows Shakespeare's early attempt to "invent the human." Aaron kills the nurse who brought him the child, his only killing in the entire play, then resolves to flee to the Goths where he hopes to raise the child to become a great warrior. At that point, the demonic power resulting from the union of Tamora and Aaron diminishes and their fortunes turn toward their ultimate demise.

In his only miscalculation of the play, Aaron is unaware that Lucius has joined with the Goths and when he arrives at their encampment he is taken prisoner. Under Lucius' threat to hang the child, Aaron negotiates a full confession in exchange for the life of his son. Meanwhile, back in Rome, Saturninus is being plagued by repeated appeals from Titus for justice and by the threat of invasion from Lucius and his Goths. Overconfident from her successes, Tamora sans Aaron proposes a parley with Lucius and boasts that she will persuade Titus to again support Saturninus.

> I will entreat the old Andronicus...
> For I can smooth and fill his aged ears
> With golden promises, that, were his heart
> Almost impregnable, his old ears deaf,
> Yet should both ear and heart obey my tongue.
>
> (TA, IV, 4, 90, 96-99)

In her second miscalculation of the play, her first being to allow Aaron to impregnate her, Tamora with her two sons goes to Titus in the disguise of Revenge, deluded that she will not be recognized because of Titus' reported madness. Titus easily sees through the ruse, agrees to host the parley between Lucius and the Emperor, and persuades Tamora to leave her sons with him until the meeting. As soon as she has left, Titus seizes the sons and prepares for his final revenge.

In executing his final revenge, Titus rounds out the Ovidian myth of "Progne and Philomela" first alluded to in the rape and mutilation of Lavinia. In the myth, Philomela is raped and mutilated by her sister Progne's husband, Tereus. When Progne uncovers the crime, she murders Tereus' –and her own – son and serves him up in a banquet to her husband. Titus describes his own plans to the doomed sons of the Empress,

> Hark, villains, I will grind your bones to dust,
> And with your blood and it will make a paste,
> And on the paste a coffin [pie crust] I will rear,
> And make two pasties of your shameful heads,
> And bid that strumpet, your unhallowed dam,
> Like the earth, swallow her own increase.
>
> (TA, V, 2, 187-192)

He then slits their throats on-stage while Lavinia collects their cascading blood in a bowel. The scene then changes to the banquet hall. Lucius and his Goth allies, Marcus, Saturninus, and Tamora enter followed by Titus, Lavinia and young Lucius. The dinner is served and while Saturninus and Tamora eat, Titus poses a question to the Emperor,

> Was it well done of rash Virginius
> To slay his daughter with his own right hand,
> Because she was enforced, stained, and deflow'r'd?
>
> (TA, V, 3, 36-38)

When Saturninus agrees that it was indeed well done, Titus enquires of his reasoning. Saturninus responds, saying

> Because the girl should not survive her shame,
> And by her presence still renew his sorrows.
>
> (TA, V, 3, 41-42)

In response, Titus kills Lavinia in what is the play's most chilling indictment of Titus and Rome's misogynistic patriarchy. At this point, any lingering sympathy for Titus that has survived the excesses of his revenge on Tamora and her sons vanishes in the horror of Lavinia's murder. The action accelerates as Titus reveals to Tamora the contents of his dinner, and then kills her. Saturninus kills Titus, then Lucius kills Saturninus. In the wake of this cataclysm, Lucius assumes the Empery and condemns the still proud and cussing Aaron.

Once we recover from the shock of the final act, we can look back at the play and try to grapple with the extent of villainy and evil we have witnessed. The witch-devil alliance of Tamora and Aaron reflects the misogyny and racism of the age. These principal villains reflect the fear of the stranger and the stereotypes associated with women and blacks, but Shakespeare does not turn Tamora and Aaron into cartoons. Instead, he grants them the one virtue that humanizes them and places them in opposition to the "hero" of the drama, Titus himself. Tamora and Aaron are caring parents, intent on caring for their own. Titus is directly responsible for the murder of two of his children, Mutius and Lavinia, who have offended him. Mutius defies the father and Lavinia, through no fault of her own, sorrows her father with her mere presence. That Tamora and Aaron are the clear villains of the drama is self-evident. But in the end, what do we make of Titus? When we count up the bodies, Titus kills five with his own hands. Tamora's sons kill one (Bassianus). Aaron kills one (the nurse). Titus kills two as a result of his offended honor and the remaining three in an act of revenge. Tamora's brutish sons kill Bassianus as a means to attain their lustful ends. Aaron kills the nurse to protect his child. The physical act of murder, however, is less important to Shakespeare's definition of villainy than the joyfully Machiavellian planning of murder. In this, Tamora and Aaron excel.

Titus, on the other hand, is a marginal Machiavel at best. Outside of preparing the "unpleasant" final meal for Tamora, his opportunity for executing revenge is one of convenience, ironically arranged by Tamora herself. Nevertheless, Titus cannot be allowed to escape the consequence of executing revenge regardless of how justified it might appear. Fredson Bower notes that Titus, like Hieronimo and other stage-revengers meet their death either because "they turn from sympathetic wronged heroes to bloody maniacs ... or else that the strain of the horrible situation in which they found themselves so warped their character that further existence in the normal world became impossible and death was the only solution."[17] The latter situation defines the case of Titus. While Titus is fatally flawed by his rigid pride and sense of honor, while many of his actions, particularly related to his children, are less than admirable, and while he ends a brutally bloody revenger, he is in the final analysis, not as a villain, but as a man more sinned against then sinning.

THE GREEN-EYED MONSTER: *OTHELLO*: IAGO

If Aaron is Shakespeare's most maligned villain, Iago is his most revered. Critics almost universally rank Iago as one of Shakespeare's finest creations, comparing him favorably to Hamlet and Falstaff. That said, one aspect of Iago that continues to provoke critical debate is the disparity between his motives and his actions. "[The] question 'Why?' " according to A. C. Bradley, is the question about Iago?"[18] Probably the most repeated critical comment concerning the "Why?" of Iago comes from Samuel Taylor Coleridge who wrote a note in his copy of Shakespeare referring to Iago's soliloquy in Act 1, Scene 3,

> The last Speech, **the motive-hunting of motiveless Malignity**--how awful! In itself fiendish--while yet he was allowed to bear the divine image, too fiendish for his own steady View.--A being next to Devil--only not quite Devil--& this Shakespeare has attempted-- executed--without disgust, without Scandal![19]

Coleridge further suggests that Iago's only motive for his mischief is his "love of exerting power" and that his malignity is "motiveless" because his professed motives are merely rationalizations. Thus, Coleridge's famous phrase is often taken to mean that Iago has no real motive and does evil only because he is evil. G. D. Gunther in *Shakespeare as Traditional Artist* says "The play opens by presenting Iago to us as the devil, the devil as he appears in human guise, as adversary and slanderer."[20] To accept the opinions of Coleridge and Gunther, is to place Iago on the same level as Aaron and to marginalize the greatness of the character. I have suggested earlier that Aaron is not a fully believable (human) character because he is drawn as a demonic familiar to the witch-queen Tamora. Aaron's malignity is in fact motiveless malignity unless he is seen as an extension and tool of Tamora's vengeful will. While Aaron is a somewhat humanized devil, a figure of allegorical evil, I would argue that Iago is devilish, but very fully human.

Iago explains his grievances against Othello plainly: he has been passed over for promotion and he suspects Othello of having bedded his wife, Emilia. In Act 1, scene 1, he says:

...Three great ones of the city,
In personal suit to make me his lieutenant,

Off-capp'd to him, and by the faith of man,
I know my price, I am worth no worse a place.
But he (as loving his own pride and purposes)
Evades them with a bombast circumstance
Horribly stuff'd with epithites of war,
And in conclusion,
Nonsuits my mediators; for "Certes," says he,
"I have already chosen my officer."
And what we he?
Forsooth, a great arithmetician,
One Michael Cassio, a Florentine

(O, I, 1, 8-20)

He speaks this to his dupe and toady, Roderigo, and although critics caution that Iago is a pathological liar and that his speeches are not to be believed, there is no reasonable cause here to doubt what he says. Later, while speaking to himself at the close of the first Act, Iago expresses a second grievance:

...it is thought abroad that t'wixt my sheets
H's done my office. I know not if't be true,
But I, for mere suspicion in that kind,
Will do as if for surety.

(O, I, 3, 387-390)

He tells us that this is more than a lonely suspicion as his suspicion is also "thought abroad." When we come to know Iago's wife better as the play progresses, the possibility of infidelity on her part is less than unlikely.

Somehow, these two grievances seem to the critics insufficient to warrant the depth of the evil perpetrated by Iago against Othello. This has set them off on a mission of "motive-hunting" that results in Iago being labeled a racist, a latent homosexual, a psychopath and much more. The history of race relations in the West, particularly in England and America makes a discussion of race and *Othello* unavoidable. We are forced to ask "Is *Othello* a racist play?" "Was Shakespeare a racist?" "Was Shakespeare's audience racist?" And most important to this study, "Is Iago a racist driven to evil by racial hatred?"

To be sure, Shakespeare's England was not without racial stereotypes and prejudices. The official attitude toward blacks in England was clearly expressed in 1596, when Queen Elizabeth issued an "open letter" to the Lord Mayor of London, announcing that "there are of late divers blackmoores brought into this realme, of which kinde of people there are already here to manie," and ordering that they be deported from the country.[21] One week later, she reiterated her "good pleasure to have those kinde of people sent out of the lande" and commissioned the merchant Casper van Senden to "take up" certain "blackamoores here in this realme and to transport them into Spaine and Portugall."[22] Finally, in 1601, she complained again about the "great numbers of Negars and Blackamoors which are crept into this realm," defamed them as "infidels, having no understanding of Christ or his Gospel," and, one last time, authorized their deportation.[23]

The travelogues, Richard Hakaluyt's *Principal Navigations* and Africanus' *A Geographical Historie of Africa*, did much to shape the English attitude toward blacks and they generally portrayed blacks more as animals than men describing them as unpredictable, devious, lascivious, cruel and intellectually weak. *The History and Description of Africa* by John Leo defined blacks by their credulity, their high regard of chastity, their jealousy and the fury of their wrath. They were also credited with some unusual power of attraction over white women.

There was also a tradition formed at the nexus of religion and theater found in the Mystery Plays of the late Middle Ages. By the time of Shakespeare, the color black had been firmly positioned to represent the opposite of Christian values. In Mysteries, the image of the black person came to solidify grotesqueness and foolery. The stage devils were usually clad in black or represented as black men. The most frequently cited instances of blackness being identified with evil in the English theater tradition would be found in the Wakefield mystery cycle's The Creation, and the Fall of Lucifer (ca. 1460). In these, the fallen angels lament "We, that were angels so fare, and sat so hie aboue the ayere,/ Now ar we waxen blak as any coyll [coal]...."[24]

As the religious trappings of the dramas fell away, the early modern theater was born, but the black = evil equation remained. Now when a black character appeared in a production, they were uniformly villains: Muly Hamet in the *Battle of Alcazar* (1594), Aaron in *Titus Andronicus* (1594), and Eleazer in *Lust's Dominion* (1600). In 1596, eight years before *Othello*, Shakespeare broke with the pattern of the evil black with a minor character in *The Merchant of Venice*. A noble, well spoken, but foolish Moor, the Prince of Morocco comes to win Portia in the game of caskets. He is described as "tawny" in the stage direction, so he is probably not meant to be as fully black as Othello. Like Othello, he is a proud and great warrior and, in spite of the "shadowed livery" of his complexion, he is well received by Portia who tells him:

> But if my father had not scanter me
> And hedg'ed me by his wit to yield myself
> His wife who wins me by that means I told you

Yourself, renowned Prince, then stood as fair
As any comer I have look'd on yet
For my affection.

(MOV, II, 2, 17-22)

He of course fails the challenge of the caskets and is spared the issues of a Moor who marries a white woman.

After this "experiment," Shakespeare is ready to tackle a fully realized black character and with Othello he uses the existing racial stereotypes in creating his noble Moor, but then works with character to subvert the stereotype and humanize his creation. So is *Othello* a racist play? I think not. It does adhere to some of the racial stereotypes of the period, as does *The Merchant of Venice* with respect to Jews, but Othello is not the stereotyped black villain of the English stage tradition. That there are racist undercurrents running through the play is undeniable and most are linked to the "problem" of a black man "unnaturally" married to a white woman. Barbantio is the character most given to racist outburst, but he is also a father deceived by his daughter. Is it not likely he would seize upon any avenue of attack to disparage any man who had eloped with his daughter? Roderigo and Iago are given to uttering racial comments, but they are hardly representative of Venetian society and both have reason to resent and attack Othello. The fact is that the majority of the cast seem to have nothing but respect and admiration for Othello. They take him as they find him. In the final analysis, Othello's race is certainly a factor in the tragedy because it highlights the exotic "otherness" of Othello, but as a character Shakespeare does not treat him as anything other than a sad and noble outsider capable of capturing the imagination and sympathy of the audience.

The critical response to and the performance history of *Othello* speaks more to the attitude of critics and audiences than to any inherent racism is the play. In 1692, Thomas Rymer found the play unbelievable, suggesting that the playwright stretched credibility too far in presenting Othello as a General in the Venetian army or as husband to a well-born white woman.

> *The character of [Venice] is to employ strangers in their wars; But shall a poet thence fancy that they will set a Negro to be their General; Or trust a Moor to defend them against the Turk. With us a Black-amoor might rise to be Trumpeter; but Shakespeare would not have less than a Lieutenant. With Us a Moor might marry some little drab, or small-coal Wench; Shakespeare would provide him the Daughter and Heir of some great Lord or privy-councellor.* [24]

This clearly racist attitude continued throughout the 18th century and into the 19th century when we find Samuel Coleridge suggesting that the character of Othello would be more believable if the Negroid characteristics of Othello were substituted with those of the lighter skinned North Africans. Applauding the performance of the famous Shakespearean actor, Edmund Kean who introduced the first nonblack (i.e., non-black faced white actor) Arabian Othello in 1816, Coleridge wrote "Othello must not be conceived as a negro, but a high and chivalrous Moorish chief."[25] Kean's "tawny" Othello continued through the 19th and first half of the 20th century. Although Kean's method of portrayal went a long way toward defusing the racial tensions raised by *Othello* in England, the tragedy continued to flame racial anxieties in America. Surprisingly, Othello enjoyed some popularity in the American South prior to the civil war, being performed in Charleston sixty-three times, Memphis twenty times, Mobile forty-one times and so on.[26] James Dorman explained this by advancing the idea that southern audiences saw *Othello* as a cautionary tale against the evil of miscegenetation.[27] Nevertheless, American audiences would not accept a "black" Othello having physical contact with a white Desdemona, and the Kean vision of the Arabian (or "bronze") was the only acceptable portrayal on the American stage. Great Britain saw its first notable black actor take the stage as Othello in the 1830's. Ira Aldridge, an African-American, enjoyed his initial success in the role at Dublin's Theater Royal in 1831-2 and his performance there was applauded and endorsed by none other than Edmund Kean. Aldridge's performances in England at first received mixed reviews, but gradually won general acceptance and Aldridge went on to perform the role throughout Europe to great acclaim. Sadly, Aldridge was never able to take his performance of Othello to the American stage. That distinction was reserved to Wayland Rudd who in 1930 became the first black actor to play Othello in a white professional company in America. In 1932, according to an article by Jack El-Hai, the Communist International party paid to send a cast of American blacks to Moscow to make a movie about American racial injustice. Wayland Rudd was one of the actors selected and though the plan subsequently failed for the movie, Rudd remained in the Soviet Union where he studied acting and directing in Moscow and attempted to use his American stage experience as a springboard for Soviet theater work. Unfortunately, as probably would have happened in the United States, he found himself restricted to portrayals of exotic natives and such roles as Jim in *The Adventures of Huckleberry Finn*. He became a Soviet citizen and died sometime after 1959.[28] Twelve years after Rudd's performance as Othello, another African-American actor, Paul Robeson, opened in New York as Othello and triggered with his strong noble portrayal of the Moor a slow transition that would so firmly establish the "Africanized" Othello that by the beginning of the twenty-first century, it seems improbable that a "blacked-up" white actor would ever be able to credibly perform the role. Today, watching the coal-black Sir Laurence Olivier in Stuart Burge's 1967 film version of *Othello* is nearly painful as it is so clearly a white man's interpretation of a black man. With little subtlety, Olivier lunges from sensual lover to raging beast with barely a pause between the two. His too white eyes roll in his too black face in a performance that reminds today's viewer of minstrel shows and the shamefully racist portrayal of blacks in the films of the 1930's, 40's, and 50's. When compared with the naturalistic performance of Laurence Fishburne in Oliver Parker's 1995 *Othello*, the Olivier portrayal highlights the insidious racism that can inform the tragedy if actor or director chooses to adopt a currently popular stereotype.

The curse and beauty of *Othello* is that it is so susceptible to performers and audiences pouring into the characters their particular empathies and anxieties. If an actor chooses to present Othello as a caricature of a stereotypical black man it can be easily (and sometimes unconsciously) done. If an audience chooses to view Iago as society's racist avenger for Othello's "unnatural" union, it is easy enough to do; but if an actor attempts to portray Iago's hatred of Othello as racially motivated, I believe it will be an up-hill climb. We do well to remember that Iago served Othello as ensign, a position of trust and responsibility. Is it probable that a rabid racist would serve the object of his contempt? Indeed, as the play opens, he explains why he serves Othello:

> *I follow him to serve my turn upon him.*
> *We cannot all be masters, nor all masters*
> *Cannot be truly followed...*
> *...Others there are*
> *Who trimmed in forms and visages of duty,*
> *Keep yet their hearts attending on themselves*
> *And throwing but shows of service on their lords,*
> *Do well thrive by them, and, when they have lined their coats,*
> *Do themselves homage: these fellows have some soul*
> *And such a one do I profess myself...*
> *...In following him, I follow but myself;*
> *Heaven is my judge, not I for love and duty,*
> *But seeming so, for my peculiar end...*
>   (0, I, 1, 40-42, 48-54, 58-60)

So we can conclude that Iago could by his own admission serve any master so long as that service worked to the ultimate advantage of Iago. Othello's race or Iago's distaste for it would be no bar to Iago's "seemingly" loyal service to the Moor. Throughout the play, Iago shows himself to be the consummate actor, able to play many roles and convincingly deceive all his fellow players. He could surely smile and smile and yet be brimming with racial hatred, but once again, it is important to recall the responsibility of the ensign in military affairs. The ensign would as the commander's standard bearer vowed to die rather than allow the commander's colors to be taken. Iago's position, as Harold Bloom points out, testifies both to Othello's trust and to Iago's devotion. For this reason, I find it more convincing that Iago was in truth a loyal ensign to Othello and served him out of admiration, more than self-interest.

When preparing to stage *Othello* in the 1950's, Laurence Olivier consulted Dr. Ernest Jones, a friend and devotee of Sigmund Freud, for insights into the characters. According to Felix Barker writing in *The Oliviers,* Dr. Jones believes:

> ...the clue to the play was not Iago's hatred for Othello, but his deep affection for him. His jealousy was not because he envied Othello's position, not because he was in love with Desdemona, but because he himself possessed a subconscious affection for the Moor, the homosexual foundation of which he did not understand. [29]

Inspired by Jones, Olivier turns the Act III scene where Iago and Othello knell together as they plot the death of Cassio into a mock marriage where they swear fealty to one another. Iago, falling on this kneels before the already kneeling Othello says,

> Witness that here Iago doth give up
> The execution of his wit, hands, and heart,
> To the wrong'd Othello's service. Let me command.

Othello responds,

> I greet thy love
> Not with vain thanks, but with acceptance bounteous...
> ...Now art thou my lieutenant.

To which Iago responds,

> I am your own for ever.

(O, III, 3, 465-67, 469-70, 479-80)

Enamored with the idea, Olivier adopted a "gay" persona for his Iago and met with notable failure. It seems no one could quite figure out what Olivier was doing and why he was doing it. He became more of a comic figure, robbing Iago of his essential wickedness. In retrospect, Olivier came to reject Jones' theory, noting that while he could "still accept a psychological interpretation involving homosexuality as it exists entirely in the subconscious, there is no object for toughing on it in any detail of performance"[30]

Nevertheless, psychoanalytic discussions of Iago's supposed latent homosexuality regularly capture the attention of scholars. M. D. Faber in *The Design Within* renewed discussion in 1970, and in 2006 David Somerton, Linford S. Haines and J.P. Doolan-York devoted several chapters of *Notes for Literature Students on the Tragedy of Othello* to arguing the case for 'Sexuality and Sexual Imagery' in the play. They concluded that Iago is "a pre-Jungian expression of Shakespeare's shadow, his own repressed homosexuality," and that Iago's unrequited love for Othello is the explanation for his otherwise motiveless but passionate loathing.

Oliver Parker's 1995 film treatment of Othello touches visually on the theme of Iago's latent homosexuality with Kenneth Branagh taking the role of the vengeful ensign and Laurence Fishburne in the role of the Moor. In it, the knelling scene is performed under a cloudy sky, with Othello and Iago exchanging vows and conducting a blood bonding to seal their loyalty. At the end of the ceremony, the two embrace and the camera focuses on Iago's emotion wracked face. In a voice thick with passion, Iago speaks his line, "*I am your own for ever,*" then closes his moistening eyes is a look of complete devotion. In the final act, after Othello commits suicide, Lodovico pulls the wounded Iago to the side of the bed now crowded with bodies and Lodovico hisses,

> *I look on the tragic loading of this bed;*
> *This is thy work; the object poisons sight;*
> > *(O, V, 2, 363-64)*

Iago's face shows no emotion, but moments later he also crawls on to the bed and rests his head on Othello's thigh demonstrating his continued devotion to his fallen general.

Marvin Rosenberg argues against a homosexual motivation for Iago saying that, if present, it should have explicitly emerged in Iago's soliloquies. He goes on to say that a visual statement of homosexuality, such as that in Parker's *Othello,* (especially lacking, as it does, a supporting verbal statement) would distort the whole context of Iago's actions. Rosenberg insists that Iago is, in fact, incapable of love, homosexual or otherwise.[31] I am inclined to agree. If I were to look for some submerged subconscious motivation, I would suggest that Iago is drawn to Othello not by a sexual attraction, but by a search for the approval and affection of a surrogate father. The relationship between Othello and Iago puts me in mind of the Biblical story of Jacob and Esau where the younger brother, Jacob, deceitfully robs the elder, Esau, of the blessing of their father, Isaac. Esau, outranged at the brother's deception, intends to kill him, but being a Bible story, the two are ultimately reconciled. While not a direct parallel, the story does portray the importance of a father's acceptance (blessing) to a son. Othello, as the father figure of his tragedy, rejects the elder son, Iago, in favor of the younger son, Cassio. By passing over the devoted and proven Iago for promotion in favor of the less experienced Cassio, Othello ignites a fire of rage in Iago directed not only at the younger "brother," but also at the rejecting father. As I've said before, Shakespeare invites the audience to invent the backstory of his characters. In Othello's case, the Moor's history is unusually complete; in Iago's case, the history is completely absent. Harold Goddard in *The Meaning of Shakespeare, Volume 1* writes

> ....that some situation or event early in Iago's life...produced a profound sense of injustice or inferiority and instigated a revolt against it [that] could alone have produced such a twisted nature.[32]

Psychoanalyst Carl Goldberg in his article "Iago's Malevolence" published in *Jihad and Sacred Vengeance* explains the "twisted nature" of Iago this way:

> The two most important psychological factors in regard to the development of the destructive personalities of the people I treated were the roles of shame and self-contempt in shaping their personal identities.
> There is no more unbearable virulence visited upon any of us then unremitting, unrelieved self-contempt resulting from a person's sense of goodness and self-worth. Boyce (1990) points out that Iago 'senses that the open and virtuous qualities others may point up his own worthlessness [the most important of these are] Othello's steadfast, loving character [The Moor, howbeit, that I endure him not/Is of a constant loving, noble nature' (II, 1, 328-329) and the nobility of Cassio ['He hath a daily beauty in his life/That makes me ugly' V, 1, 21-22]"[33]

Goldberg goes on to say that a number of these destructive people he treated came from authoritarian families were expectations were high and failure to attain them was punished either physically or emotionally. The father figure becomes a god to be worshipped and pleased, but the father's love comes with conditions and expectations. The inability of the child to satisfy the father's expectations leads to feelings of shame and rejection. Many of Goldberg's patients had attempted to overcome their self-contempt through shows of bravado, choosing careers in the military or law enforcement where they could fit in to a well ordered and clearly defined power and status system. Their superiors become surrogate fathers whose expectations are fair and achievable and who reward their "sons" for achievement. This kind of environment encourages a compensatory sense of exaggerated self-worth. When this system breaks down as it does for Iago, the "son" feels betrayed and the feelings of shame from childhood threatens the stabilizing self-image the "son" has manufactured for himself. This according to Goldberg, forces shame to morph into shamelessness. The offended person adopts the position that the "chips are stacked against him" and on that basis, he feels justified to strike back against the system and its representatives to restore his fragile sense of self-worth. Viewed in this light, the intensity of Iago's hatred for Othello and Cassio is easier to understand. At once, Iago seeks to destroy Othello while simultaneously trying to win back his love and approval. If he can eliminate his rival's for the Moor's affection, he can receive the approval of the rejecting father and enjoy the promotion he feels he has earned. By eliminating Desdemona and Cassio, he can isolate Othello and he expects to become the Moor's sole source of support.

With that psychological groundwork laid, I would like to suggest that Iago is the first clearly psychopathic character in modern literature. Part of the difficulty of Iago is that he is a 21st century villain in a 16th century play. Perhaps Coleridge and his contemporaries could not imagine a man so petty and so vindictive that he could inflict so much evil for so little an injury as being overlooked for a promotion. Even as late as 1958, Bernard Spivack in *Shakespeare and the Allegory of Evil* says "that in Iago we encounter a form of evil which is fundamentally inscrutable from the perspective of modern psychological criticism."[34] Today, in the narcissistic age of the early 21st century, such a man is all too believable, even if still inscrutable.

Noted 20th century criminal psychologist, Dr. Robert Hare studied psychopaths and developed a checklist of characteristics common to their pathology. The following reads like a character sketch of Iago:

- *Grandiose Sense of Self*
  Feels entitled to certain things as "their right."

- *Manipulative and Cunning*
  They never recognize the rights of others and see their self-serving behaviors as permissible. They appear to be charming, yet are covertly hostile and domineering, seeing their victim as merely an instrument to be used. They may dominate and humiliate their victims.

- Pathological Lying
  Has no problem lying coolly and easily and it is almost impossible for them to be truthful on a consistent basis. Can create, and get caught up in, a complex belief about their own powers and abilities. Extremely convincing and even able to pass lie detector tests.

- Poor Behavioral Controls/Impulsive Nature
  Rage and abuse, alternating with small expressions of love and approval produce an addictive cycle for abuser and abused, as well as creating hopelessness in the victim. Believe they are all-powerful, all-knowing, entitled to every wish, no sense of personal boundaries, no concern for their impact on others

- Lack of Remorse, Shame or Guilt
  A deep seated rage, which is split off and repressed, is at their core. Does not see others around them as people, but only as targets and opportunities. Instead of friends, they have victims and accomplices who end up as victims. The end always justifies the means and they let nothing stand in their way.

- Glibness and Superficial Charm

- Shallow Emotions
  When they show what seems to be warmth, joy, love and compassion it is more feigned than experienced and serves an ulterior motive. Outraged by insignificant matters, yet remaining unmoved and cold by what would upset a normal person. Since they are not genuine, neither are their promises.

- Incapacity for Love

- Need for Stimulation
  Living on the edge. Verbal outbursts and physical punishments are normal. Promiscuity and gambling are common.

- Callousness/Lack of Empathy
  Unable to empathize with the pain of their victims, having only contempt for others' feelings of distress and readily taking advantage of them.

- Early Behavior Problems/Juvenile Delinquency
  Usually has a history of behavioral and academic difficulties, yet "gets by" by conning others. Problems in making and keeping friends; aberrant behaviors such as cruelty to people or animals, stealing, etc.

- Irresponsibility/Unreliability
  Not concerned about wrecking others' lives and dreams. Oblivious or indifferent to the devastation they cause. Does not accept blame themselves, but blames others, even for acts they obviously committed.

- Promiscuous Sexual Behavior/Infidelity
  Promiscuity, child sexual abuse, rape and sexual acting out of all sorts.

- *Lack of Realistic Life Plan/Parasitic Lifestyle*
  Tends to move around a lot or makes all-encompassing promises for the future, poor work ethic but exploits others effectively.
- *Criminal or Entrepreneurial Versatility*
  Changes their image as needed to avoid prosecution. Changes life story readily.[35]

Consider the first point: the "grandiose sense of self." From the first scene of the first act, Iago expresses his elevated self-image. His principle reason for hating Othello is that he was passed over for promotion by someone he resents as possessing inferior military skill. Michael Cassio is a "great arithmetician," a book scholar, "that never set a squadron in the field/ Nor the division of a squadron knows" (O, I, 1, 19, 22-23). Iago explains to Roderigo, his dupe and toady, that Othello has seen his (Iago's) martial skills first hand on battlefield "[a]t Rhodes, at Cyprus, and on other grounds." So why was Cassio promoted over Iago to Lieutenant, the second in command, when the position became available? Iago's explanation is one familiar to all of us:

> *Preferment goes by letter and affection,*
> *And not by old gradation, where each second*
> *Stood heir to th' first?*
> $\qquad\qquad$ *(O, I, 1, 36-38)*

In other words, Cassio received the promotion because of private recommendations and favoritism rather than on the basis of proven ability and seniority. It is for this reason, Iago asserts he hates the Moor. Is this sufficient grounds for the mayhem he will create throughout the course of the play? To the 18th century critics like Coleridge, Iago's malignity seemed unthinkable, but to the 21st century reader used to the slighted employee shooting-up an office and co-workers because he feels "diss'd" by the boss, we marvel more at Iago's means rather than at his motive. Does Iago have reason to feel "diss'd"? Was he unfairly passed over for promotion? Is his sense of self in fact grandiose?

It is noteworthy that Iago's companions universally praise the man. He is first and always "honest Iago." Coarse, but in the rough way of the soldier, cynical, but friendly and good natured, Iago is the confident of all: Othello, Desdemona, Cassio, Roderigo. They all turn to Iago for advice and consolation. Are we to conclude that they have all been taken in by the pathologic villain we see in the drama or can we conclude that their opinion of Iago is grounded in the true nature of the pre-drama Iago? If the former, is it credible that Iago's psychopathology would not have manifested itself by the age of 28? And if the psychopathy was present and simply escaped the notice of those around him, why does Iago not gloat upon prior nefarious deeds as we saw happen in the cases of Aaron and Barabas? If the latter, which I suspect is the case. It is the loss of promotion that triggers Iago's attack on Othello and that invites us to examine the fairness of Othello's choice of lieutenant.

If Iago is (or was) as honest as his companions believe, if his experience in combat exceeds that of Michael Cassio, if his judgments and suggestions are unquestioned by all, why would Othello promote the callow Michael Cassio over the experienced and respected Iago? There is nothing in the play to suggest that Michael Cassio is in any manner superior to Iago. Cassio is hardly an exemplary leader. In spite of a self-professed weakness for alcohol, he allows himself with minimum persuasion to become drunk and in his intoxicated state, he allows himself to become embroiled in a brawl. Cassio show contempt for his subordinates as is evidenced by this exchange with Iago:

> **Cas.**   ...there be souls that must be sav'd
> and there be souls must not be sav'd
> **Iago.**   It's true, good lieutenant.
> **Cas.**   For my part—no offence to the general,
> nor any man of quality—I hope to be sav'd.
> **Iago.**   And so do I too, lieutenant.
> **Cas.**   Ay, but by your leave, not before me;
>   the lieutenant is to be sav'd before the ancient.
> (O, II, 3, 103-110)

This is hardly a speech to inspire loyalty among the ranks! All in all, Cassio comes off as a spoiled, ivy-league "pretty boy" promoted as Iago says because of his charm and his connections instead of proven talent or skill. So I believe it is reasonable for the audience to accept Iago's contention that he was unfairly passed over for promotion and that his hatred of Othello, though out of proportion to the harm, is understandable. The problem for the motive hunting critics is, of course the magnitude of Iago's rage. Hare in his checklist of traits defining the psychopathic personality notes that the psychopath carries around a "deep seated rage, which is split off and repressed, is at their core." When offended, the psychopath's rage will overflow the walls of repression and manifest itself in exaggerated acts of violence and revenge. So it is in the case of Iago.

Many of Iago's psychopathic traits are so self-evident that they hardly need detailed discussion. That he is cunning, manipulative and a pathological liar is undeniable. His charm and his lack of remorse are equally apparent. Other traits on Hare's list do not seem to apply to Iago at all. He is neither promiscuous nor unreliable. We know nothing of his childhood or of any childhood delinquency. One trait, however, cries out for discussion because it so importantly reflects an aspect of Shakespeare's world view.

The psychopath's need for stimulation, to live on the edge, is apparent in Iago's joy of the game he plays with the lives of Othello, Desdemona and Cassio. He is both the director and lead actor in the drama of his own making. He sees the world of Cypress as the stage on which the he will produce the tragedy of Othello. Venice is his prelude. New to his role as director, Iago's script is unformed. He knows he hates the Moor and that he wants revenge for the slight he has received, but the form of that revenge is still to be worked out. In the beginning, it does not appear that Iago intends a mortal attack on Othello. He stirs up Brabantio in the hope that that he will bring shame and possible demotion to the Moor and perhaps deprive him of the happiness of his new wife. Iago tells Roderigo

> Call up her father,
> Rouse him, make after him, poison his delight, (here he means Othello)
> Proclaim him in the street, incense her kinsmen.
> And though he in a fertile climate dwell,
> Plague him with flies, though that his joy be joy
> Yet throw such changes of vexation on't
> As it may lose some colour.
>
> (O, I. 1, 67-73)

When this plan fails, he needs to plot a new strategy. Bob Hoskins captures this moment perfectly in the BBC *Othello* where he as Iago ponders to himself his next steps. Instead of directing the soliloquy directly to the audience, Hoskins allows the audience to overhear his private thoughts as he develops the broad strokes of his new plan.

> Cassio's a proper man: let me see now;
> To get his place, and to plume up my will
> In double knavery – How, how – Let's see --
> After some time, to abuse Othello's ear
> That he is too familiar with his wife.
> He hath a person, and a smooth dispose,
> To be suspected; framed to make women false.
> The Moor is of a free and open nature.
> That thinks men honest that but seem to be so,
> And will as tenderly be led by the nose
> As asses are.

I have it. It is engender'd.

(O, I, 3, 392-402)

The scene changes to Cyprus and Iago has an opportunity to observe the close familiarity between Cassio and Desdemona and their conduct encourages Iago that his plot may work. The first task is to discredit the young lieutenant that to achieve this, he scripts a brawl where his dupe, Roderigo plays the role of provocateur opposite unwitting Cassio. To assure success, Iago plays the 'good fellow" encouraging Cassio to indulge his weakness for wine. Intoxicated, Cassio is easily drawn into conflict with Roderigo and Montano, the former governor of Cyprus intervenes to restore peace, Cassio turns on him and injures him. Othello, roused from his bed by the uproar, interestingly queries Iago and not his lieutenant how the fray was begun. With false reluctance Iago lays the blame on Cassio and Othello dismisses Cassio from his office. After Othello has retired, Iago ever the false friend attempts to cheer Cassio and encourages him to recruit "the general's general" Desdemona to plead for his reinstatement to office.

> *And by how much she strives to do him [Cassio] good*
> *So shall she undo her credit with the Moor.*
> *So will I turn her virtue into pitch;*
> *And out of her own goodness make the net;*
> *That shall enmesh them all.*
>
> *(O, II, 3, 358-63)*

The trap is set and Iago now sits back and waits for the right moment to spring it.

> *Two things are to be done:*
> *My wife must move for Cassio with her mistress;*
> *I'll set her on;*
> *And bring him jump when he may Cassio find*
> *Soliciting his wife; aye, that's the way.*
>
> *(O, II, 3, 382-7)*

Two short scenes later, Iago leads Othello upon the very scene he has envisioned: Cassio and Desdemona in conference. Cassio, leaving the scene quickly, prompts Iago to huff "Hah? I like that not." This "startled" outburst leads to an exchange between Iago and Othello where the former sets the hook in the mouth of the latter. Through inference and innuendo Iago plants the seeds of jealousy in the heart and mind of the Moor and by the end of their discussion,

Othello has gone from happy husband to enraged cuckold. Hoping against hope, Othello turns his fury upon Iago. Grabbing him by the throat, Othello demands

> *Villain, be sure thou prove my love a whore;*
> *Be sure if it. Give me the ocular proof,*
> *Or by the worth of mine immortal soul*
> *Thou hath been better have been born a dog*
> *Than answer my wak'd wrath!*
>
> (O, III, 3, 259-63)

This is, I believe the precise turning point where Iago, heretofore willing to rob Cassio of his office and reputation, slander Desdemona's virtue and destroy Othello's future happiness, is first convinced that the death of the principals is the only safe outcome possible as a result of the schemes he has placed in motion. Ever quick on his feet, Iago reassures Othello of his loyalty further inflames Othello's jealously and promise to kill Cassio for his fantasized adultery with Desdemona. But before Iago can kill Cassio, he still must provide Othello with the "ocular proof" of Desdemona's infidelity. To accomplish this, Iago again assumes the role of director and actor in a scripted interlude. Using Desdemona's stolen handkerchief, Iago stages a scene with the unwitting Cassio where the dialogue is contrived to convince the listening, but hidden Othello that Cassio is confessing to adultery with Desdemona. Othello's darkest fears now confirmed, the Moor, encouraged by Iago, announces his intention to kill his wife.

The prelude to Desdemona's murder provides one of the plays most interesting scenes. How this scene is played by an actor can define the extent of Iago's malignity. In Act 4, scene 2 Othello has brutally confronted Desdemona with his suspicions, and then after he has left the room, she seeks comfort from Iago and Emilia, his wife. The tearful heroine say

> *Alas Iago,*
> *What shall I do to win my lord again?*
> *Good friend, go to him, for, by the light of heaven,*
> *I know not how I lost him*
>
> (O, IV, 2, 249-52)

And Iago, "compassionately" consoles her, blaming Othello's behavior on the pressure of his office. In this scene, for the first time, he is confronted with the suffering he has caused the one true innocent of the play. In the small space between Desdemona leaving the scene and Roderigo entering, what does the facial expression or the body language of the actor communicate? Does he manifest the psychopath's inability to empathize with the pain of victim? Does he watch Desdemona leave the stage with an expression cold indifference or gleeful satisfaction at her distress? Or does he stare after her with an expression of pained compassion, suggesting that he has some regret that this good lady will be devoured in the jaws of the trap he has laid for the Moor? Is he, as Tucker Brooke suggests in *The Romantic Iago* simply a cleaver and petty man who for vengeance sets in motion a series of actions that quickly grow beyond his ability to control.[36] He started the play as scriptwriter, star and director of his own little revenge tragedy with Othello as the sole protagonist. Soon Cassio and Desdemona are added to the victim list. Iago's first mistake is to underestimate Othello's violent response to the suggestion of Desdemona's infidelity. For his own safety, Iago is forced to amend his script, now to include the deaths of the actors. He is untroubled by the thought of Othello's fate and even less so by the death of Cassio. In his distorted sense of justice, Othello and Cassio have earned their fates. But Desdemona, fully innocent of offending Iago's elevated sense of self, is drawn in to Iago's tragedy as a tool, as the "net to enmesh them all." Does Iago regret Desdemona's involvement? I have seen Iago played this way; manifesting regret that Desdemona will be destroyed in his plots and resignation that there is no other way forward.

For Iago to show no misgivings at the Act IV, scene 2 interlude is to stamp the villain as one of Hare's classic narcissistic psychopaths, just a more subtle version of Aaron, a human aberration of malignant evil. But for the actor to use this brief space in time to show empathy with the suffering of Desdemona and some small gesture of resigned regret elevates the character of Iago from stage villain to a tragic figure himself. Like Othello, Iago is a basically good man (remember "honest Iago") destroyed by jealousy, the famous green-eyed monster. His actions are impelled by jealousy of Cassio and resentment of Othello. He is in some way similar to Macbeth, another good man who by a single, though certainly horrendous act of ambition sets himself upon a path of and to destruction. Like Macbeth, Iago in Act III, scene 3 when he faces the ignited wrath of Othello, realizes that he has wadded so far into his plots that there is no safe way back. Certainly, Iago is not given the explicit speeches of introspective regret we find in Macbeth. Since Shakespeare chose not to explicitly show any regret on Iago's part, it is fully consistent to simply label Iago as a classic stage villain, an evil narcissistic psychopath. But I would suggest, since the central theme of the play is jealousy, it works well to have both Othello and Iago destroyed by it. By adopting this interpretation, Othello and Iago are doubled: Othello destroys his beloved Desdemona because he feels betrayed, because he feels someone has taken from him that which is rightfully his. Similarly, Iago destroys his beloved Othello because he feels betrayed, because he feels someone has taken from him that which is rightfully his. Both are impelled by their jealousy; both are doomed by their actions.

In either case, Iago steadfastly pursues the path he has set upon, plotting with Roderigo to murder Cassio in the street. The attack fails, both Cassio and Roderigo are wounded and Iago finishes Roderigo off assuring his silence about Iago's leadership role in the attack. Meanwhile, Othello is murdering Desdemona in her bed. Discovered by Emilia immediately following the murder, her shrieks bring all, including the Venetian envoy Lodovico and Iago to the bedchamber. Othello explaining his action calls upon Iago to support his contention that Desdemona was unfaithful. When Iago agrees, Emilia is shocked, then outraged and proceeds to unveil Iago's nefarious plotting. For her honesty she is killed by her husband. Now aware that he has been undone by Iago's plots, Othello wounds Iago and then asks

> Will you, I pray, demand that demi-devil
> Why he has thus ensnared my soul and body?
>
> (O, V, 2, 301-2)

Iago replies defiantly with one of his best remembered statements,

> Demand me nothing; what you know, you know:
> From this time forth I never will speak word.
>
> (O, V, 2, 303-4)

Othello commits suicide and the tragedy closes with Iago led off, like Aaron, to torture and death. The play scripted and directed by Iago is also over, but not necessarily to his liking. He has encountered complications in his script and has been able to improvise adjustments that kept the play going, but in the end one actor, Emilia, unexpectedly steps out of her assigned role as compliant wife and turns into a raging Fury straight from Greek tragedy. When improvisation cannot work, Iago flees but cannot escape. Still, Iago's plot of revenge on Othello is accomplished and although Iago is also enmeshed in the net he has constructed, he must in the end feel a certain satisfaction that he has bested the proud Moor. His little play of destruction is his supreme work of artistic drama and like the stereotypical artist, he will not explain his art, but lets the art speak for itself. It is up to Othello, Lodovico and the audience to make of it what they will.

STAND UP FOR BASTARDS: KING LEAR: EDMUND MUCH ADO ABOUT NOTHING: DON JOHN

Most readers would characterize Iago as a real bastard, meaning what the *Compact Oxford English Dictionary* defines informally as "an unpleasant or despicable person." As to the formal definition of a bastard, "an illegitimate person, a child born out of wedlock," Iago probably does not fit the term. Further, *Wiktionary* adds to the definition of "bastard" the following characteristics: "something of no value or worth, of irregular or inferior or of dubious origin." Again Iago would probably not fit this definition as he is clearly is valued by Othello and is irregular and inferior only in his moral compass. For Shakespeare to have made Iago a literal bastard, i.e. an illegitimate person, would have weakened the chilling malignity of Iago by boxing his character into a stock villain whose evil could be easily explained away by his tainted birth. The disparaging attitude of Elizabethans toward bastards is a tradition that literally spans the ages. In Deuteronomy 23:2, the law of the Hebrews specifies "[a] bastard shall not enter into the congregation of the LORD; even to his tenth generation shall he not enter into the congregation of the LORD." In Medieval England, the Latin phrase "filius nullius" was applied to bastards and literally means "nobody's son." In England's canon and common law, bastards received no automatic inheritance in land. In manorial law "a bastard can never be heir unto any man, nor yet have heir unto himself but his children." Henry Swinburne's *Treatise of Testaments, Part 5* specifically lays out the rules governing bastards.

> Bastards begotten and bourne in Adultery or Incest, are not capable any benefit by the Testament or last will of their incestuous or adulterous parents...
> ...by the Laws Ecclsiatical they are ...capable of so much of that which is bequeathed unto them by their incestuous and adulterous parents, as will suffice for their competent alimentation or relief: that is to say, for their food, clothing, lodging, and other meet and convenient necessaries, according to the wealthy and ability of the parents, and although the civil Law in detestation of this heinous sin of incest and adultery did deprive this incestuous and adulterous issue of the hope of all testamentary benefit, ...to restrain the unbridled lusts of some and to preserve the chastity of others.

In 17th century England, the bastard child might even be denied baptism; when allowed, the parish register would explicitly note the child as "bastard." [37]

The bastard was believed to be tainted from birth by the sin of his parents and as such it was assumed that he would have a twisted moral compass. Even if acknowledged, the bastard bore the stigma and shame of illegitimacy and the social isolation of someone outside the norm.

There are four bastards in Shakespeare's canon, two are outright villains, one is cowardly and craven, and one is a heroic figure who rises above his stained paternity. The latter is Philip "the bastard: Faulconbridge in *King John* (1595-6). A play focused on a weak and cowardly king and on the machinations of real politick and the wrangling over the right to rule the throne of England, *King John* like *Titus Andronicus* is a story nearly bereft of an admirable character let alone of a heroic one. The central plot focuses on the conflict between King John who sits upon the English throne and the claim of Arthur, son of John's deceased older brother, Geoffrey, as the rightful ruler. Arthur's claim is supported by the King of France who at the beginning of the play is prepared to go to war with John to forcibly place Arthur on throne and John vows to match the French blow for blow. In the midst of his preparations, King John is asked to settle a dispute between two brothers, the sons of Sir Robert Faulconbridge, Philip the elder and Robert the younger. Robert asserts to the King that his father told him on his deathbed that Philip was a bastard and that Robert had the right to inherit the family lands. Further, Robert relays that the true father of Philip was none other than the late King Richard Cordelion, the lion-hearted. Both John and his mother, Queen Elinor, recognize the stamp of Richard on the face of Philip and they persuade him to give up his claim to the Faulconbridge lands and join them in their war on France. In return, Philip (henceforth called "the Bastard" by Shakespeare) is knighted and renamed Sir Richard Plantagenet. What follows for Philip is to serve as an observer and chorus reflecting on the ways of his new world among the royals. In France, as the armies join in battle, he sees King John and King Philip barter for peace. A marriage is arranged between John's niece, Blanche and Philip's son, Lewis. In exchange, Philip will withdraw support for Arthur and Arthur will be compensated by being made Earl of Richmond and Duke of Anjou. Philip the Bastard is appalled at the ease with which the Kings set aside their principles in favor of advantage and expedience. Still in France, Faulconbridge encounters the Duke of Austria who claims to have killed King Richard and he looks for an opportunity to avenge his father's death. Meanwhile, because King John refuses the Pope's demand to name Stephen Langton as Archbishop of Canterbury, he is excommunicated and King Philip is pressured by Rome to abandon his truce with John. War again breaks out, Arthur is seized and Faulconbridge has his opportunity to take his revenge on the Duke of Austria. Arthur is shipped off to England under John's death sentence. The English lords urge John to free Arthur and, under duress, the King agrees, but Arthur, attempting to escape falls to his death from a tower. The outraged Lords join with an invading French force led by Lewis. While Faulconbridge encourages the King to prepare to repulse the invasion, the cowardly John hopes that Rome, now reconciled with the English king, will call off the French force. Finally, John authorizes Faulconbridge to marshal the country's defenses. The rebellious Lords, learning that the French Dauphin plans to betray them, return to beg and receive pardon from the King. John then falls ill and is taken to an abbey where he is inexplicably poisoned by a monk. John's son Henry is now king and Faulconbridge continues his efforts to repulse the French invaders, but then learns that the French have withdrawn from the field, having lost their reinforcements in a channel storm. The play concludes with a patriotic speech by Faulconbridge asserting that *"This England never did, nor never shall/Lie at the proud foot of a conqueror."* (V, vii, 121-2)

I have given this synopsis because *King John* is one of Shakespeare's least memorable plays and Faulconbridge far from one of Shakespeare's most memorable characters. He only shines in *King John* because the other characters in the play appear so lifeless (excepting the hysterical Constance, mother of Arthur). With his frequent asides and soliloquies, his wry and cynical tone, and his speeches concerning honor and expedience, Faulconbridge is tailored to be the sole character that the audience can applaud. It is a commentary on the darkness of the time of King John that Shakespeare is required to invent the Bastard to provide the audience with a point of identification. It is also a remarkable that Shakespeare would invent a bastard as the single positive character in the play. That in itself serves as an indictment of the characters that surround him. His courage, integrity and loyalty amplify the craven nature of the kings and nobles that make up his new world. Like his stereotypical brother bastards, Faulconbridge stands apart from his surrounding society, but in his case it is a good thing.

The taint of Faulconbridge's bastard birth seems to have been over-written by the stronger influence of his noble and revered father, still lauded as one of England's greatest kings at the time of Shakespeare's play. It is as if the magnificence of the noble genes of Richard Cordelion as sufficiently strong so as to overcome the stain of carnal sin. Faulconbridge is strangely permitted to choose his paternity. Elinor asks

> *Whether hadst thou rather be a Faulconbridge,*
> *And like thy brother, so enjoy thy land;*
> *Or the reputed son of Cordelion...?*
>
> (KJ, I, 1, 134-6)

Faulconbridge freely adopts his title as Richard's bastard and a life of service to King and country rather than the quiet life of the landed gentry. Faulconbridge also has the unique situation of not growing up a bastard. He was raised to adulthood as the true son of Sir Robert Faulconbridge, with the entire societal acceptance that entails. Until the moment when he accepts his true paternity, Faulconbridge was not subjected to the social isolation and rejection that often accompanied illegitimacy.

By his choice of bastard as hero, Shakespeare challenges the stereotype of his age just as he challenged the stereotype of the Jew in *The Merchant of Venice* and of the Moor in *Othello*. With Faulconbridge, Shakespeare raises the question of nature versus nurture in the development of a man. He seems to suggest that the twisted moral compass associated with the stereotypical bastard does not derive from the act of conception but from the treatment of the bastard by his society as somehow stained or polluted from birth.

The nature/nurture controversy goes back to Greek and Roman philosophers, and to the writings of the early Christian fathers. In Augustine's view, for example, the soul of man was created pure, but the body, composed of matter was corrupt and prone to the "animal instincts." Though knowledge and the exercise of free will, man could learn to reject his animal nature and aspire to the things of God. A war raged within each man between the purity of the soul and the corruption of the body. What determined which propensity dominated was the will to choose guided by grace and knowledge. In the 13th century, a French romance called *Silence* dramatized the roles of nature and nurture in determining the choices made in life. Written by Heldriss of Cornwall, *Silence* is the story of a young girl raised as a boy to enable her to receive the family inheritance. Her training as a boy proved so successful that she dominated in contests of riding, skills of war, and musical talent. At the onset of adolescence, two allegorical figures, Nature and Nurture, appear to the girl and argue their cases, Nature tells the girl that she should be true to her gender and renounce her boyish behaviors.

> *This is a fine state of affairs,*
> *You conducting yourself like a man,*
> *running about in the wind and scorching sun*
> *when I used a special mold for you,*
> *when I created you with my own hands,*
> *when I heaped all the beauty I had stored up*
> *upon you alone! (2502-2509)*

Nature nearly, or quite, convinces the girl to drop her facade, and take up more suitable pass-times; a decision to which Silence seems initially inclined, by her strong moral conviction that her constant act of deception must be in some way wrong. We are told that:

> She wanted to go and learn to sew,
> just as Nature demanded of her;
> she should not cultivate such savage ways
> for fief or inheritance. (2542-2545)

and later she laments:

> Was any female ever so tormented
> or deceived by such vile fraud
> as to do what I did out of greed?
> I certainly never heard of one! (2583-2586)

At this point, Nurture arrives on the scene and banishes Nature with the angry words:

> Nature, leave my nursling alone,
> or I will put a curse on you!
> I have completely dis-natured her. (2593-2595)

The girl, persuaded by Nurture, continues on her boyish path saying, "I am on top, why should I step down." (2640)

Later, Nature and Nurture meet again and argue about which of them the true author of the person is. Nurture attempts to win by bringing up the example of Adam and Eve, who though lacking parents, and thus presumably nurture, are nonetheless capable of committing original sin. Nature turns this ploy to her advantage arguing that in their natural state Adam and Eve were without sin. It was only the undue environmental influence of the serpent the caused the fall of humanity. Nature thus wins this round by means of a sophistic trick, though it should be noted that while this debate is couched in theological terms, its conclusion has to do with the moral character of a person, as the true nature of an individual.

Heldriss intrudes on the story to summarize by writing:

> I can prove it by this example:

a little tumbler-full of gall
would harm a measure of honey
more than a measure of honey
could improve a quart of gall, if you poured it in.
A little bad nurture
harms a good nature more
than lengthy instruction in doing good
can mend a heart intrinsically evil. (2334-2342)[38]

Thus, Heldriss suggests what Francis Galton makes explicit in *English Men of Science: Their Nature and Nurture (1874).*

> *The highest natural endowments may be starved by defective nurture, while no carefulness of nurture can overcome the evil tendencies of an intrinsically bad physique, weak brain, or brutal disposition. Differences of nurture stamp unmistakable marks on the disposition of the soldier, clergyman, or scholar, but are wholly insufficient to efface the deeper marks of individual character.*[39]

In the character of Falconbridge, Shakespeare challenges the idea that bastardry insures a weak or corrupt disposition. In his other bastards, Shakespeare is less generous and open-minded. Don John in *Much Ado About Nothing* and Edmund in *King Lear* are noble, if not royal, bastards and are thoroughly villainous. Thersites in *Troilus and Cressida* is neither high born nor villainous. He is, in fact, nearly the polar opposite of Faulconbridge: base-born, acerbic and cowardly. When the play begins, Thersites is the unruly servant of Ajax who after incurring the wrath of his master for his insolence, turns to serve Achilles. Thersites is the common clown and fool for this cynical comedy. He is, as Achilles notes, "*a privileged man*" (*T&C*, II, 3, 93) meaning that like Lear's fool and Feste in *Twelfth Night*, he is privileged to speak his mind with relative impunity. He serves as a cynical commentator on the action of the play, underlining the folly of a war over a woman and the bumbling antics of the "heroes" on each side. Because he stands outside the circle of kings, he is, like Faulconbridge, an objective if bitter observer of the world around him. He summarizes his observations in probably his most remembered comment, "*Lechery, lechery, still wars and lechery, nothing else holds fashion.*" (*T&C*, V, 2, 194-5).

Like Faulconbridge, Thersites embraces his bastard status, but for a very different reason. When confronted in combat by the bastard son of Priam, Thersites comically cries out,

I am bastard begot, bastard instructed, bastard in mind,
bastard in valor, in everything illegitimate. One bear
will not bite another, and wherefore should one
bastard? Take heed the quarrel's most ominous
to us. If the son of a whore fight for a whore, he
tempts judgment. Farewell bastard.   [Exit]

                                    (T&C, V, 7, 116-22)

This speech shows that Thersites is an emblem of the stereotypical bastard, corrupted from birth by the sin of his parents. Since they, unlike Richard Cordelion, had not extraordinary virtues to pass on to their bastard son, Thersites is doomed to play the debased, embittered and craven bastard of the popular imagination. Touching on another related stereotype, the bastard birth was often associated with a deformed body reflecting the bastard's deformed moral nature. This is true of Thersites who is listed in the Dramatis Personae as "a ***deformed*** and *scurrilous Greek.*" Later, we will discuss the significance of physical deformity in one of Shakespeare's most notable villains, Richard III, but for now it will suffice to say that the character with a physical deformity will be automatically suspect by Shakespeare's audience.

Thersites is a relatively minor character in *Troilus and Cressida* whose chief function is to amuse the audience with his crude remarks and knock-about antics. Don John in *Much Ado About Nothing* is also a relatively minor character, but one who performs a far more significant function: to be the villainous catalyst to the play's complicating plot twist. Don John is the malicious bastard brother of Don Pedro, Prince of Aragon. Just prior to the play's beginning, Don John has led a failed rebellion against his half-brother. Don Pedro has crushed the rebellion and has magnanimously forgiven Don John and his followers. As the play begins, the reconciled forces arrive at Messina and take up temporary residence on the estate of Don Pedro's friend and the town's governor, Leonato. Don John, smoldering from his recent defeat and true to his "bastard" nature, is dejected. In his first of his few scenes, we find him in discussion with his man, Conrade.

Con.   *...! why are you thus out of measure sad?*
*   *   *   *
D. John. *...I cannot hide what I am: I must be sad*
when I have cause and smile at no man's jests,
*   *   *   *
Con.   *...You have of late stood out against your brother,*

76

and he hath ta'en you newly into his grace;

*   *   *   *

D. John. *I had rather be a canker in a hedge than a rose in*
his grace, and it better fits my blood to be
disdained of all than to fashion a carriage to rob
love from any: in this, though I cannot be said to
be a flattering honest man, it must not be denied
but I am a plain-dealing villain. I am trusted with
a muzzle and enfranchised with a clog; therefore I
have decreed not to sing in my cage. If I had my
mouth, I would bite; if I had my liberty, I would do
my liking: in the meantime let me be that I am and
seek not to alter me.

(MAAN, I, 3, 13-4, 21-2, 27-37)

Like Faulconbridge and Thersites, Don John accepts and embraces his bastard nature, but in its most malignant form. When he says "I cannot hide what I am," he means more than his present emotional state. He is known to be a bastard and accepts the culturally assigned role of villain, plain-dealing or otherwise. He, like his brother bastards, has his character dictated by the quality of his birth. The noble character of Faulconbridge's royal sire is sufficient to raise the character of the son above that which an ordinary bastard could hope to attain. The base and illegitimate birth of Thersites produces a base and scurrilous bastard true to the nature of his parents and their illicit act. Don John is born of nobility, therefore by nature is not as base as Thersites but not sufficiently redeemed as Faulconbridge. Instead, he is simply villainous, gratified only by the making of mischief.

At the core of Don John's malignity is the medieval doctrine of primogeniture that would bar Don John from inheritance hence his grab for power against his legitimate half-brother. When this endeavor fails, he is reduced to simply creating mischief to assuage his bitterness. His first opportunity comes when he learns that Don Pedro intends to woo Leonato's daughter, Hero, on behalf of his young friend Claudio. To drive a wedge between the two, Don John informs Claudio that Don Pedro is in fact in love with Hero and is wooing her on his own behalf. Though Claudio is initially angered, Don John's pathetic plot is so quickly overturned that no one even takes note of his intention. Claudio and Hero are betrothed and a wedding is quickly planned. When he learns that his mischief has failed and that Claudio and Hero are soon to be married, he immediately seeks out another way to embarrass Don Pedro and upset the impending nuptials. It is his comrade Borachio who shows him the way. Don John, following Borachio's instruction, goes to Don Pedro and Claudio and impugns the chastity of Hero. By way of proof, he leads them to a grove outside Hero's bedroom where they witness Borachio "dallying" with Margaret, Hero's attendant. Convinced in the low lighting that Margaret is Hero, Claudio decides to shame her before the entire wedding party. He literally leaves Hero at the altar, publicly denouncing her as "an approved wanton." It is only through the chance discovery of the plot by the bumbling constable Dogberry that the truth of Don John's slander comes out. The couple is reconciled and married and in the final act Don John who had fled Messina is captured and returned to face "brave punishments."

Don John is certainly Shakespeare's most incompetent villain. His every plan is easily discovered and quickly overthrown. His mischief is petty and his motives vague. Shakespeare makes no effort to explain or understand Don John; he is simply a necessary trigger to the complicating action of the play. *Much Ado About Nothing* is after all a comedy and it is entirely appropriate that its villain should be a bumbling cartoon character. Like the Coyote to the Road Runner, Don John acts the way he does because it is his nature and he us constantly thwarted, no so much because of the cleverness of his opponents, but because the convention of the genre requires it.

Now we come finally to *King Lear's* Edmund. Considered by many to be the evil equal of Iago, Edmund like Aaron in *Titus Andronicus* is only one of many villains who occupy the world of Lear. Although critics have called Edmund one of the most interesting villains ever concocted by Shakespeare, I find Edmund to be one of Shakespeare's most transparent villains. Unlike Iago, there is no mystery in Edmund. He is the only character in Lear who directly addresses the audience and when he does so, he is plain spoken about to his motive and his plan. We meet Edmund in the very first Scene of the very first Act. He and his father, Gloucester are walking with Lear's loyal friend, Kent. Kent asks, "Is not this your son, my Lord?" and the conversation following is most revealing.

> ***Glou.***   *His breeding, sir, hath been at my charge,*
> *I have so often blush'd to acknowledge him,*
> *That now I am braz'd to't.*
> ***Kent.***   *I cannot conceive you.*
> ***Glou.***   *Sir, this young fellow's mother could;*
> *whereupon she grew round-womb'd, and had indeed*
> *sir, a son for her cradle ere she had a husband for her*
> *bed. Do you smell a fault?*
> ***Kent.***   *I cannot wish the fault undone, the issue of it*
> *being so proper.*

Glou.   But I have a son, by order of the law, some
year elder than this, who yet is no dearer in my
account. Though this knave came something saucily
To the world before he was sent for, yet was his
Mother fair, there was good sport at his making, and
the whoreson must be acknowledged.

                                        (KL: I, 1, 9-24)

Gloucester's callous and cruel comments about Edmund and his mother are certainly not the basis for loving and loyal feeling by the son for the father. Clearly Gloucester is embarrassed by his past indiscretion and Edmund is the physical reminder of it. Gloucester regards Edmund off as a cruel joke perpetrated against him by the boy and his mother. As a result, he has removed Edmund from his sight and from the sight of the court. He tells Kent "He hath been out nine years, and away he shall again." (*KL*, I, 1, 31-2). How could Edmund feel any filial bond, let alone affection for a man who has treated him so dismissively? In his first soliloquy, Edmund makes a convincing case that he has been wronged and that the laws of inheritance stand in his way of getting what should justly be his.

Thou, Nature, art my goddess; to thy law
My services are bound. Wherefore should I
Stand in the plague of custom, and permit
The curiosity of nations to deprive me,
For that I am some twelve or fourteen moonshines
Lag of a brother? Why bastard? wherefore base?
When my dimensions are as well compact,
My mind as generous, and my shape as true
As honest madam's issue? Why brand they us
With base? with baseness? bastardy? base, base?
Who, in the lusty stealth of nature, take
More composition and fierce quality
Than doth, within a dull, stale, tired bed,
Go to the creating a whole tribe of fops,
Got 'tween asleep and wake? Well, then,
Legitimate Edgar, I must have your land.
Our father's love is to the bastard Edmund
As to the legitimate: fine word -- legitimate!
Well, my legitimate, if this letter speed
And my invention thrive, Edmund the base

Shall top the legitimate. I grow, I prosper!
Now, gods, stand up for bastards!

(KL, I, 2, 1-22)

More than any of Shakespeare's bastards, Edmund chafes at his status and his treatment by his father in particular and by society in general. He is condemned as "base" through no fault of his own. His "dimensions," he says, "are as well compact, [his] mind as generous, and [his] shape as true" as his legitimate brother, Edgar, but Edmund has been distained by his father, shut away from the sight of polite society, and deprived of any inheritance by "curiosity of nations." His goal, he plainly tells the audience, is to have Edgar's inheritance (*Edgar, I must have your land*) and thereby to grow and prosper. To achieve his goal, he must eliminate Edgar and he devises a plan to estrange Gloucester from his legitimate son.

It is interesting that Edmund shows none of the venom we found in Iago. He needs to eliminate Edgar but he does not chose" to catch the nearest way", i.e., to murder Edgar, as most of Shakespeare's other villains would have. Edmund does not rail against either his father or brother, but seems total indifferent to their fates. If they live, fine. If they die, fine. So long as Edmund gets his land, all will be well with the world.

Edmund's plot is not as complex and convoluted as Iago's: he simply forges a letter that convinces the gullible Gloucester that Edgar is plotting against his life. Edgar is forced to flee the family home and Edmund assumes the role of the favored son. Later, after Lear is also banished onto the hearth, Gloucester attempts to aid the elderly king despite the warning of Regan, Lear's middle daughter, against such aid. Gloucester has learned that Lear's youngest daughter, Cordelia, has mounted a force from France to come to Lear's aid. Before following Lear onto the hearth, Gloucester shares this information with Cornwall, Regan's brutal husband, and Cornwall swears to repay Gloucester's treachery when he returns. Edmund, advised by Cornwall that "the revenges we are bound to take upon your traitorous father are not fit for your beholding'" is dispatched with Goneril, Lear's eldest daughter to prepare for Cordelia's invasion. Cornwall, true to his word and with the enthusiastic assistance of Regan, tortures and blinds old Gloucester. So appalling is their treatment of the old man that one of Cornwall's servants attempts to intervene and mortally wounds Cornwall before being killed himself.

It becomes apparent in a subsequent scene that the married Goneril is much taken with Edmund. Her amorous fancy is suddenly upset when, after sending Edmund back to Regan to urge her to bring her forces to the front, discovers that Regan is now a widow and thus a rival for Edmund's affection. Her fears are justified. We learn that Edmund and Regan have "talked" and that she considers herself a fitter mate for Edmund than her sister. When the two sisters meet as their forces gather for battle with Cordelia, the rivalry for Edmund intensifies. Edmund is both amused and unsettled by the attentions of the sisters and seems to resolve to accept the more ruthless of the two, i.e., the last sister standing.

> To both these sisters have I sworn my love;
> Each jealous of the other, as the stung
> Are of the adder. Which of them shall I take?
> Both? one? or neither? Neither can be enjoy'd,
> If both remain alive: to take the widow
> Exasperates, makes mad her sister Goneril;
> And hardly shall I carry out my side,
> Her husband being alive. Now then we'll use
> His countenance for the battle; which being done,
> Let her who would be rid of him devise
> His speedy taking off.
>
> (KL, V, 1, 55-65)

The battle is joined between the English and French forces and the French forces are defeated. Lear and Cordelia are taken captive. With the battle won, the victors begin to fall out. Goneril has poisoned Regan, and her husband, Albany, and Edmund are at odds. Into the fray comes a disguised challenger who calls Edmund out as a miscreant and traitor. In the ensuing single combat, Edmund is mortally wounded and the challenger is revealed to be his brother, Edgar. As he lies dying, a servant enters and informs the assembly that both sisters are dead, Regan poisoned by Goneril and Goneril dispatched by her own hand. The bodies are brought in and Edmund seems uncharacteristically touched.

> Edmund was beloved:
> The one the other poison'd for my sake,
> And after slew herself.
>
> (KL, V, 3, 240-42)

It is as if Edmund, all his life deprived of love because of his bastard status, is surprised that he was sufficiently lovable (or lustable) for two women to fight and die for love of him. Now suddenly repentant, Edmund reveals that he has ordered the execution of Cordelia and Lear and encourages Albany to save them. His warning comes too late. Lear enters with the dead Cordelia in his arms and then dies himself, ending the play.

    King Lear is among other things an analysis of the result of poor parenting. Lear's relationship with his three daughters is the play's dramatic driver and with be discussed in greater detail in a subsequent chapter, but Edmund's relationship for his father, Gloucester, compliments the theme. Both Freud and Jung emphasized the role of the father in the psychological development of the son's sense of self. The superego they say is the legacy of the father and if the father is removed physically or emotionally, normal development of the regulating conscience is impaired. Gloucester has removed Edmund physically and emotionally from his presence, and this has resulted in an emotionally stunted personality, outwardly loyal and charming, but inwardly hollow, feeling unloved and unlovable. Unlike Iago, Edmund is utterly without emotion. His plots are not motivated by the sense of outrage we find in Iago; they are completely utilitarian, designed to establish his place in the world. He betrays Edgar to usurp his inheritance. He betrays Gloucester to accelerate his inheritance. He joins with Goneril and Regan for the purpose of advancing his position. None of his actions are motivated by any emotion; they are undertaken only to consolidate his position, not to punish Gloucester for his rejection. In fact, Edmund does not blame Gloucester, but instead blames "custom" and "the curiosity of nations" for depriving him of acceptance and inheritance. In spite of Gloucester's unkind words in the first act, Edmund even appears to delude himself into believing that Gloucester cares for him saying "Our father's love is to the bastard Edmund as to the legitimate (Edgar)." Or is this remark intended to show that Gloucester is no better a father to Edgar than he is to Edmund? Gloucester is surely quick enough to accept that Edgar could betray him. This supposition is, however, called into question by the devotion Edgar shows to Gloucester throughout the play. If Gloucester were in fact as indifferent to Edgar as to Edmund, is it likely that Edgar would have been so devoted? So in the final analysis, Edmund imprints his own sense of rejection on Edgar as well: Edgar is as loved (or unloved) as Edmund, thus it is not Gloucester's fault (nor Edmund's) that Edmund must resort to villainy: it is simply the way of *Lear's* cruel world.

THINKING MAKES IT SO: HAMLET

In the final scene of the final act of *Hamlet*, Shakespeare's most famous avenger has taken his revenge on his murderous uncle King Claudius, but has himself been poisoned and dies on stage in the arms of his only trusted friend, Horatio. After the noble Hamlet draws his last breath, Horatio looks upon his friend and whispers in a grief choked voice, *"Good night, sweet prince, and flights of angels sing thee to thy rest."* (H, V, 2, 359-60). A consoling thought and a fitting benediction for the character who we have come to like and feel sympathy for, but can we really expect that the sweet prince is winging his way heavenward in the company of angels at the end of the play, or do we have the nagging discomfort that he may be headed in the opposite direction to perhaps dine with his fellow avengers, Tamora and Titus.

Hamlet is probably Shakespeare's best known and best studied protagonist. Often called the hesitant hero, Hamlet is Shakespeare's most internalized characters, immobilized some have argued by the tendency of his over-active mind to over-think everything. *Hamlet* (the play), to use Marjorie Garber's metaphor is "like a series of Russian dolls, nested one inside another... [repeated] until we are no longer sure where to place the boundaries of reality and illusion."[40] I believe the metaphor extends not only to the play with its self-conscious theatrical references and plays within plays, but also to the character of Hamlet and to the fictive world where he exists. Throughout the play, Hamlet is constantly taking off one shell after another to revel the next "inner doll" of self until by the end of the play, there only remains the inner most man who at last discovers that the freedom "to be or not to be," to act or not to act, is only an illusion born of an over-active intellect.

Hamlet is a play of questions. It even opens with a question: "Who's there?" and then proceeds immediately to one of the play's central mysteries, who or what is the ghost? Is the ghost "honest?" Is Claudius really guilty of murdering his brother? Is Hamlet obligated to obey the ghost's demand for revenge? Will Hamlet endanger his soul if he follows the ghost's command? Does Hamlet turn from hero to villain, like Titus Andronicus, when he puts on the mantle of revenger?

Hamlet, for all its depth of thought and beauty of language, is a revenge tragedy in the tradition of Kyd's *The Spanish Tragedy*. It features all the key checkpoints on Fredson Bowers' list of defining features. To repeat, the revenge tragedies according to Bowers all share, to a greater or lesser degree, these common motifs:

1. The fundamental motive for the action is revenge.
2. The revenge extends not only to a specific offender, but also to his/her kindred.
3. The revenger and the object of the revenge are both aided by accomplices who commit suicide or are otherwise killed during the course of the action.
4. A ghost appears on stage and in some manner figures into the action.
5. There is a justifiable delay in exacting revenge because of a lack of evidence, lack of opportunity, or a failure on the part of the State's legal machinery.
6. Madness is important as a dramatic device.
7. Machiavellian intrigue is used by and against the revenger.
8. Actions are bloody and numerous.
9. Revenge is accomplished in some horrific fashion, accompanied by intense violence and a high body count.[7]

One aspect not listed by Bowers is that the revengers are universally condemned. Eleanor Prosser, in *Hamlet and Revenge*, argues convincingly that noted Shakespeare critic A. C. Bradley and others have been wrong in assuming that "Shakespeare's audience endorsed blood revenge as an unquestioned duty."[41] Prosser reviews the establishment view on revenge by quoting from numerous treatises and sermons of the Elizabethan age. Revenge is viewed as blasphemy, the attempt by man to usurp the prerogative of God to meet out judgment.

> No matter how righteous a man might think his motives, the act of revenge would inevitably make him as evil as the injurer in the eyes of God...Not only is the revenger guilty of blasphemy and malice, he cuts himself off from the possibility of forgiveness and thus is damned forever...[42]

Revenge is not only a danger to the soul, but is also a danger to the mind and body of the revenger. Quoting from Sir Thomas Elyot's *The Governour* (1531)

> To be short, after that anger hath once got the bridle at will, the whole mind and judgment is so blinded & carried head-long that an angry man thinks of nothing but revenge, insomuch the he forgetteth himself, and careth not what he doth, or what harm will light upon himself in so doing, so that he may be revenged.[43]

This was certainly evident in the cases of Hieronimo and Titus, and it is also true of Hamlet.

But what, critics have argued is the proper response of the wronged party when circumstances deny justice? Titus and Hamlet are both denied the normal justice of the State, God's rightful representative on Earth, because the heads of the State are also the offending parties. What is there proper recourse? Elyot speaking the mind of the "Establishment" counsels *"the best waye to be advenged is to contemne Injurie and rebuke, and lyve with suche honestie, that the doer shall at the laste be therefore a shamed."*[44] Hard counsel, to be sure, and yet that was the standard that man was expected to strive for as a Christian and a subject of the crown.

> *The law was absolute: murder, as such, was never justified. Even if a man's entire family had been massacred by the most vicious criminal, even if the magistrates themselves were so corrupt that the knowingly would let the guilty go free—even then, the man who planned and executed the death of the murderer would be equally a murderer in the eyes of the law.*[45]

In response, defenders of private revenge turn to William Perkins' well-known 1613 statement that *"God puts the sword into the private man's hands"* when the magistrate is absent.[46] Prosser argues that this statement does not, if fact, justify private revenge except when committed in "hot blood," that is, in defense of self or others. I would not support Prosser's conclusion although contextually her conclusion is supported by Perkins' latter condemnation of revenge executed in "cold blood." *"For if there is delay, and it* [violence] *come afterward, it loses the name of just defense, & becomes a revenge, a rising of prepensed malice."*[47]

Nevertheless, human execution of God's vengeance is clearly delegated to God's representatives on Earth. St. Paul in the popular *"Vengeance is mine; I will repay, saith the Lord."* passage of his letter to the Roman's also notes *"The ruler...beareth not the sword in vain; for he is the minister of God, a revenger to execute wrath upon him that doeth evil."*[48] The ruler of course delegates his power as revenger to his ministers and magistrates. When ministers and magistrates and even the ruler are absent or ineffectual, doesn't it seem likely that God, as Perkins suggests, might delegate his prerogative to revenge to "lesser" individuals, e.g., a Prince of State? So how would God make His will known to the extra-legal representative? Might he dispatch a spokesperson? An angel? A burning bush? A ghost?

I would agree with Prosser that the ghost is the key to plucking out the mystery that is Hamlet. Is the ghost truly sent from God to charge Hamlet with avenging the murder of his father or is the ghost a devil sent from Hell to capture the soul of the melancholy Prince? Prosser demonstrates that the ghost can be evaluated by two religious standards: that of the Protestant Elizabethan audience or that of the play's Catholic context. Protestant doctrine would suggest three explanations: the ghost is a hallucination, an angel or a devil. Catholic doctrine would add a fourth explanation: a spirit released from Purgatory, which is, exactly what the ghost insists that he is. Since this explanation would not be acceptable to the Protestant audience, and since the ghost seen by so many people cannot be a hallucination, they would be left with two choices: to accept the ghost as an angelic messenger from God placing the sword of retribution in Hamlet's hand or an evil spirit sent from Hell to ensnare Hamlet's soul. The very fact that the ghost insists he is the spirit of Hamlet's father returned from Purgatory would signal to the Protestant audience that the ghost is a liar and therefore must be a devil. But for the closet Catholics in the audience and the Catholic characters of the play, the possibility that the ghost is true exists. For those, Shakespeare piles up evidence to show that the ghost is up to no good. First, the ghost appears at midnight. When charged "By heaven" to speak, it is "offended" and "stalks" away. When the cock crows signally the coming of day, it "started like a guilty thing" and vanished. All of these actions would scream "devil" to the Elizabethan audience. The ghost if from Purgatory should be humble and conciliatory, not angry and vengeful. The Purgatory ghost should be only concerned about its own sins and not the sins of others. And the Purgatory ghost would _never_ suggest anything that would be contrary to the Word of God or the tenants of the Catholic faith.[49]

One significant command of the ghost has been used to defend its honesty: it enjoins Hamlet

> Taint not thy mind, nor let thy soul contrive
> Against thy mother aught.
> Leave her to heaven,
>   (H, I, 5, 85-6)

Critics have used this to show that the ghost is only concerned about avenging its murder, not punishing his spouse for his infidelity. I would suggest the ghost warns against action against Gertrude because such action would be a "bridge too far" for Hamlet. He is no Orestes, who could slaughter his mother to avenge his father. There is, in any case no evidence that Gertrude was complicit in or even aware of Hamlet, Sr.'s murder. But that aside, the ghost only asks Hamlet to do what Hamlet already wants to do. The ghost takes all Hamlet's suspicions and suppressed desires and feeds them back to him: allowing him to act "sinfully" without having to take personal responsibility for his actions. "After all," he can say, "it was the ghost that made me do it."

I believe it is clear that the ghost has been dispatched to trap the soul of a man already prepared to perform the "damnable" act, e.g. the murder of Claudius. The ghost is just the goad he needs. And yet Hamlet delays. Why? That has been the central mystery of Hamlet. Does Hamlet doubt the ghost? Is he hampered by the impediments surrounding any attempt to murder the King? Is he worried about the consequences he will face as a regicide? Is he worried about the state of his soul?

In answer to the first question, after the encounter with the ghost, Hamlet tells Horatio

> *Touching this vision here,*
> *It is an honest ghost, that let me tell you.*
>
> $\qquad$ *(H, I, 5, 37-8)*

Here "honest" has two possible meanings: real as in an actual ghost, not an illusion, and truthful in what he has said. Both seem to apply. We, the audience, believe what the ghost has to say is true, but would we believe the ghost to be the true ghost of Hamlet's father, I think not. Caught up in the moment of his harrowing encounter, Hamlet seems to accept the ghost at face value.

Later, Hamlet seems to have some doubts and decides to use the visiting theater troupe to put the ghost to the test.

> *The spirit that I have seen*
> *May be a devil, and the devil hath power*
> *To assume a pleasing shape, yea, and perhaps*
> *Out of my weakness and melancholy*
> *As he is very potent with such spirits,*
> *Abuses me to damn me. I'll have grounds*
> *More relative than this. The play's the thing*
> *Wherein I'll catch the conscience of the King.*
>
> $\qquad$ *(H, II, 2, 598-605)*

The presumption is that if Claudius is guilty, then the ghost must be "honest" and not a devil sent from Hell to entrap Hamlet's soul. But we do well to remember that in the *Merchant of Venice* we hear from Antonio that

The devil can cite Scripture for his purpose.
An evil soul producing holy witness
Is like a villain with a smiling cheek,
A goodly apple rotten at the heart:
O, what a goodly outside falsehood hath!.

(MOV, I, 3, 98-102)

As predicted by Hamlet, the King does react to the staged murder in a way that makes clear his guilt. The King races from the performance and when he finds himself alone, he confesses his guilt,

O, my offence is rank it smells to heaven;
It hath the primal eldest curse upon't,
A brother's murder. Pray can I not,
Though inclination be as sharp as will:
My stronger guilt defeats my strong intent;
And, like a man to double business bound,
I stand in pause where I shall first begin,
And both neglect. What if this cursed hand
Were thicker than itself with brother's blood,
Is there not rain enough in the sweet heavens
To wash it white as snow? Whereto serves mercy
But to confront the visage of offence?
And what's in prayer but this two-fold force,
To be forestalled ere we come to fall,
Or pardon'd being down? Then I'll look up;
My fault is past. But, O, what form of prayer
Can serve my turn? 'Forgive me my foul murder'?
That cannot be; since I am still possess'd
Of those effects for which I did the murder,
My crown, mine own ambition and my queen.
May one be pardon'd and retain the offence?
In the corrupted currents of this world
Offence's gilded hand may shove by justice,
And oft 'tis seen the wicked prize itself
Buys out the law: but 'tis not so above;
There is no shuffling, there the action lies
In his true nature; and we ourselves compell'd,
Even to the teeth and forehead of our faults,
To give in evidence. What then? what rests?

Try what repentance can: what can it not?
Yet what can it when one can not repent?
O wretched state! O bosom black as death!
O limed soul, that, struggling to be free,
Art more engaged! Help, angels! Make assay!
Bow, stubborn knees; and, heart with strings of steel,
Be soft as sinews of the newborn babe!
All may be well.
Retires and kneels

(H, III, 2, 36-72)

The audience now knows as does Hamlet that Claudius is guilty and that the ghost has been "honest" in that respect. The King in this scene is genuinely sorry for his crime; he rightly fears for the state of his soul and yet is too weak to confess his crime, give up his gains and take his punishment. He kneels as a penitent to pray that "all may be well." This is a remarkably sympathetic scene and we are likely to see the tragedy of Claudius in the same way we see the tragedy of Macbeth or Doctor Faustus. Like Macbeth he is doomed by his ambition and like Doctor Faustus he finds his prayerful "mouth stopped" by the enormity of his crime.

My words fly up, my thoughts remain below:
Words without thoughts never to heaven go.

(H, III, 2, 97-8)

Hamlet comes upon Claudius at his prayers and it is frequently played so that Hamlet is in a position to overhear the King's soliloquy. Hamlet prepares to strike and conclude his task of revenge but then draws back.

Now might I do it pat, now he is praying;
And now I'll do't. And so he goes to heaven;
And so am I revenged. That would be scann'd:
A villain kills my father; and for that,
I, his sole son, do this same villain send
To heaven.
O, this is hire and salary, not revenge.
am I then revenged,
To take him in the purging of his soul,
When he is fit and season'd for his passage?
No!

trip him, that his heels may kick at heaven,
And that his soul may be as damn'd and black
As hell, whereto it goes.

(H, III, 3, 73-9, 84-7, 93-95)

And thus Hamlet lets pass his opportunity for revenge, fearing that the prayers of Claudius might be heard in Heaven and his soul purged of his sins. The thought of Claudius in Heaven while his father languishes in Purgatory is abhorrent to Hamlet and he stays his hand to await a fitter opportunity.

This scene again shows the dominate Catholic theology of the play, suggesting the idea that the old King landed in Purgatory because he died without benefit of last rights, while the murderous Claudius, if killed at the point on praying for forgiveness, would have a straight road to Heaven. This scene also shines an unflattering light on Hamlet who wishes not only the death of Claudius, but to ensure his damnation. Here the young Prince not only intends to usurp God's prerogative of judgment and revenge, but also to determine the disposition of the King's immortal soul. His hubris combined with his vindictiveness move him closer to the conventional realm of villainy similar to that found in Hieronimo and Iago.

In the next scene we find Hamlet badgering his mother in her bedchamber. So enraged is he that when he hears a noise behind arras, he strikes with his dagger, mistaking the eavesdropping Polonius for the King. Hamlet is now a wrathful murderer and though the act is committed in "hot blood," his fate is sealed and there is no turning back. His action not only causes the death of Polonius, but also destroys Ophelia and perpetuates the emerging cycle of revenge by creating yet another avenger, Laertes.

Laertes, another son of a murdered father is the perfect foil for Hamlet. While Hamlet thinks and talks, Laertes is a man of action. He returns from France after the death of Polonius ready to avenge his father without hesitation. At the head of a mob he comes to the palace ready to unseat and slay the King and is only dissuaded by the calm persuasiveness of Claudius and the sight of his deranged sister. Presumably, in an off-stage conversation Claudius lets Laertes in on his plot to have Hamlet killed in England and Laertes is temporarily satisfied that justice has taken its course. However, when Hamlet unexpectedly returns to Elsinore, Claudius asks Laertes

...what would you undertake
To show yourself your father's son in deed
More than in words?

(H, IV, 7, 124-6)

Laertes replies "To cut his throat i' the church."

This brief exchange recalls two incidents that highlight the difference between Laertes and Hamlet. Earlier in the play Polonius comes upon Hamlet reading. He asks, "What do you read, my Lord?" Hamlet replies "Words, words, words." Words, not deeds are what drive Hamlet the character and *Hamlet* the play. For most of the play, all Hamlet does is talk. In this longest of all Shakespeare's plays, 39% of all the lines are spoken by Hamlet. Laertes rarely speaks in more than simple sentences. Hamlet is a man of the mind; Laertes a man of action.

Laertes is ready to slit Hamlet's throat in a church, but Hamlet when afforded this very opportunity throws away his chance. He justifies his inaction by explaining he does not wish to send the repentant soul of Claudius to Heaven, but just moments later, he mistakenly kills Polonius while in a rage. Is Hamlet a victim of his own interior dialogue? Does conscience make a coward of the Prince? Laertes would certainly have no such quibbles.

Claudius persuades Laertes to execute his revenge in a Machiavellian plot. The audience would know that this signals Laertes' imminent doom since adopting such tactics inevitably results in the downfall of the plotter. If Laertes simply killed Hamlet on sight, he might have maintained the sympathy of the audience even if the audience would know objectively that his action was wrong. By allowing himself to be led by Claudius who becomes in an instant his surrogate father, Laertes is led like Hamlet by his father to execute an action that will likely doom his soul. The King's plot, however, raises a significant question. Punishing Hamlet for the murder of Polonius is the rightful obligation of the State, meaning the obligation of the King. Keep in mind that St. Paul in his Letter to the Romans wrote "The ruler... is the minister of God, a revenger to execute wrath upon him that doeth evil."[49] The ruler delegates his power as revenger to his ministers and magistrates. Could it not be argued that Laertes is acting in the plot as the sanctioned minister to the State's revenge? Is this argument weakened by the illegitimacy of this particular ruler or by the Machiavellian methods used to exact the "justice of the State?"

In Shakespeare's time, the medieval doctrine of "the divine right of kings" still held sway, though the Protestant reformation was eroding its authority. The doctrine held that rulers derived their position and power directly from God and that any attempt to depose the king or to restrict his powers runs contrary to the will of God. The problem of the ineffective or tyrannical ruler and the appropriate response of the people to such a ruler is a theme that dominates Shakespeare's history plays from *Richard II* to *Richard III*. We will explore this issue extensively in the next chapter, but for now, consider the legitimacy of Claudius as king. In the first Act it appears clear that Claudius is competent. He deals effectively with the threat of young Fortinbras and has the apparent support of the people. It is worth recalling that in Denmark, kingship was elected and not necessarily passed from father to son. Claudius, in spite of his secret crime, has been selected by Denmark to rule. It might be argued since the people have selected his as King and God has not opposed it, that Claudius the agent of both the people and of God in Denmark.

On the other hand, we know that Claudius "played most foully" to achieve the crown and it could be argued that God for His own inscrutable purposes allowed this, as he allowed the eminently evil Richard III to usurp the throne of England. Claudius has taken into his own hands his destiny and the destiny of his country and for that he must pay. Because his rule is illegitimate, his orders and plots are also illegitimate. His authority to punish the murder of Polonius is undermined by the illegitimacy of his rule. Laertes cannot be seen as the legitimate tool of the State's justice because what is done by the State in executing justice must be done in the light of day. Neither Claudius nor Laertes acts for the benefit of justice; Claudius acts from self-interest and Laertes acts for a thirst for revenge.

So we come back to the question of Hamlet as the scourge of God, selected to right the wrong done to his father and his country. While Hamlet's actions are largely of his own choosing, there is a sense of inevitability wholly appropriate to tragedy that implies a greater hand guiding the events. In the final scene of the final act, Hamlet speaks of "a special providence in the fall of a sparrow" that reflects the Protestant belief that the will of God controls even the smallest of events. In the end, does Hamlet give himself over to the will of God?

> there's a special
> providence in the fall of a sparrow. If it be now,
> 'tis not to come; if it be not to come, it will be
> now; if it be not now, yet it will come:
> the readiness is all:
>
> (H, V, 2, 219-23)

"(I)f it be not now, yet it will come" speaks to the inevitability of a divine plan, perhaps incomprehensible in its larger design, perhaps appearing unfair that Hamlet has been placed against his will in the role of God's instrument. Nevertheless, Hamlet in the final analysis resigns himself to his assigned role and is ready to accept that which will come.

"The readiness," as he says, "is all."

Notes

1. Exodus 21: 23-24. *King James Bible.*
2. Matthew 5: 38-39. *King James Bible.*
3. Romans 12: 19. *King James Bible.*
4. Francis Bacon, *On Revenge.*
    http://people.brandeis.edu/~teuber/bacon.html .
5. Fredson Bowers, *Elizabethan Revenge Tragedy* (Princeton: Princeton University Press, 1940) 34-35.
6. Ibid, 74
7. Ibid, 71-72.
8. Sylvan Barnet, "*Titus Andronicus* on Stage and Screen" in *Shakespeare: The Tragedy of Titus Andronicus*, ed., Sylvan Barnet (New York: Signet Classics, 2005) 151.
9. Ibid, 153.
10. "Introduction to Titus Andronicus" in *Shakespeare: The Tragedy of Titus Andronicus*, ed., Sylvan Barnet (New York: Signet Classics, 2005) 2.
11. Leslie A. Fiedler, *The Stranger in* Shakespeare (New York: Barnes and Noble, 1972) 43.
12. *Shakespeare's Moor: The Sources and Representations*, *http://www.geocities.com/Wellesley/7261/gripes5.html?20084* .
13. Isaac Asimov, *Asimov's Guide to Shakespeare* (New York: Avenel Books, 1970) 402.
14. Jeffrey Burton Russell, *The Prince of Darkness* (Ithaca, NY. Cornell University Press, 1988) 114-115.
15. Fiedler, 181.
16. Quoted in Steven Katz, *The Holocaust in Historical Context, Vol. I* (New York: Oxford University Press, 1994) 438-39.
17. Fredson Bowers, *Elizabethan Revenge Tragedy* (Princeton: Princeton University Press, 1940) 40.
18. A. C. Bradley, *Shakespearean Tragedy* (London: McMillian, 1981) 181.
19. Samuel Taylor Coleridge, *Notes on the Tragedies* (published 1836-9).
20. G. D. Gunther, *Shakespeare as Traditional Artist* (Whitehorn: Johansen Printing and Publishing, 1994) 239.
21. Queen Elizabeth to the Lord Mayor et al., 11? July 1596, in *Acts of the Privy Council of England*, n.s., 26 (1596–97), ed. John Roche Dasent (London: Mackie, 1902), 16-7.

22. Queen Elizabeth to the Lord Mayor et al., 18 July 1596, in *Acts of the Privy Council*, pp. 20–1.

23. Quoted in Eldred D. Jones, *The Elizabethan Image of Africa* (Charlottesville: Univ. Press of Virginia, 1971), p. 20. See also "Licensing Casper van Senden to Deport Negroes [draft]," in *The Later Tudors (1588–1603)*, vol. 3 of *Tudor Royal Proclamations*, ed. Paul L. Hughes and James F. Larkin, 3 vols. (New Haven and London: Yale Univ. Press, 1969), pp. 221–2.Thomas Rymer, *A Short View of Tragedy*, 1692 quoted in S. E. Ogude " Literature and Racism: The Example of *Othello*" in *Othello: New Essays by Black Writers*, Ed. Mythili Kaul (Washington, D.C.: Howard University Press, 1997) 152.

24. "The Creation, in The Towneley Plays," ed. Martin Stevens and A. C. Cawley (New York: Published for the Early English Text Society by the Oxford University Press, 1994), vol. 1, ll. 132-36, 7;

25. Samuel T. Coleridge, *Coleridge's Shakespearean Criticism*, 2nd volume quoted in Mythili Kaul "Background" in *Othello: New Essays by Black Writers*, Ed. Mythili Kaul (Washington, D.C.: Howard University Press, 1997) 8.

26. Charles Lower, "*Othello* as Black on Southern Stages, Then and Now" quoted in Mythili Kaul "Background" in *Othello: New Essays by Black Writers*, Ed. Mythili Kaul (Washington, D.C.: Howard University Press, 1997) 9.

27. James H. Dorman, *Theater in the American South 1815-1861* quoted in Mythili Kaul "Background" in *Othello: New Essays by Black Writers*, Ed. Mythili Kaul (Washington, D.C.: Howard University Press, 1997)

28. Jack El-Hai, "Black and White and Red" *American Heritage.* http:www. americanheritage.com/articles/magazine/ah/1991/3/1991

29. Felix Barker, *The Oliviers* quoted in Marvin Rosenberg, *The Masks of Othello*, (Berkley: University of California Press, 1961) 158.

30. Bernard Spivack, *Shakespeare and the Allegory of Evil* (New York: Columbia University Press, 1958) 182

31. Marvin Rosenberg, *The Masks of Othello*, (Berkley: University of California Press, 1961) 182.

32. Harold Goddard, *The Meaning of Shakespeare, Volume 1.* (Chicago: University of Chicago Press, 1960) 75.

33. Carl Goldberg, "Iago's Malevolence" in, *Jihad and Sacred Vengeance*, Ed. Jerry S. Piven and Chris Boyd (iUniverse, 2002) 127.

34. Bernard Spivack, *Shakespeare and the Allegory of Evil* (New York: Columbia University Press, 1958) 67.

35. R. Hare, PCL-R 20-item checklist.
   http://www.angelfire.com/zine2/narcissism/psychopathy_checklist.htm

36. Tucker Brooke, *The Romantic Iago.*
   http://www.theatrehistory.com/british/iago001.html

37. Peter Laslett, Karla Oosterveen and Richard M. Smith (eds.), *Bastardy and its Comparative History* (Arnold, 1980).

38. Heldriss of Cornwall. *Silence.* Roche-Mahdi, Sarah (ed. and trans... East Lansing, MI: Colleagues Press Ltd, 1992).

39. Francis Galton, *English Men of Science: Their Nature and Nurture.* (London: Macmillan and Co., 1874) 13.

40. Marjorie Garber. *Shakespeare After All.* (New York: Anchor Books, 2004) 470.

41. Eleanor Prosser. *Hamlet and Revenge,* 2nd ed. (Stanford, California: Stanford University Press, 1971) 3.

42. Ibid, 5.

43. Ibid, 8.

44. Ibid, 11.

45. Ibid, 18.

46. Ibid, .20.

47. Ibid, .21, fn 56.

48. Romans 12:17, 13:4.

49. Prosser, 116.

49. Romans 12:17, 13:4.

THE USURPERS

Usurper (lat. *usurpare* = to seize for use, to use) is a derogatory term used to describe either an illegitimate or controversial claimant to the power; often, but not always in a monarchy, or a person who succeeds in establishing himself as a monarch without inheriting the throne, or any other person exercising authority unconstitutionally. Wikipedia, the free encyclopedia

While most people can sympathize with the revenger without necessarily condoning their actions, few people will at least consciously identify with the usurper, a character who takes that which is not rightfully his (or hers). With a few notable exceptions, the usurper on the Elizabethan/Jacobean stage is inevitably a villain. He is someone who has acquired political power through illegitimate or at least questionable means. More often than not he employs Machiavellian stratagems and murder to advance his position. And always there is a price he will pay for his crimes.

The usurper is an interesting character. Considering the very real threat of rebellion in Elizabeth's England, any playwright depicting events where a ruler is overthrown, had to be very careful to soundly denounce the usurper. Shakespeare's *Richard II* serves as an example. The play which included a scene showing the king's deposition was politically suspect and while the deposition scene could be shown on the stage, it was omitted from any quarto published during Elizabeth's reign. Elizabeth's fears were not without basis. In 1601, the Earl of Essex along with Shakespeare's friend and patron, the Earl of Southampton, disaffected with Elizabeth's rule decided that it was a time for a change. The conspirators hired Shakespeare's group, the Chamberlain's Men to perform *Richard II* on the eve of the rebellion in order to garner public support for the seizure of parliament and imprisonment of the queen. Elizabeth was outraged when she learned of this, allegedly saying "I am Richard II, know you not?" The rebellion failed, Essex was executed, Southampton was jailed and members of Shakespeare's company were brought in for questioning. Augustine Phillips, one of the heads of the company was questioned by government officials but the company was ultimately cleared of any wrong doing. In a cruel ironic twist, the

Chamberlain's Men were "invited" to perform for the Queen at Whitehall on 24 February 1601, the night before Essex was executed.

The political sensitivity about a ruler's overthrow went beyond an individual ruler's security. In the still theocentric world view of Elizabethan England, the position of the ruler was seen as divinely ordained as was the position of every element in what Alexander Pope called the "great chain of being." Born of an amalgam of Plato and the Bible, the world view of the Elizabethan was according to E. M. W. Tillyard "that of an ordered universe arranged in a fixed system of hierarchies, but modified [and modifiable] by man's sin and the hope of his redemption."[1] The chain stretched from the foot of God's throne to the meanest of inanimate objects. Each speck of creation was a link in the chain. There could be no gaps. Angels were situated between God and man and were arranged in three orders. The highest grouping included Seraphs, Cherubs and Thrones. The next included Dominations, Virtues and Powers. The lowest order, those closest to man included the Principalities, Archangels and Angels. The best known of this lower order are Michael, Gabriel and Raphael who served as God's agents in His dealings with man. Below man was the animal world comprised of beings endowed with life and movement. Again in hierarchical order the animals descended from the strongest, fastest and most intelligent down to the weakest, slowest and least intelligent. In some traditions the lion was the king of the beasts and in other traditions the honor fell to the elephant. Grouped below the animals were the birds ruled by the eagle, the fish and other sea creatures ruled by the whale or dolphin, than the insects ranked by their usefulness or attractiveness. At the very bottom of the animal order were the snake and other serpents. Below animals comes the division for plants which are endowed with life but not movement. Trees were at the top of this division, with all subsequent plants ranked based on their usefulness or attractiveness. Finally, at the very bottom of the great chain of being were the minerals which had neither life nor movement. At the top of this grouping were jewels with the diamond ranked the highest. The jewels were followed by the metals, then the rocks, soil, sand, dust and dirt.

Man like all the other groupings in the Great Chain was arranged in in a strict hierarchy with the king at the top of the social order. Below the king were the nobility consisting of dukes, earls and barons; then the gentry defined by land ownership and including knights and esquires. Below these were the common classes that included merchants; yeoman including farmers, tradesmen and craft workers; and laborers including servants and others who worked for wages.

The position of the king on the Great Chain gave rise to the doctrine of the divine right of kings which asserted that the king derived his right to rule directly from God and was not subject to the will of his subjects, the nobility or, in the case of protestant England, even the church. The king came to represent God's anointed and appointed on earth, subject only to God's judgment. The roots of this idea in the Christian West could be found in the Old Testament where Moses tells the Jews:

> "When you come into the land which the Lord your God is giving you and inherit it and live in it, and you say, 'Let us appoint over me a king like all the nation around me,' [then] you will appoint over yourself a king **whom the Lord your God shall choose.**" (Deut. 17:14-15)

The implication is that the people will appoint the king, but that God will really be deciding who that king will be. The Jewish king was established to be a model for the rest of the nation to emulate: a leader, a scholar, pious, righteous and God-fearing. The first king among the Jewish people was Saul who was appointed by the prophet Samuel. He almost immediately lost favor with God by disobeying an order to destroy the nation of Amalek down to the last cow. As a result, Samuel tells Saul:

> "Though you may be small in your own eyes, you are the head of the tribes of Israel; and God anointed you to be king over Israel... Why did you not obey the voice of God?... I shall not return to you for you have rejected the word of the Lord and the Lord has rejected you from being King over Israel."
> And Samuel turned to go and he [Saul] seized the hem of his robe and it tore. And Samuel said to him, "The Lord has torn the kingdom of Israel from you today and has given it your fellow who is better than you.'"
> (1 Samuel 15:17-28)

David was Samuel's next appointee and ascended to the throne of Israel after Saul's suicide following his military defeat at the hands of the Philistines.

The idea of the divinely ordained nature of human authority was affirmed in the New Testament by Jesus when at his trail he says to Pilate *"You would have no power over me at all if it had not been given you from above"* (John 19:11). Peter when writing his first letter said *"For the sake of the Lord, accept the authority of every human institution: the emperor, as the supreme authority and the governors as commissioned by him to punish criminals and praise those who do good."* (1 Peter 2:13-14). And Paul when writing to the Roman's was even more explicit:

> Let every person be subject to the governing authorities. For there is no authority except from God, and those that exist have been instituted by God. Therefore whoever resists the

> *authorities resists what God has appointed, and those who resist will incur judgment. For rulers are not a terror to good conduct, but to bad. Would you have no fear of the one who is in authority? Then do what is good, and you will receive his approval, for he is God's servant for your good. But if you do wrong, be afraid, for he does not bear the sword in vain. For he is the servant of God, an avenger who carries out God's wrath on the wrongdoer.*
> *(Romans 13:1-7)*

From these and similar Church teachings it came to be accepted that kings and all those in authority ruled with God's approval and as a part of God's divine plan, but this created a problem. How was one to come to terms with an unwise, unjust or tyrannical ruler? St. Augustine postulated that the world of history can be divided along two trajectories. The first trajectory is the human history of wars, government, authority, taxes, conquests, and laws and the second trajectory is the sacred history of human salvation. Whatever happened in secular history, good or bad, advanced sacred history. Rulers were put into place as a part of the grander scheme advancing human salvation—even if those rulers were immoral or non-Christian. This argument—that temporal authority in any form essentially advances human sacred history—would become the basic political theory of the Middle Ages.[2] Thus, in the face of an unjust ruler, the Christian was expected to accept that the tyranny he experienced was all part of the Divine Plan and was to be endured. Although the king might be ungodly, to question their authority is in essence to question God's purpose and plan. Further, any attempt to depose a king or restrict his power was seen as contrary to God's will and serious offense against the divine order of the universe.

By the time of Shakespeare, the doctrine of the divine right of kings was well entrenched. King James I of England explained his understanding of the doctrine in Chapter 20 of his *Works*.

> *The state of monarchy is the supremest thing upon earth; for kings are not only God's lieutenants upon earth, and sit upon God's throne, but even by God himself are called gods. There be three principal similitudes that illustrate the state of monarchy: one taken out of the word of God; and the two other out of the grounds of policy and philosophy. In the Scriptures kings are called gods, and so their power after a certain relation compared to the divine power. Kings are also compared to fathers of families: for a king is truly Parens patriæ, the politique father of his people. And lastly, kings are compared to the head of this microcosm of the body of man.*
> *Kings are justly called gods, for that they exercise a manner or resemblance of divine power upon earth: for if you will consider the attributes to God, you shall see how they agree in the person of a king. God hath power to create or destroy, make or unmake, at*

> *his pleasure, to give life or send death, to judge all and to be judged nor accountable to none; to raise low things and to make high things low at his pleasure, and to God are both souls and body due. And the like power have kings: they make and unmake their subjects, they have power of raising and casting down, of life and of death, judges over all their subjects and in all causes and yet accountable to none but God only.*
>
> *I conclude then this point touching the power of kings with this axiom of divinity, That as to dispute what God may do is blasphemy, so is it sedition in subjects to dispute what a king may do in the height of his power. But just kings will ever be willing to declare what they will do, if they will not incur the curse of God. I will not be content that my power be disputed upon; but I shall ever be willing to make the reason appear of all my doings, and rule my actions according to my laws.[3]*

It is ironic that the author of such a pronouncement was only one generation from the popular overthrow and execution of a royal monarch, his son King Charles I.

Combined with the theory of the divine right of kings was the concept of the King's Two Bodies: the king's body natural that has physical attributes as do all human bodies and the king's spiritual body, the body politic that transcends the earthly body and serves as a symbol and the essence of the office. Upon the death and perhaps upon the disposition of the king there is a separation of the two bodies and the body politic is transferred to a new body natural. The notion of the two bodies allowed for the continuity of monarchy and was used to defend the idea of a feminine ruler who might, as Elizabeth I famously said "have the body of a weak and feeble woman, but ... the heart and stomach of a king, and of a king of England too."[4]

Implicit in the metaphor of the Great Chain is a degree of inflexibly that suggests mobility of the individual links is rigidly restricted. A lamb cannot aspire to be a lion and a rose cannot evolve to become an oak. Only in the links representing mankind is the possibility of mobility apparent. Although possible, mobility is not viewed as desirable. Remember that the Great Chain represents God's divine design and any attempt to manipulate the design through the exercise of free will is explicitly a prideful challenge to God's wisdom. If the links in the Chain are broken, rearranged and forged anew, the result will invariably lead to a social structure less perfect then the structure originally designed by God. As a result, the newly formed Chain would be at best a flawed imitation of God's divine design and at worst a sinful travesty that would require God's retribution and correction.

Tinkering with the Chain also could have more global implications. There existed correspondences between the individual groupings along the Great Chain so that disorders on one plane could impact those on others. Iirregularities of the heavenly bodies mirror the loss of order in the state. Storms and unnatural events were duplicated by commotions and disasters in the state. This idea is seen in many of Shakespeare's play, but a single example will serve for now. When Macbeth murders Duncan, the cosmos respond. Lennox speaking to Macbeth says:

> The night has been unruly: where we lay,
> Our chimneys were blown down; and, as they say,
> Lamentings heard i' the air; strange screams of death,
> And prophesying with accents terrible
> Of dire combustion and confused events
> New hatch'd to the woeful time: the obscure bird
> Clamour'd the livelong night: some say, the earth
> Was feverous and did shake.
>
> (M, II, 3, 54-61)

By the time of Shakespeare and King James I, the metaphor of the Great Chain was being challenged by a second metaphor, that of a ladder. The rungs of a ladder suggest a greater mobility among the individuals located on the ladder. The individuals on one rung need only exert the energy necessary to step up to the next. If God's design is represented by a ladder, it implies that God allows for movement (within limits) up and down on the ladder and that his divine plan will not be altered regardless of who occupies a particular rung. The reason for this new way of viewing the design of the universe came from growing merchant and trade classes that aspired to improve their status in society through acquisition of wealth and property. Upward mobility based on skill and the will to power became an attractive theme that led to a reimagining of the classical archetype of the "over-reacher." Like the usurper, the over-reacher aspires to position or status that is not rightfully his. Unlike the usurper, the over-reacher is not a villain, but usually an admirable or heroic character who reaches too high and meets with a tragic end as a result of his hubris (overweening pride). Phaeton and Icarus served as two popular figures from Greek mythology that embodied the spirit of the over-reacher. Phaeton was the son of Apollo who aspired to drive the chariot of the sun. Without his father's permission, Phaeton steals the chariot and discovers he is unable to control. The sun weaving wildly through the sky comes too close to the earth causing death and destruction and finally Zeus is required to intervene by blowing Phaeton from the chariot with a thunderbolt. Icarus was the son of the great Greek inventor, Daedalus. Father and son were imprisoned by King Minos on the island of Crete and to affect an escape, Daedalus constructed a set of wings for each made of feathers bound together by wax. The pair flew away from their prison, but Icarus intoxicated by the power of flight flew higher and higher until the warmth of the sun melted the wax on his wings and he fell to his death.

The over-reacher reemerged in Elizabethan drama as the product of the creative energy of Shakespeare's contemporary and chief rival, Christopher Marlowe. Marlowe is a murky figure reputed to be a spy, an atheist, a homosexual and an all-round libertine and rebel. This reputation if true would in part explain his attraction to rebellious over-reachers. Marlowe's first play performed on stage in London was *Tamburlaine* (1587) about the Scythian shepherd, Tamburlaine (Timur) who, moved by an ambition far beyond the circumstances of his humble birth, makes himself leader of a gang of bandits that prey upon rich merchant trains crossing Persia. When Mycetes, the King of Persia, sends troops to suppress Tamburlaine, the eloquent shepherd persuades the king's troops to join him and with the help Mycetes' brother, Cosroe, Tamburlaine marches on and defeats Mycetes, then turns on Cosroe and takes control of Persia himself. His remarkable success in Persia and his insatiable ambition impels him next to try his fortunes against the emperor of Turkey. After another successful campaign, Tamburlaine turns his eyes on Egypt which he conquers in turn and the play ends with the conqueror marrying the daughter of the defeated Sultan. *Tamburlaine* was so wildly popular with playgoers that Marlowe penned a sequel which further documented Timur's expanding empire until his untimely death.

This celebration of human potential was an example of evolving Renaissance humanism which placed an increased value on the individual and encouraged the intellectual inquiry into the source, function and legitimacy of temporal power. Once it became apparent that upward mobility within the hierarchy of society was both possible and to some extent desirable, the ideas that upward mobility within the ruling class might also be acceptable. Certainly, this was the view of Niccolo Machiavelli who believed a ruler should not come to power by dynastic inheritance (or divine appointment), but as the result of his own initiative, skill, talent or strength. In England, jurists represented by Sir Edward Coke who was writing during the reign of James I were arguing that the King was not the exclusive appointee of God, but was in fact a creation of the laws of England and was subject to those laws. This theory would allow the law to judge the actions of the King and if they were found wanting, the law had the authority to replace the King with one better suited.

This conflict is the core theme of Shakespeare's *Richard II*. In this 1595 play that so troubled Elizabeth I and her supporters, the audience sees the weak and corrupt Richard replaced with popular support by his cousin Henry Bolingbrook. The play opens with Richard mediating a dispute between Henry and one of the King's henchmen, Thomas Mowbray. Mowbray has been accused by Henry of fiscal malfeasance and is suspected of the murder of the Thomas of Woodstock, Duke of Gloucester, the King's uncle. Thomas was the leader of a group of powerful nobles whose ambition to wrest power from Richard culminated in a successful rebellion in 1388, which significantly weakened the king's power. Richard bided his time and managed to imprison Thomas nine years later on a charge of treason, but Thomas was murdered prior to going to trial and probably on behalf of Richard. Thomas Mowbray was at the time the Governor of Calais, in whose charge Thomas was held after his arrest.

Bolingbrook leaves behind his aging and ailing father, John of Gaunt who serves the play as the spokesperson for the traditional view of kingship. Even though he shares his suspicion that Richard was responsible the murder of Gloucester, he steadfastly supports the divine right of Richard to rule. In Act I, scene 2, John of Gaunt explicitly expresses his suspicion of Richard in conversation with his widowed sister-in-law, the Duchess of Gloucester

> Alas, the part I had in Woodstock's blood
> Doth more solicit me than your exclaims,
> To stir against the butchers of his life!
> But since correction lieth in those hands [Richard's]
> Which made the fault that we cannot correct,
> Put we our quarrel to the will of heaven;
> Who, when they see the hours ripe on earth,
> Will rain hot vengeance on offenders' heads.
>
> (RII, I, 2, 1-8)

The Duchess rebukes him for his passive response to the murder of his brother and he responds

> God's is the quarrel; for God's substitute,
> His deputy anointed in His sight,
> Hath caused his death: the which if wrongfully,
> Let heaven revenge; for I may never lift
> An angry arm against His minister.
>
> (RII, I, 2, 37-41)

Gaunt clearly indicates his faith that Richard, though complicit in murder is beyond the judgment and condemnation of man because Richard is God's deputy on Earth. Only on his deathbed does Gaunt finally confront Richard with his crime, calling him "Landlord of England ..., not king."

Gaunt's death presents Richard with the opportunity to fund his impending war in Ireland by confiscating Gaunt's wealth and estate. With

Bolingbroke, the rightful heir, banished, no one openly resists, but the Duke of York, another of the king's uncles, disapproves, noting that:

> *What will ensue hereof, there's none can tell;*
> *But by bad courses may be understood*
> *That their events can never fall out good.*
>
> *(RII, II, 1, 212-214)*

Other nobles object more covertly and when they discover that Bolingbroke is returning under arms to reclaim his rightful inheritance, they see this as their opportunity to

> *...shake off our slavish yoke,*
> *Imp out our drooping country's broken wing,*
> *Redeem from broking pawn the blemish'd crown,*
> *Wipe off the dust that hides our sceptre's gilt*
> *And make high majesty look like itself,*
>
> *(RII, II, 1, 291-295)*

They are not at this point plotting to depose Richard but to force him to behave in a more kingly manner. After the king has departed for Ireland, these nobles join with Bolingbrook and set out to establish their power in the king's absence. At Bristol, the rebels capture and execute several of the king's favorites for the crime of "misleading" the king. Meanwhile, hurrying from Ireland, Richard lands in Wales. Confident of his divine appointment as God's anointed on Earth; Richard assures his followers and himself:

> *Not all the water in the rough rude sea*
> *Can wash the balm off from an anointed king;*
> *The breath of worldly men cannot depose*
> *The deputy elected by the Lord:*
> *For every man that Bolingbroke hath press'd*
> *To lift shrewd steel against our golden crown,*
> *God for his Richard hath in heavenly pay*
> *A glorious angel: then, if angels fight,*
> *Weak men must fall, for heaven still guards the right.*
>
> *(RII, III, 2, 54-62)*

No sooner does Richard utter these words then he learns that his Welsh
allies have deserted him in favor of Bolingbrook. Next, he learns that Bolingbrook
has won the popular support of the common folk. Richard, so confident a moment
ago, quickly falls to despair as political reality confronts political theory and
speaks his most famous speech:

> No matter where; of comfort no man speak:
> Let's talk of graves, of worms, and epitaphs;
> Make dust our paper and with rainy eyes
> Write sorrow on the bosom of the earth,
> Let's choose executors and talk of wills:
> And yet not so, for what can we bequeath
> Save our deposed bodies to the ground?
> Our lands, our lives and all are Bolingbrook's,
> And nothing can we call our own but death
> And that small model of the barren earth
> Which serves as paste and cover to our bones.
> For God's sake, let us sit upon the ground
> And tell sad stories of the death of kings;
> How some have been deposed; some slain in war,
> Some haunted by the ghosts they have deposed;
> Some poison'd by their wives: some sleeping kill'd;
> All murder'd: for within the hollow crown
> That rounds the mortal temples of a king
> Keeps Death his court and there the antic sits,
> Scoffing his state and grinning at his pomp,
> Allowing him a breath, a little scene,
> To monarchize, be fear'd and kill with looks,
> Infusing him with self and vain conceit,
> As if this flesh which walls about our life,
> Were brass impregnable, and humour'd thus
> Comes at the last and with a little pin
> Bores through his castle wall, and farewell king!
> Cover your heads and mock not flesh and blood
> With solemn reverence: throw away respect,
> Tradition, form and ceremonious duty,
> For you have but mistook me all this while:
> I live with bread like you, feel want,
> Taste grief, need friends: subjected thus,
> How can you say to me, I am a king?

Richard and Bolingbrook confront each other at Flint Castle in Wales. It does not appear that Bolingbrook is at this point considering the overthrow of Richard. He sends his most powerful ally, the Duke of Northumberland, to Richard saying:

> *Henry Bolingbrook*
> *On both his knees doth kiss King Richard's hand*
> *And sends allegiance and true faith of heart*
> *To his most royal person, hither come*
> *Even at his feet to lay my arms and power,*
> *Provided that my banishment repeal'd*
> *And lands restored again be freely granted:*
>
> (RII, III, 3, 35-41)

However, he does inform Richard and all present that he is willing to use force of arms to enforce his demands should Richard fail to abide by his conditions. Richard for his part still boldly mouths the assurances that God will defend his minister on Earth should Richard resist, but no longer believing this in his heart, Richard concedes to Bolingbrook 's demands on the pretense of avoiding bloodshed and civil unrest. Foreshadowing the dark times to come for England that will culminate in the War of the Roses, Richard says:

> *...though you think that ,*
> *... we are barren and bereft of friends;*
> *Yet know, my master, God omnipotent,*
> *Is mustering in his clouds on our behalf*
> *Armies of pestilence; and they shall strike*
> *Your children yet unborn and unbegot,*
> *That lift your vassal hands against my head*
> *And threat the glory of my precious crown.*
>
> (RII, III, 3, 82-90)

His threat to children yet unborn is presaging the working out of the so-called Tudor myth that laid the blame for the continual turmoil starting with the reign of Henry Bolingbroke and ending with the establishment of the Tudor line under Henry VII upon the country and the men who deposed God's elect on Earth. England's willful overthrow of God's appointed king breaks and re-forges the Great Chain. God's divine plan is altered by man's exercise of free will as it was in

Eden and dire consequences are incurred for the correction of man and the fulfillment of God's plan. This working out of England's punishment will become the overarching theme in all of Shakespeare's histories from *Richard II* to *Richard III*.

When Bolingbrook and the subdued King Richard arrive in London, Bolingbrook seems to have had a change of heart. Without back-grounding or explanation, Richard offers Bolingbrook the crown and Bolingbrook without hesitation accepts it. Up until this point the Bishop of Carlisle had been a supporter of Bolingbrook, but he is shocked at Bolingbrook's ready acceptance of Richard's crown. He too foretells of the horrors to come as a result of the usurpation:

> *My Lord of Hereford here, whom you call king,*
> *Is a foul traitor to proud Hereford's king:*
> *And if you crown him, let me prophesy:*
> *The blood of English shall manure the ground,*
> *And future ages groan for this foul act;*
> *Peace shall go sleep with Turks and infidels,*
> *And in this seat of peace tumultuous wars*
> *Shall kin with kin and kind with kind confound;*
> *Disorder, horror, fear and mutiny*
> *Shall here inhabit, and this land be call'd*
> *The field of Golgotha and dead men's skulls.*
> *O, if you raise this house against this house,*
> *It will the woefullest division prove*
> *That ever fell upon this cursed earth.*
> *Prevent it, resist it, let it not be so,*
> *Lest child, child's children, cry against you woe!*
>
> (RII, IV, 1, 134-149)

For speaking out not so much on Richard's behalf, but on behalf of the theory of the Divine Kingship, the Bishop is promptly arrested for treason. Richard is brought before Bolingbrook who asks "Are you contented to resign the crown?" to which Richard replies:

> *I give this heavy weight from off my head*
> *And this unwieldy sceptre from my hand,*
> *The pride of kingly sway from out my heart;*
> *With mine own tears I wash away my balm,*

> With mine own hands I give away my crown,
> With mine own tongue deny my sacred state,
>
> (RII, IV, 1, 204-209)

The defeated king is forced to publicly un-king himself as if he ultimately had any ability to transfer the body politic to another independent of God's will. If the body politic is transferable by the still living king, it is transferred in a debased form. After the formal deposition before the nobles, Richard is paraded through London where the crowds become complicit in Bolingbrook's crime as they cheer him and humiliate Richard: "rude misgoverned hands from windows' tops / Threw dust and rubbish on King Richard's head" (V.ii.5-6). The Duke of York describes the scene:

> As in a theatre the eyes of men,
> After a well-graced actor leaves the stage,
> Are idly bent on him that enters next,
> Thinking his prattle to be tedious,
> Even so, or with much more contempt, men's eyes
> Did scowl on gentle Richard. No man cried "God save him!"
>
> (RII, V, 2, 23-28)

Richard is taken to Pomfret castle and imprisoned there until one of Bolingbrook's knights, Sir Pierce Exton hearing the new king say "Have I no friend will rid me of this living fear [referring to Richard]?" Taking Bolingbrook at his word, Exton goes to Pomfret and murders Richard. Expecting praise and thanks, Exton brings the slain body before Bolingbrook but is surely surprised by the response. "[T]hough I did wish him dead," says Bolingbrook, "I hate the murderer, love him murdered." Bolingbrook banishes Exton and vows to undertake a pilgrimage to the Holy Land to do penance for his part in Richard's death.

UNEASY LIES THE HEAD THAT WEARS A CROWN: HENRY IV, PART II: HENRY BOLINGBROKE

The central question for our purposes is what are we to make of Henry Bolingbrook? Is he a villainous usurper, and admirable over-reacher, or a reluctant savior who replaces a corrupt and ineffectual ruler? What does history make of Henry Bolingbrook and what is Shakespeare's take on the man?

In spite of the fact that that Henry appears as a major player in three separate plays, two of which bear his name as the titled role, he is one of Shakespeare's most underdeveloped characters. In *Richard II*, we see him as the wronged subject seeking only his rightful inheritance who suddenly and without clear explanation seizes the crown with the support of both the nobles and commons. Shakespeare offers the audience no soliloquy to provide insight into Henry's thinking or motivation. In Act IV, scene I, the Duke of York enters a council of the nobles presided over by Bolingbrook and suddenly announces that Richard has adopted Bolingbrook as his heir and is prepared to yield the throne. In response, Bolingbrook simply states "In God's name, I'll ascend the regal throne." Immediately, Richard is brought before Bolingbrook and compelled to publicly resign the throne. In this poignantly written deposition scene, the defeated Richard is humbled before the assembled nobles and yield the crown into Henry's hands.

> I give this heavy weight from off my head
> And this unwieldy sceptre from my hand,
> The pride of kingly sway from out my heart;
> With mine own tears I wash away my balm,
> With mine own hands I give away my crown,
> With mine own tongue deny my sacred state,
> With mine own breath release all duty's rites:
> All pomp and majesty I do forswear;
> My manors, rents, revenues I forego;
> My acts, decrees, and statutes I deny:
> God pardon all oaths that are broke to me!
> God keep all vows unbroke that swear to thee!

Make me, that nothing have, with nothing grieved,
And thou with all pleased, that hast all achieved!
Long mayst thou live in Richard's seat to sit,
And soon lie Richard in an earthly pit!
God save King Harry, unking'd Richard says,
And send him many years of sunshine days!

(RII, IV, 1, 204-222)

The "show" is to make the usurpation appear as an abdication, making Bolingbrook, now Henry IV, innocent of any crime. In spite of its intent, the badgering Duke of Northumberland even makes Henry uncomfortable and the success of this staged abdication is threatened when Northumberland insists that Richard read a prepared document that outlines all of Richard's shortcomings. Henry says "Urge it no more, my Lord Northumberland," but Northumberland responds that "The commons will not then be satisfied." With this, the intent of this public humiliation is baldly revealed. At its conclusion, Richard is led off to imprisonment at Pomfret to the jeers of the assembled commons in the street. All however is not comfortably settled for Henry as in third scene of Act V a plot against Henry is already uncovered. Now feeling threatened as long as Richard lives to reclaim the throne, Henry utters the fateful statement, 'Have I no friend will rid me of this living fear?" According to Exton, a knight in attendance:

he wistly look'd on me,
And who should say, 'I would thou wert the man'
That would divorce this terror from my heart;'
Meaning the king at Pomfret. Come, let's go:
I am the king's friend, and will rid his foe.

(RII, V, 4, 7-11)

Since these statements are not spoken by Henry on stage, the audience can take them as literal truth or as a misunderstood utterance wrongly interpreted by Exton. After murdering Richard, Exton brings the body to Henry fully expecting the new king's gratitude. Instead Henry responds with anger and regret.

HENRY BOLINGBROKE
Exton, I thank thee not; for thou hast wrought
A deed of slander with thy fatal hand
Upon my head and all this famous land.
EXTON

From your own mouth, my lord, did I this deed.
HENRY BOLINGBROKE
They love not poison that do poison need,
Nor do I thee: though I did wish him dead,
I hate the murderer, love him murdered

(RII, V, 6, 34-40)

It is noteworthy that Henry does not deny he wished Richard dead. Was he only musing when he expressed this wish out loud or was he slightly dangling bait for some over-eager lackey to snatch? Since we only see Henry in public speech, we never know with certainty what is going on in his mind. Are we to take his speeches at face value or as simply Machiavellian lies intended to advance and hold his power? The only clue is in his sudden change from supplicant for justice to usurping subject. I believe we can only conclude that Henry returned to England from exile with the intention of seizing the throne. All his talk of only seeking restoration of his inheritance was only cover for his real intention. While Richard was clearly unfit to rule, Henry needed to be assured of popular support before making his play for the throne. By showing himself as the injured party, sympathy with the commons was garnered. If support for his seizure of power had failed to materialized, he had the fallback position that he was simply petitioning for that which was rightfully his. Once it was clear he had overwhelming support, he dropped the mask of the loyal but wronged subject and agreed to ascend the throne. He staged managed the deposition to show Richard as a willing participate, giving up the throne to ease his cares and woes, In this charade, Northumberland played the "heavy," and Henry the kindly cousin willing to shoulder Richard's kingly burdens for the benefit of Richard and the State. If one accepts this interpretation of Henry as a fore-thinking and ambitious man, it is likely we are intended to see Exton's interpretation of Henry's desire for Richard's death as a veiled invitation to murder. Richard's death accompanied by the discovery of the conspiracy against Henry's crown would seemingly eliminate the major threats to the king. By his choice of words, Henry makes clear his intention but retains plausible deniability in the murder of Richard. In the final analysis, I think we are forced to see Henry Bolingbrook as a villainous usurper, as guilty as Claudius, and one whose crime is even further far-reaching, throwing his country into war and savagery for the next 85 years.

Once the precedent of replacing one king with another is established, subsequent usurpations become easier for dissatisfied subjects. The historical Henry took control of the throne of England in 1400 and almost immediately subjects still loyal to Richard went into revolt. They rallied to the Welsh leader, Owen Glendower who led a national uprising asserting the independence of Wales.

By the middle of 1401, the rebellion was gaining ground and a year later, Sir Edmund Mortimer, Henry's cousin, was captured at the Battle of Bryn Glas. Mortimer was the grandson of King Edward III's second son and in fact had a better claim to the throne than did Henry whose father was Edward's third son. In spite of this, Mortimer was loyal to Henry, but when Glendower offered to release Mortimer for a large ransom, Henry refused to pay. Angered by the betrayal, Mortimer negotiated an alliance with Glendower and married one of his daughters.

Meanwhile, the ever rebellious Scots were making trouble in the north of England. In the spring of 1402, the Scots launched a major offensive in Northumberland but were beaten back at the battle of Nesbit Moor. In part to avenge the killing and capture of Scottish nobles at Nesbit Moor the Scottish army led by Archibald, Earl of Douglas, invaded England on a pillaging expedition. While returning to Scotland, they were intercepted and defeated at Humbleton Hill by English forces led by the Northumberland and his son Henry Percy, Shakespeare's Hotspur. Archibald, along with many Scottish nobles, was captured, but rather than cheering Henry, the Percy victory raised his pique. The victory underscored his own lack of success against Glendower and to humble the proud Northerners, Henry demanded that all Scottish prisoners be turned over to him. Henry Percy was outraged and refused to surrender Douglas to the King. A bitter argument developed between the two and was further fueled by Henry's refusal to allow the Percys to ransom their kinsman, Edmund Mortimer (Hotspur was married to Mortimer's sister) from Owen Glendower. Faced with what they saw as a petty and ungrateful King who they had helped to plant on the throne of England, the Percys began to plot his overthrow.

Playing on the disaffection of the Percys from Henry, Owen Glendower negotiated the so-called "Tripartite Indenture" with Edmund Mortimer and the Percys. The Indenture agreed to divide England and Wales among the three of them with Wales going to Glendower, the south and west of England going to Mortimer and the north of England falling to the Percys. All these key events occurred in 1402-1403 and are either reported or seen in Act I, scene iii of Shakespeare's *Henry IV*. As in Richard II, Shakespeare only allows us to hear Henry's public discussions and witness his public actions. Again we have no insight into the mind of the man. His pronounced motives for refusing the ransom of Mortimer and the provocation of Hotspur are neither objectively confirmed nor denied. When first hearing of Hotspur's victory over the Scots, Henry's first thought is to contrast the valiant Hotspur to his wassail son, Prince Henry. He then turns to Hotspur's refusal to give up his Scottish prisoners. Seeming perplexed, Henry asks

What think you, coz,
Of this young Percy's pride? the prisoners,
Which he in this adventure hath surprised,
To his own use he keeps; and sends me word,
I shall have none but Mortimer

(1HIV, I, 1, 91-95)

In scene III, Henry seeks the answer from the principles. Asserting his position Henry again demands the prisoners who Hotspur agrees to release into the hands of the King. Henry then moves on to the matter of Mortimer who he accuses of conspiring with Glendower instead of being held as a prisoner. The Percys vigorously deny the accusation, but the King is unmoved by their defense and leaves the matter as a fait accompli. Hotspur flies into a rage. Of the prisoners, he says "An if the devil come and roar for them, I will not send them. He then boldly pronounces his treasonous intentions:

But I will lift the down-trod Mortimer
As high in the air as this unthankful king,
As this ingrate and canker'd Bolingbroke.

(1HIV, I, 3, 135-39)

King Henry does not appear again until Act III, scene ii where we find him upbraiding his son for his debauched lifestyle. He says:

I know not whether God will have it so,
For some displeasing service I have done,
That, in his secret doom, out of my blood
He'll breed revengement and a scourge for me;
But thou dost in thy passages of life
Make me believe that thou art only mark'd
For the hot vengeance and the rod of heaven
To punish my mistreadings.

(1HIV, III, 2, 4-11)

Many fathers have probably thought or said such stuff about a wayward son, but in Henry's case this takes on a special meaning because he has reason to suspect Heaven of conspiring against him, after all, he usurped Richard's throne. Henry's life, both private and public is in constant turmoil and as he prepares for battle to defend his throne, he has the additional worry about the suitability of his heir apparent. Finally, however, Prince Henry is won over by his father's chastisement and vows to put aside his wanton ways.

King Henry then disappears again until Act V which depicts the climactic battle of Shrewsbury. Prince Hal makes good his promise when he meets his nemesis Harry Hotspur on the field and slays him in single combat (a historical error; Hotspur died from a well-placed arrow to the face). The rebels are soundly defeated, but many of Henry's enemies, including Northumberland, Mortimer and Glendower, survive to fight another day.

Henry IV, Part II picks up immediately follows the battle of Shrewsbury and telescopes the next 10 years into a single play. The first two Acts focus almost entirely on Falstaff and the rebel conspirators. King Henry does not even appear until Act III, scene 1 where for the first time in three plays we are given a glimpse of Henry's inner thoughts. We find the King plagued by insomnia, an ailment also experienced by Shakespeare's most famous usurpers: Richard III and Macbeth. Insomnia is not in Shakespeare seen exclusively as the product of a guilty mind. Not all insomniacs are villains and not all villains are insomniacs, but when the context fits, it is not difficult to interpret sleeplessness as a curse placed upon the guilty as punishment   Ironically, Henry has taken on the cares and woes of leadership just as he promised to do when assuming Richard's crown. His reign has been without peace. He is beset by would-be usurpers. His very sleep is disrupted by paranoia and guilt. He belatedly understands that "Uneasy lies the head that wears a crown," particularly if that head has donned that crown without the endorsement of God.

While in discussion with Warwick, Henry informs us that it has now been nearly ten years since Richard's deposition. That makes the year 1409. Almost seven years have passed since the Battle of Shrewsbury and the northern rebellion still continues. The Glendower rebellion has been put down and Warwick reports, historically inaccurate that Owen Glendower is dead. We also learn that Henry has been sick "this fortnight." In fact the historical Henry is said to have suffered from a disfiguring skin disease, and more seriously, some acute disorder, possibly epilepsy that manifested in 1405 and recurred in the winter of 1408-9, again in 1412 and then killed him in March of 1413. After this short expository scene, Henry again fades into the background of the play until Act IV, scene 4. Here Shakespeare telescopes time dramatically. We learn that the rebellious Bishop Scroop has been captured (which actually happened in1405) and that Northumberland has been defeated (which occurred in both 1405 and again fatally in 1408). The King is again ill and forced to his sickbed never again to rise, placing the scene in 1413. In his deathbed scene, Henry laments his troubled reign and notes

God knows, my son,
By what by-paths and indirect crook'd ways
I met this crown; and I myself know well
How troublesome it sat upon my head.

(2HIV, IV, 5, 183-86)

Importantly, however, Henry confesses neither regret nor guilt over the seizure of the crown. Nor does Henry make any justification for taking the "crook'd" path to the crown. He dies unapologetic inviting us still to ponder the true character of the man: reluctant ruler or ambitious villain.

HOW SWEET A THING IT IS TO WEAR A CROWN: HENRY VI, PART III: RICHARD, DUKE OF YORK

The *Henry VI* tetralogy which concludes with *Richard III* is primarily concerned with the events of the War of the Roses where the House of York led by Richard Duke of York contended with the House of Lancaster, led by the sitting king, Henry VI, for control of the English crown. Considered Shakespeare's earliest group of plays, the *Henry VI* tetralogy was performed between 1590 and 1593. Of all the Shakespeare plays, this tetralogy is probably the most complex and convoluted. It has a very large cast and covers 63 years of English history from the death of Henry V in 1422 until the death of Richard III in 1485. Its history is remarkably inaccurate, manipulated for dramatic purposes and its characters are less well developed than we are accustomed to in Shakespeare's plays. The tetralogy, like *Titus Andronicus* which was written during the same period, is filled with villains, each one worse than the one before and ultimately terminates in Shakespeare's master villain, Richard III. While Richard III will be the chief focus of our study, it is his father, Richard, Duke of York that we will first consider as we review the background leading up career of the infamous "crook-backed" king.

Henry VI, part 1 opens following the funeral of King Henry V. This places the scene in 1422. The new king, Henry VI was only 9 months old. The rule of the realm has been placed in the hands of Henry V's brothers John, Duke of Bedford who has been appointed Regent of France, and Humphrey, Duke of Gloucester, as Protector. Henry Beaufort, Bishop of Winchester and Humphrey's uncle, feels he is better fit to be Protector and plots to gain control of the infant King and rule on his behalf. While these power struggles emerge, the French are reclaiming land conquered by Henry V. We are told in Act I, scene 1 that "Guienne, Champagne, Rheims, Orleans, Paris, Guysors, Poictiers, are all quite lost." Bedford quickly resolves to return to France and set things right.

In scene 2, we are introduced to Charles, Dauphin of France, as he meets Joan La Pucelle, AKA Joan of Arc. This scene takes place during the siege of Orleans making the year no earlier than 1428. In scene 3, we are back in England and the conflict between Gloucester and Winchester breaks into open confrontation. Scene 3 shifts back to France and the narrative remains there detailing the English victory at Orleans until the fourth scene of Act II.

Act II, scene 4 describes the source of the impeding War of the Roses. Meeting in the Temple Garden of Parliament, the Earl of Somerset and Richard Plantagenet (latter Duke of York) are involved in a petty argument over Plantagenet's noble birth. The surrounding nobles are asked to pick a white rose to show their support for Somerset or a red rose to show their support for Richard. Plantagenet and Somerset trade insults about their flowers and scorn each other. Somerset criticizes Plantagenet's father, who was put to death as a traitor by Henry V. Plantagenet says his father was accused and put to death, but his treason was never proven. He says he will remember this slight for a long time, and Somerset should expect to see results from his insults in future dealings with Plantagenet. Somerset for his part is the grandson by the second marriage of John of Gaunt and nephew to Winchester. Scene 5 is expository, using the imprisoned Edmund Mortimer, Richard's maternal uncle, to explain the root of the argument dramatized in scene 4. Mortimer says the same deed that caused him to be in the tower all these years was the reason for Plantagenet's father's demise. Mortimer explains that his family was next in line to the throne after Richard II, but because Henry IV deposed Richard, Henry's line came to power instead. When he attempted to reassert himself as the rightful heir, Mortimer was thrown in jail. Early in the reign of King Henry V, Richard's father (yet another Richard) raised an army to install Edmund on the throne, but he was captured and executed in 1415, and the Mortimers were suppressed. This leads Richard to conclude that he has a better claim to the English throne than the sitting King, Henry VI.

House of Mortimer-York

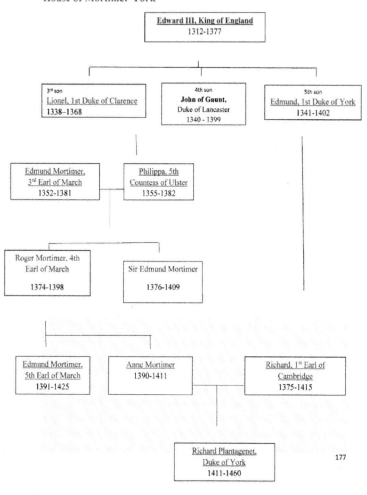

Edward III, King of England
1312-1377

3rd son
Lionel, 1st Duke of Clarence
1338–1368

4th son
John of Gaunt,
Duke of Lancaster
1340 - 1399

5th son
Edmund, 1st Duke of York
1341-1402

Edmund Mortimer,
3rd Earl of March
1352-1381

Philippa, 5th
Countess of Ulster
1355-1382

Roger Mortimer, 4th
Earl of March
1374-1398

Sir Edmund Mortimer
1376-1409

Edmund Mortimer,
5th Earl of March
1391-1425

Anne Mortimer
1390-1411

Richard, 1st Earl of
Cambridge
1375-1415

Richard Plantagenet,
Duke of York
1411-1460

177

118

This confusing succession contention is complicated by Shakespeare's poor use of history. Edmund Mortimer the 5th Earl of March was imprisoned by King Henry IV, but was freed by Henry V whom he accompanied on the first expedition to France. He fought with distinction at Harfleur and after the death of Henry V; he was placed in charge of the English settlement in Ireland where he died in 1425 of the plague. Richard's dialogue with him in prison and the preceding garden scene are pure fabrications, but they build the foundation upon which the subsequent two *Henry VI* plays are built.

The young King Henry VI makes his first appearance in Act III, scene 1 and assumed the role of peacemaker, trying to calm the contention between Humphrey and Winchester that has threatened the peace on the streets of London. The antagonists acquiesce to the King's request, but make it clear that their animosity is unabated. Henry then turns his attention to the status of Richard Plantagenet and reinstates his rights as the Duke of York, much to the chagrin of the Earl of Somerset. Finally, at the urging of Humphrey, Henry agrees to journey to France and be crowned as king there, thereby asserting English control over France once and for all. The remainder of Act III returns to the progress of the wars in France. This first introduction to the king portrays him as a gentle and peace-loving soul ill-suited to manage the nest of vipers that surround him. As this scene occurs shortly after the death of Mortimer, we can assume it takes place at the Parliament of 1426. Historically, Henry would only have been five years old at the time.

Act IV, scene 1 now has Henry in Paris for his coronation. The date would be December 17, 1430 and Henry would now be nine years old. Here again, the young king is required to take on the role of peacemaker as the feud between York and Somerset threatens to erupt into violence. Henry orders York and Somerset to forget their quarrel and to remember where they are. Here in France, "amongst a fickle and wavering nation"(IV.i.138), the lords must make an effort not to reveal dissention, for if the French see disagreements among the English forces, then they will again dare rebellion. To pacify the feuding nobles, Henry appoints York as regent to France, replacing the Duke of Bedford who died four months before, and Somerset as commander of the English cavalry and infantry in France. He urges them to "Go cheerfully together and digest [their] angry choler on [their] enemies." Such a naïve strategy is of course doomed to failure. Here again, history suffers as Bedford did not die and York did not assume the role of regent until 1436.

The remainder of the fourth Act focuses on the siege of Bordeaux which results in a resounding English defeat. Recriminations fly between

York and Somerset with York accusing Somerset for failing to send reinforcements to Bordeaux and Somerset accusing York of launching an ill-conceived and undermanned expedition. The actual battle described in Act IV did not occur until 1452.

Act V opens in London where Henry and his advisers contemplate a plea from the Pope for a peace agreement between France and England. Henry who is always predisposed to peace says

> I always thought
> It was both impious and unnatural
> That such immanity and bloody strife
> Should reign among professors of one faith.
>   (1HVI, V, 1, 11-14)

Humphrey agrees with Henry and suggests a royal wedding between Henry and the daughter of   Earl of Armagnac, a close relative of the French dauphin. Winchester, now a cardinal of the Church, predictably opposes Humphrey's peace plan. Oddly, again we have a break from the historical truth. This scene would have taken place in 1444. Henry would have been 23 years of age and the siege of Bordeaux would have been eight years in the future.

The action then shifts again to France where York is launching an offensive against the city of Angers in the province of Anjou. In the course of the battle, Joan La Pucelle is captured, then placed on trial and condemned to death. Here the history is breathtaking is its inaccuracy. Joan was in fact captured in 1430 by the Burgundians while attempting to free Compiègne, a town in northern France. They in turn sold her to the English forces still under the leadership of the Duke of Bedford. Her trail for heresy was conducted in an ecclesiastical court headed by the bishop of Beauvais in 1431 at Rouen, not in the camp of York and under his supervision. It would be inconceivable that Shakespeare would not have known the facts of matter, so we must conclude that Shakespeare consciously places these scenes where they are to strengthen a favorable impression of the Duke of York by having him dispose of this "evil" opponent of the English. At the end of the trail, Winchester arrives with a letter from Henry instructing York to make peace with the French forces. York is outraged to think that so many died and were captured for their country, only to now be dishonored by what he considers "effeminate peace"(V.vi.107). He however complies with the King's command and a peace agreement is concluded.

Sandwiched between the capture and trial of Joan is a scene that introduces us to Margaret of Anjou who will become the queen of King Henry VI. She has been taken captive by the William de la Pole, Earl of Suffolk who is immediately taken with her beauty. Though he lusts for the maiden, de la Pole is married. He ruminates on how he can have Margaret and lights upon a strategy; he will woo her on behalf of his king. Margaret is technically the daughter of a "king"—Reignier, the titular and penniless king of Naples. Suffolk pitches his idea to father and daughter and both agree. In the final scene of the play, Suffolk persuades Henry to marry Margaret even though Henry must break off his engagement from the daughter of Earl of Armagnac. Suffolk has the final word:

> Thus Suffolk hath prevail'd; and thus he goes,
> As did the youthful Paris once to Greece,
> With hope to find the like event in love,
> But prosper better than the Trojan did.
> Margaret shall now be queen, and rule the king;
> But I will rule both her, the king and realm.
>
> (1HVI, V, 7, 103-8)

Most scholars agree that *Henry VI, Part 1* was written after the remainder of the *Henry* plays and *Richard III*. Of all the history plays, *Henry VI, Part 1* is probably the most historically inaccurate. Shakespeare plays fast and loose with the characters and the timeline, but manages to create a reasonably compelling, if frequently confusing, drama. He uses the play as background for the War of the Roses that will dominate the subsequent three plays and sets up two dominant themes that permeate the subsequent plays. First, that a weak king is more dangerous to welfare of the kingdom than a strong one. During Shakespeare's time, the line of succession was far from certain as Elizabeth, the Virgin Queen had brought forth no heirs and who would ascend the throne had not been determined. Thinking back to the turmoil of King Henry VI's reign when warring factions all but exterminated the nobility of England, the Elizabethans looked forward to the future after the Queen with great anxiety. Second, it promotes the Tudor myth that all the events dramatized in the tetralogy were evidence of God's justice being wrought on England for the deposition of King Richard II. First the English lose all their possessions in France and then they wallow in the blood of their own countrymen in a destructive civil war. It is not until the Plantagenet line pretty well burns itself out with the death of Richard III that peace can return to the land.

The political machinations for control of the King continue in Henry VI, Part 2 with Humphrey, Duke of Gloucester and Henry Beaufort, the former Bishop of Winchester (now Cardinal) jockeying for influence. Into the mix is added Margaret of Anjou, the future queen who is introduced to the court in the first scene of the first Act. This would set the scene in 1445; Henry would have been 23 years old and Margaret just 15. It is revealed that the peace treaty negotiated by Suffolk includes terms yielding the provinces of Anjou and Maine to the French in exchange for Margaret's hand in marriage. Gloucester and York are outraged, but the King is so taken with Margaret that he readily agrees to the terms and elevates Suffolk to the rank of Duke (this promotion did not in fact take place until 1448). Margaret quickly learns that Gloucester is the true power behind the throne and that

> *Beside the haughty protector, have we Beaufort,*
> *The imperious churchman, Somerset, Buckingham,*
> *And grumbling York: and not the least of these*
> *But can do more in England than the king.*
> > *(2HVI, I, 3, 68-71)*

Together with Suffolk, the new Queen resolves to eliminate all her rivals for power starting with Gloucester who is most vulnerable through his proud and ambitious wife. Suffolk has already laid a trap to disgrace the Duchess and dishonor Gloucester and tells the Queen

> *Although we fancy not the cardinal,*
> *Yet must we join with him and with the lords,*
> *Till we have brought Duke Humphrey in disgrace.*
> > **   *   *   **
> *So, one by one, we'll weed them all at last,*
> *And you yourself shall steer the happy helm.*
> > *(2HVI, I, 3, 94-6, 99-*
> > *100)*

The details of the plot against the Duchess will be discussed in detail later, but it is sufficient to say that it succeeds in disgracing the Duchess and driving the Duke to his doom. In the third Act, his rivals, Cardinal Beaufort, York, Margaret, and Suffolk unite to poison the mind of the King against Gloucester. He is accused of undermining the troops in France, inflicting unnatural tortures on offenders at home, and general treason against the King. At the same time, a revolt in Ireland presents the Cardinal, Margaret, and Somerset, who has newly returned from France, an opportunity to remove the ever-grumbling York from the power equation. York is dispatched to Ireland to squelch the rebellion, but before he leaves he hatches a plot to stir up revolt at home by instigating "a headstrong Kentishman, John Cade of Ashford, [t]o make commotion, as full well he can, [u]nder the title of John Mortimer." (2HVI, III, 1, 356-9) With troops at his disposal, York plans to return to England as its savior from the Cade revolt and as usurper of the Lancastrian crown.

Meanwhile, unsure of their ability to make a convincing case against Gloucester and fearful of Henry's forgiving nature, the Cardinal and Suffolk take the surer way and contract with murderers to take the life Gloucester, Henry immediately suspects foul play and he is encouraged in his belief by two of York's most powerful allies at court, the Earl of Salisbury and his son, the Earl of Warwick. Heated words are exchanged as Warwick boldly accuses Suffolk of Gloucester's murder and stirs up the populace who demand that King Henry either execute or banish the Duke. Henry believing Suffolk guilty exiles him to the deep distress of the Queen. In the midst of all this, the Cardinal takes ill and dies a raving and writhing death. Suddenly with Gloucester and Beaufort dead, York dispatched to Ireland, and Suffolk banished and ultimately executed, Margaret and Somerset (who is the last of the Lancastrian line besides the King), are the last two powers standing to lead and control the King. This action packed third Act takes place in 1447 and Shakespeare is required to make only comparatively minor compressions of time. The Duke of Gloucester died in February; Winchester in April. York was appointed to suppress the Irish rebellion in August. The chief historical inaccuracy centers on the Duke of Suffolk. He was not immediately implicated in the death of Gloucester nor was he the paramour of Queen Margaret as Shakespeare implies. If fact, over the course of the next two years, he received promotion after promotion culminating in the Dukedom in 1448 that Shakespeare had awarded him three years earlier. However, the people of England where generally suspicious of Suffolk and their suspicion was magnified when Suffolk seized the estates of Gloucester who had died without an apparent heir. By 1450, fate had turned against him. The loss of nearly all the English possessions in northern France again recalled attention to Suffolk's role in the loss of Maine and Anjou. Further, although he was never officially implicated on Gloucester's death, the popular suspicion attached to Suffolk vented itself in insurrections in 1450. Suffolk was arrested by

123

Parliament at the insistence of the Commons and sentenced without trial to five years' banishment. For many, the sentence seemed grossly insufficient and on his journey into exile, his ship was intercepted by a ship of war, and probably under the covert orders of the government, the Duke was beheaded.

The very long fourth Act focuses almost exclusively on the Cade rebellion and I will cover it in some detail in a later chapter; meanwhile, we will leap forward to the fifth Act and the return of York from Ireland. He immediately makes his intentions known:

> *From Ireland thus comes York to claim his right,*
> *And pluck the crown from feeble Henry's head:*
> *Ring, bells, aloud; burn, bonfires, clear and bright,*
> *To entertain great England's lawful king.*
> > (2HVI, V, 1, 1-4)

Historically, York did return to England in 1450 and did stir up some trouble in London, but did not confront the Lancastrians with military force for another five years. York's public stance was that of a reformer, not a usurper. He carried on an escalating feud with the Duke of Somerset and in 1453 when the King suffered a catastrophic mental breakdown; York managed to have himself appointed Protector of the Realm and promptly imprisoned Somerset. Somerset was subsequently saved only by the King's recovery late in 1454 which forced York to surrender his office. Henry swiftly released Somerset. Seeing armed conflict as the only means of eliminating Somerset once and for all, York gathered his forces and marched for London. In the play York is met between Dartford and Blackheath. Here again, Shakespeare is compressing time and manipulating fact. The meeting that took place between Dartford and Blackheath actually occurred in 1452 when York with military backing attempted to be recognized as Henry VI's heir apparent (Henry was still childless at this time), although Henry preferred the Earl of Somerset to succeed him as a Beaufort descendant of the Lancastrian line. Gathering men on the march from Ludlow, York headed for London, to find the city gates barred against him on Henry's orders. At Dartford in Kent, with his army outnumbered, and the support of only two of the nobility, York was forced to come to an agreement with Henry and dismiss his army.

At the meeting which Shakespeare clearly intends to take place just before the Battle of St Alban, the opening volley in the War of the Roses, York is met by Humphrey, Duke of Buckingham on the King's behalf. Buckingham inquires about York's intention in arriving with so large a military force at his back. York in spite of his previous bluster dissembles:

> *The cause why I have brought this army hither*
> *Is to remove proud Somerset from the king,*
> *Seditious to his grace and to the state.*
>
> (2HVI, V, 1, 35-7)

York is informed that Somerset has already been imprisoned and that his military force is not needed to achieve his goal. Henry then enters the scene giving further assurances and York dismisses his troops. No sooner are they dismissed then Margaret enters the scene with Somerset on her arm. York drops all semblance of deference and explodes:

> *Shall I endure the sight of Somerset?*
> *False king! why hast thou broken faith with me,*
> *Knowing how hardly I can brook abuse?*
> *King did I call thee? no, thou art not king,*
> *Not fit to govern and rule multitudes,*
> *Which darest not, no, nor canst not rule a traitor.*
> *That head of thine doth not become a crown;*
> *Thy hand is made to grasp a palmer's staff,*
> *And not to grace an awful princely sceptre.*
> *That gold must round engirt these brows of mine,*
>
> (2HVI, V, 1, 90-9)

All pretense now gone, the battle lines are drawn. Buckingham and the Cliffords (father and son), powerful nobles from the northwest of England, stand with Henry and Somerset. The Earls of Salisbury and Warwick enter to throw their support to York. Also on hand are "the bastard boys of York" (so-called by Margaret), Edward and Richard, the future kings. It is important to note that in 1445, Edward was only 10 years old and Richard had not yet been born! The first words from Richard could serve as his motto for the next two plays: "...if words will not [serve], then our weapons shall." Richard will wield both with equal skill, as comfortable with violence as with diplomacy. Equally significant are the first words addressed to him: "... heap of wrath, foul indigested lump as crooked in thy manners as thy shape!" His physical deformity will at once be the prick that spurs his ambition and a disguise that encourages others to underestimate this diminutive devil.

The antagonists separate to gather their forces and they meet in battle on May 22, 1455 in the town of St. Alban, about twenty miles north of London. The Yorkist force of 3,000 men outnumbered and soundly defeated the Lancastrians who fielded 2,000. While York launched a frontal assault, a flacking maneuver by the Earl of Warwick resulted in the collapse of the Lancastrian defender and the death of the Duke of Somerset. During the same action, the King and the Duke of Buckingham were injured by Warwick's archers. In Shakespeare's description of the battle, he has York killing the elder Clifford and Richard (III) killing the Duke of Somerset in single combat. Richard is also credited with saving the life of the Earl of Salisbury three times on the field of battle, evidence of his prowess and courage. The King and Queen flee to London and the play ends with the victors planning to follow.

Henry VI, Part 3 is a retelling of the key events in the War of the Roses. After the victory of St. Alban, Shakespeare shows York ready to mount the throne, but in a parley with Henry, he agrees to allow Henry to remain on the throne until his death in exchange for Henry's promise that he will name York as his heir apparent. By so doing, Henry essentially disavows the right of his son Edward to ascend the throne. Margaret naturally objects as does the young Clifford who has sworn blood revenge against the house of York for the death of his father. Nevertheless, the King agrees to York's terms and the parties separate. These events in fact occurred in 1460, almost five years after the Yorkist victory at St. Albans. During the intervening years, Henry was at first held as York's prisoner. When Parliament met in November 1455, the throne was empty, and it was reported that the king was ill again. York deferred his claim to the throne and resumed the office of Protector, but surrendered it when the king recovered in February 1456. An uneasy peace held until June 1459 when a great council was summoned to meet at Coventry. York and his allies refused to appear, fearing arrest and as a result of their failure to appear, they were indicted for treason. York gathered his forces and moved south. On October 12, the forces of York and Lancaster met again at Ludford Bridge and the Yorkists were driven back. York fled for Ireland and Salisbury, Warwick and York's son Edward fled to Calais. York's wife Cecily and their two younger sons (George, Duke of Clarence, age 10 and Richard, age 8) were captured in Ludlow Castle and imprisoned at Coventry. The Yorkist forces regrouped and again confronted the forces of the King at Northampton in July 1460, this time with a favorable outcome. King Henry was again taken prisoner and on October 7, 1460 Parliament recognized the Duke of York's stronger claim to the throne and agreed that Henry VI should rule England until his death when the crown would pass to York. King Henry agreed to this but his fugitive wife (she had fled to Scotland where she rallied her supporters) certainly did not; no sooner was the Act of Accord passed than Queen Margaret marched south with an army of twenty thousand men. Her forces met York at Wakefield on December 30, 1460 and this is where Shakespeare picks up the narrative in Act I, scene 3.

In Shakespeare's account, York's sons Edward and Richard urge York to take the throne immediately, rather than await Henry's death. York insists he has sworn an oath to let Henry rule, but Richard easily convinces him that the oath was not binding. Richard reveals his cunning logic and his manipulation of an argument:

> An oath is of no moment, being not took
> Before a true and lawful magistrate,
> That hath authority over him that swears:
> Henry had none, but did usurp the place;
> Then, seeing 'twas he that made you to depose,
> Your oath, my lord, is vain and frivolous.
>
> (3HVI, I, 2, 22-7)

Richard concludes the argument with an encouragement to his father: "And, father, do but think/How sweet a thing it is to wear a crown/ Within whose circuit is Elysium." (3HVI, I, 2, 29-30). The final sentence reveals Richard's personal view of kingship and echoes the words of another great over-reacher, Christopher Marlowe's Tamburlaine who says ""Is it not passing brave to be a king, / And ride in triumph through Persepolis?" (Tam 1, II, 5, 51-2).[7] The influence of Marlowe's writing on the early works of Shakespeare is well accepted as fact and that influence will be particularly evident in the creation of Richard III.

Meanwhile, the Lancastrian forces arrive to challenge York at Wakefield. Queen Margaret has assumed command of the King's army and, reminiscent of Joan la Pucelle, she arrives in full armor. York's second son Edmund, Earl of Rutland (age 17) is captured and killed by Clifford. York is also captured by Margaret and Clifford and in an excruciating scene of cruelty he is tormented and executed by Margaret and Clifford. Make to stand on a molehill, York is crowned with a paper crown and taunted as a false king. To dry his tears of humiliation, Margaret offers him a handkerchief dipped in Rutland's blood and as he rails against her; she and Clifford stab him to death.

So as Richard, Duke of York passes into eternity, how are we, the audience, expected to judge his actions. Is he a failed usurper, a villain who meets his just reward? Or is he like Hamlet who has a legitimate claim to a throne occupied by a usurper? For comparative purposes, the actions of York are most similar to those of Henry Bolingbroke: both are provoked by the irresponsible acts of the seated kings. King Richard II seized Bolingbroke's inheritance; King Henry VI attempted to deceive York with a false report of Somerset's imprisonment. King Richard is ruled by his arrogance; King Henry is ruled by his advisors. King Richard is a bad king; King Henry, an incompetent one.

Henry Bolingbroke has no legitimate claim to Richard's throne. Richard, Duke of York, has a legitimate claim to Henry's throne. Shakespeare takes pains in *Henry VI, Part 1*, Act 2, Scene 5 to use the imprisoned Edmund Mortimer to explain the legitimacy of York's claim to the throne. York's mother was Anne Mortimer, daughter of Richard II's legitimate heir Roger Mortimer who was the grandson of Lionel of Antwerp, Duke of Clarence, and Edward III's second surviving son. When Roger died in Ireland in 1398 his son Edmund became heir apparent, but this right was usurped when Henry Bolingbroke seized the throne a year later. By strict interpretation of the laws of primogeniture, Edmund should have been king after Richard's fall and his nephew York, by his sister Anne Mortimer, should have succeeded him if the laws of primogeniture had been followed. This gave York a stronger claim to the throne than Henry VI, who descended from Edward III's third son and from the usurping Henry Bolingbroke. Henry himself acknowledges this:

> KING HENRY VI
> Henry the Fourth by conquest got the crown.
> YORK
> 'Twas by rebellion against his king.
> KING HENRY VI
> [Aside] I know not what to say; my title's weak.--
>
> (3HVI, I, 1, 132-4)

Even given his superior claim, York is prepared to defer ascension to the throne until after the death of Henry to avoid civil war and bloodshed. Henry readily agrees, but Margaret and her allies reject the peace as such an agreement disinherits her son, Edward. Similarly, it is the York's sons,

Edward and Richard, who persuade to Duke to renege on the agreement and seize the throne immediately.

York's capture, torture and death at Wakefield is treated sympathetically by Shakespeare, portraying York in the mode of a tragic figure, rather than as usurping rebel receiving his just reward. He endures the torments of Margaret and Clifford stoically until confronted with the death of his son, Rutland. At that point, he rails against Margaret in such moving language that Margaret's ally Northumberland says:

> Had he been slaughter-man to all my kin,
> I should not for my life but weep with him.
> To see how inly sorrow gripes his soul.
>
> (3HVI, I, 4, 169-71)

Shakespeare's sympathetic handling of the death of York, I think, argues that Shakespeare did not intend the audience to have the same misgivings about York that they may have had about Henry Bolingbroke. York is open where Bolingbroke is closed. York throughout the plays takes pains to establish his legitimacy as a claimant to the throne; Bolingbroke never argues his legitimacy. York's enemies are painted with the black brush of villainy gleefully tormenting the helpless York while Bolingbroke's enemies, most notably, Henry "Hotspur" Percy, are treated with respect for their nobility. Although not a paragon of virtue, York is the least villainous of Shakespeare's usurpers. Finally, I would suggest that York is really the prototype for the tragic protagonists of Shakespeare's later plays, a great and noble man who is brought to woe by a flaw or mistake in judgment.

WHY, I CAN SMILE, AND MURDER WHILES I SMILE: HENRY VI, PART III: RICHARD III

There is no ambiguity in Shakespeare's Richard III. He is one of Shakespeare's most popular and transparent villains. Developed over the course of three plays, *Henry VI, Parts 2* and *3 and Richard III*, Richard constantly proclaims his villainy to the audience. Part Tamburlaine, part Machiavelli, and part medieval Vice, Richard is one of Shakespeare's earliest and greatest creations, combining Aaron's overt love of evil, Iago's malignant cunning, and Macbeth's overweening ambition. But unlike Shakespeare's other creations, Richard was once a living, breathing man and a King of England too. As such, Shakespeare did not have the option of significantly changing the facts of the man beyond his popularly accepted history. For historical source information, Shakespeare frequently relied upon Raphael Holinshed's *Chronicles of England, Scotland, and Ireland* (2nd edition, 1587) and Edward Hall's *Union of the two noble and illustre famelies of Lancastre and Yorke* (1550). Hall's version, in turn, was based on other texts, specifically Sir Thomas More *History of King Richard the Thirde* (1513) and Polydore Vergil's *Anglica Historia* (1534). In 1505, Vergil, an Italian priest living in England, was commissioned by Henry VII to write an "official" history of England. Sometimes called "the Father of English History," Vergil's task was to embellish and perpetuate the version of Richard current at the court of Henry VII and he gave the King what he wanted – an account making King Richard III the monster that has come down to us through Shakespeare's play. Vergil's Richard is an accomplished Machiavellian who determines to seize the throne by "artifice". More's account is a bit more complicated. Predating Virgil's account, More's *History of King Richard the Thirde* portrays Richard as such a monster that some scholars have argued that it was written as an attack on royal tyranny, rather than on Richard III, himself. More, unlike Vergil was no supporter of Henry VII. His history barely mentions the first Tudor king, the hero of Vergil's works, perhaps because Henry persecuted his father, Sir John More Thomas it seems incurred the royal wrath in 1504, when as a newly elected burgess he persuaded parliament not to allow the king the full grant which he was seeking. In revenge, Henry VII had More's father imprisoned and fined. When, after five more years of extortionate taxation, the king died unlamented, More's congratulatory verses to Henry VIII on his coronation contained a message of hope that tyranny was dead and even a specific reference to the end of a 'gloomy reign'.   More's *History* includes only the period between the death of Richard's older brother, King Edward IV, in the spring of 1483 and Buckingham's rebellion in the autumn of the same year.   It excludes specific reference to Henry Tudor's victory at Bosworth Field in 1485.   Twentieth century historian Paul Murray Kendall in *Richard III* (1955), a scholarly defense of the controversial monarch arguing for a more favorable view of Richard, has pointed to the significance of this exclusion by suggesting Richard may have been serving as a substitute target for More, who endowed Richard with Henry's own dissimulating character.

Prior to Vergil and More, recorded history in Christianized Europe tended to be universal, providential and apocalyptic.   History was treated as an illustration of the working out of God's judgment in human affairs and thus it tended to emphasize an intelligible and "objective" narrative pattern of events which inevitably affirmed the justice of God.   History was often used and studied to teach moral lessons. It fulfilled a dual purpose; it was for people to learn about and to learn from.   This approach is particularly apparent in the histories penned by Vergil and adapted by Hall and gives rise to the fundamentally religious "Tudor myth" which identifies a pattern of events set into motion by the deposition of Richard II that evolve under a law of blood atonement, and that result in the glory of Tudor England.   On this tradition, More and to a lesser extent Vergil layered the influence of the new historical schools of Renaissance Italy that were predominantly secular, intensely nationalistic, and deliberately propagandistic. The Italian historians offered three reasons for the writing of history: "that it is a form of literature, highly regarded by the ancients and presenting attractive opportunities for the exercise of style; that it has great practical value since it teaches moral, ethical, and political lessons; and finally, that his history celebrated the past and present glories of his native land..."[6]   To achieve these goals, the "new" histories tended to be more subjective and dramatic. Objective reality could be manipulated or omitted in favor of "improving" the story or advancing an agenda.

While Vergil is both nationalistic and propagandistic, Thomas More's *History of King Richard the Thirde* is more strictly subjective and secular.   It can be read as a meditation on power and corruption as well as an abridged history of the reign of Richard III.   The religious undertones of the "Tudor Myth" are entirely absent from More's work and emphasis is placed on the creative dramatic writing rather than jingoistic cheerleading.   More creates whole scenes and dialogues that cannot be factually accurate, but that are intended to reveal character and circumstances. *The oracion of the kyng, in his death bed* section of the *History* serves as an excellent example.   Here Edward IV is imagined trying to reconcile the differences between his family and the family of his wife, Elizabeth Woodville.

Since it is highly improbable that someone sat at his bedside recording his every word, More imagines an eloquent speech that shows the character of man and dramatically relates that underlying issues that ultimately lead to the coronation of Richard III. More introduces the scene by writing

> When these lordes with diuerse other of bothe the parties were comme in presence, the kynge liftinge vppe himselfe and vndersette with pillowes, as it is reported on this wyse sayd vnto them.[8]

More then launches Edward into a lengthy speech which concludes dramatically with the death of the King. Similar lengthy orations occur throughout the *History* and include Richard speaking on the institution of sanctuary and the Duke of Buckingham speaking on the bastardry of the sons of Edward IV and Richard's right to the throne.

More also takes pains to assign motives to the actions of the principle players, creating characters as well as mere actors on the stage of history. Again, an example will suffice. More in describing the relative minor character of Richard Ratclif says:

> Richard Ratclif knight, whose seruice the protector specially vsed in the counsel and in thexecucion of such lawles enterprises, as a man that had ben long secret with him, hauing experience of the world & a shrewde wit, short & rude in speche, rough & rough & boistiouse of behauiour, bold in mischief, as far from pitie as from al fere of god.[9]

Ratclif by this description becomes a man the reader can visualize, understand and instantly dislike. Similarly, in describing James Tyrell, the man directly credited with the murder of the young princes in the Tower, says:

> sir Iames Tyrell, which was a man of right goodlye parsonage, and for natures gyftes, worthy to haue serued a muche better prince, if he had well serued god, and by grace obtayned asmuche trouthe & good will as he had strength and witte. The man had an high heart, and sore longed vpwarde, not rising yet so fast as he had hoped, being hindered and kept vnder by the meanes of sir Richard Ratcliffe and sir William Catesby, which longing for no moo parteners of the princes fauour, and namely not for hym, whose pride thei wist would beare no pere, kept him by secrete driftes out of all secrete trust. Whiche thyng this page wel had marked and knowen. Wherefore thys occasion offered, of very speciall frendship he toke his time to put him forward, & by such wise doe him good, that al the enemies he had except the deuil, could neuer haue done him so muche hurte.[10]

So here More creates a degree of sympathy for a man he deems guilty of the most heinous of crimes: the murder of children.

Finally, More does takes every opportunity to climb into the pulpit and preach to the reader. Following the account of the murder of the Princes, More writes about *"The out & inward troubles of tyrauntes."*

> *I haue heard by credible report of such as wer secrete with his chamberers, that after this abhominable deede done, he neuer hadde quiet in his minde, hee neuer thought himself sure. Where he went abrode, his eyen whirled about, his body priuily fenced, his hand euer on his dager, his countenance and maner like one alway ready to strike againe, he toke ill rest a nightes, lay long wakyng and musing, sore weried with care & watch, rather slumbred then slept, troubled wyth fearful dreames, sodainly sommetyme sterte vp, leape out of his bed & runne about the chamber, so was his restles herte continually tossed & tumbled with the tedious impression & stormy remembrance of his abominable dede.[11]*

Shakespeare draws on all these sources either directly or indirectly. It should be kept in mind that Shakespeare was first and always about delighting the theater audience. He was an entertainer, not an academic or a historian. His first tetralogy is frequently criticized for its convoluted story line and its historical inaccuracies, but the Richard plays develop the theme of God working out His divine plan for England, while showing how individual choices and actions, freely taken impact the course of history. Shakespeare is true to the theory of history dominating in his time, i.e., he entertains, he teaches, and he promotes the government line.

Richard appears in three of Shakespeare's plays: *Henry VI, part 2, Henry VI, part 3,* and the play that bears his name. His first appearance is in the next to the last scene of the final act of *Henry VI, part 2.* The scene is that preceding the battle of St. Albans and "the bastard boys of York" (so-called by Queen Margaret), Edward and Richard, are on stage. The first words from Richard could serve as his motto for the next two plays: *"...if words will not [serve], then our weapons shall."* Richard will wield both with equal skill, as comfortable with violence as with diplomacy. Equally significant are the first words addressed to him: *"... heap of wrath, foul indigested lump as crooked in thy manners as thy shape!"* His physical deformity will at once be the prick that spurs his ambition and a disguise that encourages others to underestimate this diminutive devil. In the subsequent scene, Richard kills the Duke of Somerset in single combat and is credited with saving the life of the Earl of Salisbury three times on the field of battle, evidence of his prowess and courage.

Richard's physical description has been a sore spot for the defenders of Richard. They argue that there are no objective contemporary documents or portraits that would the support the misshapen Richard we see on the stage. Only one panel painting of Richard III could have been taken from life, perhaps in the last few months of his reign, and that is the round-topped portrait in the Society of Antiquaries. It shows a man with a pensive face and long delicate fingers, revealing no gross deformity of the arm or back.

Reproduced by kind permission of the Society of Antiquaries

Vergil provides his physical description of Richard at the end of his history.

> He was slight of stature, misshapen of body, with one shoulder higher than the other, and had a pinched and truculent face which seemed to smack of deceit and guile. While he was plunged in thought, he would constantly chew his lower lip, as if the savage nature in that miniature body was raging against itself. Likewise with his right hand he was constantly pulling the dagger he always wore halfway in and out. He had a sharp, clever, wily wit, fit for pretence and dissimulation. His spirit was lively and fierce, and did not fail him even in death.[12]

More on the other hand describes Richard early in this narrative.

> Richarde the third sonne, of whom we nowe entreate, was in witte and courage egall with either of them, in bodye and prowesse farre vnder them bot, little of stature, ill fetured of limmes, croke backed, his left shoulder much higher then his right, hard fauoured of visage, and suche as is in states called warlye, in other menne otherwise, he was malicious, wrathfull, enuious, and from afore his birth, euer frowarde. It is for truth

> reported, that the Duches his mother had so muche a doe in her travaile, that shee coulde not bee deliuered of hym uncutte: and that hee came into the worlde with the feete forwarde, as menne bee borne outwarde, and (as the fame runneth) also not vntothed, whither menne of hatred reporte aboue the trouthe, or elles that nature chaunged her course in hys beginninge, whiche in the course of his lyfe many thinges vnnaturallye committed.[13]

Both agree that Richard was small of stature one, hard favored, and that one shoulder was higher than the other. More adds the now famous hunched back and the story of his strange nativity, probably borrowed from John Rous, historian and antiquary to the House of Warwick who wrote the *Historia Regum Angliae* shortly after the death of Richard. According to Rous, Richard was "retained within his mother's womb for two years, emerging with teeth and hair to his shoulders." From this, More than concludes that because "nature chaunged her course in hys beginninge, whiche in the course of his lyfe many thinges vnnaturallye committed."

Shakespeare adopted More's description of Richard, including More's conclusion that Richard's physical deformity accounts for his "unnatural" behavior. More's conclusion was consistent with that of the ancient Greeks and Romans who believed that physical features revealed a person's natural disposition. Aristotle in his *Prior Analytics* noted that "It is possible to infer character from feature." This idea that "you can tell a book by its cover" enjoyed varying degrees of popularity and although it had fallen into disrepute by the time of Shakespeare, it features prominently in many of his plays, including *Richard III*. For example, Caesar in *Julius Caesar* says:

> Yond Cassius has a lean and hungry look,
> He thinks too much; such men are dangerous.
>
> (JC, I, 2, 194-5)

Here as in *Richard III*, the villain's appearance reveals his character. However, in the writing of *Macbeth*, Shakespeare has Duncan reject the reliability of appearances. Speaking of the traitorous Thane of Cawdor Duncan says:

> There's no art
> To find the mind's construction in the face:
> There's no art
> To find the mind's construction in the face
>
> (M, I, 4, 12-5)

The character of Richard III anticipates the "nature vs. nurture" argument that has persisted in criminology. The central question is does nature or genetics determine individual differences in behavioral traits or does the environment control how the individual will behave. Traditionally, human nature had been thought of as not only inherited but divinely ordained, but as noted above, by the time of Shakespeare differences among individuals were more associated with socialization rather than with inborn qualities. With Richard III, Shakespeare decides to have it both ways. Supporting the "Tudor myth" that sees Richard as "scourge of God," sent as the final and most terrible of the punishments visited on England for the deposition of Richard II, Richard III is born deformed as an external sign of his internal evil. His physical appearance should have served as a warning to his countrymen, but they ignore the obvious, instead repeatedly underestimating the self-serving evil of the man. Was Richard born bad? His appearance and his strange nativity would suggest it. But even if not, his physical appearance would surely have guaranteed a rough life during the tumultuous reign of Henry VI. His father would have been frequently absent and his mother shows us in *Richard III* that she has no great affection for her misshaped son. In Act II, scene 2 when Richard encounters his mother, the Duchess of York, he asks for her blessing, to which she indifferently replies

> *God bless thee; and put meekness in thy mind,*
> *Love, charity, obedience, and true duty!*
> *(RIII, II, 2, 107-8)*

She clearly sees these virtues lacking in her youngest son. Later, in conversation with the young Duke of York (Edward IV' youngest son) and the Archbishop, she is more direct in speaking of Richard:

> *DUCHESS OF YORK*
> *He was the wretched'st thing when he was young,*
> *So long a-growing and so leisurely,*
> *That, if this rule were true, he should be gracious.*
> *ARCHBISHOP OF YORK*
> *Why, madam, so, no doubt, he is.*
> *DUCHESS OF YORK*
> *I hope he is; but yet let mothers doubt.*
> *(RIII, II, 4, 18-22)*

And by the fourth Act of Richard III, she lets vent to her full feelings about her youngest son,

> Thou camest on earth to make the earth my hell.
> A grievous burthen was thy birth to me;
> Tetchy and wayward was thy infancy;
> Thy school-days frightful, desperate, wild, and furious,
> Thy prime of manhood daring, bold, and venturous,
> Thy age confirm'd, proud, subdued, bloody,
> treacherous,
> More mild, but yet more harmful, kind in hatred:
> What comfortable hour canst thou name,
> That ever graced me in thy company?
>
> (RIII, IV, 4, 167-175)

Raised in such a loveless world, if not born bad, the cards were stacked against young Richard and his personality would surely be warped by upbringing. Like Iago, Richard shows most of the characteristics criminal psychologist, Dr. Robert Hare identified as common to the psychopathic personality.

Bullying has become a cause célèbre in the early years of the 21st century and perhaps can also shed some light on Richard's malignant personality. One can easily imagine the abuse young, small and deformed Richard would have endured at the hands of his older and more vigorous brothers and companions. The popular understanding is that Columbine killers, Eric Harris and Dylan Klebold, were taking revenge against the bullies who had made school miserable for them. While this explanation is certainly an oversimplification of such a horrific crime, it does highlight the fact that bulling was a significant contributing factor. A paper presented at the annual meeting of the American Psychology - Law Society in 2010 described a study exploring whether bullies and bully-victims exhibited unique patterns of criminal thinking, aggression, psychopathy, and criminal behaviors in comparison to victims or controls. The researchers found that bully-victims had significantly higher scores on criminal thinking, aggression, psychopathy, and criminal behavior than did their control subjects.[14] Victims of bullying most often show depression, withdraw, poor self-esteem and suicidal tendencies, but some find means for to cope with bullying by finding and enhancing their own strengths. They may come to see their oppressors as inferior to themselves in all aspects of save their superior strength or size or physical attractiveness. The victims may find and develop "super-competence" in certain equalizing skills, e.g., skill with a particular weapon. They may exhibit cunning or ruthlessness or disarming charm and wit. They may cultivate relations where companions because tools in executing actions that are incapable of executing on their own. They, in short, may over-compensate for their low self-esteem with a psychopathic exaggeration of self-worth where those around him become either inferiors to be destroyed or tools to achieve his narcissistic wants, needs and desires. This is how I see young Richard. Imagine the self-discipline required to not only equal but to surpass his "normal" peers. Consider the physical and emotional control he had to exercise to be even marginally accepted in the tempestuous world of the War of the Roses. It would require what Nietzsche refers to a true will to power, rejecting traditional values in preference to his own needs and world view.

With his portrait of Richard, Shakespeare is able to endorse the notion that God used Richard as the climatic curse on England for the deposition of Richard II while preserving the humanity of Richard. Richard acts like a devil, but he is not one. Ultimately he is a man, with the free will to reject evil. That his physical deformity might predispose him to persecution and that the bellicose and loveless environment of his childhood might predispose him to violence, he was always free to determine his course. God does not create him evil, but does set the circumstance that would turn him to evil. Like Job, Richard is plagued with hardship, but unlike Job, he turns his back on God and heartily embraces evil. In the famous soliloquy that opens *Richard III*, Richard announces this: "*I am determined to prove a villain*" (*RIII*, I, 1, 30).

To return to Shakespeare's narrative, the role of Richard continues to develop in *Henry VI, part 3* as the war between the Houses of Lancaster and York escalates in ever increasing savagery. Following the death of the Duke of York, the Yorkists now lead by York's eldest son Edward marched on London where he was joined by the forces of Warwick. When Edward and Warwick entered London, a largely Yorkist-supporting city, they were welcomed with enthusiasm, money and supplies. The popular opinion was quickly confirmed by Parliament, and Edward was unofficially crowned in a ceremony at Westminster Abbey, although Edward vowed he would not have a formal coronation until Henry and Margaret were executed or exiled. He also announced that Henry had forfeited his right to the crown by allowing his queen to take up arms against his rightful heirs under the Act of Accord. The Yorkist forces than marched northward to meet the Lancastrians in a final climatic battle. The armies met near Towton, a town just southwest of York and what followed was the largest battle of the Wars of the Roses which an estimated 60,000—80,000 men took part in, with over 25,000 men being killed, the greatest recorded single day's loss of life on English soil. Just three months after the death of the Duke of York, the Yorkists under the leadership of Edward, now King Edward IV, and Warwick won a decisive victory.

Henry and Margaret, who were waiting in York with their son Edward, fled north when they heard the outcome.

The greater part of Shakespeare's second act is taken up with the Battle of Towton and the third act opens with the capture of King Henry VI whose wife and son have left him when they fled to France. Historically, these events did not occur until 1465, four years after Henry lost his throne. The next scene depicts King Edward's wooing of his future queen, Lady Elizabeth Grey, which affords his two remaining brothers, George, Duke of Clarence and Richard an opportunity to comment on the King's lascivious nature. It is at the end of this scene that Richard in his first great soliloquy turns to the audience and reveals himself:

> *Ay, Edward will use women honourably.*
> *Would he were wasted, marrow, bones and all,*
> *That from his loins no hopeful branch may spring,*
> *To cross me from the golden time I look for!*
> *And yet, between my soul's desire and me--*
> *The lustful Edward's title buried--*
> *Is Clarence, Henry, and his son young Edward,*
> *And all the unlook'd for issue of their bodies,*
> *To take their rooms, ere I can place myself:*
> *A cold premeditation for my purpose!*
> *Why, then, I do but dream on sovereignty;*
> *Like one that stands upon a promontory,*
> *And spies a far-off shore where he would tread,*
> *Wishing his foot were equal with his eye,*
> *And chides the sea that sunders him from thence,*
> *Saying, he'll lade it dry to have his way:*
> ***So do I wish the crown, being so far off;***
> ***And so I chide the means that keeps me from it;***
> ***And so I say, I'll cut the causes off,***
> ***Flattering me with impossibilities.***
> *My eye's too quick, my heart o'erweens too much,*
> *Unless my hand and strength could equal them.*
> *Well, say there is no kingdom then for Richard;*
>
> (3HVI, III, 2, 124-146)

Richard begins by expressing his ambition for the crown and lamenting all the obstacles that stand between him and his goal. First Edward, then any children who proceed from Edward's union with Lady Grey, then brother Clarence and his off-spring; all must be removed before Richard can claim the throne. At first he doubts his ability to "cut the causes off" that stand in his way to achieving the crown. He searches for an alternative future:

> What other pleasure can the world afford?
> **I'll make my heaven in a lady's lap,**
> **And deck my body in gay ornaments,**
> **And witch sweet ladies with my words and looks.**
> O miserable thought! and more unlikely
> Than to accomplish twenty golden crowns!
> Why, love forswore me in my mother's womb:
> And, for I should not deal in her soft laws,
> She did corrupt frail nature with some bribe,
> To shrink mine arm up like a wither'd shrub;
> To make an envious mountain on my back,
> Where sits deformity to mock my body;
> To shape my legs of an unequal size;
> To disproportion me in every part,
> Like to a chaos, or an unlick'd bear-whelp
> That carries no impression like the dam.
> And **am I then a man to be beloved?**
> **O monstrous fault, to harbour such a thought!** (Emphasis added)
>   (3HVI, III, 2, 147-164)

Shall he seek his future in the love of a woman? "O miserable thought!" he says "and more unlikely/Than to accomplish twenty golden crowns! / Why, love forswore me in my mother's womb." He rallies against nature for providing him with such a misshaped body, believe that anyone so shaped could never attain the love of a woman. He has grounds for this belief: he could not even manage the love of his own mother! His comments also demonstrate a belief in the shallow nature of women suggesting they can only love a thing of superficial beauty. Since love is beyond his grasp, he can find no third way. The crown must be his.

> Then, since this earth affords no joy to me,
> But to command, to cheque, to o'erbear such
> As are of better person than myself,
> I'll make my heaven to dream upon the crown,
> And, whiles I live, to account this world but hell,
> Until my mis-shaped trunk that bears this head
> Be round impaled with a glorious crown.

And yet I know not how to get the crown,
For many lives stand between me and home:
And I,--like one lost in a thorny wood,
That rends the thorns and is rent with the thorns,
Seeking a way and straying from the way;
Not knowing how to find the open air,
But toiling desperately to find it out,--
Torment myself to catch the English crown:
And from that torment I will free myself,
Or hew my way out with a bloody axe. (Emphasis added)
(3HVI, III, 2, 165-181)

He resolves to pursue the throne by any means necessary. At this point he has no specific strategy on how he will accomplish this, but having the over-compensating self-confidence of Iago, he is sure he can find his way.

Why, I can smile, and murder whiles I smile,
And cry 'Content' to that which grieves my heart,
And wet my cheeks with artificial tears,
And frame my face to all occasions.
I'll drown more sailors than the mermaid shall;
I'll slay more gazers than the basilisk;
I'll play the orator as well as Nestor,
Deceive more slily than Ulysses could,
And, like a Sinon, take another Troy.
I can add colours to the chameleon,
Change shapes with Proteus for advantages,
And set the murderous Machiavel to school.
Can I do this, and cannot get a crown?
Tut, were it farther off, I'll pluck it down. *(Emphasis added)*
(3HVI, III, 2, 182-195)

While Edward is seducing Lady Grey, Warwick is in France negotiating a peace predicated on the marriage of Edward to the daughter of the King of France. At the same time, Queen Margaret is at the French court trying to persuade the King to support her efforts to reclaim the throne of England on behalf of her husband. To Margaret's chagrin, the French king is supporting Edward's claim on the throne and seems favorably dispose to the marriage of Edward to his daughter. Moments before the final agreement is reached, the parties are notified that

Edward has married Lady Grey. The King is insulted and Warwick humiliated. They decide to throw in with Margaret to remove Edward from the throne and reinstate Henry.

At home in England, the royal brothers are also falling out over Edward's marriage. Clarence feels particularly offended since Edward has deprived him of the wealthy bride he sought, giving her to Lady Grey's brother instead. As a result, when the brothers learn of Warwick's defection and the impending invasion of England from France, Clarence announces he will join with Warwick's forces against his own brother and thereby gain a worthy bride in the youngest daughter of Warwick. Richard, for his part, remains loyal, not so much out of love for Edward as from his own ambition. With Edward as king he has a slight chance of achieving the crown; with Henry VI on the throne he has none.

What actually happened between Edward's marriage to Lady Grey in 1464 and the events leading up to the climatic battles of Barnet and Tewkesbury was a seesaw of actions where Warwick instigated several rebellions in the north. After winning the Battle of Edgecote Moor on 26 July 1469, the earl found the Yorkist king deserted by his followers, and brought him to Warwick Castle for "protection".[13] Lancastrian supporters took advantage of Edward's imprisonment to stage uprisings. Because most Yorkist-aligned warlords refused to rally to Warwick's call, the earl was pressured to release the king. Warwick engineered another rebellion, this time to replace Edward with Clarence. The two conspirators, however, had to flee to France when Edward crushed the uprising in March, 1470. Warwick invaded England in September, 1470 at the head of a Lancastrian army, and in October, 1470 forced Edward to flee the country. The throne of England was temporarily restored to Henry VI on March 14, 1471. Edward returned to England in March, 1471 precipitating the Battle of Barnet a month later.

Shakespeare's account telescopes and abridges these events. At Coventry, he shows the belligerents meeting and unexpectantly, Clarence again changes sides and rejoins Edward. On the field of Barnet (a town outside of London) on April 14, 1471, Edward forces overwhelm the forces of Warwick and Warwick is killed in the battle. Poor Henry is sent back to the Tower. Meanwhile, Queen Margaret who had remained in France hoping for a Warwick victory landed in Wales to provide him assistance on the day of the Battle of Barnet. Learning of Edward's victory, she returned to France, but then at the urging of her son, she set sail again for England with her French forces. Marching on London, she met Edward's forces on May 4, 1471 at the town of Tewkesbury, just east of the England/Wales border. The battle turns against the Lancastrians and Queen Margaret and Prince Edward, her son, are captured. In a scene reminiscent of the death of the Duke of York, Prince Edward is stabbed to death by Edward, Richard and Clarence as the Queen is forced to watch. Immediately following, Richard moves to also kill the Queen, but his hand is stayed by Edward who decides to let her live. Thwarted in his bloodlust, Richard leaves the field for London where, Clarence tells the King, he intends "to make a bloody supper in the Tower." (3HVI, V, 3, 85)

In scene 4, Richard confronts Henry in the Tower and informs him of his son's death. Henry, past caring about his kingship or his life, confronts Richard with these prophetic words:

> ... many a thousand,
> Which now mistrust no parcel of my fear,
> And many an old man's sigh and many a widow's,
> And many an orphan's water-standing eye--
> Men for their sons, wives for their husbands,
> And orphans for their parents timeless death--
> Shall rue the hour that ever thou wast born.
> The owl shrike's at thy birth,--an evil sign;
> The night-crow cried, aboding luckless time;
> Dogs howl'd, and hideous tempest shook down trees;
> The raven rook'd her on the chimney's top,
> And chattering pies in dismal discords sung.
> Thy mother felt more than a mother's pain,
> And, yet brought forth less than a mother's hope,
> To wit, an indigested and deformed lump,
> Not like the fruit of such a goodly tree.
> Teeth hadst thou in thy head when thou wast born,
> To signify thou camest to bite the world:
> And, if the rest be true which I have heard,
> Thou camest—
>
> (3HVI, V, 3, 37-56)

Again, Richard confronted with insults about his appearance and his nativity, stabs the King to death, not only to vent his fury, but also to eliminate another potential obstruction to his royal ambition. Standing over the body of Henry, Richard restates his plans:

> since the heavens have shaped my body so,
> Let hell make crook'd my mind to answer it.
> I have no brother, I am like no brother;

And this word 'love,' which graybeards call divine,
Be resident in men like one another
And not in me: I am myself alone.
Clarence, beware; thou keep'st me from the light:
But I will sort a pitchy day for thee;
For I will buz abroad such prophecies
That Edward shall be fearful of his life,
And then, to purge his fear, I'll be thy death.
King Henry and the prince his son are gone:
Clarence, thy turn is next, and then the rest, (Emphasis added)
(3HVI, V, 6, 72-90)

He sees himself as utterly alone in the world, unlike any other man, even his kin. It is for him a point of pride in that being like no other; he is not bound by the normal laws by which a man is judged. Freed of love or guilt or fear, he is above all others and free to take what he wants from a world filled with "others." As if to prove the point, he reveals his next target will be his own brother, Clarence.

The play concludes with Edward now securely on his throne, saying:

we swept suspicion from our seat
And made our footstool of security.
Come hither, Bess, and let me kiss my boy.
Young Ned,
(3HVI, V, 4, 13-16)

He is completely unaware of Richard's ambitions and believes that his heir, young Ned, will be able to grow in a world of security and love, unlike the nightmare of suspicion and violence that has passed away with the death of all his foes.

Edward of March advanced towards London from the west where he had joined forces with Warwick's surviving forces. This coincided with the northward retreat by the queen to Dunstable, allowing Edward and Warwick to enter London with their army. Edward could no longer claim simply to be trying to free the king from bad councilors; it had become a battle for the crown. Edward needed authority, and this seemed forthcoming when Thomas Kempe, the Bishop of London, asked the people of London their opinion and they replied with shouts of "King Edward". This was quickly though it was being widely argued that Edward's victory was simply a restoration of the rightful heir to the throne, which neither Henry nor his Lancastrian predecessors had been. It was this argument which Parliament had accepted the year before

Finally, we come to the play that all the events of the preceding three Henry VI plays lead up to. It is variously titled *Richard III*, *The Life and Death of Richard III*, and *The Tragedy of Richard III*. In the table of contents of the first folio it is titled *The Life and Death of Richard III* and is grouped with the Histories, but it is interesting to note that the title page uses *The Tragedy of Richard III* as does the first quarto published in 1597. It is also interesting to note that only one other history play bares the designation of Tragedy in any of its iterations and that is *Richard II*, called *The life and death of King Richard the Second* [sic] in the first folio both in the table of contents and on the title page. However, the first quarto bares the title *The Tragedie of King Richard the second* [sic]. In neither of the *Henry IV* plays, nor in *Henry V*, *Henry VIII*, or *King John* is the label "tragedy" employed. *Henry VI, parts 1 and 2* exclude the label "tragedy" as well, but the *Henry VI, Part 3*, 1595 First Octavo, has the subtitle *The true tragedie of Richard Duke of York, and the death of good King Henrie the Sixt, with the whole contention betweene the two houses Lancaster and Yorke*, [sic].

Genre definition is always difficult because genre represents a value judgment as well as labeling system. One need only look at today's film criticism to see the truth in this. Drama is considered superior to an action film. Romantic comedy is considered superior to slapstick comedy. Film noir is superior to the psychological thriller. And tragedy is superior to either comedy or historical fiction. Before the age of Shakespeare, dramatic genres existed as either tragedies or comedies handed down from classical Greece and Rome, or that uniquely medieval form of the mysteries and moralities emerging from the Christian traditions. However, in the decades just prior to Shakespeare's arrival on the scene, dramatist began exploring other forms of dramatic expression. The historical drama actually originated in a poetical work by Thomas Sackville entitled *The Mirror for Magistrates* (1557) which has notable figures from history (including Richard II and Richard III) describing their rise and fall in the first person. Sackville joined by Thomas Norton and encouraged by the positive response to *The Mirror* composed the first historical tragedy existing in English literature—*Ferrez and Porrex*, also known as *Gorboduc*. Written in 1561, *Gorboduc* was performed for Queen Elizabeth I on January 18, 1562. Briefly, Gorboduc was a

King of Britain who divided his realm in his lifetime to his sons, Ferrex and Porrex. The sons fell to dissention and the younger killed the elder.

The mother that more dearly loved the elder, for revenge killed the younger. The people, moved with the cruelty of the fact, rose in rebellion and slew both father and mother. The nobility assembled destroyed the rebels and afterward fell into civil war. Anticipating both King Lear and the War of the Roses tetralogy of Shakespeare, *Gorboduc* is the first drama set on English soil and grounded in English history. What followed was some few anonymous "Chronicle Plays" including *The Famous Victories of Henry Fifth* (c. 1583?) and *The Troublesome Raigne of King John* [sic] (c. 1589) of little artistic significance.

It fell to Shakespeare to take these early experiments and invent the historical drama as a distinct dramatic genre. During the 1591-2 play season, the novice Shakespeare had his first plays, *Henry VI, Parts 2 and 3*, presented on the English stage. The audience response was apparently favorable because in the next season, 1592-3, Shakespeare followed up with a prequel, *Henry VI, Part I* and the culminating play of the tetralogy, *Richard III*. Since History did not yet exist as a genre, the tetralogy would most likely have been viewed as Tragedy at the time of performance. Each play did in fact present the death of a notable person, a hallmark of Tragedy as it came down from the Classical writers. In *Henry VI, Part 1* we have the heroic death of Talbot, commander of the English forces in France, who is betrayed by the petty squabbling of the Dukes of York and Somerset. In *Henry VI, Part 2*, it is the murder of the honorable Humphrey, Duke of Gloucester. In *Part 3*, the deaths include Richard, Duke of York and his son Rutland paired with the deaths of Henry VI and his son, Prince Edward. In *Richard III*, death is so pervasive that nearly every important character including the chief protagonist is dispatched before the end of the play. So the question we are left to answer is: is the Henry VI tetralogy meant to be seen as Tragedy or History?

In *An Apology for Actors* (1612), Thomas Heywood proposes that the deeds of worthies constitute the core of the history play, held up for emulation and, in the case of the English histories, patriotic pride. By its most basic definition, the recounting of events in a life constitutes a history. History, I would contend, is concerned with who said what or who did what, where and when certain events take place, and how and why certain actions came to be. Historical fiction adds to history speculation about "the inner things" of history, inferring from words and deeds the passions and motives of historical personages. It focuses on what might be fact as opposed to what is verifiably fact. It has a point of view. As we have seen earlier, Vergil and More wrote historical fictions of Richard III where facts are subordinated to the monstrous portrait of the man they were attempting to create. For them, historical truth became a matter of relatively small importance. The importance of history was for the support it might lend to political theory. Thus, the authors of historical fiction can reinvent actions and timelines in the service of advancing their particular thesis. Another example might be instructive.

Immediately upon the death of the King Edward IV, his brother, Richard contrives to gain control of the new king, Edward V, his nephew and the King's younger brother also named Richard. At the same time, he takes the opportunity to imprison his chief enemies, the family and friends of Edward's mother, Elizabeth. Young King Edward was seized on his way to London and sequestered in the Tower of London. Upon hearing this Elizabeth sought sanctuary with the King's young brother at Westminster. These are historical facts. Vergil, moving into historical fiction, gives the reader a long speech reportedly made by Richard to persuade the clerics and nobles that he intends no harm to the young King and his brother. Further he argues that the young king's younger brother has no right to sanctuary and should be released into Richard's tender care. The speech which was surely Vergil's invention show Richard's persuasive powers and is clearly intended to demonstrate his ability to manipulate the hearts and minds of otherwise good men. Richard persuades the Archbishop to act on his behalf and we are told that with "great difficulty" the Archbishop was able to turn young Richard over to his uncle.

Throughout his narrative, Vergil takes every opportunity to comment on the moral implications of Richard's actions. His description of the events immediately following the seizure of the young princes serves as an example.

> This done, Richard, whose mind was partly afire with lust for gaining the crown, and partly tormented by guilt *(for conscience always makes punishment hover before the eyes of those who have done amiss),* henceforth regarded nothing more important than to mollify the masses by largesse, and to win over his adversaries by gifts, rewards, and promises, began to stay in the Tower together with his nephews, daily discussing, conferring, and scheming with his nobles, by cleverness and craft hatching new plans to deal with pressing matters. This was his artifice that while expectation made the people look forward to the new ceremony, by gradual consultations he might sound out the nobles' minds, always pretending he was not seeking the highest power, but doing everything for the good of the realm. Therefore, by hiding and veiling his greed under the name of public utility, he so misled the nobles' minds that, with the exception of those few from whom he had never concealed his true intent, they could in no wise perceive why he was creating delays, or to what end his counsels were tending: he proposed many things, and explained few, *for a guilty mind is wont to vacillate*[5] (Emphasis added)

It is also worth noting Vergil's word choice in describing Richard's actions. Richard "schemes," "by cleverness and craft hatch(es) new plans," "hid(es) and veil(s) his greed," "mislead(s) the nobles' minds, " and "conceal(s) his true intent." Vergil goes on to describe the elimination of Lord Hastings, a powerful noble who has indicated he will not support Richard's play for the crown. In this scene adapted almost exactly in Shakespeare's play Richard accuses Hasting's of complicity in a plot led by the former Queen to murder Richard through witchcraft.

> For the last few days I have no peace by day or by night, I have been unable to eat or drink, and so gradually my blood, my strength, and my spirit has grown feeble, and my limbs are more emaciated than usual (here he showed them his arm). This mischief in me comes from that evil woman Queen Elizabeth, who has attacked me with her witchcraft. Damaged by it, I am gradually being undone.[6]

It is interesting to compare this description to More's description of the same event.

> Then said the protectour: ye shal al se in what wise that sorceres and that other witch of her counsel shoris wife with their affynite, haue by their sorcery & witchcraft wasted my body. And therwith he plucked vp hys doublet sleue to his elbow vpon hist left arme, where **he shewed a werish withered arme and small, as it was neuer other.** And thereupon euery mannes mind sore migaue them, well perceiuing that this matter was but a quarel.[7] (Emphasis added).

More, who early in his history described Richard's deformities, makes it clear that the withered arm is a preexisting disorder and one well known to the nobles and clerics in attendance. Through this bit of theater that ends in the death of Hastings, Richard in true Machiavellian fashion inspires fear in the remaining nobles and thereby insurers their continued if reluctant support. By adopting a particular point of view and then inventing/manipulating history to support it, Vergil and More become moralists and propagandists instead of historians. Their purpose is not to simply report the facts of Richard's rise and fall, but to support the image of the man as monster.

  Shakespeare, in his *Henry VI* tetralogy and most importantly in *Richard III*, supports the accepted monstrosity of Richard as handed down from Vergil and More, but a good deal more is going on than simple propaganda. Shakespeare's historical fiction is more cavalier with fact and chronology than that of Vergil and More. Historical events are telescoped and rearranged; commentary is placed in the mouths of characters experiencing the events. Shakespeare is less concerned with illustrating the consequences of bad behavior then he is with entertaining an audience and exploring bigger ideas than justifying the actions and legitimacy of one political party. Big ideas are the province of dramatic Tragedy: ideas about death and suffering, good and evil, right and wrong, loyalty and betrayal. Tragedy according to Plato is dangerous, provoking dangerous passions and showing the world as dark, violent and incomprehensible. Aristotle in response to Plato's criticism defended Tragedy in his *Poetics* by arguing it aroused those "dangerous" passions, specifically pity and fear, with the intention of expunging them through the mysterious action of "catharsis." How catharsis is achieved is not addressed by Aristotle so it has been explored and argued for more than two millennia. Aristotle also identified the specific elements that defined a Tragedy:

> Tragedy is, then, an enactment of a deed that is important and complete, and of [a certain] magnitude, by means of language enriched [with ornaments], each used separately in the different parts [of the play]: it is enacted, not [merely] recited, and through pity and fear it effects relief (catharsis) to such [and similar] emotions.[16]

Aristotle went on to define the "best" kind of tragedy in this way:

> ... one should not show worthy men passing from good fortune to bad. That does not arouse fear or pity but shocks our feelings. Nor again wicked people passing from bad fortune to good. That is the most untragic of all, having none of the requisite qualities, since it does not satisfy our feelings or arouse pity or fear. Nor again the passing of a thoroughly bad man from good fortune to bad fortune. Such a structure might satisfy our feelings but it arouses neither pity nor fear, the one being for the man who does not deserve his misfortune and the other for the man who is like ourselves—pity for the undeserved misfortune, fear for the man like ourselves—so that the result will arouse neither pity nor fear.
> There remains then the mean between these. This is the sort of man who is not pre-eminently virtuous and just, and yet it is through no badness or villainy of his own that he falls into the fortune, but rather through some flaw in him, he being one of those who are in high station and good fortune, like Oedipus and Thyestes and the famous men of such families as those...[17]

While it is unlikely that Shakespeare had any direct knowledge of Aristotle's *Poetics*, the influence of Aristotle would have come down to Shakespeare through his principle role model, Seneca. The question immediately raised by *Richard III* is can this play be a tragedy when the central protagonist is such an outright villain. Does Richard's story inspire fear and pity? Certainly we may fear for and pity the murdered nephews in the Tower, but do we fear for and pity all the other victims:

Clarence, Hastings, Buckingham? At the end of the play do we fear for or pity Richard himself? Does his death purge those emotions? If *Richard III* is a tragedy, then whose tragedy is it?

In the context of the Tudor myth where the War of the Roses and the kingship of Richard III are the culminating curses on England for the crime of condoning the deposition of Richard II, England herself can be seen as the tragic protagonist required to do penance for her great sin. From the deposition of Richard II to the crowning of Henry VII, England faces ever escalating violence at the hands of increasingly ruthless rivals until Richard III finally gathers all wickedness into himself and is cast out by the redemptive figure of Henry Tudor. The horrors of civil war are dramatically and pathetically portrayed in the memorable fifth scene of the second Act of *Henry VI, Part 3*. King Henry VI enters alone on the field of battle and sits on a molehill to await the battle's outcome. The stage direction has a man only known as "a Son that has killed his father," dragging in the dead body. Upon discovering the identity of the corpse, the son laments:

> O heavy times, begetting such events!
> From London by the king was I press'd forth;
> My father, being the Earl of Warwick's man,
> Came on the part of York, press'd by his master;
> And I, who at his hands received my life, him
> Have by my hands of life bereaved him.
> Pardon me, God, I knew not what I did!
> And pardon, father, for I knew not thee!
>
> (3HVI, II, 5, 63-70)

From the other side of the stage, "Enter a Father that has killed his son, bringing in the body." He too upon discovering the identity of his victim cries out:

> O, pity, God, this miserable age!
> What stratagems, how fell, how butcherly,
> Erroneous, mutinous and unnatural,
> This deadly quarrel daily doth beget!
> O boy, thy father gave thee life too soon,
> And hath bereft thee of thy life too late!
>
> (3HVI, II, 5, 88-93)

This scene demonstrates that God's judgment on England extends not only to the offending and contending nobles, but to the common folk caught up in the civil war.

I would like to posit the unusual position that Richard is also a tragic character who can inspire pity and fear in an audience. Richard is a villain and a victim and a tool. As the play opens, Richard is on the stage, appropriately alone, and delivers one of Shakespeare's most famous soliloquies.

> **Now is the winter of our discontent**
> **Made glorious summer by this sun of York;**
> And all the clouds that lour'd upon our house
> In the deep bosom of the ocean buried.
> Now are our brows bound with victorious wreaths;
> Our bruised arms hung up for monuments;
> Our stern alarums changed to merry meetings,
> Our dreadful marches to delightful measures.
> Grim-visaged war hath smooth'd his wrinkled front;
> And now, instead of mounting barded steeds
> To fright the souls of fearful adversaries,
> He capers nimbly in a lady's chamber
> To the lascivious pleasing of a lute.
> **But I, that am not shaped for sportive tricks,**
> Nor made to court an amorous looking-glass;
> I, that am rudely stamp'd, and want love's majesty
> To strut before a wanton ambling nymph;
> I, that am curtail'd of this fair proportion,
> Cheated of feature by dissembling nature,
> Deformed, unfinish'd, sent before my time
> Into this breathing world, scarce half made up,
> And that so lamely and unfashionable
> That dogs bark at me as I halt by them;
> Why, I, in this weak piping time of peace,
> Have no delight to pass away the time,
> Unless to spy my shadow in the sun
> And descant on mine own deformity:
> **And therefore, since I cannot prove a lover,**
> **To entertain these fair well-spoken days,**
> **I am determined to prove a villain**
> And hate the idle pleasures of these days.
> Plots have I laid, inductions dangerous,

> By drunken prophecies, libels and dreams,
> To set my brother Clarence and the king
> In deadly hate the one against the other:
> And if King Edward be as true and just
> As I am subtle, false and treacherous,
> This day should Clarence closely be mew'd up,
> About a prophecy, which says that 'G'
> Of Edward's heirs the murderer shall be. (Emphasis added)
> (RIII, I, 1, 1-40)

"I am myself alone." summed up Richard's final speech in *Henry VI, Part 3* and could easily be his key defining signifier in the play that bears his name. In this opening scene he is alone on stage, serving as his own prologue, the only principle character in Shakespeare's canon to do so. The Prologue (sometimes called the Chorus) is a stock character who appears on stage prior to the main action. In performance, announced by trumpets, the actor would come to the stage without makeup and dressed all in black to set him apart from the main players. He might carry a book or scroll, or maybe a placard displaying the title of the play. His purpose was to focus the attention of the audience and to usher it from the real world into the world of the play. He would introduce the play, provide any necessary background and set the tone for what was to follow.[18] This description should not suggest that the Prologue was a ubiquitous feature of Elizabethan drama. Of Christopher Marlowe's seven published plays, four employed a Prologue. Shakespeare used the Prologue only seven times in his 37 plays. In five of the seven, the Prologue is unnamed. In one, *Pericles, Prince of Tyre*, the Prologue is identified as dead poet John Gower. And then alone stands Richard.

As Prologue, Richard first orients the audience to the setting. "Now is the winter of our discontent/Made glorious summer by this son of York." The war between the Lancastrians and the Yorkist have come to an end with the victory and crowning of Edward IV, "this son of York." England has entered a time of peace when all are now engaged in amorous and sensual pursuits instead of feats of courage and arms. All seems to be happy. Richard, however, undercuts the mood right from the beginning. His first line "Now is the winter of our discontent" can be read as declarative; that is, Richard is saying "Now" meaning present time is our (**his** in the sense of the royal "we") time of discontent. He is not happy while all those around him are. The next line combined with the first turns the meaning to say that "Now" the time of discontent is in the past. The meaning of the second line undermines the initial meaning of the first, but the double meaning has registered with the audience. Marjorie Garber and others have commented on the legal format used in the soliloquy.[19] The first third starting with the first line and ends at line 13. It is a kind of major premise where the general circumstances are described prologue-like. The middle third, the minor premise, shows Richard as the exception to these general circumstances. It starts with "But I" in line 14 and concludes at line 27. In it Richard leaves his Prologue persona and becomes a particular character in the play. He explains his current "winter of discontent" that he hinted at in line one. He is, he says, ill-suited for this time of peace. Being deformed, he is "not shaped for sportive tricks," as his lusty brother Edward is. Because he cannot play the lover, he has "no delight to pass away the time." In short, he is bored. The concluding section begins with "Therefore" to demonstrate the outcome of his reasoning. The country is at peace and concerned with lust and love. He is bored and unable to participate as others do amorous games. Therefore, he concludes, the only thing left to him is "to prove a villain."

When an actor speaks a soliloquy we usually think of him as speaking to himself. Think of Hamlet's "To be or not to be" or Macbeth's "Tomorrow, and tomorrow, and tomorrow." The audience has the sense that they are overhearing the actor's thoughts. This is not the case in Richard's opening speech. He is addressing the audience directly making them confidents and co-conspirators. His directness, which suggests fellowship with the audience, draws the audience to him. He seduces the audience as he will seduce Lady Anne in the next scene. Even though he tells the audience he is "subtle, false and treacherous," we trust that what he is telling us is true. Are we, the audience, being manipulated? We tend to like Richard even though we know the terrible things he has done and the terrible things he plans to do. He is charismatic and brilliantly evil; we can't wait to see what he is up to. Some of us may even feel a bit sorry for this misshaped man whose mind and spirit are overshadowed by his deformity. If we are to view *Richard III* as a Tragedy of a man as well as of a land, it is important that we be drawn to Richard, that he is able to inspire both pity and fear. We must be awed by size of the character, even when we are forced to disavow his action. He must be bigger than life. He must be grander than ourselves. Richard seems to fits the bill. But beyond all this, we are nagged with a touch of doubt. "I am subtle, false and treacherous," like the glittering, beautiful snake in the Garden of Evil.

"Plots have I laid, inductions dangerous," aligns Richard with one of England's great villains and theatrical stock characters, Machiavelli. Nicole Machiavelli was an Italian political philosopher who authored a short work titled *The Prince*. Although written around 1513, its printed version was not published until 1532. Dedicated to Lorenzo di Piero de' Medici, grandson of "Lorenzo the Magnificent", and a member of the ruling Florentine Medici family, *The Prince* advanced an innovated political theory that encouraged rulers to embrace realism as opposed to idealism in obtaining and retaining power. Machiavelli proposed the theory that the goal of retaining power superseded all other consideration including morality and legality. He encouraged rulers to leave as little to chance as possible by planning and plotting ahead. At the same time, Machiavelli encouraged rulers to be risk-takers and innovators. His "ends justify means" philosophy was extended in xenophobic England to include all contemporary Italians as plotters and schemers willing to perpetrated criminal deeds for sake of politics. Richard embodies the English understanding of the Machiavellian philosophy.

Richard's first plot is against his brother, George, Duke of Clarence. By spreading about news of a prophesy predicting the end of Edward IV's line by "G", Richard leads Edward to suspect and imprison George. The irony, of course, is the prophesized "G" is Gloucester, not George. By this point early in the play, Edward is a sick man and is not expected to live. If Edward should die before Clarence is disposed of, Richard's plot will fail since Edward is Richard's tool for the demise of Clarence. After assuring Clarence that he will speak on his behalf to Edward, Richard again alone turns to the audience, saying:

> I'll in [to Edward], to urge his hatred more to Clarence,
> With lies well steel'd with weighty arguments;
> And, if I fall not in my deep intent,
> Clarence hath not another day to live:
>
> (RIII, I, 1, 147-150)

The ease with which he slides from Machiavel to concerned brother and back again is breathtaking.

Richard's second plot is to achieve a noble bride. He sets his eye on the most unlike of women, Lady Anne, daughter of the dead Earl of Warwick and wife of the murdered Prince Edward, son of the murdered King Henry VI.

> not all so much for love
> As for another secret close intent,
> By marrying her which I must reach unto.
>
> (RIII, I, 1, 157-9)

His "secret close intent" is to claim the Warwick fortune which Anne shares with her older sister, Isabella and her husband, Clarence. To add to the audacity of his plot, he undertakes the wooing of Anne as she follows the corpse of her father-in-law to its grave. Against all expectations, Richard seduces the Lady with his wit and charm. Chameleon-like, he shifts from charming suitor to gloating Vice following his success:

Was ever woman in this humour woo'd?
Was ever woman in this humour won?
I'll have her; but I will not keep her long.
What! I, that kill'd her husband and his father,
To take her in her heart's extremest hate,
With curses in her mouth, tears in her eyes,
The bleeding witness of her hatred by;
Having God, her conscience, and these bars
against me,
And I nothing to back my suit at all,
But the plain devil and dissembling looks,
And yet to win her, *all the world to nothing!*
Ha!

(RIII, I, 2, 227-238)

The Vice is yet another stock character, predating Machiavelli and even the stage as Shakespeare knew it. The character of the Vice was a product of the Morality plays of the Middle Ages and featured prominently in the psychomachia or "Contest of the Soul," where the Vice tempted the protagonist away from his journey towards salvation. He was obviously diabolical and originally meant to be taken seriously, but over time his part became largely comical. He often presented with a strange appearance, engaged in bawdy banter and slapstick humor and would take the audience into his confidence in asides and soliloquies. He took great delight in his cleverness and in evil for its own sake. In his scene with Lady Anne, Richard takes on himself the character of the Vice, tempting the virtuous Lady and leading her to a kind of living Hell as his wife.

Anne does not figure prominently in the play; she is not seen again until as the Duchess of Gloucester in Act IV, Scene 1 she appears before the Tower to see the young princes. Along with Queen Elizabeth and the Duchess of York, she is denied entry. Suddenly, she is summoned by her husband to be crowned Queen and she laments her fate and the extent of her misery;

O, when, I say, I look'd on Richard's face,
This was my wish: 'Be thou,' quoth I, ' accursed,
For making me, so young, so old a widow!
And, when thou wed'st, let sorrow haunt thy bed;
And be thy wife--if any be so mad--
As miserable by the life of thee
As thou hast made me by my dear lord's death!
Lo, ere I can repeat this curse again,

> *Even in so short a space, my woman's heart*
> *Grossly grew captive to his honey words*
> *And proved the subject of my own soul's curse,*
> *Which **ever since hath kept my eyes from rest;***
> ***For never yet one hour in his bed***
> ***Have I enjoy'd the golden dew of sleep,***
> ***But have been waked by his timorous dreams.***
> *Besides, he hates me for my father Warwick;*
> *And will, no doubt, shortly be rid of me. (Emphasis added)*
>
> *(RIII, IV, 1, 70-86)*

Her final line is more prophetic than she realizes. The newly crowned King Richard in the next scene informs his lackey, Catesby to "Rumour it abroad/That Anne, my wife, is sick and like to die" (*RIII*, IV, 2, 41-2) and in the next scene he tells us that "Anne my wife hath bid the world good night." (*RIII*, IV, 3, 39).

In scene 3 of Act I, most of the principles of the court are introduced and the battle lines are drawn. On one side are the supporters of Queen Elizabeth, the commoner raised up by Edward to be his wife. These include her sons by a previous marriage, Lord Richard Grey (Grey in the play) and the Thomas Grey (Dorset in the play), and her brother, Lord Rivers. Opposing them are the traditional nobles aligned with Richard. These include Lord Hastings, Lord Chamberlain to Edward IV; the Duke of Buckingham; and Lord Stanley, here called Earl of Derby. Each group accuses the other of poisoning the King's opinion of another. Laced throughout the bickering, Richard interjects ironic humor by playing the victim:

> *Because I cannot flatter and speak fair,*
> *Smile in men's faces, smooth, deceive and cog,*
> *Duck with French nods and apish courtesy,*
> *I must be held a rancorous enemy.*
> *Cannot a plain man live and think no harm,*
>
> *(RIII, I, 3, 47-51)*

And later, "I am too childish-foolish for this world." (*RIII*, I, 3, 141). He accuses the Queen of conspiring to have Clarence imprisoned, knowing full well that he was the engineer of that deed and heaps insults on her "up-start" kin who have risen to positions considered above their station. Hovering around this rancor is Queen Margaret, wife of the murdered King Henry VI who inexplicably is still at court (in historical fact, she was shipped back to France in 1475 after spending four years in the Tower). Although a living being, she acts the role a vengeful Senecan ghost, hating and hated by everyone, leveling curses at both groups and uniting them temporarily in opposition to her. The contention draws to a close when Edward summons all, save of course Margaret, to his sickbed. Richard, left alone briefly before following the others to the King, meets with two murderers who have been contracted to kill Clarence. The final scene of Act I enacts the pitiful murder of Clarence in the tower and while worthy of detailed discussion; I will defer its analysis until a later chapter.

Act 2, scene 1 opens with all the principles surrounding Edward on his sickbed. Edward is trying to reconcile the opposing factions. All seems to be going well with Richard again giving a grand performance, saying

> I do not know that Englishman alive
> With whom my soul is any jot at odds
> More than the infant that is born to-night
> I thank my God for my humility.

(RIII, II, 1, 70-73)

Then Elizabeth asks Edward to be reconciled with his brother Clarence. Richard, acting shocked *says "Who knows not that the noble duke is dead?"* Edward responds, equally shocked, "Is Clarence dead? the order was reversed." and Richard tells him the reprieve arrived too late. Overwhelmed with guilt and grief, King Edward withdraws and promptly dies offstage in the next scene. Now only Edward's two sons stand between Richard and the throne.

At this point, let's pause for a moment to review Shakespeare's history. In Scene one, Clarence is on his way to the Tower. This would place the Scene in January, 1478. Clarence died in the Tower a month afterward. In the next Scene, Lady Anne is attending the burial of Henry VI which would have taken place in 1471. The seduction Scene is pure fiction. The fact of Anne's wooing by Richard is almost as strange. To prevent losing control of the entire Warwick fortune that Clarence gained through his marriage to Anne's older sister, Clarence kept Anne hidden in his estate. Richard managed to free her and subsequently married her in 1472. Although not mentioned in the play, they had a son a year later. Their son died in in April, 1484; Anne fell ill early in 1485 and died on March 16, 1485, just five months before her husband's defeat and death at the Battle of Bosworth Field. Further shuffling historical time, we learn in Act 1 that Edward IV is ill and he dies in Act II, not long after learning of Clarence's death. In fact, Edward fell fatally ill at Easter 1483 and died on April 9, 1483, five years after the death of Clarence.

Immediately upon the death of King Edward IV, Richard contrives to gain control of the new king, Edward V, his nephew and the new King's younger brother. As young Edward was brought from Ludlow in the southwest of England to London under the protection of Lord Rivers, Lord Grey and Sir Thomas Vaughan, Chamberlain to the prince, their party was beset by Richard and Buckingham. Rivers, Grey and Vaughan were taken into custody and sent to Pomfret prison where they were subsequently executed. The new King was escorted on to London where he was quickly sequestered in the Tower of London "for his protection." Upon hearing of this Queen Elizabeth sought sanctuary with the King's young brother at Westminster Cathedral, but Richard ever persuasive, convinced the clerics and nobles that he intends no harm to the young King and his brother. Further he argued that the young king's younger brother has no right to sanctuary and should be released into Richard's tender care. The Archbishop acting on Richard's behalf was able to wrest Prince Richard from his mother and turn him over to his uncle.

Now with both royal heirs under his control, Richard must decide how to deal with them and take the throne of England for his own. To achieve his goal, Richard must gain the support of the nobles and the common people, and undermine the Princes' claim to the throne. To achieve the first, in true Machiavellian fashion, he contrives the fall of Lord Hastings. Catesby is sent to "sound out" Hasting to determine if he would support Richard as king. When Catesby broaches the topic of Richard claiming the crown, Hastings replies "*I'll have this crown of mine cut from my shoulders/Ere I will see the crown so foul misplaced.*" (RIII, III, 2, 43-4) Having thus revealed himself, he must be eliminated as an obstruction to Richard's rise and as an example of Richard's ruthlessness. Hasting along with the other principle nobles, Buckingham, Stanley and the Bishop of Ely, are called to the Tower to prepare for the impending coronation of King Edward V. An amicable Richard enters the scene, greeting those in attendance and asks the Bishop of Ely to send for some strawberries. This delay allows Richard time to speak privately with Buckingham and together they briefly leave the scene. While they are absent, Hastings and Stanley discuss Richard's disposition and Hasting ironically says:

> *His grace looks cheerfully and smooth to-day;*
> *There's some conceit or other likes him well,*
> *When he doth bid good morrow with such a spirit.*
> *I think there's never a man in Christendom*
> *That can less hide his love or hate than he;*
> *For by his face straight shall you know his heart*
>
> (RIII, III, 4, 48-53)

And one could say that there's never a man in Christendom who is as blind as Hasting as he so learns to his woe. Richard returns to the chamber in a rage.

> *I pray you all, tell me what they deserve*
> *That do conspire my death with devilish plots*
> *Of damned witchcraft, and that have prevail'd*
> *Upon my body with their hellish charms?*
>
> $\qquad\qquad$ *(RIII, III, 4, 59-62)*

Hasting quickly replies, "I say, my lord, they have deserved death." Richard bares his withered arm and shrieks,

> *Look how I am bewitch'd; behold mine arm*
> *Is, like a blasted sapling, wither'd up:*
> *And this is Edward's wife, that monstrous witch,*
> *Consorted with that harlot strumpet Shore,*
> *That by their witchcraft thus have marked me.*
>
> $\qquad\qquad$ *(RIII, III, 4, 68-72)*

Now everyone at the table knows that this withered arm is not a new condition; his multiple deformities are obvious to everyone. When Hastings begins to protest, Richard cuts him off and accuses him of complicity in the plot as "that harlot strumpet Shore" is Hastings mistress.

> *Thou art a traitor:*
> *Off with his head! Now, by Saint Paul I swear,*
> *I will not dine until I see the same.*
>
> $\qquad\qquad$ *(RIII, III, 4, 75-6)*

So Richard at once eliminates an object in his path and set an example before the others that says "Either you are with me or you are dead."

Winning the good will of the commons is a somewhat more difficult matter and requires a bit of political theater worthy of the 21st century. First, Richard and Buckingham plot to call into question the legitimacy of the princes in the Tower by calling into question the legitimacy of their father, Edward IV.

> *Tell them [the citizens of London], when that my mother went with*
> *child*
> *Of that unsatiate Edward, noble York*

> *My princely father then had wars in France*
> *And, by just computation of the time,*
> *Found that the issue was not his begot;*
>
> (RIII, III, 5, 86-90)

Richard thinks nothing of calling the faithfulness of his mother into question, but does caution Buckingham "*touch this sparingly, as 'twere far off, / Because you know, my lord, my mother lives.*" and could easily deny the charge. Like a good campaign manager, Buckingham goes off to win support for his candidate while Richard goes off to Baynard's Castle to prepare his acceptance speech.

Unfortunately for Richard, Buckingham has overestimated his power of persuasion. In response to his pitch for Richard's right to the throne, "The citizens are mum." They were unmoved by the suggestion that Edward IV's marriage to Elizabeth Woodville was no true marriage owing to Edward's marital pre-contract with the French princess. They were similarly unmoved by the suggestion that Edward was himself illegitimate as a result of the adultery of his mother, the Duchess of York. And finally, they stood silent "*like dumb statues or breathing stones, /Gazed each on other, and look'd deadly pale*" when Buckingham "*bid them that did love their country's good/Cry 'God save Richard, England's royal king!*" Buckingham was however able to persuade the Lord Mayor and the citizens to come to Baynard to speak with Richard directly. Buckingham has one more trick up his sleeve.

> *... look you get a prayer-book in your hand,*
> *And stand betwixt two churchmen, good my lord;*
> *For on that ground I'll build a holy descant:*
> *And be not easily won to our request:*
> *Play the maid's part, still answer nay, and take it.*
>
> (RIII, III, 7, 47-51)

The Lord Mayor and the citizens enter and after being told that Richard is at his devotions and cannot be disturbed, Richard enters between two bishops. Buckingham exclaims:

> *Two props of virtue for a Christian prince,*
> *To stay him from the fall of vanity:*
> *And, see, a book of prayer in his hand,*
> *True ornaments to know a holy man.*
>
> (RIII, III, 7, 96-9)

Buckingham implores Richard to take on the kingship to save the kingdom from the "corruption of a blemished stock." Richard modestly demurs. Buckingham again pushes the illegitimacy of the young princes and again pushes Richard to take the throne, now with the voice of the Lord Mayor to support him. Again Richard "humbly" refuses.

> ...why would you heap these cares on me?
> I am unfit for state and majesty;
> I do beseech you, take it not amiss;
> I cannot nor I will not yield to you.
>
> *(RIII, III, 7, 204-7)*

Only when Buckingham feigns frustration and vows that if Richard will not take the throne, they will find another who will, does Richard relent.

> Cousin of Buckingham, and you sage, grave men,
> Since you will buckle fortune on my back,
> To bear her burthen, whether I will or no,
> I must have patience to endure the load:
>
> *(RIII, III, 7,227-30)*

Act IV, Scene 2 represents the zenith of Richard's journey, finding him crowned and on the throne as King Richard III. At the height of his success the wheel begins its downward turn. Richard is nagged by doubt and says to Buckingham, "I wish the bastards [the young princes] dead; /And I would have it suddenly perform'd. /What sayest thou?" Buckingham is clearly shocked and begs pause to consider his response. Richard takes this as a sign of faltering loyalty and the fate of Buckingham is sealed in that little time. "The deep-revolving witty Buckingham/No more shall be the neighbour to my counsel." Having secured his goal, Richard's self-assurance begins to crumble. He realizes he can climb no higher; decline is the only path now open to him. He begins to suspect that others may be as devious as he is and begins to imagine plots against him from every quarter. He is not far from right.

As he waits for Buckingham's return, the wheels are already turning. He determines it is time for Queen Anne to "bid the world good night." To sure up his position he tells the audience, still his co-conspirators:

> I must be married to my brother's daughter [the Princess Elizabeth],
> Or else my kingdom stands on brittle glass.
> Murder her brothers, and then marry her!

(RIII, IV, 2, 60-62)

He concludes his meditation with a remark that anticipates Shakespeare's greatest usurper, Macbeth: "But I am in/So far in blood that sin will pluck on sin." And with this, he conspires to have the princes murdered in the Tower. When Buckingham finally returns with an answer for Richard, the King dismisses the question: "let that pass." Buckingham surely takes this as a positive action and chooses to take the opportunity to lobby for his promised reward, the earldom of Hereford. Richard dismisses Buckingham briskly: "I am not in the giving vein to-day." He has already moved on to other matters, having learned that Lord Stanley's stepson, Henry Tudor is gathering a force to oppose Richard's kingship.

Henry Tudor has a legitimate if distant and convoluted claim to the throne. By 1483, Henry was the senior male Lancastrian claimant remaining. Henry's grandfather, Owen Tudor, married the widow of Henry V, Catherine of Valois. One of their sons was Edmund Tudor, Earl of Richmond and father of Henry. Henry's claim to the throne, however, derived from his mother through the House of Beaufort. Henry's mother, Lady Margaret Beaufort, was a great-granddaughter of John of Gaunt and his third wife Katherine Swynford who was Gaunt's mistress before they married. Henry's great-grandfather John Beaufort was born to them before the marriage making Henry's claim tenuous as it was from a woman and by illegitimate descent. Nevertheless, forces still loyal to the Lancastrians as well as those simply opposed to Richard found in Tudor a rallying point. Buckingham infuriated with Richard's rude response to his solicitation and remembering the fate of Hastings, prudently removes himself from court. In the next scene, we learn the princes are dead and buried in the Tower, that more of Richard's former allies are going over to Henry Tudor and that Buckingham has raised an army in rebellion against Richard.

The very long fourth Scene of Act IV contains four distinct movements. The first could be the called the "Lamentation of the Queens" where Queen Margaret reemerges to join with Queen Elizabeth and the Duchess of York to bemoan their many losses of the long dynastic wars of England. This Scene is strongly reminiscent of Euripides' The Trojan Women which depicted the losses and fates of the key female victims (Hecuba, Cassandra, Andromache and Helen) of the tragedy of Troy. While it is unlikely Shakespeare would know Euripides' work first hand, he might well have been familiar with Seneca's version of the same story, Troades (The Trojan Women). Thomas Lodge published an English translation of Seneca's works in 1614, well after Shakespeare's *Richard III*. But since Lodge was also a playwright working in the 1590's and is known to have worked with Shakespeare, it seems wholly possible that Lodge could have influenced this great Shakespearian scene with his knowledge of Seneca. In any case, this Scene helps elevate Richard III from mere History into the loftier sphere of the Tragedy by transporting the story beyond the villainous machinations of one evil man and generalizing the tragic consequence of civil war to representative grieving mothers and wives. The three women share a similar story and though they are enemies, there is a circuitry to their losses and a shared sisterhood in their grief. Like the scene of the father-son killings in *The Third Part of Henry VI* discussed earlier, this scene involves the audience on a more personal level where they can feel pity for these women (even Margaret!) and feel fear for themselves that they too could endure such a fate in the face of an unstable government and as a result of the actions of ruthless and ambitious men.

The second movement might by titled "The Denunciation of the Son." He is the final meeting of Richard and his mother. The Duchess laments having given birth to such a monster as Richard and her final words to her son are a curse.

> ... *take with thee my most heavy curse;*
> *Which, in the day of battle, tire thee more*
> *Than all the complete armour that thou wear'st!*
> *My prayers on the adverse party fight;*
> *And there the little souls of Edward's children*
> *Whisper the spirits of thine enemies*
> *And promise them success and victory.*
> *Bloody thou art, bloody will be thy end;*
> *Shame serves thy life and doth thy death attend.*
> (RIII, IV, 4, 188-196)

The third movement is "The Marriage Proposal" where Richard attempts to persuade Queen Elizabeth to allow him to marry her daughter. Again, as in Act I with the seduction of Anne, Richard undertakes a seemingly impossible task. With Anne, Richard had to persuade the widowed wife of a slain prince to love him. With Elizabeth, he has to persuade the mother of two slain princes to grant him her daughter as wife. In the first instances, Richard offers love, using a false sincerity that shocks the audience but inexplicably moves Anne against her better judgment. In the second instance, he uses similar tactics. He emphasizes first the advantage he offers the Queen and her daughter. To replace Elizabeth's murdered sons, he offers to replace them with grandchildren; to replace her lost crown, he offers a crown once removed. He then professes love for his young niece, in terms less sincere than he offered Anne. He suggests that this time Elizabeth should woo her daughter on his behalf. "With my soul," he says, "I love thy daughter, /And mean to make her queen of England." When Elizabeth reminds him that he murdered the princess' brothers and uncles, he responds "Say that I did all this for love of her." When Elizabeth protests, Richard lose patience, a characteristic that has crept up on him since gaining the crown and reduces his effectiveness,

> Look, what is done cannot be now amended:
> Men shall deal unadvisedly sometimes,
> Which after hours give leisure to repent.
> If I did take the kingdom from your sons,
> To make amends, Ill give it to your daughter.
> If I have kill'd the issue of your womb,
> To quicken your increase, I will beget
> Mine issue of your blood upon your daughter
> A grandam's name is little less in love
> Than is the doting title of a mother;
> They are as children but one step below,
>
> (RIII, IV, 4, 291-301)

Here he is counting on a cold logic to persuade the Queen instead of the wit and charm and lying insincerity that won Anne. Richard is slowly losing the eloquence that has been one of his most formidable weapons. When Elizabeth continues unmoved by his word, Richard broadens his argument:

> In her consists my happiness and thine;
> Without her, follows to this land and me,
> To thee, herself, and many a Christian soul,
> Death, desolation, ruin and decay:
> It cannot be avoided but by this;
> It will not be avoided but by this.
>
> (RIII, IV, 4, 406-11)

Now he is insisting that not only do his happiness and her happiness depend on the marriage, but that the future of the kingdom depends on the union. To this argument, she seems to weaken and offers at least to consider his proposal. As she departs, Richard is less celebratory than he was in his encounter with Anne, calling Elizabeth "Relenting fool, and shallow, changing woman!" We later learn in Act V, Scene I that Elizabeth, not in the least deceived by Richard, has contracted with Henry Tudor to join her daughter with him in matrimony when he successfully destroys Richard and ascends the throne of England.

The final movement picks up the main narrative. Through a series of messengers, Richard (and the audience) learns that Richmond is on the sea advancing toward Wales to join with assorted nobles and gentlemen to march against Richard and that Buckingham is in revolt with an army in the field. At this point, Richard for the first time seems distracted and unsure of himself. He gives fragmented orders, forgets what he has ordered, and then countermand his orders. Then suddenly, his fortunes change. Buckingham's army disserts him and flees to join with Richmond. Richmond's "Breton navy is dispersed by tempest" and when Richmond lands, he is met by forces from Buckingham whom he distrusts. Richmond elects to return to Brittany to fight another day. Buckingham is arrested and subsequently executed.

Here again, is a place to pause to review Shakespeare's history which is compressed to the point of possible confusion. Richard III was crowned July 6, 1483. Queen Anne was crowned with him and contrary to Shakespeare's history which suggests she died shortly after the coronation and certainly before Buckingham's revolt, Anne survived until March of 1485. Buckingham revolt was launched on October 18, 1483, quickly crushed by a combination of bad weather, desertions and Richard's army and Buckingham himself was captured and finally executed November 2, 1483. Meanwhile Richmond's invasion, disrupted by the same weather that was Buckingham's undoing. Richmond returned to Brittany and then fled to France from where he launched his next invasion in 1485. These acts of rebellion are described in Act 4, Scene4 and Buckingham's execution in Act V, Scene1.

In the scene immediately preceding Buckingham's execution we learn that Richmond has landed in Wales and is marching toward London. Obviously this did not occur until two years after Buckingham's execution. That would place the scenes both before and after the death of Buckingham in 1485 even though Buckingham met his death in 1483. This glaring error of history aside, the remainder of the play, featuring the fall of Richard III at Bosworth Field, takes place in summer of 1485.

The third scene of Act V is set on the eve of the climactic battle. Visually, it is one of Shakespeare's most innovative and interesting scenes. Anticipating the cinematic technique of the split screen, Shakespeare divides the stage, locating Richard's encampment on one side and Richmond's on the other, with the great expanse of Bosworth Field represented by the bare space between the two. The scene depicts the preparations for battle. Richard is again in control of himself, issuing precise orders although he confesses "I have not that alacrity of spirit,

/Nor cheer of mind, that I was wont to have." (*RIII*, V, 3, 73-4). On the other side of the stage, Richmond places his faith in God:

> *O Thou, whose captain I account myself,*
> *Look on my forces with a gracious eye;*
> *Put in their hands thy bruising irons of wrath,*
> *That they may crush down with a heavy fall*
> *The usurping helmets of our adversaries!*
>
> (RIII, V, 3, 108-112)

Both leaders fall asleep and in succession are visited by the ghosts of Richard's victims: Prince Edward and his father, Henry VI; Clarence; Rivers, Grey and Vaughan; Hastings; the two young princes; Lady Anne; and Buckingham. One by one they go to Richard, then Richmond. They remind Richard of his crimes against them and conclude with a curse, "Tomorrow in the battle think on me... despair, and die!" To Richmond the ghosts offer only encouragement. Richard awakes rattled and fearful. He is for the only time in the play seized with self-doubt.

> *What do I fear? myself? there's none else by:*
> *Richard loves Richard; that is, I am I.*
> *Is there a murderer here? No. Yes, I am:*
> *Then fly. What, from myself? Great reason why:*
> *Lest I revenge. What, myself upon myself?*
> *Alack. I love myself. Wherefore? for any good*
> *That I myself have done unto myself?*
> *O, no! alas, I rather hate myself*
> *For hateful deeds committed by myself!*
> *I am a villain: yet I lie. I am not.*
> *Fool, of thyself speak well: fool, do not flatter.*
> *My conscience hath a thousand several tongues,*
> *And every tongue brings in a several tale,*
> *And every tale condemns me for a villain.*
> *Perjury, perjury, in the high'st degree*
> *Murder, stem murder, in the direst degree;*
> *All several sins, all used in each degree,*
> *Throng to the bar, crying all, Guilty! guilty!*
> *I shall despair. There is no creature loves me;*
> *And if I die, no soul shall pity me:*

> *Nay, wherefore should they, since that I myself*
> *Find in myself no pity to myself?*
>
> *(RIII, V, 3, 182-203)*

He is torn in two: the psychopathic, narcissistic Richard who loves only himself and the "normal" man who has a conscious and regrets his crimes. "I love myself. Wherefore? for any good/That I myself have done unto myself?" is followed by "no! alas, I rather hate myself/ For hateful deeds committed by myself!" He says, "I am a villain: yet I lie. I am not." He has spent the entire play telling us he is a villain, but now at the end of all things, he wants to deny it, but he can't deny it even to himself: "All several sins, all used in each degree/Throng to the bar, crying all, Guilty! guilty!" He laments: "I shall despair. There is no creature loves me." He has been and continues to be alone. "I am myself alone." he said in Act I, scene 1. Nothing has changed; all the scheming and murdering that has carried him to his great dream of kingship has been for naught. He confides to Ratcliff, "shadows to-night/Have struck more terror to the soul of Richard/Than can the substance of ten thousand soldiers." But in the end, Richard remains Richard, brave and defiant and ultimately unrepentant.

> *Let not our babbling dreams affright our souls:*
> *Conscience is but a word that cowards use,*
> *Devised at first to keep the strong in awe:*
> *Our strong arms be our conscience, swords our law.*
>
> *(RIII, V, 4, 308-11)*

Does this single scene raise Richard to the end of a tragic protagonist? Does the humanizing breakdown Richard experiences after the ghostly visitations generate sympathy? Does the audience feel fear for Richard's impending doom? Is his brave defiance in the face of battle sufficient to inspire admiration and awe? These are questions raised by Richard's encounter with the ghosts. From the beginning of the play, we have been attracted to Richard. Some of us might even like him. But with each successive murder, we are more and more distanced from the character. In the first Act, the audience is Richard's confidant and he speaks to them often. In the second and third Acts, he speaks less and less to the audience, taking Buckingham on as his confidant. As long as he is speaking with the audience as co-conspirators, they are with him. They can excuse his actions because all of the deaths up to the point are people who are far from innocent. Once he is crowned king and is abandoned by Buckingham, Richard only speaks his thoughts to himself. The audience, like Buckingham, cannot stomach the murder of the innocent princes in the Tower. When he resolves to act, the audience recoils from him and can no longer be complicit in his crimes, so he wastes no words on them. In his final soliloquy following his visit by the ghosts, although he is alone on the stage with the audience around him, the audience has no sense that he is speaking to anyone but himself. Nevertheless, depending on the skill of the actor, this soliloquy can renew some audience sympathy for Richard as they see a multi-talented man, twisted by his physical deformity, who chooses a life path that can only lead to misery and damnation.

There is a sense of inevitability in Richard's fall. Nature and nurture have predisposed him to a life devoid of love and mired in violence. Only Richard loves Richard, but he also hates Richard for his deformity and his crimes. He has replaced the pursuit of love for the pursuit of power, but to what end? Once he becomes king, what does he do with the power he has obtained? Nothing except to defend it. Did he become king to be loved? To perform great deeds? To reclaim France? No. He becomes king and then doesn't know what to do. All his effort has gone into attaining the crown, but no planning has gone into what he should do once he has it.

Inevitability is also central to the nature of Tragedy and to the Tudor myth which posits Richard as God's last plague on England in payment for the deposition of Richard II. If we accept this premise, then Richard is both God's tool and God's victim. The idea of Richard as tool assumes first that God has a plan for mankind and that His laws keep mankind on the path of the plan. When God's rules are violated by man as they were by the deposition of God's anointed, King Richard II, God takes action. Sometimes God's judgment takes the form of retribution against the offending man or nation. In the Old Testament, whole nations were destroyed by the wrath of God either through divine action, as was the case with Sodom and Gomorrah, or through His agents. To the Babylonians who at the height of their power practiced idolatry held other nations including Israel in captivity, God said,

> Wherefore, behold, the days come, saith the LORD, that I will do judgment upon her graven images: and through all her land the wounded shall groan. Though Babylon should mount up to heaven, and though she should fortify the height of her strength, yet **from me shall spoilers come** unto her, saith the LORD. A sound of a cry cometh from Babylon, **and great destruction from the land of the Chaldeans**...
> (Jeremiah 51: 52-54)

Babylon was so utterly destroyed that it was thought of as a mythical city until discovered by archaeologists in the twentieth century.

These punishments were visited upon the nations in retribution for some collection of sins committed by the nation collectively, not the actions of a single ruler. In the case of Sodom, for example, the angel of God agreed to spare the city if they could find ten righteous men dwelling there. They could not. The city was corrupted to the extent that it was irredeemable and the only recourse was to destroy them completely to prevent the spread of their wickedness. These Old Testament retributions were not exclusively to punish the wicked, but to serve as an example for other nations: this could happen to you if you fail to follow God's laws.

God's punishments can also be corrective; that is, designed to bring the man or nation back in line with God's plan. The pain and suffering inflicted are intended to make the man or nation recognize the error of their ways, to repent, and be reconciled with God. It is this form of punishment that Tillyard posits as Shakespeare's overarching theme in his two great historical tetralogies. England as a nation is punished with ever escalating civil violence just as Egypt was punished with the ten escalating plaques for her failure to release the enslaved Israelites. The first Diaspora of the Jews and the destruction of Jerusalem resulted from the impiety of the kingdom of Judah. God intended and affected the restoration of a revitalized Nation after a punishment of 70 years under the rule of Babylon. Similarly, after years of losses both at home and abroad, God restores a chastened England under the revitalizing reign of the Tudor dynasty.

Richard, according to Tillyard's reading is God's final instrument of England's punishment. Can we then compare Richard III to Judas Iscariot, the great villain of the New Testament? Could the correction of England have occurred without a Richard? Could the Passion of the New Testament have occurred without Judas? If both villains are acting to fulfill God's grand plan, is God the author of their villainy? And are they to be damned for their evil acts even though they are acting as God intends them to act? The gospels paradoxically suggest that Judas' betrayal of Jesus was both necessary and unavoidable, yet leads to Judas' condemnation. In Matthew 26:24 Jesus says of Judas, "The Son of man goeth as it is written of him, but woe unto that man by whom the Son of man is betrayed! It would have been good for that man if he had not been born." In John 17:12, Jesus refers to Judas as the "*son of perdition*" which has been interpreted to mean "the one doomed to destruction." In John 7:70 he refers to Judas as "*a devil.*" In John 13:27, the writer tells us that "Satan entered him [Judas]." So is Judas evil from the beginning or does he only become evil when Satan enters him? Is Judas in control of himself at the time of the betrayal or is he possessed of the devil? Is the act of betrayal an act of free will or is it predetermined? The same questions we ask about Judas could be asked about Richard.

In considering these questions one might start from the conventional Christian position that God is omniscient and knows all beginnings and ends. His omniscience allows Him to foreknow the future; hence He is able to communicate the future to mankind through His prophets. Because God knows all things does not require us to make the leap that He causes all things. But a second Christian premise proposes that God has a master plan for mankind and takes an active role in life of man. Here things become more difficult. If God has a master plan, wouldn't that suggest that God is in control of all things, large and small? Hamlet says. "there's a special providence in the fall of a sparrow" suggesting that everything has meaning and purpose in God's plan. However, it would appear that God allows for at least temporary deviations from the grand design in that He permits man free will to go along with the plan or reject it. This brings us to the third Christian premise that God does not will sin, but does allow it. Sin came into the world according to the Genesis story when man disobeyed God's law. As a result of this sin man was punished with death and exile from the Garden of Eden. The omniscient God would have known that this would happen, but God apparently valuing the exercise of free will above enforced obedience allowed men the great fall. God however also had a plan for man to live with Him in perfect harmony; therefore, through the laws and the prophets, God attempted to bring mankind, through the test case of His chosen people, the Jews into union with God's plan. The Old Testament describes a cycle of sins, punishments and reconciliations between God and the Jewish people leading up to the final reconciliation through the blood sacrifice of Jesus Christ. In the Passion, the omniscient God knows that Judas will betray Christ to his death. This is an integral part of God's plan and is prophesied in the Old Testament. Nevertheless, Judas is a free agent; God does not force him to betray Jesus, but knows that he will.

Now let's look at Richard's case. The omniscient God knows that England will violate His laws by deposing His anointed king, Richard II. Since the sin is a political one in which the entire nation is complicit, the punishment is political in nature, designed to show the worst in government existing without God's endorsement and support. The kingdom is absorbed in civil wars at home and foreign military adventure. The subsequent kings are the constant target of would-be usurpers and never entirely at peace. The people of England are torn by shifting allegiances and divided loyalties. The culminating horror is the War of the Roses and the final reign of Richard III. God's plan, according to Tillyard, is to restore a God endorsed king upon the throne and to warn the nation of England that usurping the rightfully anointed king can only result in horrific consequence, not because God sends them villainous or incompetent rulers, but because His absent endorsement allows rulers and would-be rulers to indulge their worst characteristics: ambition, greed, ruthlessness, and cruelty. Richard is not evil because God wishes him to be evil, but because God permits him through the exercise of free will to be evil. Richard, as I have shown, is a product of his environment and his environment is a product of England's rejection of God's plan manifested in the deposing of God's anointed king.

Thus we come back to the question of Richard III as a tragic character. I suggested that he is a villain, a victim and a tool. His villainy needs no further explanation than already provided and his murder of the two young princes in the Tower is all but irredeemable. He is also a victim both of his deformity and the bellicose, loveless environment in which he was raised. His victimhood does not in itself make him a tragic figure. No, what makes Richard tragic is that such a multi-talented character squanders his talent in the pursuit of evil for evil's sake. He is not tragic because he is unlovable, but because he cannot love. Anne is proof that he has the potential to be loved, but he cannot see that potential in himself. That he has the power to lead men is apparent, but once he finally achieves his goal of ultimate authority, he loses that awesome skill of persuasion. His courage on the battlefield is unquestionable and he only waivers briefly after the ghostly visitation. In the end he is unwilling to denounce himself and repent of his evil, but having set his own course, he is willing to face the consequences of his actions without pleading for mercy or forgiveness. To the end he is a solder, willing to stand alone against Richmond and his followers. In spite of his rank villainy, there is nobility in Richard that places him above the other hero-villains of the age and finally takes him to the lofty height of Tragedy.

Finally, is Richard a tool of God's punishment of England? The word tool is perhaps a bit too strong. A tool is something mindlessly that is wielded by another. Still operating under the premise that God does not do evil, Richard must voluntarily inflict God's punishment without God's prompting. To be a tool would be to deprive Richard of free will. To allow Richard to be the villain he freely elects to be, God's corrective plan proceeds without God having to directly intervene. Richard, like Judas, does have an important role in God's grand design, but God never intervenes to direct that role.

O, MY OFFENCE IS RANK IT SMELLS TO HEAVEN: CLAUDIUS: HAMLET

From the beginning of *Hamlet*, the character of King Claudius is ambiguous. In Act I, Scene ii, he is presented as an intelligent and capable ruler. In his first lengthy speech to the court, he opens with a statement decided to expel concerns about his sudden marriage to the wife of his brother and former king. Claudius realizes that such a hasty marriage could breed scandal and undermine the smooth change in government. His speech juxtaposes the people's loss of their departed king with the new beginning they will have under his care, and he uses the death of Hamlet's father to create a sense of national solidarity, "the whole kingdom/To be contracted in one brow of woe" (*H*, I, 2, 3-4). He implies that the marriage is as much for the welfare of the State as for the mutual "delight" of the royal couple, for the marriage results in a kind of continuity that is intended to bridge the old and new administrations. He also notes that the marriage has endorsed, at least passively, by the people of Denmark, saying "nor have we herein barr'd/Your better wisdoms, which have freely gone/With this affair along" (*H*, I, 2, 14-16). With these few lines, Claudius shows himself a shrewd politician who is sensitive to his subjects need for continuity and desire to feel unified with their king.

Claudius next turns his attention to an impending national crisis. The audience learned in Act I, Scene I that preparations are underway to repeal a possible attack from neighboring Norway. The "daily cast of brazen cannon" and the urgent procurement of "implements of war" shows Claudius is preparing for the worst, but in his speech we learn he is also working toward a diplomatic solution. The source of the threat to Denmark is from the bellicose prince of Norway, Fortinbras whose father was slain by old King Hamlet in combat.

> *young Fortinbras,*
> *Holding a weak supposal of our worth,*
> *Or thinking by our late dear brother's death*
> *Our state to be disjoint and out of frame,*
> *Colleagued with the dream of his advantage,*
> *He hath not fail'd to pester us with message,*
> *Importing the surrender of those lands*

Lost by his father, with all bonds of law,
To our most valiant brother.:

> (H, I, 2, 17-25)

Claudius, to avoid warfare, dispatches messengers

To Norway, uncle of young Fortinbras,--
Who, impotent and bed-rid, scarcely hears
Of this his nephew's purpose,--to suppress
His further gait herein

> (H, I, 2, 28-31)

Concluding these matters of State, Claudius turns to more personal matters. Turning to young Hamlet who he addresses as "my cousin...and my son," he gently scolds the Prince for protracted grieving over his dead father. His words are consolatory and reasonable, and he concludes by pronouncing Hamlet his heir apparent.

We pray you, throw to earth
This unprevailing woe, and think of us
As of a father: for let the world take note,
You are the most immediate to our throne;
And with no less nobility of love
Than that which dearest father bears his son,
Do I impart toward you

> (H, I, 2, 106-112)

On the whole, Claudius emerges as a King who is well qualified for and competent in his office. His words to Hamlet seem sincere, appropriate to a man of compassion and intelligence. In fact, at first brush, Claudius is an exemplary ruler, particular when compared with the rulers we see in Shakespeare's History play.

There is, however, one dissenter among the court, young Hamlet, who compares Claudius to a "satyr," a man no more like the former king than Hamlet is like Hercules. Hamlet's complaint is not grounded in Claudius' kingship or right to rule, but in the swift marriage of his mother to him. Hamlet is more contemptuous of Claudius than angry at him. He sees Claudius as lascivious, incestuous drunkard, so inferior to the former king in character (though not in political skill) that it is inconceivable to Hamlet that Gertrude could have taken him as husband at all, let alone in such a brief time. Hamlet's rage is principally aimed at his mother, but it is vented in Claudius' direction. Much has been written about Hamlet's Oedipal subtext and some will be said later, but for now it is enough to say at this point in the play, Hamlet is angrier at his mother than at Claudius. This quickly changes when Hamlet meets the Ghost.

The Ghost informs Hamlet that contrary to public report the King was not slain by the sting of a serpent, but by a poisoning brother:

> 'Tis given out that, sleeping in my orchard,
> A serpent stung me; so the whole ear of Denmark
> Is by a forged process of my death
> Rankly abused: but know, thou noble youth,
> The serpent that did sting thy father's life
> Now wears his crown.
>
> (H, I, 5, 35-39)

At the news, Hamlet cries out "O my prophetic soul!" implying that he had suspicions of Claudius all along, but implies a willingness on Hamlet's part to leap at a worthy excuse to direct his anger away from his mother to a more acceptable target, the "incestuous, ... adulterate beast." Not only does the Ghost give Hamlet an excuse to exact revenge on Claudius, but it also provides him an excuse to "leave her [Gertrude] to heaven." The Ghost instructs Hamlet:

> Let not the royal bed of Denmark be
> A couch for luxury and damned incest.
> But, howsoever thou pursuest this act,
> Taint not thy mind, nor let thy soul contrive
> Against thy mother aught: leave her to heaven
> And to those thorns that in her bosom lodge,
> To prick and sting her.
>
> (H, I, 5, 82-88)

It is noteworthy that the Ghost devotes 22 lines bemoaning the incestuous lust between his brother and his wife, and only once mentions the loss of his crown. For the Ghost and for Hamlet, the marriage seems the chief offense and cause for the murder of the king, not the desire for the throne. Again this is an opinion that mirrors that of Hamlet's own predisposition and one that generates more rage in Hamlet than ambitious regicide ever could. So it could be said that the Ghost tells Hamlet just what he wants to hear, but is it true? By now, of course, everyone knows that the Ghost is telling the truth about Claudius, but when the play was new, the audience would have reason to doubt. The nature of the Ghost is central to the question of its motives and reliability. Is the Ghost truly sent from God to charge Hamlet with avenging the murder of his father or is the Ghost a devil sent from Hell to capture the soul of the melancholy Prince?

Elizabeth Prosser demonstrates that the nature of the Ghost can be evaluated by two religious standards: that of the Protestant Elizabethan audience or that of the play's Catholic context. Protestant doctrine would suggest three explanations: the ghost is a hallucination, an angel or a devil. Catholic doctrine would add a fourth explanation: a spirit released from Purgatory, which is, exactly what the Ghost insists that he is. Since this explanation would not be acceptable to the Protestant audience, and since the ghost seen by so many people cannot be a hallucination, they would be left with two choices: to accept the Ghost as an angelic messenger from God placing the sword of retribution in Hamlet's hand or an evil spirit sent from Hell to ensnare Hamlet's soul. The very fact that the Ghost insists he is the spirit of Hamlet's father returned from Purgatory would signal to the Protestant audience that the ghost is a liar and therefore must be a devil. But for the closet Catholics in the audience and the Catholic characters of the play, the possibility that the ghost is true exists. For those, Shakespeare piles up evidence to show that the ghost is up to no good. First, the ghost appears at midnight. When charged "By heaven" to speak, it is "offended" and "stalks" away. When the cock crows signally the coming of day, it "started like a guilty thing" and vanished. All of these actions would scream "devil" to the Elizabethan audience. The Ghost if from Purgatory should be humble and conciliatory, not angry and vengeful. The Purgatory ghost should be only concerned about its' own sins and not the sins of others. And the Purgatory ghost would never suggest anything that would be contrary to the Word of God or the tenants of the Catholic faith.[20]

Although initially convinced or the Ghost's honesty, Hamlet latter has some doubts and when the opportunity presents itself, he decides to use a visiting theater troupe to put the Ghost to the test.

> ...The spirit that I have seen
> May be the devil: and the devil hath power
> To assume a pleasing shape; yea, and perhaps
> Out of my weakness and my melancholy,
> As he is very potent with such spirits,
> Abuses me to damn me: I'll have grounds
> More relative than this: the play 's the thing
> Wherein I'll catch the conscience of the king.
>
> (H, II, 2, 598-605)

The presumption is that if Claudius is guilty, then the Ghost must be "honest" and not a devil sent from Hell to entrap Hamlet's soul.

The play, entitles "*The Mousetrap*" conclusively proves Claudius's guilt and to dispel any lingering doubts, the audience and Hamlet are allowed to overhear Claudius' prayerful confession:

> *O, my offence is rank it smells to heaven;*
> *It hath the primal eldest curse upon't,*
> *A brother's murder. Pray can I not,*
> *Though inclination be as sharp as will:*
> *My stronger guilt defeats my strong intent;*
> *And, like a man to double business bound,*
> *I stand in pause where I shall first begin,*
> *And both neglect. What if this cursed hand*
> *Were thicker than itself with brother's blood,*
> *Is there not rain enough in the sweet heavens*
> *To wash it white as snow?*
>
> (H, III, 3, 36-46)

This scene offers the audience its only glance into the soul of the private and vulnerable man. By now, we are perhaps wondering why Claudius did what he did. Was it for ambition, for love, for both? He usurped the throne of an apparently popular and competent king so he is unlike Henry Bolingbroke who replaced the corrupt and incompetent Richard II or Richard, Duke of York who sought to replace the weak and incompetent Henry VI. He is not the overtly evil and ambitious equal of a Richard III who plots for his amusement and personal gain. Claudius is no sociopath, devoid of moments of compassion, guilt and regret. He genuinely seems to love Gertrude as evidenced by his deference to her in matters concerning her son. One wonders if their love predates the murder of the old king. If so, which seems probable considering the haste of their marriage, was their relationship platonic or adulterous as the Ghost suggests. Was Gertrude complicit in the murder? The Ghost says no and the confrontation between Hamlet and Gertrude in her closet confirms this. Gertrude is shocked by when Hamlet reveals that the old king was murdered by the new king. There is no suggestion in this confrontation that the relationship between Claudius and Gertrude predated the murder and Gertrude, while confessing that Claudius is inferior to old Hamlet (to humor the mad young Hamlet?), offers no reason to explain their rapid marriage. The question of a preexisting affair is left open to speculation, but it can certainly be said that that love for Gertrude is at least coequal with the desire for the crown in motiving Claudius' crime.

Other than conclusively letting the audience know that Claudius is guilty of fratricide and regicide, what purpose does the scene serve? What are we to think of Claudius? Claudius' crime weighs heavy on his conscience and he wonders:

> O, what form of prayer
> Can serve my turn? 'Forgive me my foul murder'?
> That cannot be; since I am still possess'd
> Of those effects for which I did the murder,
> My crown, mine own ambition and my queen.
> May one be pardon'd and retain the offence?
>
> (H, III, 3, 51-6)

Are we intended to feel sympathy for Claudius? Is he a man who is not eminently evil like Iago or Richard III, but instead a morally weak man who succumbed to temptations of ambition and lust. Is he worthy of forgiveness and understanding? The question of religion again emerges in this scene. When Claudius prays is it to the God of the old church or the new? Since the source work places the play in the 12th Century, the action would predate the Protestant Reformation, but it is interesting to note the complete lack of clergy, Catholic or Protestant, in the play. While Claudius is at prayer, Hamlet comes upon him and is prepared to kill him, but the Prince pulls back, thinking that to kill the King at his prayers will assure Claudius free passage through Heaven's gate. According to Catholic teaching, the penitent must tell his or her sins directly to an ordained Catholic priest or bishop. In Claudius' case, this requirement is not fulfilled. He directs his prayer to God directly, without the mandatory intermediary. However, the Church does allows, if the penitent is unable to make a valid sacramental confession before death, knowing that if the penitent is truly sorry for their sins, God will allow them to formally apologize and make reparation (in some way) when they are judged. Essential to absolution are acts both by the sinner (examination of conscience, contrition with a determination not to sin again, confession to a priest, and performance of some act to repair the damage caused by sin) and by the priest (determination of the act of reparation to be performed and absolution). Presumably, if the sinner fulfills their part in the ritual, God at the Throne of Judgment will directly assume the role the priest would play in the Sacrament. In this case of Claudius, Hamlet might be correct if he subscribed to the Catholic view of repentance and salvation. Although Claudius is not engaged to the normal rituals of Penance and Absolution, he could still receive absolution if he fulfilled all requirements other than the direct confession to a priest, assuming he wished to do so before his death.

The Protestant (e.g. Puritans) view of absolution consists of the doctrine of justification by faith which makes penance and forgiveness as a more direct interaction between God and sinner. This Calvinist doctrine posits that divine forgiveness must precede true repentance and confession to God and is given without any reparation of "works." This idea would suggest that Claudius' call of conscious comes from God, affording him an opportunity for repentance and forgiveness. Like the Catholic view, the ball is placed in Claudius' court to determine the fate of his soul. The only real difference is that Catholicism requires some action, or at the least the intention to perform some action, to repair the damage caused by the sin. The Protestant view does not require reparation, but does assume that such an action would naturally follow true repentance.

In either case, Claudius is unwilling to give up the fruits of his crime: his crown or his queen. Since he is unwilling to do so, his repentance is insincere, or at least incomplete, and he renders himself ineligible for divine forgiveness. Realizing this, he knows forgiven is impossible and there is no going back from his crime. Once it has been established that he is, if fact a villain, Claudius is driven to commit increasingly criminal acts. Prior to the incriminating play, the audience sees Claudius spying on Hamlet either directly or through surrogates, but he justifies his spying by explaining that it is done out of concern for Hamlet's welfare. In concert with his wife, Claudius recruits Rosencrantz and Guildenstern to:

> ...To draw him on to pleasures, and to gather,
> So much as from occasion you may glean,
> Whether aught, to us unknown, afflicts him thus,
> That, open'd, lies within our remedy.
>
> (H, II, 2, 15-19)

When Claudius later spies on Hamlet during his encounter with Ophelia, it is at the urging of Polonius and in his company, for the sole purpose of discovering the source of Hamlet's "madness." Unconvinced that the loss of Ophelia's love is the cause of Hamlet's madness as Polonius posits and increasingly uneasy, Claudius' reveals a plan to send Hamlet to England where his madness can do no harm. Up until the performance of Hamlet's play, Claudius only seems concerned with Hamlet's welfare and the effect his behavior has on those around him, particularly Queen Gertrude.

After "*The Mousetrap*" has sprung, Claudius knows that Hamlet has uncovered his crime and after Hamlet unwittingly murders Polonius, mistaking him for the King, Claudius has both a reason and a means to eliminate the threat. As he explains to Gertrude,

> [Hamlet's] liberty is full of threats to all;
> To you yourself, to us, to every one.
> Alas, how shall this bloody deed be answer'd?
> It will be laid to us, whose providence
> Should have kept short, restrain'd and out of haunt,
> This mad young man: but so much was our love,
> We would not understand what was most fit,
>
> (H, IV, 1, 14-20)

A public trial for Hamlet is out of the question because the truth of Claudius's regicide would surely have come out. Additionally, Hamlet is popular with the populace and his punishment for the murder of Polonius might well turn the people against the current regime:

> Yet must not we put the strong law on him:
> He's loved of the distracted multitude,
> Who like not in their judgment, but their eyes;
> And where tis so, the offender's scourge is weigh'd,
> But never the offence
>
> (H, IV, 3, 3-7)

This way blocked, Claudius decides to proceed with his original plan, but with one caveat. He resolves to send Hamlet to England under the supervision of Rosencrantz and Guildenstern, but by way of a letter, he begs his English counterpart to immediately put Hamlet to death.

This well laid plan, like many such, goes awry. First, the secrecy surrounding the death of Polonius breeds suspicion among the Danish subjects and outrage in the son of Polonius, Laertes. Laertes, backed by a band of supporters, storms the court and confronts Claudius. Claudius, the consummate politician quickly calms them:

> If by direct or by collateral hand
> They [Laertes' supporters] find us touch'd, we will our kingdom give,
> Our crown, our life, and all that we can ours,
> To you in satisfaction; but if not,
> Be you content to lend your patience to us,

And we shall jointly labour with your soul
To give it due content.

(*H, IV, 5, 207-12*)

Claudius then takes Laertes apart and relates the circumstances surrounding the death of Polonius. When Laertes asks "Why you proceeded not against these feats, /So crimeful and so capital in nature (*H, IV, 7, 6-7*), Claudius explains:

O, for two special reasons;
Which may to you, perhaps, seem much unsinew'd,
But yet to me they are strong. The queen his mother
Lives almost by his looks; and for myself--
My virtue or my plague, be it either which--
She's so conjunctive to my life and soul,
That, as the star moves not but in his sphere,
I could not but by her. The other motive,
Why to a public count I might not go,
Is the great love the general gender bear him;
Who, dipping all his faults in their affection,
Would, like the spring that turneth wood to stone,
Convert his gyves to graces; so that my arrows,
Too slightly timber'd for so loud a wind,
Would have reverted to my bow again,
And not where I had aim'd them.

(*H, IV, 7, 9-24*)

His response, being both compassionate and credible, seems to satisfy Laertes and resolve the issue between them. Then, unexpectedly, he learns that Hamlet is alive and back in Denmark.

Claudius persuades Laertes to execute his revenge in a Machiavellian plot. The audience would know that this signals Laertes' imminent doom since adopting such tactics inevitably results in the downfall of the plotter. If Laertes simply killed Hamlet on sight, he might have maintained the sympathy of the audience even if the audience would know objectively that his action was wrong. By allowing himself to be led by Claudius who becomes in an instant his surrogate father, Laertes is led like Hamlet by his father to execute an action that will likely doom his soul. The King's plot, however, raises a significant question. Punishing Hamlet for the murder of Polonius is the rightful obligation of the State, meaning the obligation of the King. Keep in mind that St. Paul in his Letter to the Romans wrote "The ruler... is the minister of God, a revenger to execute wrath upon him that doeth evil."[21] The ruler delegates his power as revenger to his ministers and magistrates. Could it not be argued that Laertes is acting in the plot as the sanctioned minister to the State's revenge? Is this argument weakened by the illegitimacy of this particular ruler or by the Machiavellian methods used to exact the "justice of the State?" Indeed, it is. Laertes cannot be seen as the legitimate tool of the State's justice because what is done by the State in executing justice must be done in the light of day. Neither Claudius nor Laertes acts for the benefit of justice; Claudius acts from self-interest and Laertes acts for a thirst for revenge.

The King and Laertes contrive a complex Machiavellian plot to assure Hamlet's demise, conspiring to make his death appear an accident. In a contest of fencing skill, Laertes will meet Hamlet before the Court and during the bout Laertes will contrive to nick Hamlet with the blade of his sword which he will coat with a "unction...so mortal that... where it draws blood no cataplasm...can save the thing from death...that is but scratch'd withal." (H, IV, 7, 141-6). As a backup to Laertes plan, Claudius, who has successfully used poison in his previous crime, will have a poisoned cup at hand to give to Hamlet when he is "hot and dry" from the exertion of the contest. That the two elect to use poison as their tool of choice would signal to the audience the depth of their villainy as the use of poison was considered one of the most heinous tools of the assassin, particularly favored by the Machiavellian Italians.

As with the previous plan to eliminate Hamlet, things do not proceed as planned. Laertes successfully cut Hamlet with the poisoned blade, but during the ensuing scuffle, the swords are exchanged and Laertes is himself cut by his own poisoned sword. Gertrude unwittingly drinks from the poisoned cup Claudius has prepared. Knowing he is dying, Laertes reveals the plot, indicting Claudius as its' author, and Hamlet, with his final effort stabs Claudius with the poisoned sword, then pours the reminder of the poisoned drink down the villain's throat. His revenge complete, Hamlet dies in the arms of his only friend, Horatio, who he charges to tell his tale.

It is obvious by the end of the play we are intended to see Claudius as a murderous villain, but he is a nuanced villain; not a devil like Aaron or Richard III, but a man who cannot refrain from indulging his human desires. He is not a monster; he is morally weak, content to trade his humanity and very soul for a few prized possessions. As critic Harley Granville-Barker observes: "we have in Claudius the makings of the central figure of a tragedy," a complex and fully human villain who is on equal footing with Shakespeare's other great and completely human villain, Macbeth.

LOOK LIKE THE INNOCENT FLOWER, BUT BE THE SERPENT UNDER IT: LADY MACBETH: MACBETH

Shakespeare's *Macbeth* is considered one of the greatest explorations of evil in the literary canon on the West. Like Claudius in Hamlet, *Macbeth* begins the play as a relatively admirable character. Claudius is a consummate politician; Macbeth a consummate warrior. Both have and are providing good service to their countries: Claudius in obverting a war and Macbeth in winning one. Both enjoy good opinions of those around them. The chief difference between the two is that at the opening of Hamlet, Claudius has already played most foully in achieving his crown; Macbeth has yet to do so. In the case of Claudius, the audience is not privileged to see the events leading up to the murder of the old king by his own brother. The murder is only recounted second hand by the ghostly victim. The audience only sees a man more fearful of losing the material gains of his crime than one suffering from the spiritual pangs of guilt over his deed. In the case of Macbeth, the audience sees the evolution, execution and consequences of the protagonist's great act of evil from the perspective of the protagonist himself. In its own way, *Macbeth* is the most character focused of all of Shakespeare's plays. The story line is simple and unfolds with a straight chronological narrative, including a distinct beginning, middle and conclusion. It is uncharacteristically devoid of secondary plots and other than Macbeth and his wife, there is little in the other characters to draw and hold our attention. While *Macbeth* is Shakespeare's shortest play, it contains proportionally more soliloquies than either the introspective *Hamlet* or the Vice-like protagonist of *Richard III*. Because of this, we have a clearer vision into the struggling mind and soul of Macbeth than we do into that of any other character in the canon. By the end of the play, there is nothing about the character of Macbeth that really defies our understanding. There are no nagging questions left unanswered, just the unsettling feeling that we have seen the tragic destruction of a relatively good man who gives into the allure of evil and subsequently pays the price. The genius of Macbeth is that he is so clearly drawn that we in the audience can sufficiently identify with him that we are forced to wonder about the potential for evil in all of us.

Like *Hamlet*, *Macbeth* begins on a supernatural note foreshadowing dark events ahead. The witches in this opening scene introduce a world of inversion where *"Fair is foul, and foul is fair"* (M, I, 1, 10), signaling the play's focus on the reversal of values and the collapse of natural order. Their withered and wild attire, their aged and forbidding physical feature's and their devilish incantations mark them out as witches of vulgar superstition. Before meeting with Macbeth in Act 1, scene 3 they wind up a charm presumably in preparation for their attack on his soul. Macbeth is clearly the focus of their malignant intentions, but why he specifically is targeted is not revealed. We have been introduced to Macbeth in the preceding scene when his warrior feats are related to King Duncan by wounded and "bloody" soldier. We have learned that Macbeth has bested the rebel Macdonwald in single combat, *"unseam[ing] him from the nave to the chaps,"* (M, I, 2, 10), before turning on and routing Macdonwald's allies, the Thane of Cawdor and the King of Norway. Macbeth's battlefield prowess is credited with saving the day and the kingship of Duncan. It is this battlefield hero fresh from battle and victory who is confronted by the three witches on the heath. When the witches greet him with titles, "All hail, Macbeth! hail to thee, thane of Glamis!...All hail, Macbeth, hail to thee, thane of Cawdor!...All hail, Macbeth, thou shalt be king hereafter!" he is naturally started, but significantly seems to fear hearing their words. Why fear? It has been suggested that Macbeth shows fear because his secret ambitions have been spoken aloud. A. C. Bradley writes:

> But when Macbeth heard them [the witches] he was not an innocent man. Precisely how far his mind was guilty may be a questioned -- but no innocent man would have started, as he did, with a start of fear at the mere prophesy of a crown, or have conceived there upon immediately the thought of murder. Either this thought was not new to him, or he had cherished at least some vaguer dishonorable dream, the instantaneous recurrence of which, at the- moment of his hearing the prophecy revealed to him an inward and terrifying guilt.[23]

That Macbeth might at some time in the future be king is not improbable. Scotland we know from Shakespeare's source material was not governed by strict primogeniture and Macbeth as kinsman to Duncan could reasonable expect to succeed. It is not the promise of kingship that unnerves Macbeth, but the images of murder to achieve it that are brought immediately to mind by the prophecy.

> *Present fears*
> *Are less than horrible imaginings:*
> *My thought, whose murder yet is but fantastical,*
> *Shakes so my single state of man that function*
> *Is smother'd in surmise, and nothing is*
> *But what is not.*
>
> (M, I, 3, 137-42)

Although Macbeth's mind immediately turns to regicide when confronted with the prophesy of the witches, he is at heart, basically an honorable man who is at least initially able to brush aside his murderous ambition: "If chance will have me king, why, chance may crown me," (M, I, 3, 142-3). We learn later from Lady Macbeth that her husband is "too full o' the milk of human kindness/To catch the nearest way." (M, I, 5, 17) and can assume he would likely have deferred his ambition had chance not placed an unexpected obstacle between him and the crown. Unexpectedly, King Duncan names Malcolm, his eldest son, his royal heir, assuring that Macbeth will not succeed upon Duncan's death. Thus chance provides Macbeth with motive and, scarcely a breath later, with opportunity when Duncan announces his intention to spend the night at Macbeth's castle.

To what extent are the witches responsible for Macbeth subsequent crime? Their prophesy does not plant the seed of regicide in Macbeth's mind, it simply reawakens his half-forgotten dream of kingship. They don't exercise any direct influence over the man or the events leading up to Duncan's murder. The witches have the ability to see things to come; they say they have the power to call up storms; but they also have limitations. They can torment, but not ultimately destroy as their curse on the seaman shows.

> *He shall live a man forbid:*
> *Weary se'nnights nine times nine*
> *Shall he dwindle, peak and pine:*
> *Though his bark cannot be lost,*
> *Yet it shall be tempest-tost.*
>
> (M, I, 3, 21-25)

The witches are "imperfect speakers," that is, they use their half-truths to lead men to their destruction. Banquo warns Macbeth not to trust the witches:

> *oftentimes, to win us to our harm,*
> *The instruments of darkness tell us truths,*

> *Win us with honest trifles, to betray's*
> *In deepest consequence.*
>
> (*M, I, 3, 123-126*)

This warning reminds us of Hamlet's words about the intentions of the Ghost:

> *...The spirit that I have seen*
> *May be the devil: and the devil hath power*
> *To assume a pleasing shape;*
>
> (*H, II, 2, 598-605*)

Like Hamlet's Ghost, the witches have the ability to point a man down the evil path, but they do not have the power to drag him there. That job falls to Lady Macbeth.

While I will be exploring the character of Lady Macbeth in detail in a later chapter, it is necessary to explore the role she makes in Macbeth's decision making at this point. Lady Macbeth is, of course, the ambitious wife of Macbeth who encourages her husband to "catch the nearest way" (*M*, I, 5, 17) to the throne. Some have referred to Lady Macbeth as the "fourth witch," but I am inclined to see Lady Macbeth as Macbeth's Jungian shadow, that dark unconscious aspect that is repressed yet tugs him toward regicide. Lady Macbeth becomes the physical manifestations of shadow and plays out the devil's part in the play's psychomachia for the soul of husband. Before modern psychology, the internal struggle between good and evil was envisioned as an internal dialogue between a good and bad angel given to each man. The good or tutelary angel was spoken of as far bad as Socrates who wrote of "a voice which comes to me and always forbids me to do something which I am going to do, but never commands me to do anything."[25] Later thinking saw the tutelary spirit as a manifestation of the "Higher Self that knows its own true nature, its place within the grand scheme of things, and ... understands why the individual exists in the first place and how to best go about accomplishing whatever it is here to do."[26] E. C. Knowlton tells us that in the 4th Century Servius suggested the presence of a second voice or angel that represented a Manichean Lower Self whose function was to assail and tempt man toward evil.[27] In the debate over the fate of Duncan, Macbeth speaks for the good angel and Lady Macbeth for the bad.

Psychomachia

Macbeth articulates all the reasons for not murdering Duncan.

> He's [Duncan] here in double trust;
> First, as I am his kinsman and his subject,
> Strong both against the deed; then, as his host,
> Who should against his murderer shut the door,
> Not bear the knife myself. Besides, this Duncan
> Hath borne his faculties so meek, hath been
> So clear in his great office, that his virtues
> Will plead like angels, trumpet-tongued, against
> The deep damnation of his taking-off;
> And pity, like a naked new-born babe,
> Striding the blast, or heaven's cherubim, horsed
> Upon the sightless couriers of the air,
> Shall blow the horrid deed in every eye,
> That tears shall drown the wind. I have no spur
> To prick the sides of my intent, but only
> Vaulting ambition, which o'erleaps itself
> And falls on the other.
>
> (M, I, 7, 12-28)

Lady Macbeth, on the other hand, articulates the reasons for performing the murder. She cannot wait to "pour [her] *spirits in [his]* ear; / And chastise with the valour of [her] tongue/ All that impedes [him] from the golden round," (M, I, 5, 26-8). The audience is unfortunately never treated to Lady Macbeth's persuasive arguments that apparently bring Macbeth over to her side. Between his homecoming and the evening feast, she has brought him around. When he tells her "We will proceed no further in this business," (*M*, I, 7, 30) she responds "What beast was't, then, / That made you break this enterprise to me?" (*M*, I, 7, 48-9). She attacks his love for her, she attacks his courage and his manhood, but she offers nothing to support the regicide. All she does is lay out her plan which has a reasonable chance of success and this is sufficient to again turn Macbeth back on his path to murder. We can infer, then, that Macbeth is less troubled by the morality of the deed than the risks associated with its execution. At the beginning of his earlier speech he says he is willing to risk the consequences of the world beyond, to "jump the life to come," but that he fears judgment here

> *in these cases*
> *We still have judgment here; that we but teach*
> *Bloody instructions, which, being taught, return*
> *To plague the inventor:*
>
> (*M, I, 7, 7-10*)

The judgment he most fears here is that once the precedent of regicide occurs it may come back to be visited on him. Interestingly enough, Macbeth does not seem particularly bothered by the thought of judgment in the afterlife. For a play dominated by images of the supernatural, religious thought and images are all but absent. Unlike Hamlet who constantly considers the state of his soul, Macbeth makes virtually no comment about the state of his soul.

Without Lady Macbeth, would Macbeth have acted on his ambition? Act I, scene vii makes it appear that he would not. Unlike the witches who only reawaken Macbeth's dark ambition, Lady Macbeth pushes and cajoles Macbeth into action. He knows what he is about to do is wrong, he rightly fears the consequences, but ultimately the risk of losing the love and respect of his wife is a greater threat than the loss of his soul.

Once the decision to murder Duncan is made, Macbeth immediately begins to mentally deteriorate. As he proceeds to Duncan's bedchamber, he hallucinates, seeing a bloody dagger guide him along darkened corridors. After the bloody deed, Macbeth is distracted and unhinged. He tells his wife that as he returned from Duncan's bedchamber:

> *Methought I heard a voice cry 'Sleep no more!*
> *Macbeth does murder sleep', the innocent sleep,*
> *Sleep that knits up the ravell'd sleeve of care,*
> *The death of each day's life, sore labour's bath,*

Balm of hurt minds, great nature's second course,
Chief nourisher in life's feast,--
..
Still it cried 'Sleep no more!' to all the house:
'Glamis hath murder'd sleep, and therefore Cawdor
Shall sleep no more; Macbeth shall sleep no more.'

(M, 2, 2, 32-6, 38-40)

In Shakespeare, there is no darker punishment than insomnia. Insomnia plagued other usurpers: Henry IV says:

How many thousand of my poorest subjects
Are at this hour asleep! O Sleep, O gentle Sleep,
Nature's soft nurse, how have I frighted thee,
That thou no more wilt weigh my eyelids down
And steep my senses in forgetfulness?
Why rather, Sleep, liest thou in smoky cribs,
Upon uneasy pallets stretching thee,
And hushed with buzzing night-flies to thy slumber,
Than in the perfumed chambers of the great,
Under the canopies of costly state,
And lulled with sounds of sweetest melody?
O thou dull god, why liest thou with the vile
In loathsome beds, and leav'st the kingly couch
A watch-case, or a common 'larum-bell?
Wilt thou upon the high and giddy mast
Seal up the ship-boy's eyes, and rock his brains
In cradle of the rude, imperious surge,
And in the visitation of the winds,
Who take the ruffian billows by the top,
Curling their monstrous heads, and hanging them
With deafening clamor in the slippery shrouds,
That with the hurly, death itself awakes?
Canst thou, O partial Sleep, give thy repose
To the wet sea-boy in an hour so rude,
And in the calmest and most stillest night,
With all appliances and means to boot,
Deny it to a king? Then, happy low, lie down!
Uneasy lies the head that wears a crown.

(2HIV, 3, 1, 4-31)

When Queen Margaret curses Richard of Gloucester in *Richard III*, she curses him with insomnia:

> *On thee, the troubler of the poor world's peace!*
> *The worm of conscience still begnaw thy soul!*
> *Thy friends suspect for traitors while thou liv'st,*
> *And take deep traitors for thy dearest friends!*
> *No sleep close up that deadly eye of thine,*
> *Unless it be while some tormenting dream*
> *Affrights thee with a hell of ugly devils!*
>
> *(RIII, I, 3, 220-6)*

Macbeth and Lady Macbeth will both suffer from sleep disorders following the murder of Duncan. In a study published online in the journal 'Schizophrenia Research', researchers reported that "in the general population individuals with insomnia were five times more likely to have high levels of paranoid thinking than people who were sleeping well."[24] This certainly plays out in the case of Macbeth.

When Duncan's sons flee the scene of the crime, fearing they may be next to be murdered, suspicion falls on them and Macbeth is crowned king, just as the witches' prophesized. The paranoia of Macbeth rapidly takes hold as Banquo confesses to the audience that he has suspicion about his friend.

> *Thou hast it now: king, Cawdor, Glamis, all,*
> *As the weird women promised, and, I fear,*
> *Thou play'dst most foully for't:*
>
> *(M, III, 1, 1-3)*

Macbeth, however, is not driven to murder his former friend because he fears him, but instead because he resents that Banquo's issue will ultimately benefit from his crime. He says

> *Upon my head they placed a fruitless crown,*
> *And put a barren sceptre in my gripe,*
> *Thence to be wrench'd with an unlineal hand,*
> *No son of mine succeeding. If 't be so,*
> *For Banquo's issue have I filed my mind;*
> *For them the gracious Duncan have I murder'd;*
> *Put rancours in the vessel of my peace*
> *Only for them; and mine eternal jewel*

Given to the common enemy of man,
To make them kings

(M, III, 1, 60-9)

   Macbeth's slide into ultimate evil that began with the murder of Duncan to achieve the crown now continues in Macbeth's futile attempt to keep it. But to what end? If Banquo and Fleance are eliminated, is Macbeth any more secure? We know Banquo is not the immediate threat because the witches prophesized that he will "get kings, though ... be none" (M, I, 3, 67). Does he worry that Fleance will grow up to usurp the crown? This would appear to be the practical explanation, but the tone of his soliloquy implies a man more driven by malignant resentment than realistic insecurity. It eats at him that Banquo's heir will come to the throne without cost while he has yielded his "eternal jewel" for the same prize. Just as Macbeth has no real justification for murdering Duncan other than to feed his overweening ambition, he has no real reason for his attack on Banquo other than displaced resent of Banquo's perceived good fortune at the expense of Macbeth's soul-killing crime.
   Unlike Richard III, Macbeth takes no pleasure in his pursuit of the crown. Unlike Claudius, Macbeth takes no joy in his kingship. His relationship with his wife, arguably close at the beginning of the play, erodes to indifference following Duncan's murder. In the initial crime Macbeth and his wife are partners. When he launches his attack on Banquo, he keeps his wife in the dark, presumably to protect her from further crime, but in electing to exclude her, he shows he no longer needs her to encourage or provoke his evolving evil. Macbeth's shadow is no longer just an externalized portion of his personality, but has been fully integrated and has absorbed all the good that may have existed in the man.
   After Banquo's murder, the supernatural again enters the play in the form of Banquo's ghost visiting Macbeth's evening banquet. Unlike old Hamlet's ghost who is seen by several people and is an objective reality, Banquo's ghost is only seen by Macbeth suggesting the ghost is only a hallucinogenic phantom of Macbeth's guilty conscience. Lady Macbeth says it plain, "This is the very painting of your fear: / This is the air-drawn dagger which, you said,/ Led you to Duncan" (M, III, 4, 60-1). For a second time following a crime we see Macbeth become unhinged. He raves madly at the air and when he is on the verge of revealing the substance of his vision to his dinner guests, Lady Macbeth is forced to intervene and dismiss the company. Composing himself after the ghost has vanished, Macbeth resolves to consult with the Weird Sisters "to know,/ By the worst means, the worst" (M, III, 4, 134). He allies himself now completely with the dark forces, convinced that he is so fouled with his crimes that there is nowhere else he can turn. He makes this point when he famously says, "I am in

blood/ Stepp'd in so far that, should I wade no more,/ Returning were as tedious as go o'er" (*M*, III, 4, 135-7).

Meanwhile, like Macbeth's soul, Scotland has also fallen into darkness. There is a sense that Shakespeare here is employing an archetypal theme that the health of a kingdom is dependent upon the health of the king. This narrative pattern can be found at least as far back as the myth of Oedipus and was popular in the Fisher King motif found in the Arthurian legends and chronicled in Chrétien de Troyes' *Perceval* late in the 12th-century. As described by de Troyes, the titular Fisher King is injured and his kingdom suffers as he does, his impotence affecting the fertility of the land and reducing it to a barren Wasteland. Little is left for him to do but fish hence his title. Knights from Arthur's court are dispatched to discover a cure (in most legends the Holy Grail) for the king and the land and it is in the end Percival (some legends say Sir Galahad or Sir Bors) who accomplishes the mission. Scotland was already in trouble when *Macbeth* begins. When we first encounter Macbeth, his first words are "So foul and fair a day I have not seen." (*M*, I, 3, 38), suggesting an ambivalence in the natural environment that could either lead to a brightening or darkening of the world. He has freshly come from putting down a rebellion intended to unseat King Duncan. The land has been thrown into turmoil by rebellion against God's anointed, but the defeat of the rebels holds out the promise of healing, but there are still dark forces in the world ready to promote chaos and manifest themselves in the Weird Sisters. After Macbeth murders Duncan, Scotland's social structure crumbles. Malcolm describes Scotland under Macbeth's rule:

> I think our country sinks beneath the yoke;
> It weeps, it bleeds; and each new day a gash
> Is added to her wounds:
>
> (*M, IV, 3, 39-41*)

Ross adds to the description:

> Alas, poor country!
> Almost afraid to know itself. It cannot
> Be call'd our mother, but our grave; where nothing,
> But who knows nothing, is once seen to smile;
> Where sighs and groans and shrieks that rend the air
> Are made, not mark'd; where violent sorrow seems
> A modern ecstasy; the dead man's knell
> Is there scarce ask'd for who; and good men's lives

Expire before the flowers in their caps,
Dying or ere they sicken.

(M, IV, iii, 164-73)

The state of Scotland mirrors the internal state of Macbeth as the evils inflicted by the man upon the country induces a soul killing indifference to the violence that envelopes both. Both move toward and embarrass the abyss of nothingness that is the ultimate goal of evil.

When Macbeth murders Duncan, even nature is cast into turmoil. Lennox describes the night,

The night has been unruly: where we lay,
Our chimneys were blown down; and, as they say,
Lamentings heard i' the air; strange screams of death,
And prophesying with accents terrible
Of dire combustion and confused events
New hatch'd to the woeful time: the obscure bird
Clamour'd the livelong night: some say, the earth
Was feverous and did shake.

(M, II, 3, 54-61)

Ross also comments on the unnatural weather,

Thou seest, the heavens, as troubled with man's act,
Threaten his bloody stage: by the clock, 'tis day,
And yet dark night strangles the travelling lamp:

(M, II, 4, 5-7)

And the weather is not the only out of order. The Old Man talking with Ross describes how "A falcon, towering in her pride of place, / as by a mousing owl hawk'd at and kill'd." (M, II, 4, 12-13) and Ross responds by reporting an even more remarkable event:

And Duncan's horses--a thing most strange and certain--
Beauteous and swift, the minions of their race,
Turn'd wild in nature, broke their stalls, flung out,
Contending 'gainst obedience, as they would make
War with mankind.
OLD MAN
'Tis said they eat each other.

ROSS
They did so, to the amazement of mine eyes
That look'd upon't.

(*M, II, 4, 14-19*)

These pathetic fallacies (the treatment of inanimate objects as if they had human feelings, thought, or sensations) suggest that man's actions influence all things. When man acts unnaturally, the normal state of things is thrown off course and chaos follows. And herein lies probably Shakespeare's clearest definition of ultimate evil.

L. C. Sears in *Shakespeare's Philosophy of Evil* posits that "the state of Absolute Evil (in Shakespeare) [is] one of utter disorder, lack of restraint, chaos, and finally Nothingness." (294). Macbeth, Scotland and Nature are all disordered after the murder of Duncan. "Foul" has become "Fair" and the momentum of one evil deed leads to the next as Macbeth careens toward personal and societal chaos. The disintegrating power of evil eats away at Macbeth with each successive crime until he is ultimately emptied of his humanity. This then is essential weakness of evil: it is self-punishing, self-destroying and therefore self-limiting. In writing about evil, philosopher Pierre La Primaudaye, one of Shakespeare's contemporaries, said

> she frameth for and of hir selfe hir own trorment, and beginneth to suffer the pains of hir mischievous deede through the remourse thereof. This is the worme that continually gnaweth the conscience of a malefactor, and accompanieth his miserable life with shame and confusion[28]

Macbeth's course following the murder of Duncan is one slow descent into Nothingness, with each successive action intended to bring security instead resulting in the hardening of his heart and smothering of his soul. This understanding is consistent with St. Augustine's view that moral evils can be traced to the absence of goodness, a state synonymous with the Nothingness Sears evokes in his definition. Macbeth sheds his final threads of humanity when he goes to the witches for consultation. After being warned against Macduff, Macbeth resolves to immediately attack his castle and "give to the edge o' the sword/His wife, his babes, and all unfortunate souls/ That trace him in his line." (*M, IV, 1, 151-53*). The attack is shown on stage and in one of Shakespeare's most horrific scenes, matching for shock value the blinding of Gloucester in *King Lear*, the audience witnesses the casual murder of Macduff's young son. After this act, Macbeth loses any residual sympathy the audience might have held. Now they can only hope for the mad dog to be put down and end the horror of his reign.

In the end, Macbeth becomes a hollow man ruling over a chaotic wasteland, so devoid of human goodness that even the death of his wife fails to move him. His only reaction is the bitter utterance of his most famous soliloquy.

> She should have died hereafter;
> There would have been a time for such a word.
> To-morrow, and to-morrow, and to-morrow,
> Creeps in this petty pace from day to day
> To the last syllable of recorded time,
> And all our yesterdays have lighted fools
> The way to dusty death. Out, out, brief candle!
> Life's but a walking shadow, a poor player
> That struts and frets his hour upon the stage
> And then is heard no more: it is a tale
> Told by an idiot, full of sound and fury,
> Signifying nothing.
>
> (M, V, 5, 17-28)

In these words, we see the depths of despair and hopelessness into which Macbeth has fallen. For him, man is now only a "walking shadow" and life is just a creeping journey toward a "dusty death" full of chaotic "sound and fury" that ultimately signifies nothing. He is ready to meet his own death, not because he is fearless but because he believes what he has said about life's futility in general and his life in particular:

> I have lived long enough: my way of life
> Is fall'n into the sear, the yellow leaf;
> And that which should accompany old age,
> As honour, love, obedience, troops of friends,
> I must not look to have; but, in their stead,
> Curses, not loud but deep, mouth-honour, breath,
>
> (M, V, 3, 22-27)

So with all the forces of Scotland and England aligned against him, Macbeth puts on his armor and goes out to "try the last," finally losing his life in single combat with Macduff.

Macbeth is not inherently a bad man like so many of Shakespeare's villains are. He is not an Aaron nor a Richard III nor an Iago. We are drawn to

Macbeth because of his humanity. As he contemplates the murder of Duncan, we want to cry out, "No! Don't do it!" because we know what will result. And we know that he knows what will result and we pity him because it all seems so tragically inevitable. It is like the proverbial train wreck that we see unfold even before it happens. But unlike the train wreck, Macbeth's crime is not an accident; it is an act of will that could have been aborted up to the point when Macbeth first stuck the dagger in Duncan. And when the deed is done, in spite of the all the internal debate we have been privy to, in spite of Lady Macbeth's cajoling and bullying, in spite of the supernatural trappings of the weird sisters, we are still left to ponder what drove this essentially good man to this foul dead. The act is no more explicable than the act of Adam, eating the apple in the Garden of Eden. Adam too knew his action was wrong, but tempted by his wife who was in turn tempted by the serpent, he exercised his free will by eating the apple and like Macbeth he immediately felt shame for his action. It is interesting to note that the eating of the fruit of the knowledge of good and evil was motivated, like Macbeth's act of murder, by ambition. What was to be gained by the act of defiance? The serpent said to Eve, "God knows that your eyes will be opened when you eat it. You will become just like God, knowing everything, both good and evil."[29] It is their desire to be as God that drives Adam to partake of the fruit and as a result, like Macbeth, he is first cursed with spiritual death followed by physical death. By mirroring the story of Eden in *Macbeth*, Shakespeare reminds the audience of the fallen nature of man and suggests that given the choice of good and evil, man is predisposed to follow the evil path. Macbeth's tragedy is the tragedy of all men whose "heart[s are] evil from ... youth" and it is only through the grace of God that man can escape his predestined fate.[30]

Notes

1. Tillyard, E. M. W. *The Elizabethan World Picture.* (New York: Vintage Books, 1942) 5-6.

2. Hooker, Richard, "Early Christianity," 1996 *http://www.wsu.edu/~dee/CHRIST/AUG.HTM*

3. King James I. *Works* (1592). http://www.wwnorton.com/college/history/ralph/workbook/ralprs20.htm

4. *Elizabeth I's Speech to the Troops at Tilbury,* 1588. http://www.nationalcenter.org/ElizabethITilbury.html

5. Polydore Vergil's *Anglica Historia,* Chapter XXV (1534). http://www.philological.bham.ac.uk/polverg/25eng.html

6.   Ferguson, Wallace K. *The Renaissance in Historical Thought.* (Toronto: University of Toronto Press, 2006) 5.

7.   Marlowe, Christopher. *"The First Part of Tamburlaine the Great"* in *Christopher Marlowe The Complete Plays.* (Baltimore, MD: Penguin Books, 1969) 129.

8.   More, Thomas.   *The history of King Richard the thirde.* http://www.luminarium.org/renascence-editions/r3.html

9.   Ibid.

10. Ibid.

11. Ibid.

12   Polydore Vergil's Anglica Historia, Chapter XXV (1534). http://www.philological.bham.ac.uk/polverg/25eng.html

13. More, Thomas.   *The history of King Richard the thirde.* http://www.luminarium.org/renascence-editions/r3.html

14. Fremouw, William., Ragatz, Laurie., Schwartz, Rebecca., Anderson, Ryan., Schenk, Allison. and Kania, Kristina. "Criminal Thinking, Aggression, and Psychopathy in Late High School Bully-Victims -poster" Westin Bayshore Hotel, Vancouver, BC, Canada, Mar 17, 2010 <Not Available>. 2011-06-05 http://www.allacademic.com/meta/p406323_index.html

15. Polydore Vergil's Anglica Historia, Chapter XXV (1534). http://www.philological.bham.ac.uk/polverg/25eng.html

16. Aristotle, *Poetics* VI 1449b, 2-3. http://www.perseus.tufts.edu/hopper/text?doc=Perseus%3Atext%3A1999.01.0056%3Asection%3D1449bPoetics, VI 1449b 2-3

17. Ibid, 1452b, 1453a.

18. Bruster, Douglas, and Robert Weimann.   *Prologues to Shakespeare's Theatre,* (New York: Routledge, 2004) 26-27.

19. Garber, Marjorie. *Shakespeare and Modern Culture.* (New York: Pantheon Books, 2008) 112-4.

20. Eleanor Prosser.   *Hamlet and Revenge, 2nd ed.*   (Stanford, California: Stanford University Press, 1971).

21. Romans 12:17, 13:4.

22. Granville-Barker, Henry. *Prefaces to Shakespeare.* (New York: Hill and Wang, 1970), 269.

23. Bradley, A.C. *Shakespearean Tragedy* (London: 1963), p. 288.

24. *Macbeth's Curse: Link Between Sleeplessness And Paranoia Identified.* http://www.sciencedaily.com/releases/2009/01/090108150857.htm

25. Plato, *Apology of Socrates,* 40 b.

26. *The Personal Tutelary Spirit: An Abbreviated Abramelin Operation.* http://neuromagick.com/the-personal-tutelary-spirit-an-abbreviated-abramelin-operation

27. Knowlton, E. C. "The Genius of Spencer," *Studies in Philology*, XXV (1928), 441.

28. La Primaudaye quoted in L. C. Sears. *Shakespeare's Philosophy of Evil.* (Quincy, Mass: The Christopher Publishing House, 1974), 303-4)

29. Genesis 3:5

30. Genesis 8:21

THE TRAITORS

Treason is a little discussed or well understood crime at the beginning of the 21st century. In the United States, there has been only one indictment for treason lodged against a citizen since 1952 when, on October 11, 2006, a federal grand jury charged Adam Yahiye Gadahn with treason for appearing in videos as a spokesman for al-Qaeda and threatened attacks on American soil. Article III, Section 3 of the U.S. Constitution says that treason "shall consist only in levying War against them, or in adhering to their Enemies, giving them Aid and Comfort." *Oran's Dictionary of the Law* (1983) expands on the definition of treason as "... [a]...citizen's actions to help a foreign government overthrow, make war against, or seriously injure the [parent nation]." Since the Constitution came into effect, there have been fewer than 40 federal prosecutions for treason and even fewer convictions.[1] The last execution for treason against the United States was conducted against Herbert Hans Haupt, a German born naturalized citizen convicted as an "enemy agent" by a military tribunal, and carried out on August 8, 1942. The last conviction for treason against the U.S. occurred in 1952 when Tomoya Kawakita was found guilty of torturing American prisoners of war while serving as a civilian interpreter for the Japanese during the Second World War. Kawakita, a natural born American citizen who defected to Japan, was given a death sentence, but President Dwight Eisenhower commuted that sentence to life imprisonment. President John Kennedy pardoned Kawakita on October 24, 1963 on the condition that he be deported to Japan for life.

Treason during the time of Shakespeare was far more pervasive and broadly, if precisely, defined. The Treason Act of 1351, still in effect during the reign of Elizabeth I, defined both "high treason" and "petty treason". One could be found guilty of high treason if they:

1. *"compassed or imagined" (i.e. planned) the death of the King, his wife or his eldest son and heir;*
2. *violated the King's companion, the King's eldest daughter if she was unmarried or the wife of the King's eldest son and heir;*
3. *levied war against the King in his Realm;*
4. *adhered to the King's enemies in his Realm, giving them aid and comfort in his Realm or elsewhere;*
5. *counterfeited the Great Seal or the Privy Seal*

6. *counterfeited English coinage or imported counterfeit English coinage;*

7. *killed the Chancellor, Treasurer (this office is now in commission), one of the King's Justices (either of the King's Bench or the Common Pleas), a Justice in Eyre, an Assize judge, and "all other Justices," while they are performing their offices*[2]

To this list Elizabeth I's Religious Act of 1580 added it was high treason for "an individual to attempt to defend the jurisdiction of the Pope over the English Church for a third time (a first offence being a misdemeanor and a second offence a felony), or for a Roman Catholic priest to enter the realm and refuse to conform to the English Church, or to purport to release a subject of his allegiance to the Crown or the Church of England and to reconcile him or her with a foreign power." The exact number of arrests and trials for high treason during Shakespeare's lifetime is not reported, but the number of plots and conspiracies against Elizabeth and her successor, James I, would suggest numbers in the hundreds if not thousands. For example, in the so-called Babington plot (1586) intended to assassinate Queen Elizabeth and place the Roman Catholic Mary, Queen of Scots on England's throne. The plot was foiled and ultimately resulted in the execution of Mary and 14 conspirators for treason. At the very beginning of Elizabeth's reign, five conspirators were executed when they attempted to supplant Elizabeth with Lady Jane Grey. Eleven traitors were executed for the more famous Gunpowder Plot of 1605 which planned to detonate casks of gunpowder under the House of Lords with the intention of killing King James I and most of England's aristocracy Many other smaller plots were also uncovered between these two and uncounted Catholic missionaries and adherents also went to the gallows convicted of high treason.

By legal definitions of high treason, all of Shakespeare's usurpers would objectively qualify as traitors to the rightful rulers they served. Most like Macbeth, Claudius and Richard III are driven by pure ambition; a few like Henry Bolingbrook and Richard, Duke of York are driven by more ambiguous motives, and at least one, Richmond (later Henry VII) is driven by the need to destroy a monster who has murdered his way to the throne. Of course one man's traitor is another man's revolutionary hero and we must keep in mind that history is written by the victor. For Richard III, Richmond would be a traitor, but for Richmond, Richard III would be an illegitimate ruler who was owed no allegiance. Since Richmond was victorious, history has painted Richard with the blackest of brushes and Richmond as the savior of England. Had Richard won, Richmond would have been relegated in history as just another failed rebellious traitor like Guy Fawkes, the principal plotter of the Gunpowder Plot.

The precise legal definition of the crime of treason in the Treason Act of 1351 and the U.S. Constitution suggests that the term can only be applied in the realm of politics, but realistically we know that there if a more general application of the term in western culture. The common definition of treason means actions by a person who "betrays their own political party, nation, family, friends, ethnic group, team, religion, social class, or other group to which they may belong."[4] The word "traitor" is derived from the Latin *traditor* which means "one who delivers" and originates with Judas' handing Jesus over to the Roman authorities. [5] In this context, one need not be a usurper or regicide to be a traitor, it is sufficient to simply betray someone you owe loyalty. Iago, then, is a traitor to Othello. Edmund is a traitor to his family. So too are Romeo and Juliet. In *Henry VI, Part II* the Duke of Suffolk betrays Henry by seducing his wife Queen Margaret, making the Duke both an adulterer and a traitor. That said, the majority of traitors in Shakespeare are involved with power politics and their actions have national implications. Of these, again, the majority are usurpers who intend to claim power for themselves, but there are three notable exception and they will be examined in detail: Brutus and Cassius as portrayed in *Julius Caesar* and Coriolanus in the play bearing his name.

THINK HIM AS A SERPENT'S EGG...AND KILL HIM IN THE SHELL: BRUTUS: JULIUS CAESAR

On November 25, 1864, a single engagement production of *Julius Caesar* was performed at the Winter Garden Theatre in New York City. The performance was arranged to help pay for the placement of a statue of William Shakespeare in Central Park and the full theater that evening raised $3,500 for this purpose. The performance was a critical as well as a financial success and in the waning months of the American Civil War, the play's themes of civil war, oppression and tyrannicide were particularly relevant. In fact the War nearly overshadowed the performance. The drama was nearly interrupted when a fire, one of the dozen set by Confederate sympathizers with the intention of burning New York to the ground, engulfed the nearby Lafarge House and almost spread to The Winter Garden Theater. *The New York Times* called the arson "one of the most fiendish and inhuman acts known in modern times." Fortunately, the fire was quickly extinguished and did not spread to the packed theater. The show went on while the fire alarms sounded outside.

The draw of the Winter Garden *Julius Caesar* was not only its thematic timeliness and its fund raising aspirations; the crowd also filled the theater to see the first and only performance of three brothers on the same stage. Each an accomplished and popular actor in his right, they were also renowned as the offspring of one of America's most famous Shakespeareans, Junius Brutus Booth. The famous children were Edwin, Junius and John Wilkes Booth. Although he once said that his favorite character was Brutus, the youngest of the three brothers, John played Marc Antony against Edwin's Brutus and Junius' Cassius. A little over four months later, John would take on the role of Brutus in a real life tragedy that cast Abraham Lincoln in the role of the doomed Julius Caesar.

The tragedy played out on Good Friday, April 14, 1865. Less than a week before, the Army of Northern Virginia lead by General Robert E. Lee surrendered to the Army of the Potomac at Appomattox Court House. The American Civil War was effectively over. Lincoln was in a celebratory mood and decided to attend an evening performance of *Our American Cousin*, an English farce, at Ford's Theater with his wife. There, at about 10:30 p.m., John Wilkes Booth silently entered the President's box and fired a single shot from a Derringer into the back of the President's head. Slashing the arm of Lincoln's guest, Major Henry Rathbone, with a large knife, Booth leapt from the box to the stage below, a drop of roughly twelve feet. In the process, Booth fractured his left fibula just above the ankle. On stage, Booth faced the audience and brandishing the bloody knife, cried out "*Sic semper tyrannis!*" the Virginia state motto, meaning "*Thus always to tyrants!*" He then fled the theater, mounted a waiting horse, and made good his escape. The President, comatose, was carried to a boarding house across from Ford's Theater, where he lingered for nine hours, before drawing his last breath at 7:22 a.m. on April 15.

The assassination of Lincoln was part of a larger plot that that intended to also murder Vice President Andrew Johnson and Secretary of State William H. Seward. Around the same time Booth fired his pistol at Lincoln's head, co-conspirator Lewis Powell was attacking the Secretary of State in his home. Powell was fought off by members of Seward' household but the would-be assassin managed to inflict near-fatal wounds on Seward. At the same time, another of the conspirators, George Atzerodt, was supposed to go to the residence of Vice President Johnson and murder him. Apparently losing his nerve at the last minute, Atzerodt got drunk and wandered the streets of Washington instead. Meanwhile, Booth rendezvoused with another conspirator, David Herold, and together they headed south into Virginia. Their first stop was in Southern Maryland at the home of Samuel A. Mudd, a local doctor who determined that Booth's leg had been broken and put it in a splint. The pair then hid out in Maryland's Zekiah Swamp near the northern shore of the Potomac River awaiting passage across the river. The crossing was achieved on April 22. On the afternoon of April 24, now in Virginia, they made their way the farm of Richard H. Garrett, a tobacco farmer. It was there that Union soldiers from the 16th New York Cavalry caught up with them. Trapped in Garrett's barn, Herold surrendered, but Booth announced that he would not be taken alive. The troopers set fire to the barn. As Booth fled the inferno, he was shot in the neck, his spinal cord severed. He died two hours later and asked a Union soldier attending him to tell his mother, "I die for my country." The rest of the conspirators were rounded up by the end of the month.

The central question for my purposes is "Did Booth see himself as a Brutus murdering a Caesar for the good of his country?" as his message to his mother suggests. Booth was known to be a Confederate sympathizer vehement in his denunciation of the Lincoln Administration. According to some reports, Booth was actively engaged in smuggling medical supplies to Confederate forces. He also strongly opposed the abolition of slavery in the United States and Lincoln's proposal to extend voting rights to recently emancipated slaves. In these beliefs he was at odds with his brother Edwin who was just as staunch in his support for the Union. In the interest of family peace, they seldom discussed politics after Edwin ordered John from his home following a particularly ugly argument. Elder brother

Junius was "neutral," but probably had southern sympathies. He, in fact, was briefly arrested following the Lincoln assassination on suspicion of having fore-knowledge of his younger brother's plans, but was soon released.

John's original plan was to kidnap President Lincoln following his re-election in 1864. Once in Confederate hands, Lincoln would be exchanged for the release of Confederate Army prisoners of war held captive in Northern prisons and, Booth reasoned, bring the war to an end by emboldening opposition to the war in the North or forcing Union recognition of the Confederate government. A change in the President's schedule on the day the kidnapping was planned thwarted the plot and before another attempt could be made, Richmond fell and the War ended. By targeting Lincoln and his two immediate successors to the presidency for assassination, Booth seems to have intended to decapitate the Union government and throw it into a state of panic and confusion, creating sufficient chaos within the Union that the Confederate government could reorganize and continue the war, that failing, to avenge the South's defeat.

In the final analysis, however, it seems that the final words ever spoken by John Wilkes Booth on the stage to an audience were " *Sic semper tyrannis!*"," a phrase said to have originated with his favorite Shakespeare character, Marcus Junius Brutus during the assassination of Julius Caesar. Booth's loathing of the tyranny he found in the administration of Abraham Lincoln and his love of the Southern way of life combined with his theatrical nature and his longing for immortality blended at that brief moment on the stage of Ford's Theater. He needed to announce to the world what he wanted to be remembered for and his choice of words, clearly well prepared, memorably defined his motive and wrote his epitaph.

It is interesting to note that *"Sic semper tyrannis!"* is not a line from Shakespeare nor does it appear in conjunction with Brutus in any of the standard classical texts. It is, however, well known to be the State motto for the Commonwealth of Virginia and while Booth may have had Brutus in mind when speaking this line, he surely also was making conscious reference to the heart of the Confederacy. In fact, on close examination of the words and actions of John Wilkes Booth, his similarity to Shakespeare's Brutus becomes increasing tenuous. Yes, both Booth and Brutus assassinated a powerful political leader, but Booth committed the act alone while Brutus was one of many. Booth was driven more by his hatred of Lincoln for perceived acts of tyranny while Brutus was driven more by fear of future acts of tyranny. Booth was full of anger; Brutus was full of sadness. Booth was a man of passion; Brutus, a man of the mind.

Shakespeare's Julius Caesar opens at the conclusion of a Roman civil war that pitted Gnaeus Pompeius Magnus, also known as Pompey the Great, against Gaius Julius Caesar. Julius Caesar was appointed governor of northern Italy, southeastern Europe, and southern France following his victories in the Gallic Wars. The term of his governorship was set at five years, and granted him immunity from prosecution for any irregularities that occurred during his tenure In 50 BC, the five years being up, the Senate of Rome, led by Pompey who had been appointed sole Consul, ordered Caesar to disband his army and return to Rome. Caesar, fearful he would be prosecuted if he entered Rome without the immunity, refused. Pompey accused Caesar of insubordination and treason and in January 49 BC, Caesar crossed the Rubicon River (the frontier boundary of Italy) and ignited civil war. A year later, Caesar decisively defeated Pompey's forces at the Battle of Pharsalus and Pompey was forced to flee to Egypt where he was promptly assassinated by agents of Egypt's young king Ptolemy XIII who hoped to gain favor with victorious Caesar. With Pompey out of the way, Caesar was appointed Dictator of Rome in 46 B.C., a position of absolute power serving as the chief executive and supreme military commander of the Republic. Normally the dictatorship was held for a period of one year, but at the end of the first year, the Senate voted to make Caesar "*Dictator perpetuo*" or "dictator for life." This effectively put an end to the Roman Republic in favor of a monarchy. All that remained was for Caesar to be named king.

Shakespeare opens his play with a street scene that sets up the basic conflict that fuels the drama. The Roman commoners are shown adorning statues of Caesar with laurel wreaths (a symbol of divinity and royalty) and generally rejoicing in Caesar's triumph over Pompey (that actually occurred four years before the start of the play). The tribunes, Flavius and Marullus, berate the commoners for their fickleness, reminding them that no so far in the past they had similarly cheered for Pompey. Dispersing the crowd they set about removing the adornments and, we later learn, are arrested for doing so. The scene tells us several things. First, the common people are fickle and support anyone in power; currently they support Caesar. Second, the common people support the idea of appointing Caesar king as evidenced by their adorning Caesar's statues with the symbols of royalty. Third, the political class represented by Flavius and Marullus oppose a monarchy and fear Caesar as a potential tyrant who will destroy the Republic. And finally that their fears are not unfounded because Caesar's agents promptly arrest them for speaking out against Caesar.

In the second scene, we meet the play's principals: Brutus, Cassius and Caesar himself. We learn a great deal of Caesar by direct observation and by the report of others. In Caesar, we discover a divided man: the weak mortal man who is subject to all the same frailties of any man and the living legend, a demi-God who "doth bestride the narrow world/ Like a Colossus." (JC, I, ii). This distinction recalls the theory of the two bodies of the king that we have encountered before.

> [T]he King has two Capacities, for he has two Bodies, the one whereof is a Body natural, consisting of natural Members as every other Man has, and in this he is subject to Passions and to Death as other Men are: the other is a Body politic, and the Members thereof are his Subjects, and he and his Subjects together compose the corporation, as Southcote said, and he is incorporated with them, and they with him, and he is the Head, and they are the Members, and he has sole Government of them: and this Body is not subject to Passions as the other is, nor to Death, for as to this Body the King never dies, and his natural Death is not called in our Law (as Harper said) the Death of the King, but the Demise of the King, not signifying by the Word (Demise) that the Body politic of the King is dead, but that there is a Separation of the two Bodies, and that the Body politic is transferred and conveyed over from the Body natural now dead, or now removed from the Dignity royal, to another Body natural.[6]

Although not yet king, Caesar has already taken on some of the accoutrements of kingship. He refers to himself in the third person. To the soothsayer he says "Speak; Caesar is turn'd to hear." (JC, I, 2, 17). And later, commenting on Cassius, he says to Antony:

> Such men as he be never at heart's ease
> Whiles they behold a greater than themselves,
> And therefore are they very dangerous.
> I rather tell thee what is to be fear'd
> Than what I fear; for always I am Caesar.
> (JC, I, 2, 208-12)

Ironically, these lines are immediately undermined when Caesar adds: Come on my right hand, for this ear is deaf, (JC, I, 2, 213). Caesar's regal bearing is backed by real power as indicated by the deference with which he is treated by others. When Antony is instructed to "touch Calpurnia" to cure her infertility as he passes her during the race being run to celebrate the Feast of Lupercal, he replies "When Caesar says 'do this,' it is perform'd." JC, I, 2, 10). But again the regal Caesar is undermined when shows his all too human faith in the supernatural. And even at the very moment when the crowd is calling for him to be king, an honor he refuses though perhaps reluctantly, he "fell down in the market-place, and foamed at mouth, and was speechless," (JC, I, 2, 252) reminding all that for all his greatness he is still a man, subject to all human weaknesses.

While the games go on, Brutus and Cassius stay back and discuss the current state of affairs. Cassius has little good to say about Caesar. He chafes at Caesar's greatness and his subordinate position in Rome. It is not so much a fear that

Caesar may be crowned that irks him, but that any man should be awarded such power over him. For Cassius, it is personal; it is not so much that he wishes to elevate his own position to that of Caesar's as he wishes to pull Caesar down to his level. He is no usurper, but instead has more in common with Iago who acted against Othello out of petty spite. He sums up his position when he tells Brutus "I had as lief not be as live to be/ In awe of such a thing as I myself. "(JC, I, 2, 95-96). He reminds Brutus:

> I was born free as Caesar; so were you:
> We both have fed as well, and we can both
> Endure the winter's cold as well as he:
>
> (JC, I, 2, 97-99)

He scoffs at Caesar's human frailty, describing Caesar's near drowning in the Tiber and an epileptic episode Caesar suffered in Spain and he concludes:

> Ye gods, it doth amaze me
> A man of such a feeble temper should
> So get the start of the majestic world
> And bear the palm alone.
>
> (JC, I, ii, 128-31)

Cassius then personalizes the argument comparing Caesar to Brutus:

> Brutus and Caesar: what should be in that 'Caesar'?
> Why should that name be sounded more than yours?
> Write them together, yours is as fair a name;
> Sound them, it doth become the mouth as well;
> Weigh them, it is as heavy; conjure with 'em,
> Brutus will start a spirit as soon as Caesar.
>
> (JC, I, 2, 142-47)

Then Cassius calls up Brutus' ancestor to appeal to Brutus' love for the Republic:

> There was a Brutus once that would have brook'd
> The eternal devil to keep his state in Rome
> As easily as a king.
>
> (JC, I, 2, 159-61)

Here Cassius is referring to Lucius Junius Brutus who Brutus counted as an ancestor. Lucius was one of the founders of the Roman Republic who overthrew the monarchy of the Tarquins in 509 BC. It is finally this argument that seems to move Brutus. Throughout Cassius' rant against the personal foibles of Caesar, Brutus has voiced only one concern: "I do fear, the people/ Choose Caesar for their king." (JC, I, 2, 78-9). He gives no thought to Cassius' slander, but because he can imagine hard times ahead, he agrees to think on what Cassius has said and talk with him again.

The character of Cassius is further exposed in the next scene. It is night and Rome is gripped in a storm of supernatural proportion, the kind of storm that always foreshadows evil events in Shakespeare's plays. Cassius encounters the cowed Casca on the street. Unlike the unnerved Casca, Cassius revels in the storm and defies its fury:

> I have walk'd about the streets,
> Submitting me unto the perilous night,
> And, thus unbraced, Casca, as you see,
> Have bared my bosom to the thunder-stone;
> And when the cross blue lightning seem'd to open
> The breast of heaven, I did present myself
> Even in the aim and very flash of it.
>
> (JC, I, 3, 46-52)

When asked his reason for such unreasonable behavior, Cassius explains that the storm is like Caesar, a thing grown beyond its normal natural, capable of inspiring awe and fear in lesser men, but not in Cassius. Cassius, he says, will deliver Cassius from bondage and Casca takes this to mean by suicide, but was Cassius means is assassination of the inevitable tyranny of Caesar. Cassius' cynical opinion of his fellow Romans says as much about Cassius as it does about the Romans.

> Poor man! I know he would not be a wolf,
> But that he sees the Romans are but sheep:
> He were no lion, were not Romans hinds.
>
> (JC, I, 3,104-6)

Cassius is unable to imagine a man not becoming a tyrant when he is given unlimited power over other humans who are so ripe for and deserving of tyranny. What we learn here is not that Caesar would necessarily become a tyrant but that if their positions were reversed and Cassius made king, by necessity Cassius would become a tyrant.

While Cassius is motivated by self-interest and personal animus for Caesar, Brutus, who says he loves Caesar, is motivated by more by patriotic concern for Rome. Like Cassius, he can only see in the kingship of Caesar the inevitable road to tyranny and the death of the Republic. However, Brutus lacks Cassius' certainty saying of Caesar "He would be crown'd:/ How that might change his nature, there's the question." (JC, II, 1, 12-3). He has no reason from Caesar's past actions to believe this. Caesar, he says, has always shown himself to be ruled by reason, but he also notes "... 'tis a common proof, / That lowliness is young ambition's ladder, / Whereto the climber-upward turns his face/... Looks in the clouds, scorning the base degrees/ By which he did ascend. So Caesar may." (JC, II, 1, 21-7). Following this logic, Brutus arrives at the same conclusion that Cassius has. He will without animus:

> think him as a serpent's egg
> Which, hatch'd, would, as his kind, grow mischievous,
> And kill him in the shell.
>
> (JC, II, i, 32-4)

Thus resolved, when Cassius and the other conspirators come to his home to learn his mind, he assumes the leader's role. While it was Cassius' plot, Brutus is essential to its successful execution because he is highly respected by the common people. Even Cassius defers to him. When it is suggested that the conspirators murder Marc Antony along with Caesar, Brutus rejects the proposal because he fears it will make the assassination appear too bloody. He cautions restraint saying:

> Let's kill him boldly, but not wrathfully;
> Let's carve him as a dish fit for the gods,
> Not hew him as a carcass fit for hounds ...
> This shall make
> Our purpose necessary and not envious:
> Which so appearing to the common eyes,
> We shall be call'd purgers, not murderers.
>
> (JC, II, 1,172-4, 177-80)

Again, the conspirators agree although Cassius is clearly uncomfortable with the decision. Finally, Brutus cautions the conspirators in words similar to those spoken by Lady Macbeth to her husband before the murder of King Duncan: "Let not our looks put on our purposes,/ But bear it as our Roman actors do" (JC, II, 1,225-6).

The conspirators gather at the Senate and when Caesar arrives they fall upon him as one, inflicting 23 cuts that extinguish the life of the great man. Brutus, in the aftermath of the murder, encourages his co-conspirators:

> ...let us bathe our hands in Caesar's blood
> Up to the elbows, and besmear our swords:
> Then walk we forth, even to the market-place,
> And, waving our red weapons o'er our heads,
> Let's all cry 'Peace, freedom and liberty!'
>
> (JC, III, 1, 106-10)

Deluded in the rightness of their actions, Cassius adds that the co-conspirator shall "be call'd/ The men that gave their country liberty." (JC, III, 1, 16-17). They solemnly believe that the mob of commoners will embrace them as liberators once they simply explain calmly and rationally the reason for their action. Marc Antony encourages them in their naïve belief when he asks "Why and wherein Caesar was dangerous." (JC, III, 1, 222). Brutus answers him, saying "Our reasons are so full of good regard/ That were you, Antony, the son of Caesar,/ You should be satisfied." (JC, III, 1, 224-6). "That's all I seek" says Antony, and an opportunity to speak over the body of his fallen friend. Accepting Antony's passivity as assent to the assassination, Brutus, over the objection of Cassius, agrees to allow Antony an opportunity to eulogize Caesar. Brutus than goes to the citizens to explain the reason for the shocking murder of the man they thought should be their king. In his address to the citizens, Brutus relies on a single explanation:

> If there be any in this assembly, any dear friend of
> Caesar's, to him I say, that Brutus' love to Caesar
> was no less than his. If then that friend demand
> why Brutus rose against Caesar, this is my answer:
> --Not that I loved Caesar less, but that I loved
> Rome more. Had you rather Caesar were living and
> die all slaves, than that Caesar were dead, to live
> all free men? As Caesar loved me, I weep for him;
> as he was fortunate, I rejoice at it; as he was
> valiant, I honour him: but, as he was ambitious, I
> slew him.

Strangely Brutus offers no specifics to demonstrate Caesar's ambition. He assumes that his audience knows of Caesar's ambition and for a brief period, the mob seems to agree with him. Similarly, he offers no explanation of why Caesar was a threat to Rome, but again the mob seems to accept his assertion at face value. They cry out "Give him [Brutus] a statue with his ancestors." and "Let him be Caesar." (JC, III, 2, 50-51). Seeming to have won over the crowd, Brutus yields the floor to Antony. Antony knows the mob better than Brutus and appeals not to their logic, but to their emotions. He attacks Brutus' assertion of Caesar's ambition by relating specific actions by Caesar that refute Brutus' accusation. Speaking of Caesar, Antony says:

> He hath brought many captives home to Rome
> Whose ransoms did the general coffers fill:
> Did this in Caesar seem ambitious?
> When that the poor have cried, Caesar hath wept:
> Ambition should be made of sterner stuff:
> Yet Brutus says he was ambitious;
> And Brutus is an honourable man.
> You all did see that on the Lupercal
> I thrice presented him a kingly crown,
> Which he did thrice refuse: was this ambition?
> Yet Brutus says he was ambitious;
> And, sure, he is an honourable man.
>
> *(JC, III, 2, 88-99)*

The citizens immediately begin to question Brutus' explanation. When Antony pauses, they begin discussing what they have heard. One says "Me thinks there is much reason in his sayings." And another says, "Mark'd ye his words? He would not take the crown; Therefore 'tis certain he was not ambitious." And yet another comments, "Caesar has had great wrong." (JC, III, 2, 108, 112).

Antony returns and unveils the butchered body of Caesar to the crowd. He shows each wound to the body, and points out where each of the conspirators struck, concluding with the wound made by Brutus.

> This was the most unkindest cut of all;
> For when the noble Caesar saw him stab,

Ingratitude, more strong than traitors' arms,
Quite vanquish'd him: then burst his mighty heart;

(JC, III, 2, 183-6)

The crowd now is turned against the conspirators. They cry out in unison "Revenge! About! Seek! Burn! Fire! Kill! Slay! / Let not a traitor live!" and "We'll burn the house of Brutus." (JC, III, 2, 205-32). But Antony is not done yet. Brutus, he reminds the citizens, has said that Caesar was a danger to the citizens of Rome. Antony refutes this by reading from Caesar's will where he has bequeathed to each of the citizens of Rome "seventy-five drachmas" and has left to the City "all his walks,/ His private arbors and new-planted orchards,/ On this side Tiber;" for the common recreation of the citizens. (JC, III, 2, 242, 247-51). Hearing this, the mob can no longer be restrained. They gather up torches and set out to take revenge on the conspirators.

Shakespeare was always contemptuous of mobs. Here he shows them as easily swayed by cleaver rhetoric and mindlessly violent once inflamed. In one of his earliest plays, *Henry VI, Part II*, he dramatizes the violence of the mob following the rebellious Jack Cade. The clownish rebel promises his followers:

There shall be in England seven
halfpenny loaves sold for a penny: the three-hooped
pot; shall have ten hoops and I will make it felony
to drink small beer: all the realm shall be in
common; and in Cheapside shall my palfrey go to
grass: and when I am king, as king I will be,-

(2HVI, IV, 2, 65-70)

His foolish followers famously cry out: "*The first thing we do, let's kill all the lawyers.*" (HVI, 2, IV, ii, 68) and they take into custody the hapless clerk of Chatham whose only crime is that he can read and write. The mob takes the Clerk away to "*hang him with his pen and ink-horn about his neck.*" (2HVI, IV, 2, 110). Cade rallies them with the words: "*Now show yourselves men; 'tis for liberty. / We will not leave one lord, one gentleman: / Spare none...*" (2HVI, IV, 2, 183-5) foreshadowing the horrors of the French Revolution and subsequent instances of class warfare. Similarly, in the next section, we will again see the mob manipulated and acting badly in *Coriolanus*.

Shakespeare long before the formal studies of mob psychology demonstrates in Julius Caesar a clear understanding of how mobs think and act. He shows how members of the mob are prone to acting in ways that they would deem immoral or unjust if in control of their behavior. Individuals tend to ignore or avoid one's conscience or rational judgment in favor of the group's dominate spokespersons. By joining the ethos of the mob, the individual subsumes his personal values and is able to deflect blame and responsibility for their actions upon the group. By demonstrating the irrationality of the mob and its propensity for creating chaos, Shakespeare endorses the need for a monarchy to control the populace. He, in fact, mirrors Cassius' opinion of the common people as sheep and hinds. Perceptively, Shakespeare demonstrates the contagious nature of ideas in forming the group's consensus by showing how Citizens One through Four play off each other in response to the speeches of Brutus and Antony. After hearing Brutus, notice how each citizen builds on the enthusiasm of his predecessor:

> FIRST CITIZEN:
> Bring him with triumph home unto his house.
> SECOND CITIZEN:
> Give him a statue with his ancestors.
> THIRD CITIZEN:
> Let him be Caesar.
> FOURTH CITIZEN:
> Caesar's better parts
> Shall be crown'd in Brutus.
> FIRST CITIZEN:
> We'll bring him to his house
> With shouts and clamours.
>
> (JC, III, 2, 49-53)

Before Antony's speech, the crowd replicated the pattern in their support of Brutus:

> FOURTH CITIZEN:
> 'Twere best he speak no harm of Brutus here.
> FIRST CITIZEN:
> This Caesar was a tyrant.
> THIRD CITIZEN:
> Nay, that's certain:
> We are blest that Rome is rid of him.
>
> (JC, III, 2, 67-70)

But when Antony speaks and unveils Caesar's mutilated body, the mood of the crowd shifts and anger flows through the assembled citizens:

> FIRST CITIZEN:
> O piteous spectacle!
> SECOND CITIZEN:
> O noble Caesar!
> THIRD CITIZEN:
> O woful day!
> FOURTH CITIZEN:
> O traitors, villains!
> FIRST CITIZEN:
> O most bloody sight!
> SECOND CITIZEN:
> We will be revenged.
> ALL:
> Revenge! About! Seek! Burn! Fire! Kill! Slay!
> Let not a traitor live!
>
> (JC, III, 2, 198-250)

The blind rage of the mob is demonstrated when they encounter the unfortunate poet Cinna who has the same name as one of the assassins and for this "crime" the mob drags him away and kills him. Again, the contagion of rage races through the mob and the rage is vented indiscriminately.

> CINNA THE POET
> Truly, my name is Cinna.
> FIRST CITIZEN
> Tear him to pieces; he's a conspirator.
> CINNA THE POET
> I am Cinna the poet, I am Cinna the poet.
> FOURTH CITIZEN
> Tear him for his bad verses, tear him for his bad verses.
> CINNA THE POET
> I am not Cinna the conspirator.
> FOURTH CITIZEN
> It is no matter, his name's Cinna; pluck but his
> name out of his heart, and turn him going.
> THIRD CITIZEN

Tear him, tear him! Come, brands ho! fire-brands:
to Brutus', to Cassius'; burn all: some to Decius'
house, and some to Casca's; some to Ligarius': away, go!

(JC, III, 2, 27-37)

The contagious nature of crowd behavior is rooted in in the then respected Galenic humoral theory that posited that the human body is essentially porous and open to the influence of outside forces including the humors of other people. Antony's observation that *"passion is catching"* (3.1.283) indicates he appreciates that humoral contagion spreads through all but the most rational and balanced of individuals in the populace. The temperament and heath of an individual depended upon the balance of four humors (black bile, yellow bile, phlegm, blood) and the excess or deficit of any of the four could influence once response to any stimulus. Caesar, for example, would likely be classified as "choleric," that is having a natural excess of yellow bile. The choleric was fundamentally ambitious and leader-like. They were excessively aggressive, energetic and passionate. They could easily dominate people of other temperaments, especially phlegmatic types, that class of individuals who are typically happy and quiet, e.g., the normal neutral state of the sheep-like citizens of Rome until they are "infected" by the humors of others. Antony, a normally sanguine (blood) ruled individual, pleasure seeking, sociable and charismatic, is infused with a "booster" of the choleric humor when he views the body of the murdered Caesar. With this excess of yellow bile, his choleric rage seems to erupt from his very pores to infect the phlegmatic crowd and transform it into a choleric mob. And just as medical treatises of the time recommended bloodletting to cure a variety of physical maladies, a form of violent bloodletting is required by to the humoral balance of the mob.

Just as Caesar is choleric, so too is he chief detractor, Cassius. Caesar, in Shakespeare, shows the more positive aspects of the choleric personality. For Cassius, he presents its darker side. Robert Burton in *Anatomy of Melancholy* (1621) writes that

> *[Cholerics] are bold and impudent, and of a more hairbrain disposition, apt to quarrel and think of such things, battles, combats, and their manhood; furious, impatient in discourse, stiff, irrefragable and prodigious in their tenents (sic); and if they be moved, most violent, outrageous, ready to disgrace, provoke any, to kill themselves and others.*[7]

Cassius certainly meets this description. It is interesting that we learn a good deal about Caesar from Cassius and about Cassius from Caesar. Caesar calls

Cassius a "great observer" who looks for hidden motives and machinations in the men he meets (*JC*, I. 2. 201). Caesar, himself a keen observer, labels Cassius' nature rightly: "*Yond Cassius has a lean and hungry look; / He thinks too much: such men are dangerous.*" (*JC*, I, 2, 199-200). When Antony dismisses Caesar's concern, Caesar rightfully replies:

> *Would he were fatter! But I fear him not:*
> *Yet if my name were liable to fear,*
> *I do not know the man I should avoid*
> *So soon as that spare Cassius. He reads much;*
> *He is a great observer and he looks*
> *Quite through the deeds of men: he loves no plays,*
> *As thou dost, Antony; he hears no music;*
> *Seldom he smiles, and smiles in such a sort*
> *As if he mock'd himself and scorn'd his spirit*
> *That could be moved to smile at any thing.*
> *Such men as he be never at heart's ease*
> *Whiles they behold a greater than themselves,*
> *And therefore are they very dangerous.*
>
> (*JC, I, 2, 203-215*)

He is a man who seems to take no pleasure in the activities of life: "*he loves no plays...he hears no music...seldom he smiles.*" In short he is a rather unpleasant fellow, but no one other than Caesar recognizes danger in the man. Caesar's perceptiveness concerning Cassius results from Caesar's ability to imagine what Cassius may do because that is exactly what Caesar, Cassius' choleric brother, would do were he in Cassius' situation.

In that Caesar's assassination was Cassius' brainchild; in that his motivation was not really love for Rome, but hatred for Caesar; Cassius is a villain on the order of Iago. That said, Iago, who was said to be "motiveless," had more reason to destroy Othello and Cassio than Cassius to destroy Caesar. Iago at least felt slighted by being unjustly passed over for promotion; Caesar has done nothing to Cassius. In many ways, the evil of Cassius is more like that of Aaron who destroyed and tormented other because that was his nature. The only difference is one of degree: Aaron committed his crimes whenever the opportunity presented itself; Cassius had a specific target. So we can safely say that Cassius is a villain, a petty plotter and murderer, but that leaves us with the question, "Is he a traitor?" Treason as we noted earlier is a political crime involving betrayal. Who does Cassius betray? Certainly not Caesar for he and Caesar clearly distrust one another from the onset. Does he wish to garner power by usurping the power of Caesar?

No, he has no personal interest in ruling Rome himself, only in making sure that no one else does. Does he murder Caesar for the benefit or safety of the people of Rome? He renders this motivation lip-service, but only as a means of drawing others, specifically the patriotic Brutus, into his plot. Is his evil equal to Aaron, Iago or Richard III? I would answer "yes."

Where then does that place Brutus? Is he equally evil? Dante Alighieri thinks so. In his epic poem, *The Divine Comedy*, written by between 1308 and his death in 1321, the poet is taken on an allegorical journal through the nine levels of Hell. The circles of Hells are concentric with each deeper level holding greater sinners and greater punishments. The deepest circle of Hell is at the center of the Earth and it is here that the chief sinner, Satan, is held bound in a lake of ice. Satan is depicted as having three heads and each head is eternally devouring the three greatest sinners in all of hell. The central head gnaws on Judas Iscariot, the betrayer of Jesus, while the head on the right tears at Cassius and the one on the left chews on Brutus. Judas' suffering for the betrayal of the Son of God is slightly greater in that he is devoured from the head down while Cassius and Brutus are devoured from the feet up.

Brutus, like Cassius, is guilty of plotting against and murdering Caesar. His actions are as evil as Cassius'. Where the two differ is in their motivation. Cassius acts from petty jealousy; Brutus has a nobler motive: to save Rome from tyranny. Does intentionality matter in judging one's actions? Dante emphatically says "no." Shakespeare on the other hand suggests "maybe." Brutus in Shakespeare is sympathetically portrayed and juxtaposed against the clearly villainous Cassius. He is portrayed as genuinely loving Caesar the man, but fearing his potential for tyranny as king. He acts, he believes, to save the Roman Republic, but in doing so, he must betray the man who has offered him friendship and kindness. Is he, like Hamlet, caught between two courses, nether correct or supportable? Is Brutus, the plotter, murderer and, yes, traitor to Caesar somehow less villainous because his motives are noble?

Caesar, in appraising Cassius comments that "*He thinks too much: such men are dangerous.*" (*JC*, I, 2, 195). In fact it is not Cassius who thinks too much, it is Brutus. Returning to the Galenic humoral theory, Brutus is of the melancholic temperament characterized as fundamentally introverted and thoughtful. Melancholic people often were perceived highly creative, but also prone to dwell upon the tragedy and cruelty in the world, seeing only the darkness and not the light. Their creativity is suggestive of a potent imagination, but that same imagination that can produce art and poetry, when preoccupied with the melancholic's dark world view, they can only imagine the worst in a situation, unable to simultaneously envision the potential for the best. Like Cassius, he can only see in the kingship of Caesar the inevitable road to tyranny and the death of the Republic. However, Brutus lacks Cassius' certainty, saying of Caesar "*He would be crown'd:/ How that **might** change his nature, there's the question.*" (JC, II, 1, 12-13). He admits "*to speak truth of Caesar,/ I have not known when his affections sway'd/ More than his reason.*" (JC, II, 1, 19-20). Nevertheless, Brutus fears that by crowning Caesar "*we put a sting in him, / That at his will he **may** do danger with.*" (JC, II, 1, 16-17). (emphasis added). He has no reason from Caesar's past actions to believe this. Caesar, like Duncan in *Macbeth*, bears his power with dignity and restraint, but Brutus notes "*... 'tis a common proof,/ That lowliness is young ambition's ladder,/ Whereto the climber-upward turns his face/... Looks in the clouds, scorning the base degrees/ By which he did ascend. So Caesar **may**.*" (JC, II, 1, 21-27). (emphasis added).

Brutus's imaginative contemplations are filled with 'mays" and "mights." The imagination according to Renaissance medical theory was subject to humoral imbalance. Although the imagination is supposed to be subject to rational control, emotional agitation and humoral imbalance can cause it to take control of common sense. In the case of Brutus, his normal melancholic temperament is unbalance under the choleric influence of Cassius and is lead to dark imaginings that he is able to ignore. Like Othello's jealousy, Brutus' fear is augmented by his overactive imagination. Whereas Cassius sees personal slights impinging on his honor at every turn, Brutus worries about the state of Rome and the security of the republican ideal. Throughout the play, the welfare of Rome is his only concern.

Can such a man be considered a villain? If a man believes his treacherous and violent actions are rendered in service to his country, without animus toward the man or men betrayed, must he be classified as evil? Can treachery and murder ever by justified? These are the questions that *Julius Caesar* raises and they lead us finally back to John Wilkes Booth, the so-called American Brutus. Let us recall a few relevant details from Booth's story. His final public words after he assassinated Lincoln were "Sic semper tyrannis!" the Virginia state motto, meaning "Thus always to tyrants!" His final dying words were in a message directed to his mother, "I die for my country." Was the assassination an act of anger and revenge, or a patriot sacrifice intended to throw the North into confusion, thereby allowing the South time to regroup and continue the already lost war. If the former, he is a villain and a traitor; if the latter, he is a patriot sacrificing his life to give his country, the South, a chance to fight on. Booth's final diary entry, written in the days following the assassination offers some insight:

> *...every man's hand against me, I am here in despair. And why? For doing what Brutus was honored for. What made Tell a hero? And yet I, for striking down a greater tyrant than they ever knew, am looked upon as a common cutthroat. **My action was purer than either of theirs.** One hoped to be great himself. The other had not only his country's but his own, wrongs to avenge. I hoped for no gain. I knew no private wrong. **I struck for my country and that alone. A country that groaned beneath this tyranny, and prayed for this end, and yet now behold the cold hands they extend to me.** God cannot pardon me if I have done wrong. Yet I cannot see my wrong, except in serving a degenerate people. The little, the very little, I left behind to clear my name, the Government will not allow to be printed. So ends all. For my country I have given up all that makes life sweet and holy, brought misery upon my family, and am sure there is no pardon in the Heaven for me, since man condemns me so.[8] (emphasis added)*

The diary was discovered on Booth's body and delivered to the War Department where Secretary of War Edwin Stanton suppressed it until 1867. William Hanchett explains the suppression in his article entitled *Booth's Diary*:

> *The government did not publicize the diary in 1865 because it would not allow Lincoln's assassin to clear his name, or try to, by describing the purity and selflessness of his motives. Stanton, who had had Booth's body secretly buried so that it could not become the object of glorification or veneration by rebels and rebel-sympathizers, knew only too well that there were many people in the North, as well as in the South, who agreed that Lincoln was a tyrant and the author of the country's sufferings. Stanton would not allow Booth to appeal to that group. Nor would he allow Booth to plead for understanding and God's forgiveness, or to reveal the torment of his dawning self-doubt; Stanton knew that there were many more people who would respond compassionately to such human suffering. He was resolved that Booth be denied any defense at all, that he be despised and execrated and, if not forgotten, then consigned to a place in history as miserable as his unknown gravesite.[9]*

Since it falls to the victors to write the history, Booth has been written into history as a villain and a traitor. Yet, if one wished to create the argument, Booth had more concrete reasons to hate and fear the Government of the North than Brutus had to fear Caesar. Yes, the Union was fighting for its life and had just concluded a war claiming over 600,000 lives. But Lincoln and his

Government had shown a shocking disregard for the Constitution. In the name of national security, the Lincoln administration had suspended Habeas Corpus, imprisoned of tens of thousands of political dissenters in the North, and shut down over 300 opposition newspapers.[10] Lincoln insisted that it made no sense for him to protect this one constitutional right (Habeas Corpus) and allow the very Union established by the Constitution, the very framework for the protection of all rights, to be obliterated. Although the times were unique and the justification probably defensible, the actions of Lincoln showed a tyrannical bent. Based on those actions, Booth would appear more justified in his attack on Lincoln than Brutus would have been on his attack of Caesar. Booth, however, has no one to portray him in the sympathetic manner that Shakespeare presents Brutus.

It is not my intention to rehabilitate the reputation of John Wilkes Booth, but to point out the issues of motivation and intentionality as we attempt to evaluate the criminal actions of another. Booth, Cassius and Brutus are all objectively treacherous murderers. Almost everyone will condemn Cassius; the majority will condemn Booth, but are uncomfortable with condemning Brutus. Why? In Shakespeare's play, the chief difference between Cassius and Brutus is motive. Cassius murders Caesar because he hates and fears him; Brutus acts because he loves Rome more than he loves Caesar. History has reported that Booth killed Lincoln because he hated him and wanted to avenge the injury to the South; Booth's own words indicate his motives were to save the South by giving it an opportunity to continue to fight on. In Shakespeare, we take the words and expressed motives of the protagonists as truth; in the case of Booth, the words and motives are clouded by the biases of the writers: historians and Booth himself.

To wander even further afield, let me also add another piece of literature to perhaps further add to the question of villainy and Brutus. Literary phenomenon Stephen King raised an interesting question about assassination in his fourth novel, *The Dead Zone*. It is the story of an everyman, Johnny Smith, who, as a result of head trauma acquires the power to see glimpses of a person's future by touching them or an object connected to them. After dramatizing several incidents that validates the accuracy of Johnny's visions, King has Johnny encountering a would-be politician, Greg Stillson, who is part charismatic orator and part thug. When, by chance, he comes in contact with the demagogue, he sees in a flash this politician rising to the level of the presidency and unleashing a nuclear holocaust. The final third of the book deals with how Johnny will react to this distant, though certain threat. He analogizes the threat in a question he asks of several characters in the book: *"...just suppose you could hop into a time machine and go back to the year 1932. In Germany. And suppose you came across Hitler. Would you kill him or let him live?"*[11] The act of killing Hitler would be murder; in 1932, he was on the cusp of rising to absolute power just as Caesar in Shakespeare's play is on the cusp of doing the same. Johnny Smith has the "luxury" of knowing with certainty what Hitler did and what Stillson will do. Brutus and the audience attending Julius Caesar have only logic and their own experience to decide if Caesar is a threat. After long deliberation, Johnny Smith decides to assassinate Greg Stillson, but he fails in his attempt. Nevertheless, Stillson's cowardly action during the assassination attempt discredits the politician leading to his downfall and ultimate suicide. Johnny is mortally wounded in the assassination attempt, but manages to learn of his success in changing the future when he manages to touch the politician before drawing his final breath. The reader, of course, knows of Johnny Smith's heroic sacrifice, but to his world he is just another crazed and/or evil would be assassin.

It is ironic that in his failed assassination attempt, Johnny still achieves his objective; Brutus, on the other hand, succeeds in assassinating Caesar, but ultimately his efforts result in that which he most feared, a monarchy in Rome. So is Brutus like Johnny Smith, an unappreciated martyr committed to saving his country at the cost of Caesar's life and ultimately his own? If he believed that Caesar was as dangerous to Rome's political life as he appears to be, wouldn't he be as heroic as Johnny Smith or must we condemn both as villains because treachery and murder are always wrong. Would the man who jumped in the time machine and killed Hitler be a hero or a villain: a Cassius or a Booth or a Smith or a Brutus? Not necessarily an easy question to answer, but this question is what makes *Julius Caesar* one of Shakespeare's most important and compelling works.

DEATH, THAT DARK SPIRIT, IN'S NERVY ARM DOTH LIE: VOLUMNIA: CORIOLANUS

Caisus Marcius Coriolanus is a monster, a killing machine, a man who lives only in the heat of battle. He is contemptuous of the people of Rome, merely tolerant of its leaders and loyal to nothing other than his mother and his code of honor which is the code of the absolute warrior. Ever though he constantly talks of his service to Rome and his loyalty, in the end he betrays her when he believes she has betrayed him. Other than respect for his military prowess which is formidable, there is little to recommend him. He is unpleasant, haughty, stubborn and imprudent, a very odd protagonist for a tragedy where the audience is expected to fear for and pity its hero.

Written between 1608 and 1609, *Coriolanus* is probably Shakespeare's last tragedy although *The Tragedy of Cymbeline* (first produced in 1611) is categorized in the 1623 *First Folio* as a tragedy. Most critics today see *Cymbeline* as a Romance or Dark Comedy. The strangeness of *Coriolanus* and *Cymbeline* relative to the traditional view of tragedy suggests that at the close of his career as a playwright, Shakespeare was perhaps exploring the flexibility of genre and questioning the essential qualities of the tragic form. In *Coriolanus*, he seems to be asking the question: can a thoroughly disagreeable person, even one who is a traitor to his own country, be a tragic protagonist? Most critics answer, "He cannot." Nevertheless, I would like to argue that Coriolanus is both villain (traitor) and yet tragic. By now, this is not a unique aspect of Shakespeare's tragic protagonist. Many if not most of his tragic heroes carry out villainous acts: Othello murders his wife, Macbeth murders his king, Brutus plots against and murders Caesar, Titus Andronicus kills his own son for defying him, Hamlet kills Polonius. How are these characters different from Coriolanus? Only in their likeability and their eloquence. And perhaps in their basic humanity.

In the first Act, Coriolanus is overtly contrasted with three characters to quickly point out his character and his weaknesses. Even before he appears on stage, we learn Coriolanus hates and is hated by the citizens of Rome, the plebeians. The plebeians call him the "*chief enemy to the people*" (*C*, I, 1, 5) and "*a very dog to the commonalty*" (*C*, I, 1, 29), and they long to kill him. When the Second Citizen reminds the crowd of the good service Coriolanus has done for the State, the First Citizen retorts that the service was not done for love of Rome or its people, but for his mother and to swell his pride. The patrician Menenius attempts to calm the crowd and demonstrates the smooth style of the born politician. He has no great love or respect for the common people, but he is able to convince them that he is with them. He uses the well-known allegory of the revolt of the body parts against the belly to explain the proper order of the new republic. Although he calls the mob "*my good friends, mine honest neighbors*" and enthralls them with his tale, but at the same time he accuses them of being "wondrous malicious" or foolish in their attacks against the "*helms o' the state, who care for* [them] *like fathers.*" (C I, 1, 77-8) He calls the leader of the crowd "*great toe of* [the] *assembly*" in an obvious insult, but he does so in such a clever way that the insult sails over their heads. When the First Citizen inquires what he means, Menenius shows his complete contempt for the mob by replying "*being one o' the lowest, basest, poorest, / Of this most wise rebellion, thou go'st foremost.*" (C I, 1, 156-7). Before the crowd can respond, Coriolanus arrives on the scene and all their attention turns to him. He makes no pretense, like Menenius, to soothe the angry mob, but seems intent upon enflaming them further. He calls the mob "*dissentious rogues and" curs.*" (C, I, 1, 164). He longs to "*make a quarry/ With thousands of these quarter'd slaves, as high/ As I could pick my lance.*" (C, I, 1, 198-200). When the Senators bring word that the Volsces have taken up arms against Rome, the First Senator attempts to disperse the mob, but Coriolanus mockingly objects,

> *Nay, let them follow:*
> *The Volsces have much corn; take these rats thither*
> *To gnaw their garners. Worshipful mutiners,*
> *Your valour puts well forth: pray, follow.*
> *(C I, 1, 248-51)*

The stage direction tells us the "*Citizens steal away.*" His contempt for the plebeians is justified: they are shown to be fickle, easily manipulated and cowardly
Coriolanus has little more respect for the soldiers that he leads. When before the walls of Corioli his troops falter under the attack of the Volsces, the General rages,

> *You shames of Rome! you herd of--Boils and plagues*
> *Plaster you o'er, that you may be abhorr'd*
> *Further than seen and one infect another*
> *Against the wind a mile! You souls of geese,*
> *That bear the shapes of men, how have you run*
> *From slaves that apes would beat! Pluto and hell!*

> *All hurt behind; backs red, and faces pale*
> *With flight and agued fear! Mend and charge home,*
> *Or, by the fires of heaven, I'll leave the foe*
> *And make my wars on you*
>
> (C I, 4, 31-40)

Hardly a speech that would endear him to the troops.

Shakespeare now contrasts the behavior of Coriolanus with that of fellow General, Cominius. When his troops retreat before the Volsces' attack, Cominius says,

> *Breathe you, my friends: well fought; we are come off*
> *Like Romans, neither foolish in our stands,*
> *Nor cowardly in retire: believe me, sirs,*
>
> (C I, 6, 1-3)

When Coriolanus arrives after nearly taking the City of Corioli single-handedly, he asks Cominius *"Where is the enemy? are you lords o' the field? /If not, why cease you till you are so?"* (C I, 6, 47-8). Even though Cominius is the commanding General, Coriolanus seems disgusted that he is not pressing the battle and begs Cominius to send him immediately into combat against his arch-nemesis, the Volsces leader, Titus Aufidius.

In contrast to Cominius, he is shown to be a highly effective warrior but an inadequate general. His behavior more befits an Elizabethan adventurer rather than a general. His most famous exploit, entering the gates of Corioli without support, is as much reckless as courageous. Plutarch's Coriolanus, in fact, does not enter the city alone.[14] Paul Jorgensen believes that Coriolanus is being compared with the Earl of Essex who was *"a brilliant fighter and bad general, [who] habitually led rather than directed the charge."*[15] Similarly, Coriolanus recalls Sir Richard Grenville's daring command of the *Revenge* when he launched his ship unaided against the Spanish fleet and did *"them great hurte."* His courage, clearly exhibited, was offset by his unpopularity as a leader. Jan van Linschoten, who witnessed the battle first hand, wrote of Grenville that

> *"he was a man very unquiet in his minde, and greatly affected to warre: ... he had performed many valiant actes, and was greatly feared in these Islands, and knowne of every man, but of nature very severe, so that his owne people hated him for his fierceness, and spake verie hardly of him.[16]*

Most contemporary military books in defining the qualities needed in a general stressed "traits making for pleasant relationships with the army, traits significantly lacking in Coriolanus. The general, according to a typical work, *"would be courteous clement, and gentle. Nothing doth more please the common souldier. ... Contrariwise, nothing doth more hurt sometimes, then the untimely rigour, and austerity of the General."* The general is also enjoined to prefer *"the safety of his owne people before the killing of his enemies,"* a trait singularly absent on Coriolanus.[17] Coriolanus' solitary battle within the gates of Corioli demonstrates his extraordinary valor, but it also serves to demonstrate his essential isolation. The contrast Shakespeare sets up between Coriolanus and Cominius shows Coriolanus is unfit to be a General because he can be neither *"courteous clement, [nor] gentle."* Further, he cares only about the victory and nothing about its' cost, thereby becoming the embodiment of all the worst stereotypes of military men.

Titus Aufidius is the only character in the play for whom Coriolanus shows a modicum of respect. He says of his foe,

> *I sin in envying his nobility,*
> *And were I anything but what I am,*
> *I would wish me only he.*
>
> (C I, 1, 230-2)

What he truly admires is not the nobility of Aufidius, but his military prowess and because his military prowess is equal to that of Coriolanus, the Roman hates him as much as he admires him. However, we quickly see that Aufidius is not as noble as Coriolanus believes. When Coriolanus begins to gain the upper hand against him in combat, Aufidius' comrades intervene and spirit him away. Although he curses his saviors saying *"you have shamed me/ In your condemned seconds"* (C I, 8, 14-5), it is noteworthy that Aufidius retreats along with them.

The contrast of Coriolanus with Aufidius is telling. While the men are evenly matched in combat skills, Aufidius is perhaps less noble, but more practical. Unlike Coriolanus, his men value him enough to risk his anger rather than see him go down under the sword of his bitter foe. The troops of Coriolanus abandon him rather than follow him through the gates of Corioli. Aufidius understands strategy: in Act 1, scene 2, he chides the Senators of Corioli for allowing the Romans to discover Corioli's aggression against Rome. *"By the discovery. / We shall be shorten'd in our aim, which was/ To take in many towns ere almost Rome/ Should know we were afoot."* (C, I, 2, 22-4). Coriolanus, on the other hand, would have felt compelled to announce his plan of attack well in advance of executing it.

Aufidius is a survivor. While he is the military equal of Coriolanus, he also has the ability to adapt to change to accommodate changing circumstances. When the banished Coriolanus comes to him and offers his service against Rome, Aufidius is able to set aside his hatred of Coriolanus and use him as tool against his larger enemy, but when Coriolanus begins to outshine him with the Volsces Aufidius begins to plot his destruction when he has served his purpose. When Coriolanus relents and makes peace with Rome instead of destroying it as he promised, Aufidius conceals his rage and plots the murder of his rival. He manipulates the crowd of disappointed Volsces, turns them against Coriolanus and they fall upon him and tear him to pieces. These are acts that Coriolanus would never be able to perform. It is inconceivable that Coriolanus could have aligned himself with his arch-foe because war for Coriolanus is not about winning or losing military objectives; it is about being the last man standing atop a field of vanquished opponents. Nor could Coriolanus manipulate others into killing his rival. Coriolanus would have to meet his enemy *mano a mano*.

Coriolanus is neither a politician, a leader, nor a survivor. He is a warrior par excellence, only truly comfortable in the heat of battle, and the exemplar of the Roman concept of *virtus* meaning both valor and "manliness," that peculiar strength of character that nourishes integrity, and patriotism. He is constantly criticized for his excessive pride, but he is neither self-promoting nor comfortable hearing the praise of others. He is contemptuous of the praise and support of the plebeians, believing them unworthy of evaluating his worth.

> To brag unto them, thus I did, and thus;
> Show them the unaching scars which I should hide,
> As if I had received them for the hire
> Of their breath only!
>
> (C, II, 2, 146-9)

When custom requires him to go to the plebeians for their endorsement as Council, he is appalled by the idea. He protests to his political mentor, Menenius,

> I cannot bring
> My tongue to such a pace:--'Look, sir, my wounds!
> I got them in my country's service, when
> Some certain of your brethren roar'd and ran
> From the noise of our own drums.'
>
> (C, II, 3, 50-54)

As to his aristocratic peers, Coriolanus is no more comfortable with earning their praise by a recounting of his deeds. When Cominius speaks to the Senate espousing Coriolanus' service to the State, Coriolanus protests and leaves the Senate chamber, saying *"I had rather have my wounds to heal again/ Than hear say how I got them."* (C, II, 2, 68-9). While such a statement might suggest humility, it is instead an expression of his pride because in the final analysis all he cares about is his own self-image. Acceptance of praise might imply that his value can be judged by opinion of others.

There is one opinion, however, that Coriolanus does value even above his own: that of his mother, Volumnia. Plutarch tells us that Coriolanus was devoted to his mother and that pleasing her was one of his primary motives in achieving success. It is Volumnia who pushes Coriolanus to seek the position of Council, a pursuit that is the proximate cause of his downfall. Coriolanus is neither suited to nor interested in a life of politics. After his triumphant return to Rome, Coriolanus is greeted by his mother and she tells him *"There's one thing wanting, which I doubt not but/ Our Rome will cast upon thee."* (C, II, 1, 201-2) meaning political power. He is reluctant from the start to pursue this role, telling her, *"I had rather be their servant in my way, / Than sway with them in theirs."* (C, II, 1, 203). In spite of his misgivings, Coriolanus is persuaded to go to the plebeians and plead for their support. Strangely, the plebeians give it, but as soon as they do so, their Tribunes, their representative in the Senate who hate and fear Coriolanus, set about inflaming the crowd and persuading them to withdraw it. When Coriolanus learns of the betrayal, he explodes, denouncing the plebeians in the harshest terms. Both the nobles and the Tribunes encourage him to go to the commons and humbly explain himself. Speaking to the nobles, he warns them that such an action encourages revolt:

> *In soothing them, we nourish 'gainst our senate*
> *The cockle of rebellion, insolence, sedition,*
> *Which we ourselves have plough'd for, sow'd,*
> *and scatter'd,*
> *By mingling them with us, the honour'd number,*
> *Who lack not virtue, no, nor power, but that*
> *Which they have given to beggars.*
>
> (C, III, 1, 69-74)

In full rage he then turns on the Tribunes with a rebuke of the plebeians:

> *They know the corn*
> *Was not our recompense, resting well assured*

> *That ne'er did service for't: being press'd to the war,*
> *Even when the navel of the state was touch'd,*
> *They would not thread the gates. This kind of service*
> *Did not deserve corn gratis. Being i' the war*
> *Their mutinies and revolts, wherein they show'd*
> *Most valour, spoke not for them: the accusation*
> *Which they have often made against the senate,*
> *All cause unborn, could never be the motive*
> *Of our so frank donation.*
>
> (C, III, 1, 120-30)

For this, he is accused of treason and the Tribunes attempt to affect his arrest. He responds with his drawn sword. After a brief melee, the patricians manage to hustle Coriolanus away. Again it falls to Menenius to restore the peace. He promises to bring Coriolanus to the market place to answer to the people and the crowd adjourns to await his arrival.

The scene shifts to Coriolanus' home where Menenius now attempts to persuade the still outraged warrior to stand before the people. It is, however, Volumnia who calms her son and sends him on his way. She sees her ambitions for him crumbling and she chides him for his rash behavior. "*I have a heart as little apt as yours, / But yet a brain that leads my use of anger/ To better vantage.*" (C, III, 2, 29-31). When told he must beg the forgiveness of the people, he is revolted at the prospect, but Volumnia argues that to dissemble at this point is nobler than to fight.

> *...now it lies you on to speak*
> *To the people; not by your own instruction,*
> *Nor by the matter which your heart prompts you,*
> *But with such words that are but rooted in*
> *Your tongue, though but bastards and syllables*
> *Of no allowance to your bosom's truth.*
> *Now, this no more dishonours you at all*
> *Than to take in a town with gentle words,*
>
> (C, III, 2, 52-9)

He is unconvinced. Finally, she plays the last gambit that every child has had to confront: she plays on his guilt.

> *To beg of thee, it is my more dishonour*
> *Than thou of them. Come all to ruin; let*

> Thy mother rather feel thy pride than fear
> Thy dangerous stoutness, for I mock at death
> With as big heart as thou. Do as thou list
> Thy valiantness was mine, thou suck'dst it from me,
> But owe thy pride thyself.
>
> (C, III, 2, 124-9)

Unable to resist, Coriolanus relents: *Pray, be content: / Mother, I am going to the market-place; /Chide me no more."* (C, III, 2, 131-2)

Needless to say, when Coriolanus arrives at the marketplace, things rapidly go from bad to worse. The Tribunes goad Coriolanus with the title "*a traitor to the people*," producing the expected result. Coriolanus again erupts into a rage. When cautioned by Menenius to control himself, he rants that he "*would not buy/ Their* [the plebeians] *mercy at the price of one fair word; / Nor cheque my courage for what they can give. / To have't with saying 'Good morrow.'*" (C, III, 2, 91-3). The people call for his banishment and, to maintain the peace, the patricians concede.

Feeling betrayed by Rome, Coriolanus becomes her enemy, joining his arch-foe Titus Aufidius to attack his home. Once unfairly accused of being a traitor, now he becomes one and he leads the conquering Volsces to the gates of Rome. His old friends, Cominius and Menenius attempt to dissuade him from his destructive path, but their pleas go unanswered. Cominius describes him as "*a kind of nothing, titleless, / Till he had forged himself a name o' the fire/ Of burning Rome.*" (C, V, 1, 12-4). Finally, in a last attempt to save the city, Volumnia along with her daughter-in-law and grandson comes to the Volscian camp to plead with her son. At first her pleas fall on the same deaf ears met by Cominius and Menenius. He tells her "*desire not/ To ally my rages and revenges with/ Your colder reasons,*" so again she turns to the mother's trick and falls on her knees before her child.

> There's no man in the world
> More bound to's mother; yet here he lets me prate
> Like one i' the stocks. Thou hast never in thy life
> Show'd thy dear mother any courtesy,
> When she, poor hen, fond of no second brood,
> Has cluck'd thee to the wars and safely home,
> Loaden with honour. Say my request's unjust,
> And spurn me back: but if it be not so,
> Thou art not honest; and the gods will plague thee,
> That thou restrain'st from me the duty which
> To a mother's part belongs.

Coriolanus crumbles before her, tears in his eyes.

> *O mother, mother!*
> *What have you done? Behold, the heavens do ope,*
> *The gods look down, and this unnatural scene*
> *They laugh at. O my mother, mother! O!*
> *You have won a happy victory to Rome;*
> *But, for your son,--believe it, O, believe it,*
> *Most dangerously you have with him prevail'd,*
> *If not most mortal to him.*
>
> $$(C, V, 3, 185\text{-}90)$$

At his word, the Volsces break off their siege and return home, but Coriolanus still has to pay for his second betrayal. Aufidius plots his death and like the Tribunes, goads Coriolanus into a rage, provokes the crowd to fall on the hero and tear him apart.

Like Frankenstein's creature, Coriolanus is wholly a creature of his mother, a product of both his innate nature and nurture. We can intuit his nature indirectly by looking at his son. Volumnia, speaking of her grandson, comments *"that [h]e had rather see the swords, and hear a drum, than/look upon his school-master"* to which Valeria, Volumnia's friend, replies *"the father's son"* implying that the son has inherited the father's nature (C, I, 3, 55-6). Like his father, the son seems to be a born killer. In a chilling narrative, Valeria describes the child playing in the garden,

> *I saw him run after a gilded*
> *butterfly: and when he caught it, he let it go*
> *again; and after it again; and over and over he*
> *comes, and again; catched it again; or whether his*
> *fall enraged him, or how 'twas, he did so set his*
> *teeth and tear it;*
>
> $$(C, I, 3, 60\text{-}4).$$

then exclaims in admiration, *"'tis a noble child."* (C, I, 3, 67)

Since the 1970's, research into the psychopathology of serial killers has uncovered childhood cruelty to animals as an early warning sign of later violence, and criminal behavior. In fact, nearly all violent crime perpetrators have a history of animal cruelty in their profiles. Albert deSalvo, the Boston Strangler found guilty of killing 13 women, shot arrows through dogs and cats he trapped as a child. As a boy, Jeffrey Dahmer impaled the heads of cats and dogs on sticks.

David Berkowitz, the "Son of Sam," poisoned his mother's parakeet. Columbine shooters Eric Harris and Dylan Klebold boasted about mutilating animals for fun. Such behaviors may well indicate about an individual's capacity for empathy or lack thereof. [12, 13] We don't know the age of Coriolanus' son, but he is old enough to have a school master meaning he would be old enough to understand that animal cruelty is wrong (at least by our contemporary standards), but in the Roman society of Shakespeare's play, animal cruelty is not wrong. Instead of being rebuked for destroying the butterfly, the boy is admired. The boy is predisposed to violence, but it is the nurture he receives that encourages it. We can infer that Coriolanus himself showed similar tendencies in childhood.

Violence in the world of Coriolanus is admired and encouraged, at least as long as it is in service to the State. Volumnia has gleefully raised her son to be the ultimate soldier.

> When yet he was but
> tender-bodied and the only son of my womb, when
> youth with comeliness plucked all gaze his way, ...
> To a cruel war I sent him; from whence he returned, his brows
> bound with oak. I tell thee, daughter, I sprang not
> more in joy at first hearing he was a man-child
> than now in first seeing he had proved himself a man.
> (C, I. 3, 5-17)

For Coriolanus, to win "honour" is to be his highest goal and Volumnia basks in his reflected honour. She professes her motivation is love of country, and patriotism is inextricably entwined with the pursuit of personal honour both for mother and son. She tells her daughter-in-law,

> had I a dozen sons, each in my love
> alike and none less dear than thine and my good
> Marcius, I had rather had eleven die nobly for their
> country than one voluptuously surfeit out of action
> (C, I. 3, 22-5)

However, patriotism is simply Coriolanus' cover; they allow him the opportunity to prove his "virtus" and exploit his violent impulses without censure. To value his native country above his personal honor would require true patriotism. This he cannot do. If not for the wars to cover his pathology, he would have been recognized for what he is: a pathological killing machine. His inborn propensity for violence has been nurtured both by his Volumnia and by the State, and Coriolanus grows to be ill-equipped for anything else. And this is the very core of his tragedy.

Coriolanus does not have the traditional "fatal flaw" often associated with Shakespeare's tragic protagonists. Some have pointed to his pride and others have pointed to his uncontrollable rage as the attributes that cause his downfall. I would contend that he *is* the fatal flaw. He is raised to be a weapon rather than an individual. He has been fashioned by Volumnia and by the State for a single purpose, to kill the enemies of the State, and when he has served that purpose, or worse yet, is turned against the State; there is no option but to destroy him. There is inevitability about the fate of Coriolanus that is Aristotelian in origin. Like Oedipus, Coriolanus appears to have the option to choose: Oedipus could have ceased the inquiries that ultimately led to his downfall, but because of who he is, because of his very nature, that option is only an illusion. To cease to inquire would be to cease being Oedipus. Similarly, Coriolanus could have been humbler or have exercised more self-control, but to do so would have required him to be other than what he is. So again, for him, these options are an allusion. Volumnia had created a grotesquery, a monster, programmed for destruction and self-destruction. Because it is she who is most responsible for his creation, it falls to her to push the button that will finally end his life. Coriolanus' tragedy is ultimately what he was created to be. In a fashion, Volumnia is more tragic than Coriolanus because she is responsible for destroying that which she loves, her own son and the hopes for her future that she had invested in him. For Coriolanus, the tragedy is not in his death, but that he has never lived as fully human. He is only an insentient *"thing of blood,"* a heartless and mindless instrument that kills without compassion. He is only really alive when in the thick of battle; all the rest of life is waiting for the next war. He is so obsessed with *virtus* and his own manhood that he betrays his country and destroys himself to assert it. His tragedy is not what he is, but what he could have been, and that he lives in a world where his only expression of humanity serves to destroy him.

Notes

1. http://en.wikipedia.org/wiki/Treason
2. http://en.wikipedia.org/wiki/Treason_Act_1351
3. http://en.wikipedia.org/wiki/Petty_treason
4. http://en.wikipedia.org/wiki/Treason
5. http://www.etymonline.com/index.php?term=traitor

6. Edmund Plowden's *Reports*, qtd in Ernst H. Kantovitz, *The King's Two Bodies: A Study in Medieval Political Theology.* (Princeton, NJ: Princeton University Press, 1959), 13.

7. Burton, Robert. *The Anatomy of Melancholy.* Ed. Holbrook Jackson. (New York: New York Review Books, 2001), 401

8. Last Diary Entry of John Wilkes Booth. http://law2.umkc.edu/faculty/projects/ftrials/lincolnconspiracy/boothdiary.html

9. Thomas James DiLorenzo, "Abraham Lincoln, U.S. Authoritarianism and Manipulated History." Exclusive interview, Sunday, May 16, 2010, *The Daily Bell.* http://www.thedailybell.com/1053/Thomas-DiLorenzo-Abraham-Lincoln-US-Authoritarianism-Free-Market-History.html

10. http://www.heritech.com/pridger/lincoln/booths_diary.pdf

11. King, Stephen. *The Dead Zone.* (New York: New American Library, 1979), 329.

12. Johnston, Joni E. "Children Who are Cruel to Animals: When to Worry." *Psychology Today.* April 27, 2011. http://www.psychologytoday.com/blog/the-human-equation/201104/children-who-are-cruel-animals-when-worry

13. Siebert, Charles. "The Animal-Cruelty Syndrome." *The New York Times,* June 11, 2010. http://www.nytimes.com/2010/06/13/magazine/13dogfightingt.html?pagewanted=all&_r=0

14. Jorgensen, Paul A. "Shakespeare's Coriolanus: Elizabethan Soldier." *PMLA,* Vol. 64, No. 1 (Mar., 1949), pp. 221-235.

15. Ibid, 222.

16. Ibid 222.

17. Matthew Sutcliffe, The Practice, Proceedings, and Lawes of Armes (London, 1593), pp.42-43. Cf. Barnaby Rich, The Fruites of Long Experience (London, 1604), pp. 29-30. "Rich, A Path-way to Military Practise (London, 1587), sig. Cl. Quoted in Jorgensen, 223.

SHAKESPEARE'S BAD GIRLS:

She is wedded to convictions - in default of grosser ties;
Her contentions are her children, Heaven help him, who denies!
He will meet no cool discussion, but the instant, white-hot wild
Wakened female of the species warring as for spouse and child.

        *   *   *

So it comes that Man, the coward, when he gathers to confer
With his fellow-braves in council, dare not leave a place for her
Where, at war with Life and Conscience, he uplifts his erring hands
To some God of abstract justice - which no woman understands.

And Man knows it! Knows, moreover, that the Woman that God gave him
Must command but may not govern; shall enthrall but not enslave him.
And She knows, because She warns him and Her instincts never fail,
That the female of Her species is more deadly than the male!

The Female of the Species
Rudyard Kipling, 1911

Women can be scary. Who from our childhood is scarier than Margaret Hamilton playing the Wicked Witch of the West in 1939 version of *The Wizard of Oz*? Motivated by a desire to avenge the death of her sister witch, the Witch of the West relentlessly pursues Dorothy and her friends until, at the very point of achieving her revenge, she is dissolved by a dousing with pure, clean water. As the stooped, green-skinned witch dressed in a long black dress with a black pointed hat, she became for subsequent generations the standard for what witches look like and an archetype for human wickedness.

Margaret Hamilton in MGM's *The Wizard of Oz* (1939)
Wkli-Commons

     Not scary enough? How about the evil queen from Walt Disney's *Snow White and the Seven Dwarfs* (1937)? Portrayed with the throaty and threatening voice of Lucille La Verne, the evil queen is the archetypal evil stepmother who is envious of the budding beauty of her stepchild, Snow White. After failing an attempt to murder the child through a surrogate, the queen adopts the appearance of an old crone (witch) through the agency of a magical potion and sets out to kill the child herself. Snow White, who has taken up housekeeping with seven mining dwarfs, is persuaded to bite into a poisoned apple and passes into a death-like sleep. The crone is discovered by the dwarfs and chased through the mountains until, as she prepares to roll a boulder down on the little people, she is struck by lightning and falls to her death, Snow White is of course awakened by the kiss of a passing prince and is carried off to a happily ever after.

Evil Queen
Wiki-Commons

The evil queen in *Snow White* was not the last of Disney's scary ladies. Mining the fairy tales of Charles Perrault (Mother Goose), the Brothers Grimm, and Hans Christian Anderson, Disney bought to the screen Maleficent, the evil fairy of *Sleeping Beauty* (1959); Lady Tremaine, the evil stepmother of *Cinderella* (1950); the evil sea witch Ursula in *The Little Mermaid* (1989); and more recently, the deceptive crone Gothel in *Tangled* (2010). All are of course appropriately (and manageably) scary for the targeted audience of children.

If looking for more adult oriented femme fatales, one might turn to classical mythology or popular Bible stories. Consider for example Circe the sorceress who entertains Odysseus' crew in Homer's *Odyssey*, and then turn them into swine? Not scary enough? Then consider Medea who when betrayed by Jason for a younger bride murders their two children in revenge. Or how about Clytemnestra who captures her husband Agamemnon in his bath and hacks him to death with an ax? Or Procne who is the sister of the raped and mutilated Philomela. She takes revenge on the ravager, her own husband, King Tereus of Thrace by murdering their son, baking him in a pie and feeding him to his father. Now that's just wrong!

The Bible is only slightly less gruesome. Jezebel, for example, was the Phoenician princess who married King Ahab of Israel and became the power behind the throne. She is depicted in First and Second Kings as patroness of the Phoenician Baal and Asherah cults and adversary of Yahweh's cult and prophets. Under Jezebel's influence the cults grew and Israel's prophets were persecuted. Her chief opponent was the prophet Elijah, who fought fiercely to preserve the monotheistic worship of Yahweh in Israel. Jezebel exerted an equally evil influence on the king in other matters: when Naboth the Jezreelite refused to sell or exchange his vineyard which Ahab desired, Jezebel had him falsely accused of "cursing God and King," and he was subsequently stoned to death (I Kgs 21:1-16, KJV). When Ahab went to take possession of the vineyard, he was confronted by

Elijah who denounced him as a murderer. The prophet predicted that, as the dogs licked up Naboth's blood, so dogs would lick up Ahab and Jezebel's blood. This came to pass when Ahab was killed in battle with the Arameans. After his death, Ahaziah and Jehoram, his sons acceded to the throne and continued Ahab's policies under the influence of their mother. In response, the prophet Elisha anointed the Israeli general Jehu as king to overthrow the house of Ahab. Jehu killed Jehoram and incited the court officials to murder Jezebel by throwing her from the palace window. Her corpse was left in the street to be eaten by dogs.

Yet another wicked woman from the Bible is Salome. The daughter of Herodias and step-daughter of Herod Antipas, Salome is the archetype of the seductive adolescent who uses her sexuality to achieve her evil goals. On the occasion of her step-father's birthday, she came in to the party and danced for the king. Herod was so pleased by the performance that he "said unto the damsel, 'Ask of me whatsoever thou wilt, and I will give it thee.' And he sware unto her, 'Whatsoever thou shalt ask of me, I will give it thee, unto the half of my kingdom.' And she went forth, and said unto her mother, 'What shall I ask?' And she said, 'The head of John the Baptist.'" (Mark 6:21-25, KJV). Herodias bore a grudge against John for stating that Herod's marriage to Herodias was unlawful and John had been languishing in Herod's dungeons for the offense. When Salome made her demand, Herod regretted his rash offer, but kept his promise, having John's head cut from his body and according to tradition had it delivered to Salome on a silver platter.

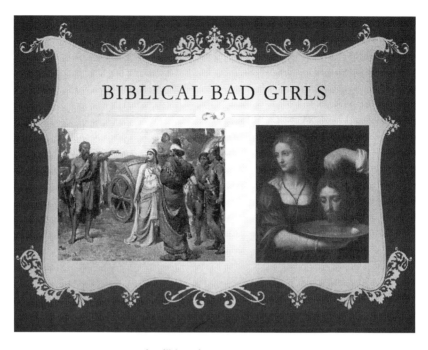

BIBLICAL BAD GIRLS

Left: Elijah confronts Jezebel and Ahab
Right: Salome presented with the head of John the Baptist

The image of the scary, wicked women is found throughout western culture: in history, mythology, literature, music and the visual arts. The same of course can be said about scary wicked men, but I would suggest that wicked women generally produce a more visceral revulsion than do their male counterparts. The reason for this is rooted in the Western cultural binary that exists between the idealization of woman as virgin/wife/mother versus the eroticization of woman as hussy/whore/tease. The male psyche that has controlled the cultural narrative of the West divides woman into these two mutually exclusive categories. From folklore to myths and from literature to history, men have consciously and unconsciously crafted the story of women to conform to their vision of the feminine "Other." In the male narrative, the female image is most importantly the vision of the mother who gives life and provides nourishment so when confronted with a woman who takes life, she is perceived as an abomination. Similarly, the woman is scripted to be the helpmate to the male and subordinate to his rule, so when the woman asserts herself in the home or in the wider world, she is seen as a disturber of the peace and a disrupter of the world's order. Even in the person of Queen Elizabeth, it is the fiction of the king's

237

two bodies that permits the masculine "body" of a king to inhabit the female body of the Queen and enables her to rule without upsetting the natural order of things.

When analyzing Shakespeare's wicked women, one must keep this potent binary in mind. How is it evidenced in his source works and in his characterizations? Is he supporting or subverting the binary? Is he working within the traditional framework for a woman's character or is he reflecting the changing attitude toward women which drifted like an undercurrent through the England of his age? Are Shakespeare's wicked women held to the same standard of villainy that adheres to their male counterparts and if not, are they condemned for the same behaviors that might be explained or excused in a male? Are they really wicked or merely self-actuated women who have personal goals and ambitions and who elect to act upon them using the tools and talents they have at hand?

In one of the earliest examinations of Shakespeare's female characters, William Richardson (1788) defends Shakespeare from critics who found Shakespeare's female characters shallow and under-developed. He excused/explained that Shakespeare's female characters "are most commonly furnished by rude, remote, or ancient ages, [and that] the poet must submit to such limitation, in his views of human life, as the manners of such periods require." Under this constraint, Richardson argues that "Shakespeare is justified in producing less varied female characters since real women show less diversity of character and occupation than men." That said, he continues, "Many persons may have received from nature similar talents and dispositions; but being differently placed in society, they exert the same power, or gratify the same desire, with different degrees of force, and different modes of indulgence. Their characters are therefore different, and if so in reality, so also in imitation.[1]

In the early decades of the 19th century, Samuel Taylor Coleridge was also defending Shakespeare's portrayal of women by praising the playwright for infusing his female characters with the ability to see "all things by the light of the affections. In all the Shakespearean women," he continued, "there is essentially the same foundation and principle; the distinct individuality and variety are merely the result of the modification of circumstances."[2]

It was not until 1832 that the first book length critical analysis of Shakespeare's women appeared in print. Anna Jameson in *Characteristics of Women, Moral, Poetical, and Historical* argued that Shakespeare's female characters were "in truth, in variety, in power, equal to his men" and that feminine weaknesses: "the mean spirit of competition, the petty jealousy of superior charms, the mutual slander and mistrust" which she sees as common faults are "the result of an education which makes vanity the ruling principle." Shakespeare, she said, in his essential love and understanding of women was able to see through the superficial societal representations of the feminine and do "justice to their natural good tendencies and kind sympathies." While seeming at first to circle back and agree with Richardson and Coleridge in their simplification and idealization of Shakespeare's women, Jameson asserts they are "not stuck up, like the cardinal virtues, all in a row for us to admire and wonder at—they are not merely poetical abstractions"[3] Nevertheless, the stereotypical idealization of Shakespeare's women was entrenched in the critical minds and persisted throughout the Victorian period.

It was not until the emergence of feminist criticism in the early 1970's that the traditional view of Shakespeare's women began to be seriously challenged. Critics and scholars lined up on either side of the question: was Shakespeare supporting the persistent patriarchal idealization of women or was he subverting it by giving his women strength and intelligence? The arguments typically focused on Shakespeare's positive female characters, Portia and Rosalind being particular favorites, but Shakespeare's "bad girls" received much less critical attention and were often dismissed as two dimensional caricatures of patriarchal nightmares. As such, the outspoken bad girls like Katherina and Beatrice had to be tamed and the ambitious bad girls like Lady Macbeth, Goneril and Regan, and Cleopatra had to be destroyed. On the other side, these bad girls were read as not really bad at all, but women acting as men would act in similar circumstances. They are condemned not because their actions are particularly evil (at least by comparison to their male counterparts), but because they do not conform to the patriarchal expectations of proper women.

In a patriarchal society, both Shakespeare's and ours, adherence to an ideal female standard dictates how the society perceives women. The Renaissance preoccupation with the definition and representation of woman grew out of the classical influence the Greek and Roman mythologies and philosophers, and the early Christian binary of Eve and Mary. In Greek mythology it was the action of the first woman, Pandora, who in defiance of her husband, opened the famous box containing all the evils of the world and released them upon mankind. Pandora's story emphasized an aspect of womankind that has been used since as a reason for the strict control of woman, i.e., woman's innate insatiability (of appetite, of curiosity, etc.).

John William Waterhouse's *Pandora*

Aristotle (384 BC – 322 BC), who was the most important Classical influence on Renaissance thinking, reflected the dominant Greek attitude concerning the nature and role of women in society. Writing in *History of Animals*, he proposed that women are less intelligent than men but possess a greater sense of enjoyment and liberty. He posited that women are more compassionate than man, more easily moved to tears, while at the same time being more jealous, more querulous, and more apt to scold and to strike. They are prone, he said, to despondency and less hopeful than the man, more void of shame or self-respect, more false of speech, more deceptive, and of more retentive memory. Women, he concluded, are physically inferior to men and that their proper place was in the home, controlled by their husbands. Therefore, he believed that women should not be educated with or like men, but should receive training in gymnastics and domestic arts to enable them to manage households, to bear and raise children, and to please and be obedient to their husbands.[4]

Like the story of Pandora, the Biblical story of the disobedient Eve provided Christian men with the reason to restrain and restrict the freedom of women and the justification to hold women responsible for all the misfortunes suffered by mankind. From Genesis, we learn that Eve was created from the rib of Adam to serve as his companion and helpmate, but she submitted to the temptation of the serpent, Lucifer, and ate of the fruit of the forbidden Tree of the Knowledge of Good and Evil. Having eaten, she persuaded he husband, Adam to eat as well, and through their actions, they introduced sin and death into the world. As a result of the story, all subsequent women, like Eve, were seen as the "mothers of sin" and, according to St Jerome writing in the 4th century, "the gate of the devil, the path of wickedness, the sting of the serpent, in a word a perilous object."5 St. Paul writing in his First Letter to Timothy said.

> For I do not allow woman to teach, or to exercise authority over men; but she is to keep silent. For Adam was formed first, then Eve. And Adam was not deceived, but the woman was deceived and became a transgressor.
> (1 Timothy 2:12-14, KJV)

Eve and the serpent

Paul's thoughts were supported by St, Augustine (354-430) who compared a husband's treatment of his wife to that of a parent and a child. Justifying this, he said "Before the Fall, the woman was oriented toward the man but this was an act of love and love leaves no room for domination, which is a burden to others. Burdensome domination is a consequence of the Fall." Pope Gregory (540-604) was even harder on women. "Woman" he said, "is slow in understanding and her unstable and naive mind renders her by way of natural weakness to the necessity of a strong hand in her husband. Her 'use' is twofold; [carnal] sex and motherhood." Even the relatively enlightened St. Thomas Aquinas (1225-1274) *in Summa Theologica* conceded Aristotle's point that woman is "misbegotten," but only when considered as an individual and only with respect to the body; her soul, however he considered equal to that of a man. Nevertheless, as a practical matter, since individuals need to be governed by others wiser than themselves, women needed to be governed by men because in men "the discretion of reason predominates."[6]

The only chance of redemption for the Christian woman was to become like the Virgin Mary who represented absolute obedience and purity. In the 2nd century, St. Irenaeus of Lyons (130-202) called Mary the "second Eve" because through Mary and her willing acceptance of God's choice, God undid the harm that was done through Eve's choice to eat the forbidden fruit. Mary became the ideal for women: pure and chaste, a mother, and a woman whose life reflected humility, sweetness, benevolence, and wisdom. While ordinary women could not be expected to achieve Marian perfection, they were expected to strive for the achievement. The institution of nuns offered women the opportunity to devote themselves to the practice of a life of perfection. By the third century, community houses were established where women, usually virgins, devoted to the religious life gathered together for mutual support and service to the community. From the beginning, nuns provided Christian education to orphans, young girls brought by their parents, and especially girls intending to embrace a religious life. They frequently took vows of poverty and at the beginning of the religious orders, the nuns came and went freely in doing the work to which they were called, but by the 13th century, nuns were being strictly controlled by the church. First local bishops and then the Holy See imposed strict enclosure of the nunneries that made it virtually impossible for sisters to undertake works of charity; the education of young girls alone was permitted to them. Latter the care of the sick who came to their enclosures was also permitted. Their principle raisons d'être, however, was contemplative, seeking personal perfection by close union with God.[7]

Virgin Mary by Raphael

In the late Middle Ages, another alternative to the Marian ideal emerged in the cult of courtly love that idealized women and presented the love of women as an exalting and ennobling spiritual and moral force. The lover is usually a knight and the idealized lady, the wife of his employer or lord, a lady of higher status, usually the rich and powerful. The knight tries to make himself worthy of her by acting bravely and honorably and by doing whatever deeds she might desire, subjecting himself to a series of tests to prove to her his ardor and commitment. These lovers would have short trysts in secret, which escalated emotionally, but never physically. That said, it was nevertheless true that the two great models of courtly love in the Middle Ages--Tristan and Isolt and Lancelot and Guinevere--both involved women who betrayed their husbands, emotionally if not physically. Unlike the unachievable icon of Mary, the cult of courtly love offered real women a redemptive alternative designed to bring out the best, not the worst, in men.

In England, as a result of Henry VIII's reformation, nunneries were dissolved. Without this avenue to redemption for women, the new Protestants had to address the "problem" of women differently. Initially, Protestant leaders were not particularly generous to women. Martin Luther (1483-1546) said, for example,

"Women are created for no other purpose than to serve men and be their helpers. If women grow weary or even die while bearing children, that doesn't harm anything. Let them bear children to death; they are created for that."[8] John Calvin (1509-1564) was kinder in saying, "as for women, this reason holdeth which Paul brought before, that God hath set an order which may in no wise be broken, and must continue even to the world's end. Seeing man is made to be the woman's head, and the woman is a part, & as it were an accessory of man, we must follow that order, and as well great as small must submit themselves unto it."[9] And from John Knox (1513-1572) we have the following: "Woman in her greatest perfection was made to serve and obey man, not to rule and command him: as Saint Paul does reason in these words, 'Man is not of woman, but woman of the man.' And man was not created for the cause of woman, but the woman for the cause of man, and therefore ought the woman to have power upon her head (that is a coverture in sign of subjection). Of which words it is plain that the Apostle meaneth, that woman in her greatest perfection should have known, that man was Lord above her: and therefore she should never have pretended any kind of superiority above him, no more than do the angels above God the creator or above Christ Jesus their head."[10]

With these quotations as a backdrop, most readers will be surprised to learn that most of the defenders of women relied on the ideas of the increasingly influential Puritan movement in England during the last part of the 16th and early decades of the 17th centuries. Juliet Dusinberre has made a scholarly study of the role of women in Shakespeare's day and her thesis, outlined in *Shakespeare and the Nature of Women*, 3rd Ed. (2003), is that "Protestant [Puritan] ideology inaugurated new attitudes to women and coalesced with the practical concerns of the Humanists like Thomas More (1478-1535) and Desiderius Erasmus (1466-1536) to reform women's education."[11] Of particular importance to the defense of women was the Puritan insistence that spiritual equality existed between men and women. From this first principle, reformers encouraged the rejection of the old Pauline views of universal feminine nature in favor of viewing women as individuals.[12] Generally ignoring what they perceived as the decadent world of the court, the Puritans and pamphleteers directed their preaching and teaching to the solid and relatively numerous middle class. Building on the framework of the spiritual equality of men and women, the reformers looked at the state of marriage and concluded that a chaste marriage was on equal footing with celibacy.[13] This was significant because the Roman Catholic traditional of holding virginity as the ideal undermined the sacrament of marriage as second best to celibacy and cast the woman in the role of seductress who pulled men down from the preferred path. St. Paul in writing to the Corinthians said of men too weak to follow a life of celibacy "... let them marry: for it is better to marry than to burn." (1 Corinthians

7:9, KJV). Rejecting virginity as the single spiritual ideal, the Puritans elevated the perception of women from spiritual corruptors to spiritual collaborators who, working in harmony with her husband, labored together to create a Christian home. While in the final analysis, the Puritans and pamphleteers endorse the patriarchal norm which placed the man at the head of the household, they placed emphasis on fellowship within a marriage where the husband was expected rule benevolently by treating his wife as a partner and not as a servant.

Against the backdrop of these traditions, the discussion and debate about what constituted the "ideal" women was a potent subject during the reign of Elizabethan and beyond. The appearance of the printing press enabled unprecedented dissemination of ideas and a growing "middle class" with an appetite for intellectual discussion scooped up an ever increasing number of pamphlets debating the proper role and behavior of women in society. These treaties placed less emphasis on the aristocratic and were more secular then the writings leading up to them. Handbooks for the education of women and the conduct for wives appeared to guide parents in the education of their children and women in the proper execution of their wifely duties. Juan Luis Vives, for example, was a Spanish humanist and educational theorist who served as tutor to Mary Tudor. In 1524, he published *De institutione feminae Christianae (The Education of a Christian Woman)*, in which he set out pedagogical principles for the instruction of women. While he supported educating women, he believed women should be submissive and educated only in a manner that would improve their role as a wife and caregiver to her husband.

The opening volley in what came to be called the "Pamphlet Wars" occurred in 1541-2 with the appearance of *The Schoolhouse for women* [sic] and *Mulierum Paeam*. *The Schoolhouse* was a comprehensive attack on womankind written in a humorous, sometimes vulgar vein. *Mulierum Paeam* was the response to *The Schoolhouse*, defending women in a scholarly and serious tone. In 1558, exiled Puritan John Knox wrote *The First Blast of the Trumpet against the monstrous regiment of Women*, an attack on Queen Mary I in particular and women in general. The next year, John Aylmer penned a defense that at once defended a woman's right to rule while simultaneously conceding their weakness and inferiority to men. In 1560, *The Schoolhouse* was reprinted followed by the reprinting of *Mulierum and A Little and Brief treatise called the defense of women* [sic] by Edward More that stated, along with the standard defenses, that English women were more chaste than Italian women because of England's cooler climate. Toward the end of the decade, C. Pyrrye published *The praise and Dispraise of Women* [sic] which argued both the virtues and vices of women and advised young men on the selection of a worthy bride. Things then went quiet for a score of years until, in 1589, Thomas Nashe published a satirical attack on the vices of womankind entitled *The Anatomy of Absurdity.* Quickly following its appearance, the first defense written by a woman was published. Jane Anger's *Protection of Women* turned her defense of women into an attack on men. She argued that men only see women as objects of sexual desire, and that once that desire was satisfied, they abandoned them.

The general thrust of the attacks against women centered on the assumption that women were all body, ruled by emotion and fundamentally opposed to the rationality and order that governed the male. They were seen in the context of natural forces: unpredictable, disorderly, and potentially dangerous. Like nature, women were seen as something to tamed, exploited, and closely controlled where possible. The patrilineal system, supported by religion, tradition, science (such as it was), and law, did what it could both by persuasion and regulation to mold women into acceptable "civilized" members of society. The underlying strategy of the masculine power base was the commodification of the women. As a commodity, women became items for barter among men. They could be used to forge alliances between competing tribes, clans, or countries. They could be bartered by fathers to improve their financial or social status. Their value came to be associated with their virtue and their virtues were defined by their potential husbands. The valued virtues as catalogued by the pamphleteers included chastity, humility, obedience, and silence. In an interesting twist of logic, the pamphleteers proposed that women given free rein would exhibit characteristics contrary to these virtues, giving into their "natures," but they then turn around to label women who did not exhibit these virtues as "unnatural."

As a commodity, women were the responsibility of first their fathers and/or brothers and then their husbands. The father was expected to regulate the daughter's behavior, to assure her proper education as becoming to her social station, to guard her chastity and to guide her to an acceptable husband. Since all wealth and titles descended through the males, the husbands were particularly concerned with the chastity of their wives because infidelity on the part of the wife could result in the man's wealth descending to a child not his own. As a commodity, women were also prohibited from owning property although by the time of Shakespeare some women, particularly widows, were being permitted by law to keep a portion of the wealth left behind by a husband. However, if the widow elected to remarry, in more cases than not, her inherited wealth would come under the control of the new husband.

As any commodity, women were meant to serve the needs of their "owners," i.e., their husbands. It was the duty of the wife, to anticipate, reflect and support their husband's wants, needs and desires. They were expected to reflect well on their husbands through their silence and obedience to his will since a man would be judged unfavorably if his wife appeared to be beyond his control.

Women were particularly criticized by the pamphleteers if they were too free with their tongues. A "scolding" wife was seen as one of the worst banes that could be visited upon a husband, second only to the adulterous wife who makes her husband a cuckold.

These are the competing conceptual frameworks that served as a backdrop for the creation of Shakespeare's women. It can be inferred that the majority of the middle class adhered to the traditional approach that women were font of all evils and that prudence required that they be controlled as a potentially dangerous animal by means kindly if possible, but violently if necessary. If not, it would have been unnecessary for the Puritan preachers and pamphleteers to devote so much energy and ink in trying to reform society's attitudes toward the natures and proper treatment of women. While the pulpit and the press can be potent shapers of public opinion, we are certainly aware in the 21st century that the entertainment industry is probably more powerful than both. Preachers typically only reached their specific congregations and pamphleteers only directly reached the literate who made up less than a third of the population. The theater, however, was opened to everyone who could pay the price of admission. Contrary to the impression given by many high school English teachers, the purpose of the playwright was not to write lofty philosophical tracts in dramatic form; it was to make money! Then, as today, people tend to pay money to be entertained, not to be lectured to about what they should think or how they should behave. Certainly many of the plays presented on the stage of the Curtain, Rose or Globe had topical relevance to the audience, but like the motion pictures of today, the social, political or theological point of view of the playwrights was subordinated to the entertainment value of the work in all but the most ham-handed of productions. If one wishes to attract the largest audience possible (and thus make the largest possible box office revenues), one would be wise not to overtly take sides on an issue of significant public debate. At best, generating controversy would result in smaller crowds or the actors being pelted on the stage with raw fruit. At worst, it could result in the closing of the theater and imprisonment of the theater staff. Nevertheless, playwrights of Shakespeare's age just as the screenwriters and directors of today, brought to their works a point of view on subjects of contemporary interest and the best of these artists, the true geniuses, were/are able to present the subject in such a way that their work would produce "buzz," that is, discussion about the underlying subject matters as well as the entertainment value of the work. I would suggest that that entertainment exploring the nature and role of women in society was certain to produce such buzz.

Notes

1.   Richardson, William. *On Shakespeare's Imitation of Female Characters (addressed to a friend).* 1788. http://www.shakespearean.org.uk/fem1-ric.htm

2.   Hankey, Julie. "Victorian Portias: Shakespeare's Borderline Heroine." *Shakespeare Quarterly;* Winter 1994; 45, 4.

3.   Ibid.

4.   Aristotle. *History of Animals,* Book IX, part 1. [Online]. http://classics.mit.edu/Aristotle/history_anim.9.ix.html

5.   Barr, Jane. *The Influence of Saint Jerome on Medieval Attitudes to Women* [Online].
      First published as Ch. 6, in <u>After Eve</u>, edited by Janet Martin Soskice, 1990. http://www.womenpriests.org/theology/barr.asp

6.   Keane, Marie-Henry. *Woman seen as a 'problem' and as 'solution' in the theological anthropology of the Early Fathers: Considering the Consequences* [Online]. Paper presented to Catholic Theological Society of South Africa, October 1987. http://www.catherinecollegelibrary.net/theology/keane1.asp

7.   "Nuns: Origins and history." *New Advent Catholic Encyclopedia* [Online]. http://www.newadvent.org/cathen/11164a.htm

8.   For context of quote, see [Online] http://beggarsallreformation.blogspot.com/2010/04/luther-if-women-wear-themselves-out-in.html.

9.   Calvin, John. *A Sermon of Maister. Iohn Caluine, vpon the first Epistle of Paul, to Timothie, published for the benefit and edifying of the Churche of God* [Online]. http://www.truecovenanter.com/calvin/calvin_19_on_Timothy.html

10. Knox, John. *First Blast of the Trumpet Against the Monstrous Regiment of Women* (1558) [Online]. http://www.gutenberg.org/files/9660/9660-h/9660-h.htm

11. Dusinberre, Juliet. *Shakespeare and the Nature of Women,* 3rd Ed. Amazon Kindle Edition, 2003, location 783

12. Ibid, location 827.

13. Ibid, location 802.

THE IMMORTAL SHREW

SHE IS MY GOODS, MY CHATTELS: THE TAMING OF THE SHREW: KATHERINA

Fie, fie! unknit that threatening unkind brow,
And dart not scornful glances from those eyes,
To wound thy lord, thy king, thy governor:
It blots thy beauty as frosts do bite the meads,
Confounds thy fame as whirlwinds shake fair buds,
And in no sense is meet or amiable.
A woman moved is like a fountain troubled,
Muddy, ill-seeming, thick, bereft of beauty;
And while it is so, none so dry or thirsty
Will deign to sip or touch one drop of it.
Thy husband is thy lord, thy life, thy keeper,
Thy head, thy sovereign; one that cares for thee,
And for thy maintenance commits his body
To painful labour both by sea and land,
To watch the night in storms, the day in cold,
Whilst thou liest warm at home, secure and safe;
And craves no other tribute at thy hands
But love, fair looks and true obedience;
Too little payment for so great a debt.
Such duty as the subject owes the prince
Even such a woman oweth to her husband;
And when she is froward, peevish, sullen, sour,
And not obedient to his honest will,
What is she but a foul contending rebel
And graceless traitor to her loving lord?

I am ashamed that women are so simple
To offer war where they should kneel for peace;
Or seek for rule, supremacy and sway,
When they are bound to serve, love and obey.
Why are our bodies soft and weak and smooth,
Unapt to toil and trouble in the world,
But that our soft conditions and our hearts
Should well agree with our external parts?
Come, come, you froward and unable worms!
My mind hath been as big as one of yours,
My heart as great, my reason haply more,
To bandy word for word and frown for frown;
But now I see our lances are but straws,
Our strength as weak, our weakness past compare,
That seeming to be most which we indeed least are.
Then vail your stomachs, for it is no boot,
And place your hands below your husband's foot:
In token of which duty, if he please,
My hand is ready; may it do him ease.

(*TOS*, V, 2, 136-179)

When reading or hearing Katharina's concluding speech in *The Taming of the Shrew*, what modern woman doesn't roll her eyes and what modern man, after checking that his wife isn't looking, doesn't smile inwardly and nod in agreement? Are we meant to take the speech seriously? Does Kate believe what she is saying? Does Petruchio believe what he is hearing? Is the audience meant to cheer or jeer at the end? Did the 16th century see the scene differently than a 21st century American audience? Commenting on the scene in the late 19th century, George Bernard Shaw wrote that "no man with any decency of feeling can sit it out in the company of a woman without being extremely ashamed of the lord-of-creation moral implied in the wager and the speech put into the woman's own mouth." Similarly, in a 2009 review of a performance of *Shrew* at London's Novello Theatre, theater critic Charles Spencer described the play as a "deeply nasty comedy in which a vainglorious fortune-hunter inflicts physical and psychological torture on the woman he has married for her money in order to break her spirit and enjoy a quiet life."[1] Although Shaw and Spencer are separated by more than a century, their response to the play represents at least the published critical impressions of the play throughout the 20th century. Why then, other than the fact it was written by Shakespeare, does such a "repulsive" work continue to attract productions and audiences?

In Shakespeare's day, "the explicit and implicit subjects of this play--arranged marriages, the authority of fathers and husbands, the obedience expected from daughters and wives, the economic helplessness of most women--were issues and experiences that touched the lives of everyone in Shakespeare's audience."[2] Although *The Taming of the Shrew* was not "officially" published until the First Folio of 1623, there is evidence that the play was quite popular during Shakespeare's lifetime. A pirated Quarto version of the play appeared 1604 that claimed the play was "sundry times acted" and *Shrew* was sufficiently popular to spawn a 1611 sequel by John Fletcher: *The Woman's Prize*, or *The Tamer Tamed*.[3] It would seem that Shakespeare's audiences were less offended by the subject matter of *Shrew* than the critics of the 19th and 20th centuries. Similarly, the response of 19th and 20th century audience appears to mirror the response of their 16th century counterparts. Notwithstanding the obvious feminist issues that have been raised since the 1970's, *The Taming of the Shrew* remained an extremely popular play in the 20th century. At Stratford-upon-Avon, for example the play has been on the boards in more than one-half of the last 100 seasons, including 5 different productions between 1979 and 1993. Because of its popularity, *The Taming of the Shrew* has been adapted to other media on numerous occasions. A condensed, silent version was made in Great Britain in 1923and Douglas Fairbanks and Mary Pickford made an early sound version of the work in 1929, and in1966 Franco Zeffirelli made a wide-screen version, starring Richard Burton and Elizabeth Taylor At least 27 operas have been crafted from the materials of *The Taming of the Shrew*, but the most notable musical rendition is the musical comedy, *Kiss, Me Kate* (1948), with a book by Sam and Bella Spewack and with words and music by Cole Porter.[4]

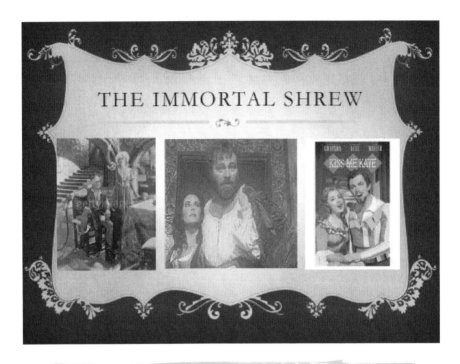

THE IMMORTAL SHREW

The popularity of *Shrew* in Shakespeare's lifetime can, I suggest, be attributed to the exploration of some very real social concerns of the period in a verbally and visually entertaining farce. Issues such as the proper conduct of wives and daughters were, as I've mentioned, being discussed in pulpit and pamphlet. The practice of arranged marriages was under attack from the advocates of romantic love. And the practice of managing one's household was of intense interest to the young husbands of the day. The popularity of the play today, I believe, has to do with modern man's hidden and guilty nostalgia for the time when man was the uncontested ruler of his household. Our Western contemporaries will of course deny such feelings and disguise their delight in Kate's speech much as they will harbor deep-seated racist attitudes while claiming that racism has been eradicated. In spite of progress, the culture of the West is still predominately paternalistic and several thousand years of misogyny are not erased in a few generations. For women, the enjoyment of the play takes on a different form. Women are likely to view *Shrew* as an anachronistic throwback to the bad old days and take solace and enjoyment from how far they have come or they may view the play as many current productions do, as an ironic farce where both Katherina and Petruchio are winners, having developed an "understanding" and a potentially loving relationship. Such an interpretation plays the concluding speech as a "nod, nod—wink, wink" collaboration between husband and wife that simply mouths all the conventional thinking of what a wife should be or do.

The *Taming of the Shrew* opens with an Induction which is seldom seen in performance. It involves an inebriated tinker found sleeping in the street by a Lord and his servants. For sport, they take the tinker in to the Lord's manor, clean him up, place him in the Lord's bed and, upon his awakening, persuade him that he is in fact a Lord who has been mad, forgetting himself for the past seven years. In his madness he has only thought himself a tinker and has now returned to health and ready to resume his rightful place in society. For his pleasure, the true Lord has arranged an entertainment in the way of a play for the befuddled tinker and that play is *The Taming of the Shrew*. The tinker, Lord and company then all but disappear from the action, excepting a brief interjection at the end of Act I, scene 1. The Induction serves no function as a part of the main narrative and is simply forgotten after the first Act. Why did Shakespeare include it? Perhaps as a clue to his intention in the telling of the story of Katherina and Petruchio. The story of the tinker is one of disguise and deception. No one is what he presents himself to be. Similarly, in the main narrative of the *Shrew*, a large number of the characters assume disguises.

When the play within a play begins, a young scholar, Lucentio arrives in Padua with his servant, Tranio. Immediately they come upon a scene in the street where the rich merchant Baptista Minola, accompanied by his daughters, Katherina and Bianca, is being petitioned by two suitors, Hortensio and Gremio, who wish to marry the younger daughter, Bianca. Baptista tells that that he will not grant Bianca in marriage until his oldest daughter, Katherina has a husband. The problem is that Katherina is such a notorious shrew that no man in Padua will have her for a wife. Katherina is not slow to show her colors. To her father, she protests, "I pray you, sir, is it your will/To make a stale of me amongst these mates?" to which Hortensio responds "no mates for you, /Unless you were of gentler, milder mould." Katherina rounds on him and replies,

> I'faith, sir, you shall never need to fear:
> I wis it is not half way to her heart;
> But if it were, doubt not her care should be
> To comb your noddle with a three-legg'd stool
> And paint your face and use you like a fool.
>
> (TOS, I, 1, 61-65)

This scene establishes that Katherine's crime as her determination to exercise free speech in a world where silence in women is a principle virtue. Bianca's suitors call her "devil," and "fiend of hell" while Tranio, looking on, describes her as "curst and shrewd" (TOS, I, 1, 180). To further emphasize his point, Tranio contrasts the two sisters, describing "The one as famous for a scolding tongue /As is the other for beauteous modesty" (TOS, I, 2, 252-3). His judgment is based exclusively on how Katherina exercises her voice and how Bianca restrains hers. Both sisters have their lines is this scene, but Katherine's words are filled with defiance and violence. Bianca, on the other hand, uses words that are full of acquiesce and humility and as such, they are the verbal equivalence of silence. One could visualize this scene as imitation of a bear-baiting with the proud and bellowing Kate hemmed in by the yelping, nipping suitors. As she has no power beyond her scathing tongue, she uses it to vent her frustration at her tormentors. When, for example, Katherina questions, "is it your will /To make a stale of me amongst these mates?" (TOS, I, 1, 57-8), the signification of "stale" as "prostitute" is her protest against the woman's role in the patriarchal culture as an object of exchange in the circulation of male desire."[5]

As fate (and the story line) would have it, an old acquaintance of Hortensio, one Petruchio of Verona comes "to wive it wealthily in Padua" (TOS, I, 2, 75). From his first appearance, he is revealed as an abusive bully by his treatment of his servant. He learns from Hortensio of the available and wealthy Katherina and immediately resolves that he will marry her, though

> Be she as foul as was Florentius' love,
> As old as Sibyl and as curst and shrewd
> As Socrates' Xanthippe, or a worse,
> She moves me not, or not removes, at least,
> Affection's edge in me, were she as rough
> As are the swelling Adriatic seas:
>
> (TOS, I, 2, 69-74)

His servant, Grumio quickly agrees:

> Why give him gold enough and marry him to
> a puppet or an aglet-baby; or an old trot with ne'er
> a tooth in her head, though she have as many diseases
> as two and fifty horses: why, nothing comes amiss,
> so money comes withal.
>
> (TOS, I, 2, 77-82)

Petruchio constructs for himself a heroic persona. For him, Katherina is a subject onto whom he will, with the strength of his words, overpower hers and enforce his will like a conqueror. He boasts to Hortensio and Gremio,

> Think you a little din can daunt mine ears?
> Have I not in my time heard lions roar?
> Have I not heard the sea puff'd up with winds
> Rage like an angry boar chafed with sweat?
> Have I not heard great ordnance in the field,
> And heaven's artillery thunder in the skies?
> Have I not in a pitched battle heard
> Loud 'larums, neighing steeds, and trumpets' clang?
> And do you tell me of a woman's tongue,
>
> (TOS, I, 2, 199-207)

When we next see Katherina, she is physically abusing her younger sister, having tied her hands and pulled her about the house as if leading an ass. She demands Bianca reveal to her who she truly loves and when Bianca's answer fails to please, Katherina escalates the violence to the level of striking her sister. At this exact moment, Baptista enters to free Bianca and chastise Katherina who, in response cries,

> She is your treasure, she must have a husband;
> I must dance bare-foot on her wedding day
> And for your love to her lead apes in hell.
> Talk not to me: I will go sit and weep
> Till I can find occasion of revenge.
>
> (TOS, II, 1, 32-36)

In both her early scenes, there is little sympathy created for Katherina. She is loud, envious of her sister, verbally and physically abusive. Shakespeare's purpose is clearly to portray Katherina in the worst possible light, savage and uncivilized, in order to justify Petruchio's "taming" of this out-of-control shrew. This portrayal is reinforced one last time before Katherina and Petruchio meet. When Petruchio arrives at Baptista's he brings along Hortensio disguised as a music teacher so that he can gain access to Bianca. While Petruchio makes his intentions clear to Baptista, Hortensio who has been sent in to begin instructing Katherina to play the lute, emerges in a state of disarray. When asked by Baptista if his daughter will make a good musician, Hortensio replies "I think she'll sooner prove a soldier." He continues, describing his encounter with Katherina:

I did but tell her she mistook her frets,
And bow'd her hand to teach her fingering;
When, with a most impatient devilish spirit,
'Frets, call you these?' quoth she; 'I'll fume with them:'
And, with that word, she struck me on the head,
And through the instrument my pate made way;

                              (TOS, II, 1, 149-154)

Again we see Katherina striking out verbally and physically with the slightest provocation. From these early scenes and descriptions, we are likely to see Katherina more as a child throwing a temper tantrum. Harold Goddard makes this point *The Meaning of Shakespeare*, seeing Katherina as a child who must be dealt with accordingly: "When a small child is irritable and cross, the thing to do is not to reason, still less to pity or pamper, or even to be just kind and understanding in the ordinary sense. The thing to do is to take the child captive"[6] The child must be brought under control to maintain peace in the environment and prevent injury to others. Baptista is obviously unable to control his child's behavior, so it will fall to Petruchio to do so.

Petruchio continues his blunt persona when he meets the father of his intended. He makes no secret of the fact that monetary gain is his chief objective, not Katherina's affection. T Baptista, he says:

...every day I cannot come to woo.
You knew my father well, and in him me,
Left solely heir to all his lands and goods,
Which I have better'd rather than decreased:
Then tell me, if I get your daughter's love,
What dowry shall I have with her to wife?

                              (TOS, II, 1, 115-120)

The terms of the dowry are acceptable, but Baptista to his credit does require that Petruchio win his daughter's love "for that is all in all." Petruchio is unfazed,

Why, that is nothing: for I tell you, father,
I am as peremptory as she proud-minded;
And where two raging fires meet together
They do consume the thing that feeds their fury:
Though little fire grows great with little wind,
Yet extreme gusts will blow out fire and all:

So I to her and so she yields to me;
For I am rough and woo not like a babe.

$$\text{(TOS, II, 1, 130-137)}$$

When the "two raging fires" meet, Petruchio immediately attacks Katherina's most potent weapon: her words. He contradicts and purposely misconstrues her word, thereby disarming her. In greeting her he addresses her as Kate, usurping her power to be called as she wills. In punning words, he engages her in bawdy banter, dragging her from her lofty position as a maid who should be wooed to the level of the tavern and the street. When he seems to get the better of her in this war of words, Kate falls back on a cruder response by striking her wooer/tormentor. Petruchio will have none of this and plainly tells her, "I swear I'll cuff you, if you strike again." (TOS, II, 1, 220). Petruchio then resumes his bawdy attack before launching his principle stratagem, that is, to redefine Kate's reality. He tells her that she is "pleasant, gamesome, passing courteous, / But slow in speech," and says:

Thou canst not frown, thou canst not look askance,
Nor bite the lip, as angry wenches will,
Nor hast thou pleasure to be cross in talk,
But thou with mildness entertain'st thy wooers,
With gentle conference, soft and affable.

$$\text{(TOS, II, 1, 247-251)}$$

While the facts are obviously counter to this praise, Kate is put off balance. The reality of words is central to Kate's defense in her patrilineal society and when words and facts are used counter to her perceived reality, she is confused and her speech is effectively neutralized. Petruchio then concludes with the only reality that really matters,

Thus in plain terms: your father hath consented
That you shall be my wife; your dowry 'greed on;
And, Will you, nill you, I will marry you.

$$\text{(TOS, II, 1, 269-271)}$$

Katherina is dumbstruck, without a doubt feeling betrayed by a father who contracted her with a husband and did so without consulting her, let alone soliciting her consent. When Baptista comes upon the couple, Katherina is only able to squeak out a protest before her words are overrun by her soon to be husband who tells Baptista and his companions,

'Tis bargain'd 'twixt us twain, being alone,
That she shall still be curst in company.
I tell you, 'tis incredible to believe
How much she loves me:

(TOS, II, 1, 304-307)

With this clever ploy, Petruchio manages to silence any protest Katherina might make by making her every word subject to question as to its sincerity. He subverts the power of her speech by imposing his own meaning on her words before she can correct him. He acts as though his words determine the very nature of reality, and because nobody is willing to defend Katherina's interests anyway, his assertion goes unchallenged. He so suppresses her reality that she concludes her protests are useless. She has no choice but to stand by in silent consent as Baptista sells her to a man she despises.

The remainder of the second Act is taken up with Baptista taking up the role of the merchant who barters with the suitors for his daughter Bianca. In Katharina's case, he was willing to bestow a generous dowry to be free of his head-strong daughter. In negotiating for the far more valuable Bianca, he establishes a bidding war between the suitors, granting the hand of Bianca to the highest bidder. Here the role of woman as commodity is most apparent. As it happens, it is Tranio who has taken on the role of his master, Lucentio, who makes the winning bid. Lucentio, like Hortensio, has disguised himself as a tutor to gain access to woo Bianca. It is interesting to note that again Baptista makes the decision concerning a husband for his daughter with consulting or seeking Bianca's consent. In fact, there is no indication in the play that Bianca has even seen Tranio, let alone spoken to him. Here Shakespeare shows the state of unmarried daughters who were still subject to arranged marriage, a practice still observed in Shakespeare's England, but one which was increasingly under attack, particularly from the Puritan community. The Puritans believed that marriage was only acceptable when both the principle parties and their parents consented to the partnership.

The second Scene of the third Act opens on the day of Katherina's wedding and to the discomfiture of the bride, the groom is a no-show. In spite of the embarrassment she must feel at being left at the altar, it seems strange that she would be distressed that the man she seemed to abhor at the end of the wooing scene had no appeared for the wedding. One would think that she would have some sense of relief. In fact, one might wonder that head-strong Katherina is there herself. Is she there in obedience to her father's wish or is she so desperate to be married that even Petruchio is acceptable as a husband? In the past she has certainly been willing to cross her father on matters far less important than her marriage to a man she calls "lunatic" and "mad-cup ruffian." Or does she see something in Petruchio that draws her to him? Does she see him as a worthy mate, able to bandy words with her on an equal footing or does she think that she will be able to have her way with him as she has successfully done with others in the past? The answer is not obvious in the play, but the final option seems most likely. After Petruchio finally arrives decked out in clothing sure to embarrass his bride and marries Katherina in a ceremony where his behavior is so unruly that it borders on blasphemy, he tells the wedding guests that he and Katherina must leave before enjoying the wedding feast. Katherina begs that they stay, but when Petruchio refuses, she reverts to her normal behavior telling her new husband:

> *Do what thou canst, I will not go to-day;*
> *No, nor to-morrow, not till I please myself.*
> *The door is open, sir; there lies your way;*
> *You may be jogging whiles your boots are green;*
> *For me, I'll not be gone till I please myself:*
>
> *(TOS, III, 2, 208-212)*

She must surely be shocked when Petruchio forcibly removes her, saying:

> *... for my bonny Kate, she must with me.*
> *Nay, look not big, nor stamp, nor stare, nor fret;*
> *I will be master of what is mine own:*
> *She is my goods, my chattels; she is my house,*
> *My household stuff, my field, my barn,*
> *My horse, my ox, my ass, my anything;*
>
> *(TOS, III, 2, 228-232)*

Here is probably the most concise and explicit statement of the woman as property philosophy that permeated the Western culture. Katherina is reduced to the level of one more object in Petruchio's household and one more animal existing to provide for and comfort their master. In this way, Petruchio is justified in bring what he owns under his control.

After a cold and miserable ride to Petruchio's country home, Katherina is thrust into an alien world where the master, Petruchio, rails madly and physically abuses the servants who surround him to serve his need. He calls for his supper and when it is brought, he calls it burnt and tosses it about the stage. Katherina protests, "The meat was well," but Petruchio again changes objective reality to his reality, says:

> *I tell thee, Kate, 'twas burnt and dried away;*
> *And I expressly am forbid to touch it,*
> *For it engenders choler, planteth anger;*
> *And better 'twere that both of us did fast,*
>
> *(TOS, IV, 1, 170-173)*

So, cold, tired and hungry Katherina is led off to the bridal chamber. There, we learn from the servants, she is subjected, not to the expected sexual consummation, but to a "sermon of contingency." He "rails, and swears, and rates, that she, poor soul, /Knows not which way to stand, to look, to speak, /And sits as one new-risen from a dream." (TOS, IV, 1, 183-185). Petruchio leaves her chamber, then in soliloquy reveals his plan:

> *She eat no meat to-day, nor none shall eat;*
> *Last night she slept not, nor to-night she shall not;*
> *As with the meat, some undeserved fault*
> *I'll find about the making of the bed;*
> *And here I'll fling the pillow, there the bolster,*
> *This way the coverlet, another way the sheets:*
> *Ay, and amid this hurly I intend*
> *That all is done in reverend care of her;*
>
> *(TOS, IV, 1, 197-204)*

Focusing exclusively on Petruchio's taming methods rather than Katherina's experiences as shrew, the objective of *The Taming of the Shrew* is to demonstrate an effective means of enforcing discipline in a household without crossing the line that separated the "permissible" discipline that was a superior's responsibility from the excessive violence of a domestic tyrant. Among the social and legal prerogatives to the husband is to employ violence to impose his will and to discipline his household. *"An Homily [of the State of Matrimony]"* argues that only the "common sort" use "fist and staff' to rule a wife. Thus a notion of civility recasts physical violence as weak and, at the same time, brutal. .... Husbands who rely on physical strength rather than reason come to be regarded as less manly and less human.[7] By nature, Petruchio is a violent man and is willing to use force if necessary, but by choosing to employ a method that supports the "wife-beating reformers" he is seen as effective and praise-worthy. The play teaches men how to dominate their wives by policy rather than force, and how to control them more effectively, principally by denying them language.

When we next see Katherina, she is "starved for meat, giddy for lack of sleep." (TOS, IV, 3, 9). Petruchio accompanied by Hortensio comes upon her and announces that they are to go to her father's house to attend the wedding of Bianca. To prepare, he has arranged for a tailor and haberdasher to deck Katherina out for the occasion. However, when the gown and cap are presented and approved by Katherina, Petruchio predictably finds fault with them and orders them taken away. As the couple prepare to depart, Petruchio off-handedly comments "I think 'tis now some seven o'clock" (*TOS*, IV, 3, 185). Just as casually, Kate responds "I dare assure you, sir, 'tis almost two" (*TOS*, IV, 3, 189). Exasperated, Petruchio finally explains his intention plainly. Speaking to Kate like he would to an exceptionally slow child, he tells her:

> *It shall be seven ere I go to horse:*
> *Look, what I speak, or do, or think to do,*
> *You are still crossing it. Sirs, let't alone:*
> *I will not go to-day; and ere I do,*
> *It shall be what o'clock I say it is.*
>
> (*TOS*, IV, 3, 191-195)

Finally, they set forth, presumably at the time set out by Petruchio, and when we see the couple they are on the road to Padua. Again, Katherina is tested:

> PETRUCHIO
> *Come on, i' God's name; once more toward our father's.*
> *Good Lord, how bright and goodly shines the moon!*
> KATHARINA
> *The moon! the sun: it is not moonlight now.*
> PETRUCHIO
> *I say it is the moon that shines so bright.*
> KATHARINA
> *I know it is the sun that shines so bright.*
> PETRUCHIO
> *Now, by my mother's son, and that's myself,*
> *It shall be moon, or star, or what I list,*
> *Or ere I journey to your father's house.*
> *Go on, and fetch our horses back again.*
> *Evermore cross'd and cross'd; nothing but cross'd!*
>
> (*TOS*, IV, 5, 1-10)

At last, the light goes on for Kate.

> KATHARINA

Forward, I pray, since we have come so far,
And be it moon, or sun, or what you please:
An if you please to call it a rush-candle,
Henceforth I vow it shall be so for me.
PETRUCHIO
I say it is the moon.
KATHARINA
I know it is the moon.
PETRUCHIO
Nay, then you lie: it is the blessed sun.
KATHARINA
Then, God be bless'd, it is the blessed sun:
But sun it is not, when you say it is not;
And the moon changes even as your mind.
What you will have it named, even that it is;
And so it shall be so for Katharina.

(TOS, IV, 5, 12-22)

Finally, Kate understands that if she is to have her way it will only be through her ability pander to her husband's demands. She must mold her reality to suit his and must disguise her thoughts and guard her tongue if she is to the things that she desires. Here we have our first sight of the tamed Kate.

Some scholars have suggested that Kate is a victim of the Stockholm syndrome. The Stockholm syndrome occurs when: 1) a person threatens another's survival and is perceived by the other as able and willing to carry out his/her threat; 2) the threatening person shows the other kindness; 3) the victim is unable to escape from the threatening person; and 4) the victim is isolated from outsiders.[13] Katherina has seen Petruchio brutalize his servants and strike a priest. She has been taken forcefully from her home and family and isolated from all she is familiar with. She has been starved and deprived of sleep. From this series of violent and controlling behaviors gives Kate has ample reason to believe that her very survival is threatened. Like the classic Stockholm captor, Petruchio shows Katherina some limited and conditional kindness, but it is always alternated with aggression, and the combination of the two conflicting gestures serves to confuse her perception of him as dominator. Victims of the Stockholm syndrome actively look for ways to please rather than upset their captors. So it becomes with Katherina. Petruchio has forced Katherina to create a bond with him which some might mistake for love but is in fact a survival technique common to victims of violence. It is this pivotal scene that prepares us for her famous speech at the end of the play where now able to anticipate he husband's wishes; she gives him exactly what he wants.

While some have seen the kissing scene in the streets of Padua as evidence of a blossoming love, it is really simply another example of Petruchio's absolute rule over Katherina. He exercises his power by forcing her to choose between the lesser of two evils: kissing him in public against her will, or returning to the isolation of the taming school. A false, involuntary gesture of love does not, however, constitute real love, only the illusion of it. Since Katherina's threat to the male social order is posed through her public speech, her submission to that patriarchal order is only complete when it is made public by the kiss and her final speech.

When they arrive in Padua, they learn along with Baptista that Lucentio and Bianca have secretly wed. The shocked Baptista can only ask "have you married my daughter without asking my good will?" (*TOS*, V, 1, 133-134). The tables have turned. The troublesome but finally obedient daughter has put on the disguise of the obedient wife while the quiet and valued daughter lets her mask slip to reveal her true nature by her willful defiance of her father and his patrilineal rights.

Recent producers and scholars have suggested that the speech can only be delivered ironically. Lynda Boose encourages us to avoid a revisionist reading Katherina's speech, in her opinion, is neither excessive nor ironic, but a reflection of traditional Elizabethan values.[8] Kate, by re-inventing herself in the role of obedient wife, finds a role that allow her to be respected and admired. The patrilineal social structure is not going to change for her, so Kate must learn to function and find love within that social structure. It can be said, though quite generously, that Petruchio has not tamed her, but has taught her play the patriarchal game so that they may both find success in their marriage. Marianne Novy remarks that Kate is finally "in a position of authority in which she can reprimand her newly married sister publicly, and displace her as the virtuous and ideal bride."[9] In the context of the time it ends up, in the current parlance, a win-win for both parties.

So, in the final analysis is *The Taming of the Shrew* misogynistic? I would suggest it is misogynistic to the same extent that *Othello* is racist and *Merchant of Venice* is anti-Semitic. I believe Shakespeare's purpose is to hold the mirror up to his society and let society see what is rather than pontificate on what should be. Does he support the idea that the woman should be subordinate to man? Quite likely. We shouldn't forget that he is not only a man "for all time," but a man in his time and would be largely adherent to the mores of his time. Does he endorse the taming of Kate? I believe he does Petruchio's methods, though abhorrent to a contemporary audience would seem almost benevolent to an audience who still found wife-beating an appropriate means of governing one's household. What Shakespeare seems to be saying to his audience is "this is the nature of the society we live in, make the best of it."

FATHER, AS IT PLEASE ME: MUCH ABO
ABOUT NOTHING: BEATRICE

In brief the play is concerned with two romances. The first is between Claudio and Hero, young lover who fall in love at first sight and speed toward marriage until malicious plot is hatched to call Hero's chastity into question. The other involves a budding romance between Beatrice and Benedick that also involves a plot hatched to bring the two together. Hero is a more fully developed version of Bianca and Beatrice is a merrier version of Katherina. Unlike Bianca, Hero is genuinely all virtue and obedience, totally submissive to her father and faithful to her intended husband. Beatrice, Hero's cousin, is her opposite: strong willed and outspoken. She generally displays contempt for the institution of marriage and reserves her acid tongue for one man, her former suitor, and future lover Benedick. We are told early in the play Leonato, Beatrice's uncle that "There is a/kind of merry war betwixt Signior Benedick and her:/they never meet but there's a skirmish of wit/between them." (*MAAN*, I, 1, 61-62). Their very first exchange proves the point:

> BENEDICK
> *What, my dear Lady Disdain! are you yet living?*
> BEATRICE
> *Is it possible disdain should die while she hath*
> *such meet food to feed it as Signior Benedick?*
> *Courtesy itself must convert to disdain, if you come*
> *in her presence.*
> BENEDICK
> *Then is courtesy a turncoat. But it is certain I*
> *am loved of all ladies, only you excepted:*
>
> (*MAAN*, I, 1, 119-125)

Benedick then announces that he loves no lady and Beatrice retorts she "had rather hear [her] dog bark at a crow than a man/swear he loves me." (*MAAN*, I, 1, 131). Benedick expands on his contempt for women and marriage when he learns that Claudio is taken with Hero,

Shall I never see a bachelor of three-score again?
Go to, i' faith; an thou wilt needs thrust thy neck
into a yoke, wear the print of it and sigh away
Sundays

(MAAN, I, 1, 199-201)

He goes on to say women "Because I will not do/them the wrong to mistrust any, I will do myself the/right to trust none." Trust, as shall be seen, is one of the central themes of Much Ado About Nothing. It is misplaced trust in the play's principle villain that will bring about the play's central crisis and it is just this mistrust of women that will be the undoing of young Hero.

Just as Benedick tries to undermine Claudio's faith in love, so does Beatrice attempt to influence Hero. Hero is completely under the control of her father Leonato, especially with regard to courtship. When, in Act Two, Leonato believes that Don Pedro, the leader of the band of men and the Prince of Padua, may seek Hero's hand in marriage, he orders Hero to welcome the prince's advances: "Daughter, remember what I told you. If the Prince do solicit you in that kind, you know your answer" (MAAN, II, 6, 1-3). Beatrice it seems would liberate her cousin Hero from her patriarchal repression. While virtually every main character in the play is conspiring to arrange Hero's marriage, Beatrice counsels Hero to follow her own desires, despite contemporary custom:

[I]t is my cousin's duty to make curtsy and say, "Father, as it please
you." But yet for all that, cousin, let him be a handsome fellow, or else
make another curtsy and say, "Father, as it please me"

(MAAN, II, 1, 49-52)

It is noteworthy that Beatrice lives with her uncle and not her father. The audience is not privy to where her father is. We can assume he is dead because no mention is made of him and when, at the end of the play she intends to marry, there is no mention of contacting him or asking his consent. Her uncle Leonato indulges her willfullness in a way he would clearly not tolerate in his daughter. Beatrice, unlike Hero and even Katherina, seems to have the luxury of speaking her mind or selecting her spouse that is denied most women in Shakespeare's plays and in Shakespeare's world. She refuses to marry because she has not come upon a suitable partner. She hints that she once thought Benedick to me the man fit to be her husband. In conversation with Don Pedro when he remarks that she has "lost the heart of Signior Benedick, she responds:

> Indeed, my lord, he lent it me awhile; and I gave
> him use for it, a double heart for his single one:
> marry, once before he won it of me with false dice,
> therefore your grace may well say I have lost it.
>
> (MAAN, II, 1, 276-282)

Just as in *The Taming of the Shrew*, disguises and misidentifications figure prominently in the plot. The wooing of Hero is undertaken by a disguised Don Pedro on Claudio's behave. Attempting to stir up trouble, Don Pedro's bastard brother, Don John convinces Claudio that Don Pedro is, in fact, wooing Hero for himself. Amazingly, Claudio immediately believes the malicious gossip about his friend and leader. Fortunately, the confusion is quickly sorted out and no harm comes from it.

With time on their hands before the wedding of Claudio and Hero, Don Pedro in league with Claudio, Hero, and Leonato resolve to bring Beatrice and Benedick together. This they achieve through staged conversation for overhearing. Don Pedro, Claudio and Leonato arrange for Benedick to overhear a conversation where Leonato tells his companions that his niece, Beatrice is mad with love for Benedick. Benedick immediately believes it and prepares himself for marriage.

> ...I may chance have some
> odd quirks and remnants of wit broken on me,
> because I have railed so long against marriage: but
> doth not the appetite alter? a man loves the meat
> in his youth that he cannot endure in his age.
> Shall quips and sentences and these paper bullets of
> the brain awe a man from the career of his humour?
> No, the world must be peopled. When I said I would
> die a bachelor, I did not think I should live till I
> were married
>
> (MAAN, II, 3, 235-244)

Similarly, Hero and her companion Ursula arrange for Beatrice to overhear their conversation where they discuss Benedick's great love for Beatrice.

> Can this be true?
> Stand I condemn'd for pride and scorn so much?
> Contempt, farewell! and maiden pride, adieu!

No glory lives behind the back of such.

And, Benedick, love on; I will requite thee,
Taming my wild heart to thy loving hand
(MAAN, III, 1, 107-112)

While this plot is hatched to bring Benedick and Beatrice together, another is underway under the direction Don John to drive Claudio and Hero apart. Don John's henchman, Borachio, seduces Hero's serving woman and describes the affair to his comrade,

I have to-night
wooed Margaret, the Lady Hero's gentlewoman, by the
name of Hero: she leans me out at her mistress'
chamber-window, bids me a thousand times good
night,--I tell this tale vilely:--I should first
tell thee how the prince, Claudio and my master,
planted and placed and possessed by my master Don
John, saw afar off in the orchard this amiable encounter
(MAAN, III, 3, 144-152)

Margaret is mistaken by Claudio and Don Pedro for Hero. They say nothing until all have gathered for the wedding and then with callous disregard for his bride, Claudio denounces Hero before the assembled guests.

Would you not swear,
All you that see her, that she were a maid,
By these exterior shows? But she is none:
She knows the heat of a luxurious bed;
Her blush is guiltiness, not modesty
(MAAN, IV, 1, 38-42)

Backed by Don Pedro he calls her "wanton," "stale" and a "rotten orange." Overwrought, Hero collapses as if dead and to his shame, her father wishes her dead, believing the accusations despite Hero's history of obedience and fidelity. He rages:

O, she is fallen
Into a pit of ink, that the wide sea

> Hath drops too few to wash her clean again
> And salt too little which may season give
> To her foul-tainted flesh!

(MAAN, IV, 1, 139-143)

Only the friar presiding at the wedding and Beatrice defend Hero's innocence. The friar cautions patience before judgment and Benedick begins to suspect some villainy initiated by Don John is the cause of the calamity. The friar councils to let out that Hero has, in fact, died as was originally thought until the matter can be sorted out. Through mere chance, bumbling constable uncovers the plot and forces a confession from Borachio. Hearing the confession, Claudio and Don Pedro are overwhelmed with grief and guilt. The incensed Leonato turns on them, adding fuel to their already burning guilt.

> I thank you, princes, for my daughter's death:
> Record it with your high and worthy deeds:
> 'Twas bravely done, if you bethink you of it.

(MAAN, V, 1, 268-270)

Claudio begs how he can make recompense and Leonato tells him,

> I cannot bid you bid my daughter live;
> That were impossible: but, I pray you both,
> Possess the people in Messina here
> How innocent she died; and if your love
> Can labour ought in sad invention,
> Hang her an epitaph upon her tomb
> And sing it to her bones, sing it to-night:
> To-morrow morning come you to my house,
> And since you could not be my son-in-law,
> Be yet my nephew: my brother hath a daughter,
> Almost the copy of my child that's dead,
> And she alone is heir to both of us:
> Give her the right you should have given her cousin,
> And so dies my revenge.

(MAAN, V, 1, 279-292)

All of this Claudio readily agrees to and in a final act of disguise, Hero poses as the brother's daughter. Masked, Hero comes to Claudio and after he pledges to marry her, Hero reveals herself and all present are reconciled one to another. As they make their way to the chapel for the wedding, Benedick calls out to the friar,

Soft and fair, friar. Which is Beatrice?

BEATRICE

[Unmasking] I answer to that name. What is your will?

BENEDICK

Do not you love me?

BEATRICE

Why, no; no more than reason.

BENEDICK

Why, then your uncle and the prince and Claudio
Have been deceived; they swore you did.

BEATRICE

Do not you love me?

BENEDICK

Troth, no; no more than reason.

BEATRICE

Why, then my cousin Margaret and Ursula
Are much deceived; for they did swear you did.

BENEDICK

They swore that you were almost sick for me.

BEATRICE

They swore that you were well-nigh dead for me.

BENEDICK

'Tis no such matter. Then you do not love me?

BEATRICE

No, truly, but in friendly recompense.

LEONATO

Come, cousin, I am sure you love the gentleman.

CLAUDIO

And I'll be sworn upon't that he loves her;
For here's a paper written in his hand,
A halting sonnet of his own pure brain,
Fashion'd to Beatrice.

HERO

And here's another
Writ in my cousin's hand, stolen from her pocket,
Containing her affection unto Benedick.

BENEDICK

A miracle! here's our own hands against our hearts.
Come, I will have thee; but, by this light, I take
thee for pity.
BEATRICE
I would not deny you; but, by this good day, I yield
upon great persuasion; and partly to save your life,
for I was told you were in a consumption.
BENEDICK
Peace! I will stop your mouth.
Kissing her

(MAAN, V, 4, 72-89)

Despite her earlier vows to requite Benedick's love (*MAAN*, III, 1, 109-16), when he at last proposes, the still proud Beatrice makes sure to emphasize that they are to be married only because she agrees, not because he wills it. Benedick, for his part, discover that the only way to conclude their merry banter is with a kiss.

In one way, I find *Much Ado About Nothing* to be more misogynistic than *The Taming of the Shrew*. *Shrew* is about behavior modification. It does not generalize about women, but concerns itself with behavior of a particular woman. *Much Ado*, on the other hand, seems to indict all women as untrustworthy. If the ideal daughter and lover, Hero, can so quickly be suspected of treachery on circumstantial evidence, it speaks poorly about how the men in the play view women in general. Drawing on classical and religious writings, men were inclined to view women as deceitful and lascivious. Aristotle, for example, believed that women are by nature more void of shame, false of speech, and deceptive than men. The early church fathers tended to see women as the origin of all sins. Against this background of tradition, the distrust of women in made immediately in *Much Ado About Nothing*. When Leonato greets his guests at the beginning of the play, Don Pedro asks, "I think this is your daughter." Leonato replies, "Her mother hath many times told me so." Inherent in his joking answer is evidence of his casual mistrust of women. Even with his own wife, he shows an underlying concern that he could have been deceived in his daughter's paternity. When Claudio and Don Pedro witness the scene that Don John has arranged for them, they immediately believe what they are led to believe without a pause to consider, based on Hero's known character, if what they perceive is likely to be true. Later, when his daughter is denounced at the altar by Claudio, Leonato immediately believes she has been unfaithful although there is no reason in her past that should lead him condemn her as guilty before the accusation can be explored. Oddly enough, in a play run through with deceit, disguises, and staged conversations, the only character indicted for deceit is the least deceitful of all.

And why is this the case? Because all the men in the play are predisposed to believe it.

LL MET BY MOONLIGHT: A MIDSUMMER NIGHT'S DREAM: TITANIA

Marital discord is the central concern of one of the three interwoven plots that make up *A Midsummer Night's Dream*. The feuding couple is Titania and Oberon, Queen and King of the Fairies. The main point of their contention is an orphaned child who has been given to Titania by the child's dying mother, a votaress of Titania's order. Oberon demands her to hand over her "little changeling boy" (*MSN*, II, 1, 120) so that he may become Oberon's "henchman" (*MSN*, II, 1, 121) and a "Knight of his train" (*MSN*, II, 1, 125). Titania, not surprisingly, refuses. Their meeting in the Athenian woods is rife with anger and recriminations.

> *OBERON*
> *Ill met by moonlight, proud Titania.*
> *TITANIA*
> *What, jealous Oberon! Fairies, skip hence:*
> *I have forsworn his bed and company.*
> *OBERON*
> *Tarry, rash wanton: am not I thy lord?*
>
> (MSN, II, 1, 60-63)

In reply, Titania reminds Oberon of his indiscretions with Hippolyta and Phillida. In response, he accuses her of similar dalliances with Theseus. These infidelities are not, however, at the core of their conflict; Titania calls them "forgeries of jealousy" (*MSN*, II, 1, 81) and relates how Oberon's childish anger at Titania has spilled over to upset even the forces of nature, resulting in misery for common men. "[T]his same progeny of evils" she says, "comes /From our debate, from our dissension" (*MSN*, 2, 1, 115-16), Oberon responds:

> *Do you amend it then; it lies in you:*
> *Why should Titania cross her Oberon?*
> *I do but beg a little changeling boy,*
> *To be my henchman.*

It is Titania' refusal to submit to Oberon's command that is the source of the discord. Although Titania is justified in retaining control over the boy, Oberon expects his wife to bend to his will, and place his needs and wants above her own. In this, his expectation of wifely obedience and submission mirrors the patriarchal expectations of the men in the Athenian world. When she refuses to submit, Oberon vows vengeance. Interestingly, Oberon chooses a love potion as his instrument of revenge. When Titania's eyes are anointed with the love juice, she will fall madly in love with the first creature she sees [a]nd ere I take this charm from off her sight, /As I can take it with another herb, /I'll make her render up her page to me." (MSN, II, 1, 183-185). After the potion is applied, Titania awakens and immediately her eyes fall on Bottom, a rustic actor who has been magically transformed into a man-ass by the mischief Puck, Oberon's chief henchman. In a scene both comedic and disturbingly grotesque, the beautiful Titania woos this bestial monstrosity and has him led to her bower where she presumably enjoys him sexually in a scene thankfully conducted off-stage. Oberon intends to strike at his wife's pride, and shame and humiliate her in order to teach her a lesson in obedience. When Oberon and Puck come upon the sleeping and spent monstrous couple, the fairy king relates how he had earlier come upon Titania "[s]eeking sweet favours from this hateful fool" (MSN, IV, 1, 49). He continues,

> When I had at my pleasure taunted her
> And she in mild terms begg'd my patience,
> I then did ask of her her changeling child;
> Which straight she gave me, and her fairy sent
> To bear him to my bower in fairy land.
> And now I have the boy, I will undo
> This hateful imperfection of her eyes:
>
> *(MSN, IV, 1, 57-63)*

Oberon having accomplished his goals, humiliating his wife and stealing her child, now feels it safe to remove the enchantment from Titania's eyes. When she is restored to herself, she is repulsed by the monster at her side, but surprisingly does not seem to be angry at Oberon's cruel trick. Oberon announces to Titania that "[n]ow thou and I are new in amity," (MSN, II, 1, 87) and Titania does not object. Oberon has restored the normal patriarchal rule to the fairy world and brought Titania back to her proper role as submissive wife.

Notes

1. Spencer, Charles. "The Taming of the Shrew at the Novello Theatre," (review). *The Telegraph:* 6 Feb 2009.
   http://www.telegraph.co.uk/culture/culturecritics/charlesspencer/468743
   1/The-aming-of-the-Shrew-at-the-Novello-Theatre-review.html

2. Kehler, Dorothea. "Echoes of the Induction in *The Taming of the Shrew.*" *Renaissance Papers* 1986, 31

3. Kolb, James J. *The Taming of the Shrew: Study Guide.* Hofstra University: Department of Drama and Dance, 1996, 10-12.

4. Newman, Karen. "Renaissance Family Politics and Shakespeare's *The Taming of the Shrew.*" *English Literals/ Renaissance.* 16:1 (1986):90.

5. Goddard, Harold C. *The Meaning of Shakespeare.* Chicago: University of Chicago Press, 1951, 70.

6. Detmer, Emily. "Civilizing Subordination: Domestic Violence and *The Taming of the Shrew.*" *Shakespeare Quarterly.* 48.3 (1997): 278

7. Qtd in Detmer, 274.

8. Boose, Lynda E. "Scolding Brides and Bridling Scolds: Taming the Women's Unruly Member." *Shakespeare Quarterly.* 42.2 (1991): 181.

9. Dash, Irene G. *Wooing, Wedding, and Power: Women in Shakespeare's Plays.* New York: Columbia University Press, 1981, 23

DEFIANT DAUGHTERS

TRUST NOT YOUR DAUGHTERS' MINDS:
DESDEMONA: OTHELLO

Trust and mistrust are at the heart of the tragedy of *Othello*. In brief, Othello trusts his "ancient "(Ensign), Iago who is secretly out to destroy him. He is led to distrust his wife Desdemona and his friend and subordinate officer, Cassio. Under Iago's guidance, he comes to believe they have betrayed him in adultery, and this leads Othello to murder his wife and order a failed attempt on Cassio's life. When he learns that Desdemona and Cassio are innocent, and that Iago has orchestrated his downfall, Othello takes his own life.

Othello is one of Shakespeare's most heart wrenching tragedies. In spite of the exquisite machinations of Iago, the audience wonders why Othello is so easily persuaded his new bride is a "whore." In answer, some critics attribute his credulity to his ethnicity. They argue that Shakespeare relied on the accepted view of African blacks posited in *The History and Description of Africa* (1526) by John Leo that defined blacks by their credulity, their high regard of chastity, their jealousy and the fury of their wrath. For sure, this stereotype plays into the Othello character; however, I would suggest that Shakespeare felt the need to provide a more compelling explanation for Othello's lack of faith in Desdemona. After all, Othello is clearly not at the beginning of the play a fool driven by passion rather than reason. He is a respected general in the Venetian army who is entrusted with the welfare of the Venetian state. He is articulate, even eloquent. In every way he is drawn as an intelligent and honorable man. In every way, I would suggest, but one: his secretive marriage to Desdemona without the consent of her father.

In the very first Act, we learn that Desdemona has snuck out of her father's house to marry Othello in the dead of night. This is a pattern of deception we have already seen in Bianca's marriage in *The Taming of the Shrew* and we will see repeated by deceptive daughters in *The Merchant of Venice*, *Romeo and Juliet*, and *A Midsummer Night's Dream*. We have already seen that the expectation for the obedient daughter was that she should rely on their father to select a suitable husband for her. Wanting that ideal situation, should a daughter to be bold enough to select a man on her own, the expectation was she would seek the consent of her father before commencing courtship, let alone consider marriage. This is evidenced in Hero's behavior in *Much Ado about Nothing* where she is attracted to Claudio, but is willing to accept Don Pedro as her husband on the basis of her father's insistence (*MAAN*, II, 1, 66-80).

Desdemona, like her sister in kind, Bianca, woos and weds Othello without her father's knowledge. One important difference is that Baptista has already approved the marriage of Bianca to Lucentio by proxy. Lucentio is a "proper" social and financial match for Baptista's youngest daughter regardless if he is the Lucentio portrayed by Tranio or Lucentio himself. Othello is clearly not a "proper" social match for Desdemona. They are in the opinion of Barbantio, Desdemona's father, so grossly mismatched that he attributes her "seduction" to witchcraft. Upon confronting Othello, he rails:

> O thou foul thief, where hast thou stow'd my daughter?
> Damn'd as thou art, thou hast enchanted her;
> For I'll refer me to all things of sense,
> If she in chains of magic were not bound,
> Whether a maid so tender, fair and happy,
> So opposite to marriage that she shunned
> The wealthy curled darlings of our nation,
> Would ever have, to incur a general mock,
> Run from her guardage to the sooty bosom
> Of such a thing as thou, to fear, not to delight.
> Judge me the world, if 'tis not gross in sense
> That thou hast practised on her with foul charms,
> Abused her delicate youth with drugs or minerals
> That weaken motion: I'll have't disputed on;
> 'Tis probable and palpable to thinking.
> I therefore apprehend and do attach thee
> For an abuser of the world, a practiser
> Of arts inhibited and out of warrant.
>
> (O, I, 2, 61-79)

In this rant, we learn several things. First, it is inconceivable to Barbantio that Desdemona would willingly bind herself "to the sooty bosom/Of such a thing as thou." Othello, in Barbantio's eyes, is not a man, but a "sooty" thing "to fear, not to delight" in. We later learn as Othello offers his defense to the Duke of Venice that this was not always Barbantio's opinion.

Her father loved me; oft invited me;
Still question'd me the story of my life,
From year to year, the battles, sieges, fortunes,
That I have passed.
I ran it through, even from my boyish days,
To the very moment that he bade me tell it;

(O, I, 3, 28-33)

Here, I would suggest is Othello's first act of misguided trust. He interprets the invitations to Barbantio's home as a show of love, but it is clear from Barbantio's words that the invitation was extended more from curiosity than affection. Othello was a novelty in Barbantio's world, a "thing" to be wondered at, but obviously not a man that he would consider the equal of himself or his daughter. Despite his protests, however, Othello was a thing to delight in for both himself and, more importantly, his daughter. I tend to think of Barbantio in the context of the 1967 film, *Guess Who's Coming to Dinner?* In this ground breaking film, Spencer Tracy in his final role portrayed a liberal father, Matt Drayton, who has brought up his daughter to think for herself. When, however, she brings home a brilliant African American physician and announces her plans to marry him, the father is forced to confront his latent racism. To his credit, Drayton, good liberal that he is, reasonably acknowledges his racism than puts it aside. Barbantio, more a product of his time, is unable to do so.

Barbantio's objections are not exclusively based on Othello's race. Charles Frey has observed that "[w]hen the [brotherless] daughter chooses radically against her father's will, she effectively shuts him off from patriarchal domination of the son-in-law and consequent son-like extension of his power and values."[1] In the culture where property normally passes down through the son, the son-in-law became the surrogate son of the father not blessed with a male child. If the son-in-law is deemed unworthy by the father, it would be a double loss: that of his daughter who was viewed as property and his property itself. These personal concerns dovetail with Barbantio's societal concerns that "male hyperagamy, or men marrying above their station has the effect of reversing the proper order of rule in the republic: free gentlemen over bond-slaves, Christians over pagans."[2] In marrying Othello without her father's consent or knowledge, Desdemona pushes against the patriarchal tradition of her culture. Brabantio calls her treachery "treason of the blood," that is, a betrayal not only of himself but of all the fathers of Venice who are warned, "from hence trust not your daughters' minds / By what you see them act" (O, I, 1, 168-170).

Desdemona, for her part, listened to Othello's tales "with a greedy ear," and

My story being done,
She gave me for my pains a world of sighs:
She swore, in faith, twas strange, 'twas passing strange,
'Twas pitiful, 'twas wondrous pitiful:
She wish'd she had not heard it, yet she wish'd
That heaven had made her such a man: she thank'd me,
And bade me, if I had a friend that loved her,
I should but teach him how to tell my story.
And that would woo her. Upon this hint I spake:
She loved me for the dangers I had pass'd,
And I loved her that she did pity them.

(O, I, 3, 158-168)

Diana Dreher suggests that "underneath the sweet and quiet surface" that Desdemona presented to Barbantio was "...a young soul yearning for adventure," drawn like a moth to a flame by the exotic life history of Othello.[3] We learn in Barbantio's rant before the Duke that Desdemona has rejected, presumably with his consent, "The wealthy curled darlings of our nation." We know that Roderigo has been rejected as a suitor, but there were obviously more and worthier courtiers who have also sought Desdemona's hand. From this we learn that Barbantio is not a tyrannical father who would insist on marrying his daughter off against her liking. Nevertheless, Desdemona, knowing her father would never consent to her marriage to Othello, simply elects to go around him, saying in effect what Beatrice advocated, "Father, as it please me" (MAAN, II, I, 52).

When Desdemona comes before the Duke, she freely states that she has taken Othello as her husband, but offers no excuse or explanation as to why she acted in secrecy. Instead she simply states:

To you I am bound for life and education;
My life and education both do learn me
How to respect you; you are the lord of duty;
I am hitherto your daughter: but here's my husband

(O, I, 3, 182-185)

Desdemona's actions however belie her words. Where was the respect she owed Barbantio when she wooed and wed the Moor without father's knowledge or consent? Even today, what father would not feel betrayed by such actions? Barbantio has been too liberal in the education of his daughter, apparently giving her sufficient free reign that she feels fully justified in acting on her feeling for Othello. Barbantio acknowledges his mistake when he says "I am glad at soul I have no other child:/For thy escape would teach me tyranny, /To hang clogs on them." (O, I, 3, 196-198)

So if Desdemona feels empowered to act independent of her father's consent, what is her reason for acting in secrecy? Did she simply wish to avoid the inevitable unpleasant "scene" that would certainly emerge from openly defying her father by confronting his with a *fait accompli?* Or was the marriage an act of impulse driven by the swift carriage of youthful passion? Shakespeare does not tell us Desdemona's age, by convention at the time would place an eligible unmarried women's age at 18 or less. If we compare her with Juliet who is 14 years old and whose actions are very similar in their impulsiveness to Desdemona, one can reasonable conclude that her marriage to Othello is undertaken without the depth of analysis one would expect from someone of greater maturity. In short, Desdemona saw what she wanted and took it, consequences be damned. As evidence of the suddenness of the marriage, Iago twice reminds Roderigo of the "violence [with which] she first loved the Moor" (O, II, 1, 222) and of their love's "violent commencement" (O, I, 3, 344). Iago also calls attention to her youth, attributing her attraction to the Moor to the hot blood of the young. Although this may or may not be true of Desdemona in particular, it is a stereotype sufficiently held about young women that Roderigo and later Othello accept his suggestion at face value.

The first consequence of Desdemona's hasty marriage is the loss of her father's love. When Othello is to be sent to war in Cypress, the Duke suggests that Desdemona remain with her father. Both Barbantio and Desdemona refuse outright, she preferring to go to war with Othello rather than "put [her] father in impatient thoughts/By being in his eye" (O, I, 3, 43-44). Although she makes it appear that she does not wish to be a continuing physical reminder to her father of the betrayal, to accompany Othello to war would be exactly the kind of exotic adventure that she longed when she selected Othello as her husband. Tragically, Desdemona's deception of her father undercuts her trustworthiness and provides a seed of distrust that Iago can cultivate in Othello's mind. It is not, however, Iago who plants the seed, it is Barbantio who tells Othello, "Look to her, Moor, if thou hast eyes to see: She has deceived her father, and may thee" (O, I, 3, 292-293). When Iago sets about laying his trap for Othello, he reminds him of Barbantio's words:

> IAGO
> She did deceive her father, marrying you;
> And when she seem'd to shake and fear your looks,

She loved them most.
OTHELLO
And so she did.
IAGO
Why, go to then;
She that, so young, could give out such a seeming,
To seal her father's eyes up close as oak-
He thought 'twas witchcraft...

(O, III, 3, 206-211)

I want to be careful here not to blame the victim for her own death, although some critics argue that the misogynist Shakespeare felt compelled to condemn her independence by showing her death as its price. I think Shakespeare did want us, to some extent, blame Desdemona in her own tragedy, but not because of a conscious or unconscious misogynistic need on Shakespeare's part to see the independent women put in her place. Instead, I believe it is Shakespeare's intention to elevate Desdemona to the level of a tragic figure and not just a victim. By playing a role in her own downfall, by exhibiting the fatal flaws of independence and impulsiveness, she meets the Aristotelian definition of a tragic hero (protagonist) as one "who is not eminently good and just, yet whose misfortune is brought about not by vice or depravity, but by some error or frailty."[4] In Othello's case, his "tragic flaws" are his gullibility and jealousy. In Desdemona's case, the "tragic flaws" are her independence and impulsiveness because these characteristics create the possibility that she could elect to betray Othello, just as she deceived Barbantio. The supreme irony of the play is that it is Desdemona's submission to Othello that leads to her death. It is not Othello "who loved not wisely, but too well," but Desdemona. Desdemona in her increasing desperate efforts to please her husband only succeeds in supplying Iago with more fodder to feed the flames of Othello's range. Even with her dying breath, she defends her husband. When her friend and serving woman, Emily asks "who hath done this deed?" Desdemona responds, "Nobody; I myself."

O MY DUCATS! O MY DAUGHTER! FLED WITH A CHRISTIAN! JESSICA: THE MERCHANT OF VENICE

In *The Merchant of Venice* we have a situation similar to the one we find in *Othello*. A daughter flees her home and marries without her father's knowledge or consent. The man she marries is as unacceptable to her father as Othello was to Barbantio. This daughter also steals ducats and jewels from her father, thus compounding her crime beyond that of Desdemona's. If Desdemona is murdered as a consequence of violating the patriarchal demands on an obedient daughter as some suggest, what is the consequence faced by this daughter who not only betrays her father's trust, but robs him? Instead of death, this daughter at the end of the play is rewarded with a promise that she will inherit all her father owns upon his death so that she and her husband can live happily ever after. Her name is Jessica and her father is the infamous Jew, Shylock.

Why is Jessica rewarded for deceiving her father and Desdemona destroyed? The easy answer is that *The Merchant of Venice* is intended to be a comedy and *Othello* a tragedy. Comedies end with marriages and celebrations; tragedies with death and mourning. This explanation, however, is only the beginning of the answer. Desdemona's father is a wealthy and respected Venetian. Jessica's father is a wealthy, but hated Jew. Desdemona, in the world of the play, "marries down" when she marries Othello. Jessica "marries up" by marrying the Christian, Lorenzo and in fact improves her social acceptability by converting to Christianity.

As a result of the horrors of the Holocaust, contemporary interpretations of the play have a tendency to accentuate Shylock as the victim of a prejudicial Venetian society and explain his excesses in those terms. The audiences of Elizabethan England, however, would have clearly seen him as the antagonist of the work, if not the outright villain. Shylock, as I noted earlier, is in part inspired by Christopher Marlowe's acclaimed Jewish villain, Barabas who is also betrayed by his daughter and is killed by his in consequence. Shylock is not so dark a villain and it is to Shakespeare's credit that he endows the Jew with an emotional depth of character sufficient to induce some sympathy for his sufferings and some understanding of his motives. Nevertheless, we should not lose sight of the fact that he is the villain of the piece and must be understood in that context.

The relationship between Shylock and Jessica is only seen in only one short interchanges. The short burst of dialogue between the two conveys distance rather than closeness and in fact sounds more like one between master and servant than between father and daughter.

> *Hear you me, Jessica:*
> *Lock up my doors; and when you hear the drum*
> *And the vile squealing of the wry-neck'd fife,*
> *Clamber not you up to the casements then,*
> *Nor thrust your head into the public street*
> *To gaze on Christian fools with varnish'd faces,*
> *But stop my house's ears, I mean my casements:*
> *Let not the sound of shallow foppery enter*
> *My sober house.*
>
> *(MOV, II, 5, 28-36)*

In Jessica's case, we learn more about her feelings for her father through her discussions with others then we ever learn about Shylock's feelings for her. In Act II, scene 3 Jessica describes her home as "hell" and goes on to say:

> *Alack, what heinous sin is it in me*
> *To be ashamed to be my father's child!*
> *But though I am a daughter to his blood,*
> *I am not to his manners.*
>
> *(MOV, II, 3, 16-19)*

At this point in the play she has already decided that she will leave her father's home to marry the Christian, Lorenzo. She recognizes that to so dishonor her father is a sin by the standards of her faith, but that causes her no pause. How the lovers managed to meet and fall in love is never explained. As soon as the opportunity presents itself, Jessica steals away with Lorenzo, taking with her a dowry stolen from Shylock's treasure trove. So far, Shylock has been portrayed as a wealth obsessed usurer and a domineering possessive patriarchic figure; and Jessica as the victimized shuttered daughter who is in love with a man outside her societal scope. There is a fairy tale quality to this setup where Shylock takes on the role of the evil ogre has trapped the beautiful princess, Jessica, in the tower and she can only be rescued by her true love, Lorenzo. However, when Jessica escapes with Shylock's ducats, she shows a wealth obsession equal to her father's.

The difference is that for Shylock wealth is an end unto itself; for Jessica, it is her ticket to freedom and acceptance in the broader society.

We learn of Shylock's reaction to Jessica's escape second hand. Salanio tells his companion,

> *I never heard a passion so confused,*
> *So strange, outrageous, and so variable,*
> *As the dog Jew did utter in the streets:*
> *'My daughter! O my ducats! O my daughter!*
> *Fled with a Christian! O my Christian ducats!*
> *Justice! the law! my ducats, and my daughter!*
> *A sealed bag, two sealed bags of ducats,*
> *Of double ducats, stolen from me by my daughter!*
> *And jewels, two stones, two rich and precious stones,*
> *Stolen by my daughter! Justice! find the girl;*
> *She hath the stones upon her, and the ducats.'*
>
> *(MOV, II, 8, 12-22)*

In his outrage, Shylock is cast as more concerned about the loss of the ducats than the loss of his daughter. He wants his daughter found not because he loves her but because "*she hath the stones upon her, and the ducats.*" (MOV, II, 8, 22). He cries out for justice, meaning he want the thief caught and punished and his goods returned, but when he finds the couple has fled the scene, he turns his wraith against a victim still within his scope, the Christian merchant Antonia who is in Shylock's debt. Shakespeare puts in Shylock's mouth what is considered one of the great appeals for racial tolerance, the "Hath not a Jew eyes?" speech. Often glossed over is that the beginning and the end of the speech and the central point of the speech is not an appeal for tolerance, but a justification for the revenge Shylock plans to visit on Antonia. When asked what use a pound of Antonio's flesh will be to him, Shylock replies:

> *...To bait fish withal: if it will feed nothing else,*
> *it will feed my revenge. He hath disgraced me, and*
> *hindered me half a million; laughed at my losses,*
> *mocked at my gains, scorned my nation, thwarted my*
> *bargains, cooled my friends, heated mine*
> *enemies;*
>
> *(MOV, III, 1, 53-58)*

While Antonia has, in fact, done all these things to Shylock, the merchant is assigned for convenience the role of scapegoat for the entire Christian community that has scorned and persecuted Shylock in particular and the Venetian Jews in general. Shylock concludes:

> *If a Jew wrong a Christian,*
> *what is his humility? Revenge. If a Christian*
> *wrong a Jew, what should his sufferance be by*
> *Christian example? Why, revenge. The villany you*
> *teach me, I will execute, and it shall go hard*
> (MOV, III, 1, 68-73)

The brilliance of this speech is that it at once inspires in the audience sympathy for Shylock on the one hand and yet maintains his role as the villain of the play. It is hard today to imagine an audience unmoved by Shylock's words and the wrongs done to him simply because he is a Jew. Even in the anti-Semitic England of Shakespeare, the audience must surely have been shocked into silence by Shylock's impassioned appeal to a common humanity while chilled by his malicious desire for murderous revenge. And it should be kept in mind that while Shylock has endured a lifetime of persecutions, it takes Jessica's act of theft and betrayal to spark his rage.

On the heels of his famous speech, Shylock is approached by his friend Tubal who has been searching for Jessica. Tubal has been unable to catch up with her and her new husband, but has learned she is burning through her purloined property at a record clip. Here in this play, we see a desire for wealth shared by both father and daughter; however, Shylock represents one extreme—the insatiable hoarding of wealth, while Jessica displays the opposite tendency—the squandering of money on unneeded luxuries. Tubal tells Shylock that "Your daughter spent in Genoa, as I heard, in one night fourscore ducats." (MOV, III, 1, 109) and then that, upon meeting some of Antonio's creditors, he learned from one of them that they bought a ring from Jessica "for a monkey." Upon hearing this, we see a second unexpected burst of humanity from Shylock,

> *... Thou torturest me, Tubal: it was my*
> *turquoise; I had it of Leah when I was a bachelor:*
> *I would not have given it for a wilderness of monkeys.*
> (MOV, III, 1, 120-123)

The poignancy of this single sentence portrays in a few words a younger, happier Shylock who once loved a woman named Leah who gave him a ring that he values beyond its monetary value. It speaks to the contempt of Jessica for her father that she would take the one thing she would know that Shylock valued among all his wealth and trade it for something as frivolous and worthless as a monkey. Jessica need not have taken this turquoise ring, the token of her parents' affection; she took with her wealth enough for a self-consigned dowry. One can only conclude that she took that particular ring for the express purpose of placing a dagger in her father's heart.

After their merry wandering, Jessica and her husband Lorenzo arrive at Belmont, the home of wealthy Portia and her new found love Bassanio. They are graciously welcomed and when Portia decides to go off to Venice to help save the beleaguered Antonia, she places her estate in the hands of Jessica and her husband. By this point of the play, Jessica's role has pretty much served its function. We will learn that Jessica will receive a court ordered inheritance from Shylock as part of the punishment dealt out to the Jew for his "attempt" on the life of Antonio. Her reward for deceiving her father is multiplied far beyond her expectation and her future is thus assured. But since the audience hears all this at the conclusion of the court scene, there is no theatrical motive to bring Jessica back to the stage other than to inform her of her good fortune. Instead Shakespeare gives her a rather extended scene with her husband in Act V where they seem to talk of nothing of specifically relevant to the play. They banter back and forth, making allusion to famous lovers: Troilus, Thisbe, Dido, and Medea. Significantly, all of these lovers ended badly and their choice if allusions suggest their love is already heading for unhappy times. To put emphasis on the point, Jessica concludes:

> In such a night
> Did young Lorenzo swear he loved her well,
> Stealing her soul with many vows of faith
> And ne'er a true one.
> (MOV, V, 1, 17-19)

Is Jessica only joking here or is there a hint that she feels in some way betrayed by Lorenzo. Does the reality of a marriage outrun her expectation of a carefree and exciting life she envisioned with Lorenzo? Has the role of surrogate "lady of the house" given her a vision of what lies before her as a wife? Does she start to see it as simply a life not much different from her life with Shylock? At his point, they are interrupted and learn that Portia is soon expected home. Lorenzo orders the household musicians to strike up some music to welcome her return.

When they play, Jessica sighs, "I am never merry when I hear sweet music." (*MOV*, V, 1, 69). Lorenzo excuses this comment, saying "The reason is your spirits are attentive." (*MOV*, V, 1, 70), that is, she dwells on it too deeply. Music, he suggests, has the ability to soothe the wild beast that does not "attend" to it, but accepts it as it is. When Portia and Nerissa arrive they also meditate on the music,

> NERISSA
> *It is your music, madam, of the house.*
> PORTIA
> *Nothing is good, I see, without respect:*
> *Methinks it sounds much sweeter than by day.*
> NERISSA
> *Silence bestows that virtue on it, madam.*
> PORTIA
> *The crow doth sing as sweetly as the lark,*
> *When neither is attended,*
>
> > (*MOV*, V, 1, 98-103)

In opposition to Jessica, Portia comments that the music coming from the house "sounds much sweeter than by day." Nerissa, taking a position opposite Lorenzo, notes that it is the absence of competing sounds that makes it so; that is, it can be "attended" to without distraction. Between the two opinions, Nerissa's explanation seems more credible. Music needs to be attended to be appreciated. If Jessica does not feel merry at the sound of music, it possibly results from sad associations that the music provokes. Shylock, as we have seen, was a man with no love of music; he ordered his house shut up to prevent the sounds of music from penetrating it. The youthful Jessica craved the forbidden music and fled her father's house to have it, then in having it, found it disappointing in its effect. Such a reading would be consistent with her earlier comment that suggested disappointment with her husband who stole "her soul with many vows of faith/And ne'er a true one." (*MOV*, V, 1, 18-19). Music does not make Jessica merry because it is a reminder that reality fails to live up to her youthful expectations. In the end, although Jessica is free of Shylock, married to Lorenzo, accepted by the Christian community at Belmont and assured financial security, one has the sense from her final scene that she is no happier at the end of the play than she was at the beginning. In fact, she may be worse off because as the daughter of Shylock, she had a dream of a better happier life; as the wife of Lorenzo, she has fulfilled the dream and found it wanting.

OR IF THOU THINK'ST I AM TOO QUICKLY WON, I'LL FROWN AND BE PERVERSE AN SAY THEE NAY: JULIET: ROMEO AND JULIET

Of all of Shakespeare's defiant daughters, Juliet is the best known and the most sympathetic. Long held as the paragons of idealized youthful love, Juliet and Romeo are frequently portrayed as victims of inflexible, insensitive patents and malicious fate. I, however, would suggest that the young lovers, particularly Juliet, have a degree of control over their circumstances that is often glossed over in discussions of the play. While I hesitate to throw disparagement upon a character thought of as all innocence and light, Juliet is precocious far beyond her tender years and is an active, rather than passive player in the events that unfold. When we are introduced to Juliet it is a discussion between her father and a potential suitor, Paris. We learn that she is "is yet a stranger in the world;" who "hath not seen the change of fourteen years." (R&J, I, 2, 8-9) More importantly, we learn her father cares for her and wishes her happiness when he says to Paris:

> ...woo her, gentle Paris, get her heart,
> My will to her consent is but a part;
> An she agree, within her scope of choice
> Lies my consent and fair according voice.
>
> (R&J, I, 2, 14-17)

We have heard this degree of fatherly concern before. Remember Baptista's words to Petruchio when they agree to the terms of Katherina's marriage. Before the covenant can be drawn Baptista places one condition, that: "the special thing is well obtain'd, /That is, her love; for that is all in all." (TOS, II, I, 28). In Baptista's case, we discover that this is a well-meaning self-deception because when Petruchio declares that Katherina loves him, Baptista accepts his assertion at face value and ignores Katherina's protests. At this point in the play, we have no reason to doubt Capulet's sincerity.

Juliet herself is introduced in the next scene when her mother comes to her to tell her Paris will seek her for his love. After praising the suitor in lofty terms, Lady Capulet asks "can you like of Paris' love?" In response, Juliet, the innocent and obedient daughter replies:

> I'll look to like, if looking liking move:
> But no more deep will I endart mine eye
> Than your consent gives strength to make it fly.
>
> (R&J, I, 3, 97-99)

Juliet is willing at this point to be guided by her mother in the matter of courtship, but in the next scene we see her dependence on her mother for guidance thrown out of the window when she meets Romeo.

Romeo, for his part, is the standard Petrarchan lover, stung by his unrequited love for Rosalind. He is in love with the idea of love and his rhetoric speaks to the lofty ideal of the perfect woman, chaste and worthy of adulation. Upon seeing Juliet, Rosaline is immediately forgotten. He sees in Juliet a "beauty too rich for use, for earth too dear!" and when he joins her, he compares her to a saint in an extended religious metaphor:

> ROMEO
> If I profane with my unworthiest hand
> This holy shrine, the gentle fine is this:
> My lips, two blushing pilgrims, ready stand
> To smooth that rough touch with a tender kiss.
> JULIET
> Good pilgrim, you do wrong your hand too much,
> Which mannerly devotion shows in this;
> For saints have hands that pilgrims' hands do touch,
> And palm to palm is holy palmers' kiss.
> ROMEO
> Have not saints lips, and holy palmers too?
> JULIET
> Ay, pilgrim, lips that they must use in prayer.
> ROMEO
> O, then, dear saint, let lips do what hands do;
> They pray, grant thou, lest faith turn to despair.
> JULIET
> Saints do not move, though grant for prayers' sake.
> ROMEO
> Then move not, while my prayer's effect I take.

Thus from my lips, by yours, my sin is purged.
JULIET
Then have my lips the sin that they have took.
ROMEO
Sin from thy lips? O trespass sweetly urged!
Give me my sin again.

(R&J, I, 5, 93-107)

Here Romeo and Juliet share their first kiss and then, at Juliet's instigation, they share another. At first glance this is a sweet scene drawing our attention to the magic of romantic love. However, when we think about what we have witnessed, we might have misgivings about what has transpired. This is not acceptable behavior from a daughter who moments before, has vowed to look on Paris only to the extent that her mother's "consent gives strength to make it fly" (R&J, I, 3, 99). Here she exchanges kisses with a boy she has just met. Such behavior by a young woman would still be surprising, if not shocking today. It Shakespeare's day, it would be scandalous. This is bold, even brazen behavior and shows Juliet is not the demure young woman she presents to her parents. Juliet says to Romeo, "You kiss by the book" (R&J, I, 5, 109). What does she mean and how does she know? Does she mean that he kisses as if he has studied the subject academically and kisses as he thinks he should, proficiently but not passionately, or does she mean that he kisses as one well studied is the practice, both proficient and passionate? How can she judge? Has she studied the same book?

At the opening of the balcony scene, Romeo still in the throes of Petrarchan idolatry compares Juliet to all things bright: the sun and the stars and the angels. When he reveals himself, Juliet's initial reaction is practical: how did he come to the place and does e understand the peril he is in. Only after being reassured does she return to talk of love. She admits she blushes at the words of love for Romeo spoken when she thought she was alone, but she then pushes forward, asking outright "Dost thou love me?" (R&J, II, 2, 90) and then demands a few lines later, "If thou dost love, pronounce it faithfully." (R&J, II, 2, 94). Juliet acknowledges that she is moving quicker than normally acceptable behavior for a proper young lady that she may appear too easily won, but since the proverbial cat is out of the bag, she sees no point in being coy.

I should have been more strange, I must confess,
But that thou overheard'st, ere I was ware,
My true love's passion: therefore pardon me,
And not impute this yielding to light love,

(R&J, II, 2, 102-105)

Juliet also recognizes that this romance is proceeding too quickly. She tells Romeo "I have no joy of this contract to-night: /It is too rash, too unadvised, too sudden" (R&J, II, 2, 117-118). She can see danger that Romeo chooses to ignore. Finally exercising a degree of caution, she prepares to withdraw, but Romeo cries out "O, wilt thou leave me so unsatisfied?" (R&J, II, 2, 125). Interestingly, she interprets this to mean sexual satisfaction and is relieved to him explain he is only asking for the exchange of her love vow for his. Juliet is far more worldly wise and sexually aware than the starry eyed Romeo and it she who is orchestrating the romance. After again expressing the depth of her love, she suddenly says:

> If that thy bent of love be honourable,
> Thy purpose marriage, send me word to-morrow,
> By one that I'll procure to come to thee,
> Where and what time thou wilt perform the rite;
> And all my fortunes at thy foot I'll lay
> And follow thee my lord throughout the world.
> (R&J, II, 2, 143-148)

Out of the blue, she is the one proposing marriage and soon. She gives no thought to her parents or to her outrageous behavior in proposing and arranging her own wedding. Surely Romeo must have been a bit shocked at Juliet's aggressive wooing and proposal of marriage, but he goes along with the plan, telling her he will arrange it. In parting, Juliet makes a final and prophetic expression of her love when she compares herself to a "wanton" with a bird,

> JULIET
> Who lets it hop a little from her hand,
> Like a poor prisoner in his twisted gyves,
> And with a silk thread plucks it back again,
> So loving-jealous of his liberty.
> ROMEO
> I would I were thy bird.
> JULIET
> Sweet, so would I:
> Yet I should kill thee with much cherishing.
> (R&J, II, 2, 178-183)

And so in the end, she does.

While Romeo is off arranging their marriage by Friar Lawrence, Juliet has persuaded the nurse as her co-conspirator in the plan. After speaking with Romeo at Juliet's behest, the nurse returns to the Capulet home and playfully keeps Juliet on pins and needles until revealing the Romeo has made arrangements for their secret marriage ceremony that very afternoon. The nurse's active participation in this betrayal of her employers speaks volumes about her devotion to Juliet and about Juliet's power of persuasion. Does the nurse, like Friar Lawrence, see this marriage as a devise to end the ancient grudge between the Capulets and Montagues? It seems unlikely; she is not one who exhibits a great deal of foresight. Instead, I think the nurse is only concerned with Juliet's immediate happiness and does not look beyond that single goal to consider possible consequences. In any case, the secret marriage is arranged and executed, and then inexplicably Juliet returns to the Capulet household as if nothing has happened and awaits consummation of the marriage under the very roof of her deceived parents. Juliet's eager anticipation of her wedding night is obvious in her speech as she awaits nightfall and Romeo's arrival:

> O, I have bought the mansion of a love,
> But not possess'd it, and, though I am sold,
> Not yet enjoy'd: so tedious is this day
> As is the night before some festival
> To an impatient child that hath new robes
> And may not wear them.
>
> (R&J, III, 2, 26-31)

One wonders where she thought all this was headed. Did she think that after the consummation she would present Romeo to her parents as her husband or did she think she would just continue to carry on the clandestine affair until time or circumstance revealed it? Why didn't Romeo just take Juliet to the house of his father who would probably be more accepting of the marriage than Capulet? Lord Montague may even have been glad of the marriage as is would surely result in heartbreak for his old adversary. To answer these questions, it might be useful to review how the "secret marriage" might be viewed by Shakespeare's audience. Juliet's definition of marriage is clearly still that of the old church, "a solemn pledge, confirmed by intercourse", her pledge is deeply tied to God, something that she is absolutely incapable of breaking. [5] As a general rule, however, daughters could not marry without parental consent until late in the 16th century. Before then, if a secret marriage did occur, it could often be annulled at the insistence of the parents.[6] In the context of the play, it is almost certain an annulment would have followed the disclosure of the marriage and Juliet would find herself not only no longer officially "married" but also, having consummated the marriage, a fallen woman, in which case the likelihood of marrying Paris or anyone else of an equal social rank would be erased. Further, if Juliet came forward with the information that she and Romeo have secretly married, she would not have the guarantee that the Nurse and the Friar would, in fact, even acknowledge the marriage took place. After all, when confronted with the prospect of marrying Paris, the Nurse is quick to advise Juliet to forget her first husband and the Friar comes up with a convoluted and dangerous plan to avoid announcing the very existence of the marriage. So even before the death of Tybalt, Juliet is in a no-win situation that can only end badly.

Things quickly go from bad to worse for Juliet after the death of Tybalt. At the very moment she is consummating her marriage; downstairs Capulet is betrothing her to Paris, arranging for a hasty marriage to stem the depth of Juliet's grief over the death of Tybalt. While more cynical readers see in Capulet's haste a ploy to firm up his influence with the Prince by taking Paris as a son-in-law, his earlier concern for his daughter's happiness gives credence to the argument that Capulet's first concern here is for his daughter's well-being. He wrongly believes his daughter is the compliant young women we saw in Act I, scene 2. "I think," he says, "she will be ruled/In all respects by me; nay, more, I doubt it not." (R&J, III, 4, 13-14). Thus, when Juliet responds to the "happy" news with a flat rejection, "Now, by Saint Peter's Church and Peter too, / He shall not make me there a joyful bride" (R&J, III, 5, 116-117), Capulet and his wife are flummoxed and enraged. The hereto caring father immediately falls back on his traditional paternal right to determine his daughter's future:

> Look to't, think on't, I do not use to jest.
> Thursday is near; lay hand on heart, advise:
> An you be mine, I'll give you to my friend;
> And you be not, hang, beg, starve, die in the streets,
> For, by my soul, I'll ne'er acknowledge thee,
> Nor what is mine shall never do thee good:
> Trust to't, bethink you; I'll not be forsworn.
> (R&J, III, 5, 189-195)

Juliet's defiance is more than the simple rebellion of a teenage daughter, but an attack on the entire patriarchal system that allows fathers to shuttle daughters around like property. Capulet's rage seems less at this point about his disappointment in his daughter's response than about the public humiliation he will face if he is shown unable to control that which is his.

Juliet in desperation turns to Friar Lawrence for assistance. She threatens suicide, an act that should surly have chilled the Friar's soul. His response is to devise a remarkably convoluted plot where by the application of a mysterious drug he will place Juliet in a deathlike trance for a period of "two and forty hours." During that time, she will be presumed dead and buried in Capulet's monument. Meanwhile, the Friar will send for Romeo who will return to Verona, await Juliet's "resurrection," and take her away to live happily ever after. Juliet jumps at this ray of hope: "Give me, give me! O, tell not me of fear!" (R&J, IV, 1, 121). She is advised by the Friar to:

> go home, be merry, give consent
> To marry Paris: Wednesday is to-morrow:
> To-morrow night look that thou lie alone;
> Let not thy nurse lie with thee in thy chamber:
> Take thou this vial, being then in bed,
> And this distilled liquor drink thou off;
>
> (R&J, IV, 1, 89-94)

She does as instructed and lies to her mother, father and nurse with remarkable ease. Alone is her chamber she begins to have doubts:

> What if this mixture do not work at all?
> Shall I be married then to-morrow morning?
> No, no: this shall forbid it: lie thou there
>
> (R&J, IV, 3, 21-23)

Laying down a dagger that serves as her backup plan, she continues to muse and questions the Friar's motivation in helping her.

> What if it be a poison, which the friar
> Subtly hath minister'd to have me dead,
> Lest in this marriage he should be dishonour'd,
> Because he married me before to Romeo?
>
> (R&J, IV, 3, 24-27)

She fears she may awaken prematurely in the tomb and be suffocated by the stagnant air or run mad from being surrounded by the decomposing bodies of her kinsmen. Not allowing herself to further consider these fears, Juliet drinks the draught and falls into a deathlike sleep. As everyone knows, fate intervenes and the plot unravels. Romeo, thinking Juliet is truly dead, takes his own life moments before she revives and when finding alone with her departed love and on the verge of being discovered alive, she takes up Romeo's dagger and without hesitation, plunges into her heart.

It is left to the Prince to sort out the details of the tragedy by interrogating the Friar; Balthazar, Romeo's servant; and Paris' page. Although it rarely staged, it should be remembered that Paris is slain by Romeo when he discovers the distraught husband at the tomb of his bride. The Friar confesses his role in the story and also, not very valiantly, implicates the nurse as his co-conspirator. The Prince condemns neither the Friar nor the young lovers for what has unfolded; instead he lays the blame at the feet of the two old men whose ancient grudge lies at the heart of the tragedy. The former enemies are shown contrite and a "glooming peace" settles over Verona as Capulet and Montague join hands in their mutual sorrow. This resolution offers some consolation to the audience as if it compensates for the deaths of five young people, but does it really offer the catharsis the tragedy demands? Can we draw the conclusion that if the feud had not existed, the tragedy would have been averted? If we remove the grudge from the narrative, would Capulet have immediately accepted his daughter's decision to choose Romeo over the Prince's kinsmen, Paris? That seems unlikely. For Juliet, marriage to Paris would be "marrying-up." In patriarchal Verona it would be unthinkable that Juliet would be allowed to choose a husband on her own, particularly given her tender age. If we posit Capulet and Montague as friends or even business rivals, Romeo may well have ended up at Capulet's "old accustomed feast" as an invited guest instead of as a party crasher. Would that have made any difference to the love that unfolds between Romeo and Juliet? It might be argued that Juliet's attraction to Romeo, the enemy of her family, was driven by her desire for forbidden fruit, but it seems obvious that she is enthralled by Romeo well before she learns his identity. It might also be said that had Romeo not been a Montague, he would not have drawn the attention and ire of Tybalt. This may be true enough, but considering Tybalt hates peace as he "hate[s] hell [and] all Montagues," (R&J, I, 1, 71) he surely could have found reason to brawl with Romeo, Mercutio or anyone else in Verona. If there had been no feud, would there have been a need for a secret marriage? Probably. Even if Capulet approved Romeo as a suitor, he surely would have placed the same constraints on Romeo as he did on Paris. It is not the feud that drives the hasty marriage but the young lover's passion.

The feud certainly complicates the situation for Romeo and Juliet, but an equally important cause of the tragedy lies in the patriarchal system that denies young women the right to act as independent agents in the planning of their future. Even though Capulet seems concerned about Juliet's future happiness at the beginning of the play, (remember he says, "woo her, gentle Paris, get her heart; /My will to her consent is but a part" (*R&J*, 1, 2, 14-17)), he reverts to the tyrannical patriarch when his will is crossed. Juliet is an unusually precocious young woman: a very smart, active character who decides to get married, resolves to take the sleeping potion, and finally decides to take her own life rather than live a life of shame without her beloved. Juliet is driven to commit more and more desperate acts to find a place for herself, which culminate in her untimely death, at her own hand. It is she who ultimately drives the piece to its pitiful conclusion. Juliet self-determination allows us to read the play as more than an indictment of her family's feud with the Montagues. Instead, the tragedy can be read as a consequence of asserting oneself against the accepted social norm. Modern audiences who are imbued with the notion that romantic love is self-justifying are likely to be more supportive of Juliet's independence than Shakespeare's audience would have been. The powerfully appealing love affair of Romeo and Juliet was so effectively portrayed by Shakespeare as, perhaps, to help change societal attitudes in later years, but at the time the Tudor audience would have viewed their actions quite ambivalently. The disobedience of children, in their minds, deserved punishment. Shakespeare ultimately upholds paternal rights and punishes filial disobedience, but to a degree *Romeo and Juliet* also calls into question the accepted rules of paternal control and filial obedience, and places these questions in the larger realm of marital choice and female freedom.

YOUR FATHER SHOULD BE AS A GOD: A MIDSUMMER NIGHT'S DREAM

As we have seen, punishment seems to follow filial disobedience as night follows day. The exception that at first glance makes the rule can be found in one of Shakespeare's most popular comedies, *A Midsummer Night's Dream*. The disobedient daughter in the play is Hermia who loves Lysander but is promised to Demetrius by her father. Unlike Shakespeare's other disobedient daughters, Hermia openly defies her father, Egeus, and is taken before Theseus, the ruler of Athens for his judgment. Like Othello, Lysander is accused of bewitching the girl:

> *With cunning hast thou filch'd my daughter's heart,*
> *Turn'd her obedience, which is due to me,*
> *To stubborn harshness:*
>
> (*MND, I, 2, 36-38*)

Egeus uses the same old saw used by nearly all of Shakespeare's fathers: "As she is mine, I may dispose of she/Which shall be either to this gentleman/Or to her death, according to our law." (*MND*, I, 1, 41-44). Other than the harshness of the penalty for disobedience, the law of Athens is no different than the laws of Padua or Venice or Verona. Theseus first appeals to Hermia's reason, saying

> *To you your father should be as a god;*
> *One that composed your beauties, yea, and one*
> *To whom you are but as a form in wax*
> *By him imprinted and within his power*
>
> (*MND, I, 1, 47-50*)

In all of Shakespeare there is no more concise and explicit statement of the father's rights with respect to daughters. Theseus as the enforcer of Athens' law and patriarchal tradition finds no grounds for leniency and tells Hermia that she must either conform to her father's will or "die the death or to abjure/ Forever the society of men." (*MND*, I, 1, 65-66). Showing more courage than any of the other defiant daughters, Hermia boldly responds:

So will I grow, so live, so die, my lord,
Ere I will my virgin patent up
Unto his lordship, whose unwished yoke
My soul consents not to give sovereignty.

(MND, I, 1, 79-82)

Disregarding her protestation, Theseus grants her a reprieve to reconsider her choice, assuring her that if she persists in her defiance of her father's will, she will surely suffer the law of Athens.

When confronted with the inflexibility of Athenian law, Hermia and Lysander resort to the path followed by Shakespeare's other defiant daughters: they determine to run away and marry without the consent of the father. Predictably, the couple encounters complications, but in the end, true love wins out, Theseus relents and allows their marriage, and it appears that ultimately Hermia is rewarded for her assertive behavior. This fairy tale ending to a festive comedy is to be expected, but a closer second reading reveals a darker misogynistic subtext. Although Hermia is not required to literally die for her filial defiance like Desdemona and Juliet, she is required to suffer and figuratively die as an independent and assertive young woman to be reborn as a silent and submissive wife.

Let's relook at the play's first scene. It opens with Theseus preparing for his wedding to Hippolyta, Queen of the Amazons who he has taken in battle and claimed as his bride. Renowned for their sense of autonomy, Amazons rejected the normative model of a patriarchal marriage, and refused to be ruled by men. Only through physical conquest can the Amazon be brought to heel and Theseus revels in his victory and his restoration of the patriarchal norm. The audience never learns Hippolyta's thoughts about being wooed by the sword of Theseus and the prospect of becoming his wifely subordinate. Except for a brief non-committal statement at the opening of the scene, she is silent throughout Theseus' schooling of Hermia. When he is done speaking, Theseus commands her, "come, my Hippolyta," (*MND*, I, 1, 122) and she follows in compliance and disappears from the play until Act IV.

When we observe Theseus interact with Hippolyta, we cannot be surprised that he sides with Egeus by seeing Hermia "as a form in wax" (*MND*, I, 1, 49) intended to conform to the will of her father and the demands of her patriarchal society which are limited to marriage or the convent. The latter option is particularly maligned by Theseus who views a life of devout chastity as a complete waste of womankind, calling it a thing to be endured, something cold, barren and fruitless. He does acknowledge, perhaps as a sop to piety, that "Thrice-blessed [are] they that master so their blood." (*MND*, I, 1, 74), but quickly adds that "earthlier happy" (*MND*, I, i, 76) are those who offer up their virginity in approved marriage. The convent serves as a threat to the patriarchy because it offers the young woman the only refuge that will preserve her autonomy and allow her to exist in a place free of patriarchal control. For the men in the play, the convent and its enforced virginity are seen as punishments for the defiant woman, but for Hermia the convent serves as the sanctuary of last resort and her virginity is her ultimate bargaining chip, the single thing that she controls. That said, Hermia's first choice is for a marriage to a mate of her choosing. The elopement plot ultimately provides for this happy ending, but not without a humbling of proud Hermia. Before the happy marriage can be achieved, Hernia needs to yield up some of that autonomy she so values; in short, she needs to be tamed to silence and obedience before she can take on the role of a proper wife.

As a foil for the independent Hermia, Shakespeare gives us her rather pathetic childhood friend, Helena. Helena is hopelessly in love with Demetrius, Lysander's rival for the love of Hermia. Demetrius and Helena have a romantic history, but Demetrius has rejected Helena in his pursuit of Hermia. Helena pines for Demetrius who takes every opportunity to discourage and disparage her. He warns her "Tempt not too much the hatred of my spirit; /For I am sick when I do look on thee." (*MND*, II. 1. 211-212). He even threatens to "do [her] mischief in the wood." (*MND*, II. 1. 237) Undeterred, she tells him

> *I am your spaniel, and, Demetrius,*
> *The more you beat me I will fawn on you.*
> *Use me but as your spaniel: spurn me, strike me,*
> *Neglect me, lose me; only give me your leave,*
> *Unworthy as I am, to follow you.*
> *What worser place can I beg in your love—*
> *And yet a place of high respect with me—*
> *Than to be used as you use your dog?*
>
> (*MND*, II, 1, 203-210)

Her demeaning devotion, so appalling to our ears, would be more acceptable to the Elizabethan audience (at least the males in the audience) than Hernia's open defiance of masculine rule. Deeming herself "unworthy" of Demetrious' love, Helena is quite ready to do anything—be anything—so long as it pleases her lover. Unlike Hermia, Helena is quick to humble herself before the object of her idolatry and will risk anything: her chastity, her reputation and her life, to be as the side of her intended mate.

Helena's plight does not go unnoticed, for in this very woods, Oberon, King of the Fairies, is having his own issues with love. He admires Helena's sense of womanly loyalty, a trait currently absent in his own head-strong wife, Titania and endorses Helena as a woman worthy of his supernatural assistance. He instructs Puck, his henchman, to find Demetrius and "[a]noint his eyes" (*MND*, II, 1, 261) with a love juice that will cause Demetrius to fall wildly in love with Helena. A case of mistaken identity results in Lysander being anointed as well as Demetrius and both men transfer their amorous attention to Helena, placing both women on unaccustomed ground. The self-effacing Helena suddenly gains self-confidence as she is wooed by not one, but two men and the proud Hermia is distraught at being an object of derision rather than one of adoration. While Helena becomes even more the ideal, deferent woman, Hermia's faults become more and more pronounced as she exhibits shrewish behavior. Helena differentiates herself from Hermia in that she possesses a "gentle tongue", while the "immodest" Hermia is vocal and aggressive, and uses her voice as a means of asserting her authority—a shrewish behavior that causes anxiety in Helena. When Helena insults her as a "puppet," Hermia responds with a threat of physical aggression, and threatens that though she may be short, "my nails can reach unto thine eyes" (*MND*, III, 2, 299). Hermia's penchant for violence is yet another marker of shrewishness, and Helena demurely shrinks from her in fear:

> Let her not hurt me: I was never curst;
> I have no gift at all in shrewishness;
> I am a right maid for my cowardice:
> Let her not strike me.
>
> (*MND*, III, 2, 301-304)

Helena's words call attention to Hermia's short-comings. Where we previously may have applauded her independence, we are now shown the dark side of this autonomous and self-assured personality, that when its will is obstructed it is quick to lash out with words and nails. For her behavior as much as for the effect of the love position, Hermia is rejected by both her previous suitors and her best friend. Finally, the confusion comes to Oberon's attention and he commends Puck to set things right. Through reapplication of the love potion to the correct parties, Lysander is restored to Hermia and Demetrius is left enamored with Helena. It is in this state of reconciliation that the couples are found by Theseus, Hippolyta, Egeus, and their hunting party. After hearing from Lysander of his plot to elope with Hermia and hearing Demetrius express his newfound love for Helena, Theseus suddenly and inexplicably reverses his earlier decision to support Egeus' parental right and Athenian law:

Egeus, I will overbear your will;
For in the temple by and by with us
These couples shall eternally be knit:

                                        (MND, IV, 1, 179-181)

It is worth noting that the previously verbose Hermia is silent throughout the scene and remains silent except for two short and inconsequential lines for the remainder of the play. While in the fifth Act the three newly-wed couples view the performance of the rustics, the men and even Hippolyta conduct a running commentary on the content and quality of the play. Hermia and Helena sit silently on the stage signaling their new status as subservient wives.

Notes

1. Frey, Charles. "Shakespeare's Imperiled and Chastening Daughters of Romance." *South Atlantic Bulletin* 43.4 (Nov. 1978): p125-140. (p. 127).
2. Delgado deTorres, Olivia. "Reflections of Patriarchy and Rebellion of Daughters in Shakespeare's Merchant of Venice and Othello." *Interpretation: A Journal of Political Philosophy.* 21:3 (1994), 333-351. (p. 345)
3. Dreher, Diane E. *Domination and Defiance: Fathers and Daughters in Shakespeare.* Lexington: University of Kentucky Press, 1986, 45.
4. Aristotle. *Poetics.*
5. Abbott, Mary. *Family Ties: English Families 1540-1920.* New York: Routledge, 1993, 34.
6. Carlson, Eric Josef. *Marriage and the English Reformation.* Cambridge: Blackwell, 1994

BITCHES AND WITCHES

SHE-WOLF OF FRANCE: HENRY VI TETRALOGY: QUEEN MARGARET

There is only one character in the entire Shakespeare canon that appears in four plays. Shakespeare's most popular character, Falstaff, appears in three. Prince Hal (later Henry V) appears in three. So too does Henry Bolingbroke. Richard, Duke of Gloucester (later Richard III) appears in three. The same is true of his father, Richard, Duke of York. The only character to physically appear in four plays is, surprisingly, a woman, and one of the most interesting and least known characters created by Shakespeare: Queen Margaret of Anjou, wife of Henry VI in Shakespeare's earliest tetralogy. The central focus of the Henry VI/Richard III tetralogy is the devastating War of the Roses that spanned 30 years and laid waste to the English nobility. Leading the rebellious White Rose of York is Richard, Duke of York and his sons. They are opposed by the seated ruler King Henry VI, a weak and ineffectual leader, and Henry's ruthless and formidable wife, the Red Queen, Margaret. The *Henry VI* tetralogy is Shakespeare's earliest attempt at Historical Drama and one of his earliest plays, first performed in 1592. Like another early work, his first effort at Tragedy, *Titus Andronicus*, the *Henry VI* tetralogy is full of villains. In four plays, the only unequivocally heroic characters are John Talbot; the English Constable of France depicted in *1 Henry VI*, and Richmond (later Henry VI) who defeats Richard III in the play of that name. All of the other characters span the gamut from weak victims to cunning plotters to ruthless murderers.

The tetralogy was one of the most popular plays during his lifetime, but has not enjoyed similar success in the centuries that followed. While the tetralogy's concluding play, *Richard III* continues to be popular; the three parts of the *Henry VI* are rarely performed. This fact can be attributed to a number of factors. First, the complexity and scope of the tetralogy's content is truly epic. The action dates from the death of Henry V in 1422 through the loss of English territories in France, the War of the Roses and the ascension of Henry VII in 1485. The cast is large and understanding their relationship to one another, their goals and motives, requires more than a rudimentary knowledge of medieval English and French history. In addition to these complications, one can add Shakespeare's confusing distortions of time and place, often compressing years in a single scene and placing people in scene where they could not possibly have been. In despite of the large cast, or because of it, there is no single male role that towers over the others until Richard III comes into his own. There are no sweeping or grandiose speeches like those found in Shakespeare's more mature works. Hence, there is little incentive for actors/producers like Olivier or Branagh to launch such a grand production. In general, the *Henry VI* trilogy is considered Shakespeare's weakest literary effort. Nevertheless, it contains flashes of brilliance that preview the talent that will show more brightly in his future works. Queen Margaret of Anjou is one of those flashes.

The audience is introduced to Margaret toward the conclusion of *1Henry VI*. She is a French princess, the daughter of Reignier, the destitute Duke of Anjou and titular King of Naples, Sicily and Jerusalem: "a man of many crowns but no kingdoms." Margaret is the prisoner of William de la Pole, Earl of Suffolk who is one of the English military commanders in France and a close ally of Cardinal Henry Beaufort and John Beaufort, the Duke of Somerset, at home. Suffolk is struck nearly speechless by her beauty, but remembering that he is already married, he realizes Margaret is beyond his reach. He instead lights on the idea of marring her off to his King and thereby having access to her and simultaneously gaining favor with Henry. His plan runs to the grandiose where at worst she might become his mistress, though he fears the potential consequence of such a treasonous course, and at best his political puppet, allowing that "Margaret shall … be queen, and rule the king;/ But I will rule both her, the king and realm." (*1HVI*, V, 5, 107-8).

For her part Margaret is understandably concerned only with her fate as a prisoner and while Suffolk ponders how to use Margaret to his best advantage, she tries to determine what must be done to gain her freedom. Suffolk at his time would be 48 years old; Margaret would have been 14. She nevertheless maintains her composure, and when Suffolk expectantly offers her the crown of England's queen, she answers with a dignity and confidence that defies her years: "To be a queen in bondage is more vile/ Than is a slave in base servility; / For princes should be free." (*1HVI*, V, 3, 112-4). When assured that freedom shall be hers, Margaret agrees to be Henry's bride if her father consents. Reignier shrewdly offers no dowry for his daughter and in fact insists that Henry return the lost kingdoms of Maine and Anjou to him in exchange for his daughter's hand. Amazingly, Suffolk agrees to his demands, convinced that foolish Henry will also agree. As they part, Suffolk asks a "loving token [for] his majesty" and Margaret sends "a pure unspotted heart," but to Suffolk she gives a kiss, not for the King, but for himself. She is clearly aware of the effect she has had on Suffolk and just as he plans to use her for his own purposes, she is already planning how to bend this infatuated old courtier to hers.

When the next play, 2 Henry VI, opens, the scene is England and Margaret has arrived and, having already been married to Henry by proxy, is presented to her new husband and his court. Immediately, court politics intervenes. When the Lord Protector, Humprey, Duke of Gloucester learns of the gifted lands in France, Margaret immediately gains a resentful and powerful enemy. Cardinal Beaufort, Gloucester's chief rival at court, seeks to see how the Lord Protector's rancor can be used against him. The assembled nobles are divided into factions: Beaufort is allied with the Dukes of Buckingham, Somerset and Suffolk. The Duke of York, allied with The Earls of Warwick and Salisbury, oppose Beaufort's faction. Gloucester stands alone, opposed by all although the Yorkist faction seems to support him because he is such a formidable foe of the Beaufort faction. This is the viper's nest into which Margaret is thrown and her only ally is Suffolk who also has his own political agenda. Margaret, however, is a quick study and rightly perceives that the Lord Protector stands between her and the power she aspires to. Margaret, coming from France where the King enjoyed absolute rule unencumbered by a Parliament or quarreling nobles, is understandably confused by her new environment. Trying to find her place, she asks Suffolk, her mentor:

> What shall King Henry be a pupil still
> Under the surly Gloucester's governance?
> Am I a queen in title and in style,
> And must be made a subject to a duke?
>
> (2 HVI, I, 3, 46-9)

As the ultimate "Other" in the English court, she is at a double disadvantage being marginalized because she is a woman and detested because she is French. As Queen, she is expected to be seen and not heard, to look good, and entertain at the banquet table. When she attempts to intrude in matters of state, Gloucester dismisses her, saying: "these are no women's matters." (2 HVI, I, 3, 117). As a Frenchwoman in the English court, she is the tangible representative of England's greatest foe at a time when England is losing her possessions in France at a starting rate.

As much as she resents the Duke of Gloucester, she equally resents "Beaufort, the imperious churchman, Somerset, Buckingham, / And grumbling York" observing that "the least of these/ But can do more in England than the king." (2 *HVI*, I, 3, 68-71). And she also resents her new husband, King Henry, whom she believes better suited to be Pope than king. But she holds a particular grudge against Gloucester's wife Eleanor:

> *Not all these lords do vex me half so much*
> *As that proud dame, the lord protector's wife.*
> *She sweeps it through the court with troops of ladies,*
> *More like an empress than Duke Humphrey's wife:*
> *Strangers in court do take her for the queen:*
>
> (2 *HVI, I, 3, 75-79*)

Unsure of herself, she selects the weakest of her enemies, another woman, as her first object of attack. When Suffolk councils her to join with the Cardinal and the lords against Duke Humphrey, she sees Eleanor as the weak link to bring him down. At their next meeting, Margaret deliberately provokes Eleanor by boxing her ears and claiming that she mistook the Duke's wife for a serving woman. Seeking to gain intelligence that might elevate her husband and revenge herself upon Margaret, Eleanor consorts with witches and conjurers and is taken in the act by York. As a result, Eleanor is banished from England and the Duke, having his protectorship revoked, is irretrievably weakened at court. His disgrace, however, is not enough for his enemies. Upon his return to court, all the nobles turn on him, accusing him of corruption and treason, but when the trusting King Henry is unwilling to take action, the Cardinal, Queen, Suffolk and York plot Gloucester's murder. Before the plot against Gloucester can be executed, an uprising in Ireland forces York to leave England to put down the rebels and, conveniently, to build up an army, following the example of the usurper, Henry Bolingbroke, for it is York's long range plan to seize the throne from young King Henry. The next scene opens with Suffolk asking two men, identified as first and second murderer, if they have "dispatch'd this thing?" The first murderer replies, "Ay, my good lord, he's dead." and we know that it is Gloucester who has been murdered. When Henry learns that the Duke is dead, he swoons and upon recovery accuses Suffolk on complicity in the Duke's death. Margaret immediately rises to the defense of Suffolk, arguing that to indict Suffolk is to indict her since Gloucester had been her enemy as well as Suffolk's. As the news of Gloucester's death spreads, Warwick and Salisbury enter the scene to inform Henry that the peasants are in revolt, calling for the arrest of the Cardinal and Suffolk who they hold responsible for the murder of Gloucester. Warwick openly accuses Suffolk of murder and the commons speaking through Salisbury inform Henry

Unless Lord Suffolk straight be done to death,
Or banished fair England's territories,
They will by violence tear him from your palace
And torture him with grievous lingering death.

(2 HVI, III, 2, 244-7)

Henry immediately accedes to their demands and over Margaret's strident protests, he orders Suffolk banished.

Margaret is genuinely distressed by the loss of her only ally and confidant. There has been speculation that Suffolk and Margaret had been lovers, but I find little in their parting speeches that would indicate anything more than a deep friendship. Margaret says:

*Even thus **two friends** condemn'd*
Embrace and kiss and take ten thousand leaves,
Loather a hundred times to part than die.
Yet now farewell; and farewell life with thee! (emphasis added)

(2 HVI, III, 2, 353-6)

Perhaps being aware of the age difference between the two or perhaps because of the risk involved with committing adultery against the king, particularly in the political snake pit of the English court where everyone is watching almost by habit for an opportunity to undo a rival, I cannot convince myself of a physical relationship between Margaret and Suffolk. Instead, I see Suffolk acting as a surrogate father to Margaret, guiding her in the path to power, certainly for his own purposes as well hers, but also out of a genuine affection for the young queen who is after all young enough to be his daughter. When the two are parted by Suffolk's banishment, Suffolk expresses the depth of his feeling:

'Tis not the land I care for, wert thou thence;
A wilderness is populous enough,
So Suffolk had thy heavenly company:
For where thou art, there is the world itself,

(2 HVI, III, 2, 359-62)

This scans as emotion far beyond carnal passion and though both Suffolk and Margaret are complicit in the cold-blooded murder of Gloucester, they part garnering the sympathy of the audience.

Five scenes later, the couple is reunited although not in a manner to the liking of the Queen. The stage direction for Act IV, scene 4 reads, "Enter KING HENRY VI with a supplication, **and the QUEEN with SUFFOLK'S head**" [emphasis added]. A lot has happened since the Queen last graced the stage. Cardinal Beaufort has died on the heels of Gloucester's death, a peasant revolt lead by Jack Cade and instigated by the Duke of York has broken out, and Suffolk on his way into exile, has been captured and murdered by pirates. The Queen is distraught, trying to drown her sorrow with thoughts of revenge, but against whom? Although Henry, having sent Suffolk away would be the likely target, her anger does not seem directed at him. The actual perpetrators are beyond her reach. Instead she seems to light upon the "Kentish rebel" led by Jack Cade as the object of her rage. While she would surely kill them all, Henry in his typical beneficence offers them pardon and the rebellion falls apart. But even as the country in on the brink of peace, Henry is warned that "The Duke of York is newly come from Ireland, /And with a puissant and a mighty power... And still proclaimeth, as he comes along, / His arms are only to remove from thee/ The Duke of Somerset, whom he terms traitor." (2 *HVI*, IV, 9, 24-8). Henry, to avoid open conflict with York, sends his ambassador to York saying he will jail Somerset "Until his [York's] army be dismiss'd from him."

York immediately reveals his true purpose when he re-enters the action at the opening of Act V: "From Ireland thus comes York to claim his right, / And pluck the crown from feeble Henry's head" (2 *HVI*, V, 1, 1-2). However, as soon as he is confronted by the King's representative, Buckingham, he demurs saying to himself: "I must make fair weather yet a while, / Till Henry be more weak and I more strong," (2 *HVI*, IV, 9, 30-31). He is told by Buckingham that the Duke of Somerset has been jailed and York satisfied by the news agrees to dismiss his army. Henry arrives on the scene followed by Queen Margaret and Somerset and the blatant lie of Somerset's imprisonment is revealed incensing York. Margaret has thrown her lot with Somerset, Suffolk's ally, to force Henry's hand against the more dangerous York. Hot words and charges of treason are exchanged. The forces on either side gather. Civil war erupts and the Battle of St. Albans is underway. In single combat, York confronts Clifford, a lord loyal to Henry, and slays him. Elsewhere on the field, York's hunchbacked son, Richard confronts Somerset and slays him. The tide of battle has turned to the Yorkist faction and the King and Queen flee the field toward London, bring the play to its conclusion with the Yorkists in pursuit.

3 Henry VI opens with the victorious York entering the Parliament House in London and claiming England throne as his own. Here he and his faction leaders are confronted by Henry and his supporters. Henry, perceiving his weak position, negotiates a resolution whereby Henry will continue to rule as sovereign until his death and then the throne will pass to York and his heirs. Henry's followers are appalled, call him "faint-hearted and degenerate," and abandon him, determined to continue the fight. Not only has Henry betrayed his followers who have lost friends and family defending him, but in his agreement to yield the throne to York, he has disinherited his son

At this point it is probably worth taking a quick look at the actual history Shakespeare is distorting and compressing. Henry and Margaret were married in 1445. The Duke of Gloucester died in 1447 as did Cardinal Beaufort. York left for Ireland in 1445 and returned to England in 1450. The Jack Cade rebellion occurred in 1450 as did the murder of Suffolk. Although in Shakespeare, the Battle of St. Albans occurs immediately after York's return to England, in fact, it did not occur until 1455. In the intervening five years, Henry had a two-year bout of insanity, and the Duke of York was appointed Protector of the Realm. When Henry regained his senses in 1454, York resumed his quest for power and gathered forces from the north of England to launch a rebellion against Somerset and the King. At St. Albans, Henry was taken prisoner and did not successfully retreat to London. Margaret was not present for the battle. Henry was locked away in the Tower of London and York, reporting that the King was again insane, took up the mantle of Protector of the Realm for a second time. By the time Henry again regained his faculties in 1456, with Suffolk and Somerset both dead, Queen Margaret became the power behind the throne. Queen Margaret also added another element to the dynastic struggle between the Lancasters and the Yorks when after eight years of marriage, she conceived and delivered a son, Edward, Duke of Westminster, in 1553. In Shakespeare's rendering of events, the negations that disinherited young Edward took place immediately following the Battle of St. Albans, but historically this agreement did not come to pass until 1460 when Parliament affirmed the agreement in the Act of Accord.

The Queen in Shakespeare's version of the story, confronts her husband and berates his cowardice:

> I shame to hear thee speak. Ah, timorous wretch!
> Thou hast undone thyself, thy son and me;
> And given unto the house of York such head
> As thou shalt reign but by their sufferance.
> To entail him and his heirs unto the crown,
> What is it, but to make thy sepulchre
> And creep into it far before thy time?
>
> (3 HVI, I, 1, 231-7)

Henry's final outrage against her and her son brings Margaret fully into her own. She tells him:

> The northern lords that have forsworn thy colours
> Will follow mine, if once they see them spread;
> And spread they shall be, to thy foul disgrace
> And utter ruin of the house of York.
>
> (3 HVI, I, 1, 251-4)

In effect she in now both king and queen, not by design but by necessity. There has been no suggestion that Margaret has held aspirations to rule. Up until this point, she has been content to exercise influence on the political scene in the traditional manner of her sex, i.e., as the collaborator of the men who surround her, Henry, Suffolk, and Somerset. Now bereft of strong men to hide behind, she is forced for her son's sake to take up the sword and put on the traditional male role of war leader. Gathering Henry's disaffected lords around her the Queen mounts an army and follows York northward to his castle near the city of York. York is informed of her approach:

> The queen with all the northern earls and lords
> Intend here to besiege you in your castle:
> She is hard by with twenty thousand men;
> And therefore fortify your hold, my lord.
>
> (3 HVI, I 1, 251-4)

Disdainful of the Queen's larger army, York decides to meet her army in the field rather than stand siege in his castle. His son Richard voices the general consensus, "A woman's general; what should we fear?" The armies meet on the field at Wakefield and the Queen's soldiers overwhelm the smaller Yorkist force. York is taken captive and confronted by his chief antagonists, Queen Margaret, hot-blooded Clifford seeking revenge on York for having killed his father at St Albans, and Northumberland, who also lost kin to York at St. Albans. They taunt the captive and at the Queens suggestion, the stand him upon a mole hill and place a paper crown upon his head. Margaret asks:

> Where are your mess of sons to back you now?
> The wanton Edward, and the lusty George?
> And where's that valiant crook-back prodigy,
> Dicky your boy, that with his grumbling voice

Was wont to cheer his dad in mutinies?

(3 HVI, I, 4, 73-7)

She asks about York's second son, Rutland, and then sadistically tells him:

I stain'd this napkin with the blood
That valiant Clifford, with his rapier's point,
Made issue from the bosom of the boy;
And if thine eyes can water for his death,
I give thee this to dry thy cheeks withal.

(3 HVI, I, 4, 79-83)

The audience is surely appalled by Margaret's brutality, unprepared by her earlier appearances for this depth of violence. It seems that all her years of frustration with Henry and the petty power brokers and seekers that surround him, her loss of Suffolk and Somerset, and the final indignity of watching her son disinherited by his father, erupt in one blinding flash of rage directed at York who serves as proxy for all the wrongs she has endured. York defeated and knowing his life is at end, attacks Margaret not for her taunts and torments, but that they come from a woman:

She-wolf of France, but worse than wolves of France,
Whose tongue more poisons than the adder's tooth!
How ill-beseeming is it in thy sex
To triumph, like an Amazonian trull,
Upon their woes whom fortune captivates!

(3 HVI, I, 4, 111-5)

He continues:

O tiger's heart wrapt in a woman's hide!
How couldst thou drain the life-blood of the child,
To bid the father wipe his eyes withal,
And yet be seen to bear a woman's face?
Women are soft, mild, pitiful and flexible;
Thou stern, obdurate, flinty, rough, remorseless.

(3 HVI, I, 4, 137-42)

So pathetic is York's final lament for Rutland that even Northumberland feels sympathy for him and is shocked by Margaret's callousness: "Had he been slaughter-man to all my kin, /I should not for my life but weep with him" (3 HVI, I, 4, 169-70). The Queen and Clifford are not moved and they fall upon York, stabbing the helpless man to death concluding one of Shakespeare's most shocking scenes.

Has Margaret transformed into something less than human? She is at the pinnacle of her power. She has successfully led an army of men in defense of her husband, the king. She has changed from a naïve *female* foreigner in the English court to a fierce warrior woman, able to negotiate the politics of power and kill the more experienced and charismatic York. She has put on the armor of a man and has taken on the cruel persona of a man, and it is that aspect of Margaret that is probably the most repulsive aspect of her scene with the defeated York. What Margaret has done is to maneuver into a position of power by imitating what she sees as the characteristics of the men of power that surround her. For her specifically and for the women of power in Shakespeare generally, they think that such modeling is the most direct path to success. Unfortunately, Margaret and the others are confounded on at least two levels. First they lack appropriate role models. This is surely the case with Margaret. Henry is a weakling. Gloucester, who would probably have been the best of a bad lot, instantly alienated Margaret through his benign misogyny and his dismissal of Margaret as anything more than a costly ornament, blind Margaret to his virtues. Beaufort, Somerset and Suffolk are all slithering back-stabbers and York is a grumbling, indecisive and ultimately traitorous trouble-maker. Who is she to learn from? Certainly none of these! Instead she seems to self-create an image of warrior queen that she believes is based on the "ideal" masculine image of leadership. While the men around her tip-toe around each other, plotting and slandering and murdering one another, Margaret's approach to power is, when the limited power of Henry is finally threatened by York, surprisingly direct and overwhelming effective. Nevertheless, Margaret and Shakespeare's other powerful women misunderstand powerful men. They mimic, even exaggerate, their perceptions of masculine ruthlessness and cruelty, believing that these attributes are both the source and manifestation of a man's power. What they fail to understand is even when these men obviously hate one another, there is a kind of brotherhood that exists that sets up certain rules of conduct and decorum they typically will not violating. Specifically, there are rules in combat, a kind of mock chivalry that Margaret does not understand and would view as hypocritical. Additionally, even though the men are enemies, they are still part of the patriarchal system that accepts any man as a part of "us" and all women as one of "them," the always suspect and never accepted alien "other."

Margaret has defied the conventional role of a woman and Queen and must be vilified and condemned even by the men she leads.

Wakefield represents the high-water mark of Margaret's power. She could in this victory have been drawn as heroic; she is the victorious defender of God's anointed ruler, King Henry VI, against a treacherous and traitorous pretender to the throne. Instead, Shakespeare chooses to demonize her. He, too, for all his sensitivity and understanding of humankind, is a member of England's patriarchal heritage and deeply suspicious of female power. His bias, however, is conflicted by virtue of the fact that a powerful and popular woman was on the throne at the time he was creating the character of Queen Margaret. Just two to three years before 3 *Henry VI* appeared on the stage, Queen Elizabeth I, said to have appeared dressed in armor and mounted on a horse, rallied her forces at Tilbury in advance of the anticipated invasion landing by the ground forces of the Spanish Armada. While this description is in doubt, she may well have appeared wearing a silver breastplate over a white velvet dress when she addressed the troops in one of her most famous speeches:

> *My loving people, we have been persuaded by some that are careful of our safety, to take heed how we commit ourself to armed multitudes for fear of treachery; but I assure you, I do not desire to live to distrust my faithful and loving people ... I know I have the body but of a weak and feeble woman, but I have the heart and stomach of a king, and of a King of England too, and think foul scorn that Parma or Spain, or any Prince of Europe should dare to invade the borders of my realm.[1]*

Although perhaps dressed in armor, Elizabeth never denies her femininity; she celebrates it and uses it to magnify her courage and commitment to her people. Margaret, on the other hand, in seeking to project her "masculine" side as a war-leader, instead creates a near caricature of the cruel and scolding woman. She attacks York most severely with her tongue, taunting and tormenting the helpless man in a manner that seems uniquely feminine. Nowhere else in Shakespeare do we find a man tormenting a defeated enemy in the manner affected by Margaret. Not even the evil Aaron is so cruel. Margaret then tortures York with the death of his son, Rutland. Here again, she acts the way she thinks a man would act, but her actions only magnify her perverse femininity. The killing of a child (Rutland was in fact 17 at the time of his murder by Clifford, but is usually played as younger) should offend anyone, but when a woman who is expected to be maternal and nurturing is shown to openly gloat over the killing, her actions do not imitate that of a man, but call attention to her perversity as a woman. She is shown to be "unnatural," neither man nor woman, but something less than human, something beastly. When at last she thrusts her sword into York, she appears merciful compared to her preceding behavior.

Margaret's fortunes quickly go into decline after Wakefield. Two of York's surviving sons, Edward and Richard, regroup at Mortimer's Cross and meet with Warwick who is smarting from a defeat at the Second Battle of St. Albans. York's third son, George, Duke of Clarence is on his way from Burgundy at the head of reinforcements. The reunited Yorkist forces launch a counter-attack against Queen Margaret's army at Towton near the town of York. This time the Queen's forces are defeated, Clifford is killed, King Henry is taken prisoner and the Queen and Prince Edward flee to France. Edward, now Duke of York, seizes the crown and becomes King Edward IV of England. Here again it is worth taking a moment to catch up on the actual history compressed in Act II, The Battle of Wakefield occurred December 30, 1460. Warwick's defeat at the second battle of St. Albans took place February 17, 1461 and the decisive Yorkist victory at Towton occurred March 21, 1461.

Margaret in France resumes her womanly role and asks aid of King Louise XI to regain her throne:

> *Now, therefore, be it known to noble Lewis,*
> *That Henry, sole possessor of my love,*
> *Is of a king become a banish'd man,*
> *And forced to live in Scotland a forlorn;*
> *While proud ambitious Edward Duke of York*
> *Usurps the regal title and the seat*
> *Of England's true-anointed lawful king.*
> *This is the cause that I, poor Margaret,*
> *With this my son, Prince Edward, Henry's heir,*
> *Am come to crave thy just and lawful aid;*
>
> (3 HVI, III, 3, 23-32)

As she pleads for help, Warwick also arrives as the representative of Edward IV to the court of Louise. Warwick is there to offer Edward's hand in marriage to Lady Bona, Louise's sister. Margaret warms Louise against an alliance with a usurper:

> *Look... that by this league and marriage*
> *Thou draw not on thy danger and dishonour;*
> *For though usurpers sway the rule awhile,*
> *Yet heavens are just, and time suppresseth wrongs.*
>
> (3 HVI, III, 3, 74-7)

Nevertheless, with honeyed words of love and accord, Warwick convinces Louise of Edward's sincerity and Louise agrees to the alliance and marriage. Just as all Margaret's hopes seem dashed, a messenger arrives bring news that Edward has suddenly married Lady Elizabeth Grey back in England. Warwick is thunderstruck, Louise outraged and Margaret ecstatic. Not only has the alliance been aborted by Edward's impulsive marriage, but the embarrassed Warwick shifts his allegiance from Edward and the Yorkists to Margaret and the Lancastrians. At the head of French soldiers, Warwick and Margaret invade England and initially manage to unseat Edward and place Henry back on the throne. All of this occurred in 1469 after eight years of Edward on the English throne. Amidst scrimmages, betrayals and shifting allegiances, Edward reasserted his claim to the throne in 1471 and in two final climatic battles, the first at Barnet and the second at Tewkesbury, Edward finally defeated the Lancastrians, ultimately killing all of the contenders for the throne: Warwick, Prince Edward and Henry VI. The only survivor of the Lancastrian alliance is Queen Margaret.

Shakespeare plays out the battle of Tewkesbury in Act V, scenes 4 and 5. Margaret is again in her armor and at the head of a great army. At her side is the 18-year-old Prince Edward. Her soldiers are cowed by the defeat of Warwick and the capture of King Henry at Barnet, but Margaret again rallies them in heroic fashion. Her speech to the troops is certainly the equal of that to Elizabeth I to her troops at Tilbury and approaches the magnificence of Henry V's rallying speech at Agincourt. Since it is so seldom heard today, it is worth printing in its entirety:

> *Great lords, wise men ne'er sit and wail their loss,*
> *But cheerly seek how to redress their harms.*
> *What though the mast be now blown overboard,*
> *The cable broke, the holding-anchor lost,*
> *And half our sailors swallow'd in the flood?*
> *Yet lives our pilot still. Is't meet that he*
> *Should leave the helm and like a fearful lad*
> *With tearful eyes add water to the sea*
> *And give more strength to that which hath too much,*
> *Whiles, in his moan, the ship splits on the rock,*
> *Which industry and courage might have saved?*
> *Ah, what a shame! ah, what a fault were this!*
> *Say Warwick was our anchor; what of that?*
> *And Montague our topmost; what of him?*
> *Our slaughter'd friends the tackles; what of these?*
> *Why, is not Oxford here another anchor?*
> *And Somerset another goodly mast?*

The friends of France our shrouds and tacklings?
And, though unskilful, why not Ned and I
For once allow'd the skilful pilot's charge?
We will not from the helm to sit and weep,
But keep our course, though the rough wind say no,
From shelves and rocks that threaten us with wreck.
As good to chide the waves as speak them fair.
And what is Edward but ruthless sea?
What Clarence but a quicksand of deceit?
And Richard but a ragged fatal rock?
All these the enemies to our poor bark.
Say you can swim; alas, 'tis but a while!
Tread on the sand; why, there you quickly sink:
Bestride the rock; the tide will wash you off,
Or else you famish; that's a threefold death.
This speak I, lords, to let you understand,
If case some one of you would fly from us,
That there's no hoped-for mercy with the brothers
More than with ruthless waves, with sands and rocks.
Why, courage then! what cannot be avoided
'Twere childish weakness to lament or fear.

(3 HVI, V, 4, 1-38)

Unfortunately for Margaret and the Lancastrian cause, the deeds of her army do not rise to the heroic words of her speech. Soon Margaret and Prince Edward are brought before the triumphant sons of York. Mother and son remain defiant and the scene mirrors that when York confronted and tormented by the triumphant Margaret and Clifford. The Yorkist victors do not torment the young Prince, but they do slay him as his mother is forced to watch. Margaret begs for death as well, but King Edward denies her plea. Margaret, now bereft of all power, is reduced to cursing the men who killed her son and is forcibly dragged from the stage.

Historically, Margaret was imprisoned following the battle of Tewkesbury and held in the Tower of London until 1472 when she was placed in the custody of her former lady-in-waiting Alice Chaucer, Duchess of Suffolk. She remained with Chaucer until she was finally ransomed by Louis XI of France in 1475. She returned to France and lived out the remaining seven years of her life in relative silence until her death at the age of 52. Shakespeare again alters history when he carries the character of Margaret into the final play of the Henry VI tetralogy, *Richard III.* The play opens with Edward IV on the throne and his brother, George, the Duke of Clarence, heading off the prison. This would place the year as 1478, but in the second scene of Act I, Shakespeare has Richard confront Lady Anne as she is following the body of Henry VI to his interment. Henry, of course was murdered by Richard in 1471, so the seduction of Anne preceded the imprisonment of Clarence by seven years. It almost seems included here as a kind of flashback to show the seductive evil of Richard and has no impact on the main narrative of the play. In the third scene of the first Act, we learn that Edward is quite ill. He will die in Act II, scene i after learning of the death of Clarence placing the time of the action as 1483. The problem here is that Clarence was executed in 1478, five years before Edward's death. Irrespective of this historical muddle, the appearance of Margaret in Act I, scene 3, whether 1478 or 1483, is historically impossible. Margaret was in France by 1478 and dead in 1483. And in some way that seems appropriate because Margaret "haunts" *Richard III* like a vengeful wraith from the past. Part vengeance seeking Fury, part fortune-telling Fate from Greek mythology, Margaret stalks the play full of venom and hatred, always emerging from the background to curse everyone she encounters, foreseeing their eventual end. "I am hungry for revenge," she boldly announces (*RIII*, IV, 4, 61), and when she is reminded that she fell in fulfillment of York's curse at Wakefield, she responds with curses of her own:

> *Can curses pierce the clouds and enter heaven?*
> *Why, then, give way, dull clouds, to my quick curses!*
> *If not by war, by surfeit die your king,*
> *As ours by murder, to make him a king!*
> *Edward thy son, which now is Prince of Wales,*
> *For Edward my son, which was Prince of Wales,*
> *Die in his youth by like untimely violence!*
> *Thyself a queen, for me that was a queen,*
> *Outlive thy glory, like my wretched self!*
> *Long mayst thou live to wail thy children's loss;*
> *And see another, as I see thee now,*
> *Deck'd in thy rights, as thou art stall'd in mine!*
> *Long die thy happy days before thy death;*
> *And, after many lengthen'd hours of grief,*
> *Die neither mother, wife, nor England's queen!*
>
> (*RIII*, I, 3, 194-208)

For Richard, she wishes:

Thy friends suspect for traitors while thou livest,
And take deep traitors for thy dearest friends!
No sleep close up that deadly eye of thine,
Unless it be whilst some tormenting dream
Affrights thee with a hell of ugly devils!

(RIII, I, 3, 222-6)

Margaret is now a mere shadow of what she had formerly been; she is impotent to have any direct impact on the events that surround her. For the men of the play, she is a harbinger of things to come. For the women of the play, she is a mirror of what they are now or what they will soon become. All that she wishes for or foresees comes to pass.

Why does Shakespeare return Margaret as a character in *Richard III*? As I have previously pointed out, the historical Margaret was dead before the main action of this play. In many productions, Margaret is totally eliminated without in any way compromising the action or enjoyment of the play. This pattern began as early as 1700 when Colley Cibber wrote her out of his revision of Shakespeare's play as part of an overall effort to make the play more stage friendly. Richard III, after all, is Shakespeare's second longest play running to just over 3 hours with an extraordinarily large cast. Some critics have suggested she is there to serve as a foil for Richard; that she is the only character in the play with enough strength to face Richard toe to toe. Others have suggested that she serves as a unifying element that holds the four plays of the tetrology together. Still others would suggest that she is the product of a talented but inexperienced author who is able to his characters. Maybe she was like Falstaff, too interesting or popular to let fade away.

I am personally inclined to view Margaret as a crucial part of Shakespeare's effort to look as the War of the Roses as God's punishment of England's crime of unseating King Richard II. Just as the previously discussed Tillyard's "Tudor myth" postulates that Richard III was God's ultimate punishment for Henry IV usurping King Richard II's crown (see above p. 145f), I would suggest that Margaret is also an instrument of God's divine corrective plan. First she is a representative of France and reminds the audience that England is losing all its hard earned influence in France and invites us to consider if these losses are punishments for England's great crime. In 1 *Henry VI*, England's greatest enemy in France is Joan Pucelle (Joan of Arc) and though she is ultimately defeated, her efforts have significantly degraded England's power in France before she is killed. It is interesting to notice that as Joan is in decline, Margaret is ascending in importance. It is as if the destructive spirit of Joan transmigrates from Joan to Margaret as Margaret becomes the new French enemy of the English. By agreeing to marry Henry, she manages without bloodshed to reacquire Anjou and Maine as a bride price. Once embedded as queen in the English court, she embroils herself in the political infighting and weakens the resolve and ability of the English to successfully prosecute their war against France. Consequently, by the end of 2 *Henry VI*, England has lost nearly all of its possessions in France. In 3 *Henry VI*, Margaret, like Joan, dons the armor of a man and personally engages in combat against the English, specifically the Duke of York and his followers. In Shakespeare's version, the war between Lancaster and York might have been avoided but for the two central villains of the play: Margaret and the man who will become Richard III. At the beginning of the play, York agrees to defer his claim on the throne of England until after the death of Henry VI. Because the agreement disinherited Henry's son, Queen Margaret elects to take up the sword and destroy York and his followers. She could have simply bided her time. Henry may have outlived York. The fickle nobles and commons could have shifted their support from York to Henry. Margaret could have worked her wiles and eventually undermined York's influence and power base. Instead, she takes the "manly" approach of open conflict that ultimately results in the demise of the Lancastrians. She is, however, not the exclusive catalyst that brings the country to civil war. After York has agreed to defer his claim on the throne, the play's other villain, Richard, persuades his father to break his oath and seize the throne immediately. It takes little persuasion. Richard's flimsy justification is that:

> An oath is of no moment, being not took
> Before a true and lawful magistrate,
> That hath authority over him that swears:
> Henry had none,
>
> (3 *HVI*, I, 2, 22-5)

Satisfied with this technicality, York resolve "I will be king, or die." and immediately begins marshaling his forces. (3 *HVI*, I, 2, 135). So, in the final analysis, the war it turns out was inevitable given the personality of the parties involved and the divine retribution postulated by Tillyard.

Consistent with the theme of God working out divine retribution against England, Margaret recalls the image of the Old Testament prophet in the concluding play of the tetralogy in the character of. Typically, the job of the prophet was to call people back to God. This frequently involved warning them of the consequences of their actions and issuing a call to repentance. At times, however, it involved simply a revelation of God's plan for the future. Popular culture tends to picture the prophets as old angry men with long white beards pointing a bony finger at God's enemies and railing against them.

Elijah, the Old Testament prophet, confronts Ahab, the murderous king.

Take for example the story of Elijah the prophet and Ahab, King of Israel after Ahab's wife Jezebel had arranged the murder of Naboth the Jezreelite so that the king could seize his vineyard. God commands Elijah to confront the rulers and say: "Have you not murdered a man and seized his property? ... In the place where dogs licked up Naboth's blood, dogs will lick up your blood—yes, yours!" When the two meet, Elijah does as commanded.

> [20]*Ahab said to Elijah, "So you have found me, my enemy!"*
> *"I have found you," he answered, "because you have sold yourself to do evil in the eyes of the Lord.* [21] *He says, 'I am going to bring disaster on you. I will wipe out your descendants and cut off from Ahab every last male in Israel—slave or free.[a]* [22] *I will make your house like that of Jeroboam son of Nebat and that of Baasha son of Ahijah, because you have aroused my anger and have caused Israel to sin.'*
> [23] *"And also concerning Jezebel the Lord says: 'Dogs will devour Jezebel by the wall of[b] Jezreel.'*
> [24] *"Dogs will eat those belonging to Ahab who die in the city, and the birds will feed on those who die in the country."*

Elijah in this passage certainly recalls Margaret's ranting in Act I, scene iii. Ahab and Jezebel are not called to repentance, but are instead condemned by Elijah, their fates foretold by the prophet of the Lord. This is not of course to suggest that Margaret is a prophet of God, but her prophet-like presentation services to remind the audience that God is still at work in the background, that no matter how bad things go in the play they are witnessing, it is all a part of working out God's plan for reconciling England to Himself.

Compare this publicity still from Richard III to the picture of Elijah and Ahab.[2]

While Margaret may remind us of an Old Testament prophet, she may also remind us of a witch. Looking forward to the more famous witches of *Macbeth*, Margaret predicts outcomes, but makes nothing happen by direct intervention. While her curses are prophetic and seem to harness the power of divine justice, Margaret also recalls an appeal to a darker power. Her curses while accurately predicting what is to come, it is not justice she calls out for, but personal revenge, not as we have seen, a commendable motive. Margaret unlike the prophets is not consciously God's mouthpiece although she participates in God's plan. Her curses and predictions are malicious and self-serving. She is full of misery and the only way she can make herself feel better is to wallow in the misery of others. This woman, like many women in Shakespeare, is reduced to powerlessness, left to mourn the dead and hate the living. Her only nourishment is her rage.

Finally, Margaret in *Richard III* is a ghost, literally and figuratively. I have already mentioned that at the time of the play's action, the historical Margaret was already dead and this is entirely appropriate to the central thread of the tetralogy, the aforementioned Tudor myth. As a ghost she is the spirit of the past recalling all that has gone before: the usurpations from and murders of Richard II and Henry VI; the loss of France; the murders of Gloucester, Rutland, York, and Prince Edward; the civil wars that killed thousands. She is the memory of the age who leads her fellow queens in a lament for and remembrance of the dead. She sits with Queen Elizabeth and the Duchess of York and summarizes the essentials of the past:

QUEEN MARGARET (to *Queen Elizabeth*)

I had an Edward, till a Richard kill'd him;
I had a Harry, till a Richard kill'd him:
Thou hadst an Edward, till a Richard kill'd him;
Thou hadst a Richard, till a Richard killed him;
DUCHESS OF YORK
I had a Richard too, and thou didst kill him;
I had a Rutland too, thou holp'st to kill him.
QUEEN MARGARET
Thou hadst a Clarence too, and Richard kill'd him.

(RIII, IV, 4, 40-46)

This exchange emphasizes the personal loss of the woman touched by those most responsible for the immediate suffering of the play. The tit-for-tat nature of their losses also emphasizes the cyclical nature of violence and revenge in 15th century England convulsing in the throes of civil war that lasted nearly thirty years.

Margaret only has two scenes in *Richard III*, but she is a powerful presence both looking forward into the eventual destruction of both the white and red rose and looking back at the deeds of treachery and murder that bring the Plantagenet's to their bloody conclusion. Is she a villain? Clearly Shakespeare tried to portray her as such, but paradoxically, he imbues her with many of the same qualities he finds admirable in his male characters. She is both resourceful and brave, willing to take up arms in an effort to protect her son and her right. She can be petty in her dealings her enemies, but she is loyal to Henry and his allies. She has a streak of cruelty, but certainly no more than the men with whom she competes. Ultimately, for Shakespeare, Margaret is a villain because she is French and a woman who asserts herself in manly ways, but there is also a grudging admiration of this strange creature that Shakespeare provides with some of the best scenes in the sweeping Henry VI tetralogy.

BRING FORTH THAT SORCERESS:

Those of us old enough to remember the 1950's probably share a picture of Joan of Arc as the beautiful, brave and saintly warrior for France portrayed by Ingrid Bergman in the 1948 Victor Fleming film titled *Joan of Arc.* Bergman for those unfamiliar with her film credits is the love interest in the classic 1942 Humphrey Bogart film, *Casablanca,* and director Victor Fleming is best known as the director of 1939's blockbuster, *Gone with the Wind.* The film garnered seven Oscar nominations at the 1949 Academy Awards, including one for Ingrid Bergman as Best Actress in a Leading Role. The film is a strait forward retelling of Joan's story from the age of 14 when she first heard the "voices from Heaven" telling her to lead France's Army against the occupying English until her betrayal and execution in Rouen. The film never questions Joan's role as a legitimate messenger of God and portrays her as the saintly Maid of Orleans who was canonized as a saint by the Catholic Church in 1920. The chief villain of the piece is the French King Charles VII, played by Jose Ferrer, who owes his crown to Joan, but betrays her to the Burgundian English. On the English side, Joan's chief antagonist is her persecutor is the corrupt, politically motivated Count-Bishop of Beauvais, Pierre Cauchon, who presides over her trial for heresy and harangues and tortures Joan until she is nearly broken. In the end, Bergman delivers a remarkably poignant, emotionally overflowing Joan who remains true to her "voices." As the flames and smoke rise about her, she devoutly stares at an upheld cross and a celestial chorus swells on the soundtrack as a heavenly light shines down through the clouds to illuminate her sublime face.

Ingrid Bergman leads the troops in Victor Fleming's *Joan of Arc* (1848)

With Bergman's image in mind, most people will be shocked when they encounter a completely different Joan in Shakespeare's *1 Henry VI*. Shakespeare's Joan is anything but saintly. She is a liar, a slut, a coward and a witch, supported by her own little band of hellish fiends until they betray her. She is introduced in the second Scene of the first Act when she has her initial meeting with Charles, Dauphin of France. Shakespeare notorious for distorting time and place for dramatic effect here places the meeting at Orleans where Charles is participating in the French attempt to raise the English siege of the city. In historical fact, the meeting took place early in 1429 in the town of Chinon, some 87 miles from Orleans. Shakespeare does dramatize the popular story of the Dauphin's test of Joan where he has one of his henchmen, in this iteration Reignier (the same man who is revealed to be Queen Margaret's father later in the play), claim to be the Dauphin to see if Joan can detect the deception. Joan instantly sees through the deception and correctly identifies the true Dauphin thereby establishing her credibility. In private conference with Charles, she reveals that she has been visited by "God's mother" and commanded to "free my country from calamity." (1 *HVI*, I, 2, 81). She further tells him that the light of the heavenly vision affected a physical change in her, saying:

> ...whereas I was black and swart before,
> With those clear rays which she infused on me
> That beauty am I bless'd with which you see.

She finally invites him to test her skill at arms and when Charles agrees, he is quickly overcome and quite won over. He *"burn[s] with thy desire,"* but Joan restrains his passion:

> *I must not yield to any rites of love,*
> *For my profession's sacred from above:*
> *When I have chased all thy foes from hence,*
> *Then will I think upon a recompense.*
>
> *(1 HVI, I, 2, 113-6)*

Charles puts his whole faith in Joan when she announces that "This night the siege [of Orleans] assuredly I'll raise" and he and his henchmen follow the Maid from the stage.

Joan next appears in Scene 5 as she leads the French troops against the English besieging Orleans. Joan drives the English troops before her and confronts the English champion, John Talbot is single combat. Lord Talbot, 1st Earl of Shrewsbury had been fighting in France for two years before encountering Joan at Orleans. Shakespeare will make him the chief hero of the play, a representative of English valor and military prowess. When he hears that the French are coming lead by Joan and the Dauphin, he confidently boasts "Pucelle or puzzel, dolphin or dogfish, / Your hearts I'll stamp out with my horse's heels, / And make a quagmire of your mingled brains." (1 HVI, I, 4, 107-9). Talbot's "Pucelle or puzzle" is a three-way play on Joan's self-selected title of Pucelle. According to Maria Warner "Pucelle means 'virgin' but in a special way, with distinct shades commutating youth, innocence, and, paradoxically, nubility" but "in English, 'pucelle' means virgin, 'puzel' means whore. The two English words can be used in performance to create a double perspective on Joan"[3] "Puzzle" in English also means a riddle or enigma which Joan clearly is, not only for the English, but also for her French allies. She is a woman who wears men's clothe and who engages in a man's profession. She is either a witch, or a madwoman, or a messenger of God. When Talbot meets Joan on the field, his confidence is shaken, Joan fights him to a standstill than breaks off combat to enter triumphantly with men to reinforce Orleans. Talbot immediately credits the victory as a witch's work because no true woman could defeat a man such as he in combat and no French force could overcome an English one unless they were aided by the forces of Hell.

> *My thoughts are whirled like a potter's wheel;*
> *I know not where I am, nor what I do;*
> *A witch, by fear, not force, like Hannibal,*
> *Drives back our troops and conquers as she lists:*
>
> (1 HVI, I, 5, 19-22)

He naturally credits his mental confusion to Joan's witchcraft and not to the more logical, but less acceptable explanation of fatigue.

Immediately following Talbot's assertion of witchcraft, Charles safely within the wall of Orleans calls Joan "Astraea's daughter," Astraea daughter being the Greek goddess of justice. She is called "glorious prophetess" identifying her as heaven's agent, but it is Charles in this scene that becomes the prophet.

> *In memory of her when she is dead,*
> *Her ashes, in an urn more precious*
> *Than the rich-jewel'd of Darius,*
> *Transported shall be at high festivals*
>
> (1 HVI, I, 6, 23-6)

He foresees Joan reduced to ashes, but at the time where cremation was prohibited by the church, the burning of the body was a penalty reserved for witches and heresy. Although he is consciously recalling the pagan's burning of the bodies of their heroes, he is also forecasting Joan's fate. Further, Charles prophetically announces that "No longer on Saint Denis will we cry, / But Joan la Pucelle shall be France's saint" (1 HVI, I, vi, xx). To this point, Shakespeare seems to be handling the enigma of Joan in an even-handed manner, portraying the distinct English and French views and showing both sides as relatively credible given their biased points of view. Shakespeare, driven by his English jingoism, cannot sustain this impartiality. In the next scene (Act II, scene i), he shows Talbot mounting an assault on Orleans, driving out Joan and the French forces and taking the city. This of course never happened. After Joan's relief of Orleans on May 7, 1429, the English troops under the command of John Talbot and William de la Pole (Earl of Suffolk) assembled the following morning in battle array for another assault on Orleans, but when the French lined up before them the English withdrew leaving Orleans in French hands. Shakespeare could not stand to let such a shameful defeat stand so he invented the taking of Orleans out of whole cloth.

We don't see Joan again until Act III, Scene ii. Shakespeare spends the intervening time developing his primary theme of treachery and corruption in the

English. When he returns to Joan she and the French forces are before the English occupied city of Rouen. She manages to infiltrate the city in disguise and open a path for French forces who evict the English. The English again under the command of Lord Talbot counterattack and reverse their defeat, retaking Rouen. This entire depiction is completely fictitious. Joan never launched an attack on Rouen, a well-fortified and defended capital of English occupation. The Duke of Bedford who Shakespeare shows dying while Talbot retakes Rouen, if fact died in September 14, 1435. The city of Rouen did not fall to the French forces until November 10, 1449 and it was never retaken. One has to wonder why Shakespeare would so dramatically alter history. The only reason is to allow a second confrontation between his chief antagonists, Joan and Talbot. He has Joan enter the city in disguise and in using this stratagem, Joan shows a disregard for the rules of chivalry that would condemn such tactics as treacherous. Talbot needs no such tactics to retake the city. He relies on the force of his arms and the courage of his English army. Thus, Shakespeare encourages his English audience's impression that the French are "sneaky" and un-chivalrous, only able to win by using under-handed tactics and that the English are forthright and chivalrous in their approach to war.

Shakespeare continues his attack on the French honor in the next scene where, after being expelled from Rouen, Joan undertakes to recruit the English ally, the Duke of Burgundy, to her side. She appeals to Burgundy as a fellow Frenchman and reminds him of his poor treatment by his English allies. With "sugar'd" words she persuades his to join her side and then in a contemptuous aside, tells the audience "Done like a Frenchman: turn, and turn again!" (1 HVI, III, 3, 85) showing the French to be morally weak and prone to treachery.

The final meeting of Joan and Talbot comes in Act IV, Scene 7 before the walls of Bourdeaux. Talbot has come to lay siege to the city, but finds himself grossly outnumbered when the combined forces of Joan and Burgundy arrive on the scene. Talbot had been expecting reinforcements from the Dukes of York and Somerset, but their squabbling and petty jealousies blocks support for Talbot and he is left alone to face the French. After a heated battle, the heroic Talbot loses both his own son and his life. When the victorious French led by Joan, Charles and Burgundy come upon the body of the slain hero, they acknowledge his prowess in battle but are contemptuous of his body is death. Burgundy even wants to desecrate the body, but Charles forbids it. When the English envoy comes to ask for the body, Joan replies, "For God's sake let him have 'em; to keep them here, / They would but stink, and putrefy the air." (1 HVI, IV, 7, 89-90). Again, Shakespeare's history is faulty: Talbot did die in battle near Bourdeaux (actually at Castillon, 25 miles from Bourdeaux) but in 1453, 22 years after Joan was burned at the stake.

After the loss at Bourdeaux, the forces of York and Somerset combine to wreak vengeance upon the French. Shakespeare has the antagonists meet at Angiers, a town about 190 miles south-west of Paris. In the course of this battle, Shakespeare shows us Joan's true colors when we see her call upon the forces of darkness to aid her.

> *You speedy helpers, that are substitutes*
> *Under the lordly monarch of the north,*
> *Appear and aid me in this enterprise.*
>
> (*1 HVI, V, 3, 5-7*)

Amazingly, the stage direction notes "Enter Fiends." This is obviously not her first experience with the fiends as she applauds them for their "accustom'd diligence" in responding to her call so promptly. She pleads "Help me **this once**, that France may get the field" (*1 HVI*, V, 3, 12) which suggests that while she is familiar with these fiends, they have not aided her in the past. Her achievements were her own. The fiends inexplicably refuse to speak to her even when she offers to feed them with her blood. They hang their heads. With increasing desperation, Joan asserts that "My body shall/ Pay recompense, if you will grant my suit." (*1 HVI*, V, 3, 18-9). The fiends shake their heads. At last, she says "Then take my soul, my body, soul and all, / Before that England give the French the foil." (*1 HVI*, V, 3, 22-3). The fiends depart in silence. She and the French forces are on their own.

What are we to make of this strange scene? Joan calls upon the powers of darkness in her hour of need and they appear, but are unwilling or unable to help. She has met with them before, but in what capacity? She asks for help "this once" telling the audience that she has not requested their help in the past. Are they the authors of Joan's voices? Did they deceive her, allowing her to assume that her mission was sent from "God's mother" or did she know from the beginning that she was doing the Devil's work? Were the fiends her guides and advisers, but powerless to interfere directly in the affair of the world? Do they refuse to aid her even when she offers both body and soul because her soul has already been lost as a result of her trafficking with the forces of darkness? I would contend that Shakespeare wishes us to believe Joan is a witch, that she knew from the beginning that her voices were not heaven sent. She used the lie that she was sent by "God's mother" to persuade the Dauphin to do her bidding. Does that suggest that France is favored by the Devil in their battle against the English? The jingoistic Shakespeare would answer with an emphatic "Yes." The English opinion of the French, both at the time of the action depicted and at the time the play was first performed, was less than complimentary. They were considered an effete and effeminate people, obsessed by fashion, leisure and sensuality. They were no way the military equal of the English and the only way they could possibly defeat an English army would be by treachery or devilry. It seems to Shakespeare's audience only natural that the French would be led by a woman.

In fact, Joan represents not only an enemy of the English, but an unnatural enemy of God's patriarchal world order. As such, she can be nothing but the "Devil's dam" as Talbot calls her. She wears a man's clothe, announcing to the world that she is the equal of the men who surround her and oppose her. The wearing of men's clothe by a woman could in itself be seen as a heresy and sign of witchcraft. It is one of the charges leveled against her during her trial. Trial transcripts show the interrogators repeatedly return to the issue of Joan's attire.

> Of all this long tissue of crimes laid to her charge, that of wearing a man's dress was made the most heinous; for the Almighty had made it a crime abominable to Himself, that women should wear men's dress.[4]

Specifically, the 5th of 12 Articles of the Indictment against Joan states:

> She affirms that her wearing a man's dress is done by her through the will of God; she has sinned by receiving the Sacrament in that garb, which she says she would sooner die than quit wearing.[5]

The ban on women dressing as men is rooted in Deuteronomy 22:5 that says "The woman shall not wear that which pertaineth unto a man, neither shall a man put on a woman's garment: for all that do so are abomination unto the Lord thy God." Even in Shakespeare's time, it was this issue was still the focus of intense debate. Puritan pamphleteers railed against 'women in breeches" as insubordinate. Phillip Stubbes, a fanatical Puritan, attacked the doublet-and-hose woman in The Anatomy of Abuses, printed in 1583:

> I neuer read nor heard of any people, except drunken with Cyrces cups, or poysoned with exorcisms of Medea, that famous and renoumed Sorceresse, that euer woulde weare suche kinde of attire as is not onely stinking before the face of God, offensiue to man, but also painteth our to the whole world the venereous inclination of their corrupt conversation.[6]

According to Juliet Dusinberre,

> "James I saw the woman in breeches as a threat to respectable society and, according to one of John Chamberlain's letters, instructed the clergy in 1620 to 'inveigh vehemently against the insolencie of our women, and theyre wearing of brode brimed hats, pointed dublets, theyre hayre cut short or shortie, and some of them stilettos or poniards, and such other trinckets of like moment.'[7]

Underlying these complaints against masculine women is the fear that they jeopardized the balance of society between male and female, and assailed the natural order. Dusinberre notes the masculine female, "by taking a man's clothes ... threatened not only to usurp his authority but to annex his nature. Men," she observes "dislike their own characteristics when they observe them in women."[8] Going further, Shakespeare seems to suggest that to some extent when women go to war, like Joan and Margaret, they cease to offer an alternative to the male world of politics and violence. In fact, they seem to heighten the viciousness of the men that surround them, encouraging the escalation of violence as if the men feel compelled to assert their masculinity in the effort to reaffirm their maleness in the presence of a powerful woman.

Like the cross-dressing women of Shakespeare's London, the actors called upon to play women on the stage were roundly condemned by Puritans. John Rainolds in *The Overthrow of Stage Playes* (1599) warned of the "filthy sparkles of lust to that vice the putting of women's attire on men may kindle in unclean affections."[9] In the face of such denunciations, there is a certain irony that Joan, the villainess, is condemned for wearing male apparel while the actor playing Joan would be a male playing a female dressing up as a male. He would be similarly condemned by the critics of the theater as "unnatural." Surely Shakespeare would not have missed the inherent humor in this situation. While the Puritan complained about the males taking on female roles and attire on the stage, could they object to a male play a female acting like a male? Joan is the first of many of Shakespeare's characters who will draw attention to this paradox and usually poke fun at it.

Joan makes her final appearance of the play is in Act V, scene 4. Here she is before the English tribunal presided over by the Duke of York. She enters denying her own father insisting that she is of noble birth, a contemptible violation of nature and the law of God. Finally angered at her rejection, the father condemns her: "I wish some ravenous wolf had eaten thee! / Dost thou deny thy father, cursed drab? / O, burn her, burn her! hanging is too good." (1 *HVI*, V, 4, 31-3). Joan insists "I never had to do with wicked spirits" (which we the audience know to be a lie) and that she "hath been/ A virgin from her tender infancy, / Chaste and immaculate in very thought." (1 HVI, V, 4, 50-51). When these protestations fail to move her prosecutors, she changes tactics and cries out, "I am with child, ye bloody homicides: / Murder not then the fruit within my womb." (1 HVI, V, 4, 62-63). This just seconds after proclaiming herself chaste and immaculate! She first names her former ally the Duke of Alencon as the father, then she names Reignier, king of Naples (the father of the future Queen Margaret). Neither claim moves her judges and she is dragged from the stage, cursing, to the stake.

While we are never particularly engaged with Joan as an audience, Shakespeare progressively reveals her evil nature as the play unfolds. We of course know from the beginning she is a villainess; she is after all a forward woman asking to lead an army and she is French to boot. We might, however, be willing to give her the benefit of the doubt: maybe she is just delusional and not evil. Her military tactics are a bit unchivalrous, but perhaps that just because she has no military training or maybe it's just her devious French nature. But later, when we see her seduce the treacherous Burgundy and then contemptuously dismiss the fallen Talbot, we begin to sense the darker side of the maid. Finally, we have ocular evidence of her complicity with the forces of Hell when she conjures the silent fiends and then her craven, cowardly behavior at her trial finally robs her of any claim on our sympathy and we, like York and Warwick, are ultimately unmoved by her execution.

Immediately on the heels of Joan leaving the scene, Margaret reemerges, reinforcing the link between Joan and Margaret. I have read that in some productions, Joan and Margaret were portrayed by the same actress and though this must have made for some interesting costume changes with the one leaving the stage and the other emerging with little time between the two, it would assert that they are in at least one important way the same character, the powerful self-asserting woman who is a threat to the patriarchy and to England. As Juliet Dusinberre writes in Shakespeare and the Nature of Women "Ferocity is bestial in Shakespeare's plays in both men and women, but ferocity in women challenges the stability of the civilized world.[10] Joan and Margaret both challenge the stability of England and become complicit with Richard III in bring about England's fall from grace and its ultimate redemption. In Richard III is accepted as God's scourge for England's crimes against Him and his anointed, these two French ladies might rightly be called scourgetts.

Notes

1. Neale, J. E. Queen Elizabeth I: A Biography. London: Jonathan Cape, 1954.

2. Steve Weingartner (Richard III) and Deborah Strang (Queen Margaret), *A Noise Within, the Classic Theatre Company* production, Photo by Craig Schwartz.
   http://onstagelosangeles.blogspot.com/2009/10/steve-weingartner-richard-iii-and.html

3. Warner, Maria. *Joan of Arc: The Image of Female Heroism*. Berkeley: The University of California Press, 2000, 22.

4. Francis C. Lowell, *Maid of Heaven*, Chapter 5 http://www.maidofheaven.com/joanofarc_gower_imprisonment_trial.asp

5. *The Trial of Joan of Arc*, Being the verbatim report of the proceedings from the Orleans Manuscript, translated by W.S. Scott, 1956, Associated Book Sellers. http://smu.edu/ijas/1431trial.html

6. Philip Stubbes, *Anatomy of the Abuses*. 1583, qtd. in Juliet Dusinberre. *Shakespeare and the Nature of Women, Third Edition* (p. 329). Kindle Edition.

7. Juliet Dusinberre. *Shakespeare and the Nature of Women, Third Edition* (p. 233). Kindle Edition.

8. Ibid, 303-4

9. John Rainolds. *The Overthrow of Stage Plays* (1599).

10. *Prefaces to Shakespeare*, ed. Muriel St. Clare Byrne (1946; rpt. Princeton, N. J.: Princeton Univ. Press, 1963),

ARE YOU OUR DAUGHTER?: KING LEAR: GONERIL AND REGAN

In a 2008 interview on the BBC's *World Book Club*, author Jane Smiley was interviewed about her 1991 Pulitzer Prize winning novel, *A Thousand Acres*, a story set in late 1970's Iowa and modeled on Shakespeare's *King Lear*. The unique spin of the novel is that it is narrated by the Lear character's eldest daughter, Ginny (Goneril), and is sympathetic the position of Lear's two eldest daughter in their struggles with their increasingly unbalanced father. Larry, the Lear figure is a domineering and generally unpleasant character who decides to incorporate his farm, handing complete and joint ownership to his three daughters, thereby avoiding paying taxes to the Government. His eldest daughters, Ginny and Rose (Regan) quickly accept the offer, but when the youngest daughter, Caroline (Cordelia) expresses doubt in the wisdom of the plan, she is quickly cut out of the deal and banished from Larry's home. Unlike Shakespeare's Lear, Larry does not spend his time in revelry, but instead sit alone in his big house, growing more isolated from human contact and sinking into drunkenness and dementia. Ginny who has been established from the beginning as Larry's principle caretaker grows increasingly concerned about her father's condition, particularly in his late night drinking and driving, is driven to try to rein Larry in after he has an automobile accident. When she and Rose confront Larry and threaten to take away his car keys, he flies into a rage, calling them "whores" and "bitches" then runs off into the cornfields at the height of a violent storm. Ginny acts from concern for Larry's safety, but Rose is driven by a need to bring Larry down, to punish him for his years of abusing his daughters, psychologically, physically and sexually. Ginny has suppressed these memories of incest and even after Rose confronts her, she continues in denial. After the episode in the cornfield, Larry with the help of Caroline attempts, but fails to regain legal control of the farm. He is finally relegated to the care of his youngest daughter until his death. Ginny, estranged from her husband, turns over her share of the farm to him, then leaves town and starts a new life. Rose loses her husband in an automobile accident, suffers a resurgence of breast cancer that has already taken one of her breasts, and dies, still bitter and enraged at her father. The farm falls into insurmountable debt and is finally lost.

Smiley in describing her reason for writing *A Thousand Acres* revealed that she never cared for King Lear because of the way the daughters were portrayed by Shakespeare and subsequent directors and critics. "They are always portrayed by [and as] dried up, middle-aged harridans." The fact that they want to stop Lear and his retinue from tuning their homes into taverns is seen as the height of selfishness and ingratitude. As the play proceeds, they go from bad to worse, indulging in adultery and torture and finally murder and suicide. Shakespeare stacks the deck against the two sisters in a way that makes them irredeemably villainous, reminiscent of Iago, paragons of "motiveless malignancy." The lack of any back story concerning the family dynamics in the Lear clan invites speculation. How did Goneril and Regan become what they are? Are they, as Smiley suggests, the products of abuse? Do they hate their father from the beginning or do circumstances lead them logically to the actions they take? Is Lear the tragic character of the play or do the sisters display tragic characteristics as well? In short, are their indications in the play that could rehabilitate the long held image of the sisters as evil incarnate?

In Act I of *King Lear*, the King decides to divide his kingdom among his three daughters so as to prevent future strife after his death. He however set the division as a contest between the daughters to determine who will receive the finest share. He asks "Which of you shall we say doth love us most? /That we our largest bounty may extend/ Where nature doth with merit challenge." (*KL*, I. 2, 51-3). Goneril, the oldest, speaks first promising love "Dearer than eye-sight, space, and liberty." (*KL*, I. 2, 56) As her reward, she is immediately awarded a plot of land already staked out for her by her father. We see that the contest is a ruse since, before the other two sisters have had a chance to speak, Lear has already determined how he will divide the kingdom. Regan goes next, trying to "one up" her sister's pronouncement: "I find she names my very deed of love; / Only she comes too short." (*KL*, I. 2, 71-2). She too receives her reward immediately: "an ample third of our fair kingdom; / No less in space, validity, and pleasure, / Than that conferr'd on Goneril." (*KL*, I. 2, 79-81). Lear then turns to Cordelia, the youngest daughter, obviously his favorite and asks "what can you say to draw/ A third more opulent than your sisters?" (*KL*, I. 2, 85-6) We see that it has already been determined that she, the favored daughter, will be the one to receive the best part of the inheritance. She answers to everyone amazement, "Nothing." Although she tries to explain to her father the absurdity of such a contest, Lear in his pride, rejects her and cuts her out of the inheritance and banishes her from his sight. When Kent, Lear's henchman, objects, Lear confesses, "I loved her most, and thought to set my rest/ On her kind nursery." (*KL*, I. 2, 123-4). What he hoped for in Cordelia was not a daughter, but a second mother to grant him unconditional love and care for him in his old age. Cordelia protests "I cannot heave/ My heart into my mouth: I love your majesty/ According to my bond; nor more nor less." (*KL*, I. 2, 91-3). While she may be admired for her truthfulness, she shows herself made of the same prideful stuff of her father. Her sisters know their father for what he is and they give him what he needs at the time; Cordelia will not humble herself to do so. Is it because she is too prideful to humble herself before her father or is she trying to show up the hypocrisy she sees in the responses of her sisters? H. Granville-Baker opined it is:

> a fatal error to present Cordelia as a meek saint. She has more than a touch of her father in her. She as proud as he is, and as obstinate, for all her sweetness and her youth. And being young, she answers uncalculatingly with pride to his pride even as later she answers with pity to his misery.[1]

It is interesting that Cordelia's rebellion against Lear's paternal and monarchial authority takes the form of silence, a normally feminine virtue, that she turns into a dagger to pierce Lear's pride. In her youthful naiveté, Cordelia's remarks reveal she believes love is a fixed commodity, divisible in a zero-sum game.

> Why have my sisters husbands, if they say
> They love you all? Haply, when I shall wed,
> That lord whose hand must take my plight shall carry
> Half my love with him, half my care and duty:
> Sure, I shall never marry like my sisters,
> To love my father all
>
> (KL, I, 1, 99-104)

In this, she is not unlike her father. For Lear, love is also "a commodity, lent out at interest and recalled at will. He has staged a public reckoning of his daughters' affections so that everyone in the court may hear how much his daughters love him. His standard, clearly, is quantitative rather than qualitative: 'Which of you shall we say doth love us most?'" (*KL*, I. 1, 51).[2] Cordelia fails to recognize that the quality of love is not at issue here, but instead the expression of it. Some critics lionize her for heroically standing up to the oppressive dual systems of paternity and monarchy, but to do so is to ignore the ultimate consequence of her petty rebellion: the collapse of the kingdom and the deaths of most of the principal players, including her own.

Goneril and Regan, on the other hand are demonized as power-hungry hypocrites, for replying to Lear's demands in an oily and flattering manner. They feel nothing and profess everything and that is enough for Lear. They have given Lear what he demands, but some will see his demands as monstrous. Johannes Allgaier writes that:

> Lear is demanding no less than the surrender of that inner worth of a person, of that sovereign sanctuary within the human heart the integrity of which enables human beings to love. To allow anyone, even a father or a king, to tear open that sanctuary with the brutality of power and authority means nothing less than submitting to spiritual rape; to accept a reward for it, even a kingdom, spiritual prostitution...Goneril and Regan have allowed their power of love to be usurped by a tyrant. What is worse, they have accepted payment for it.[3]

Thus, according to Allgaier, Lear's payment for this abuse of power is found in the cruelty the sisters inflict on him, "the cruelty of the slave turned loose."[4] This seems to me a bit of overstatement. First, is it so wrong of Goneril and Regan to play Lear's game? Agreed, he is neither the ideal father nor the ideal King, but to call his vain ceremony "spiritual rape" seems to me a bit over the top. Even if we accept that Goneril and Regan feel nothing for their father, while hypocritically professing all, what harm is done by humoring the old man's vanity? Do we have any indication that the elder sisters were in any way abused by their father in such a way that they would have justified inflicting cruelty upon him? In fact, by feeding his vanity, are they not acting kinder toward the old King than Cordelia?

We soon see there is little affection between Cordelia and her sisters. As she departs the kingdom, Cordelia says to Goneril and Regan:

> I know you what you are;
> And like a sister am most loath to call
> Your faults as they are named. Use well our father:
> To your professed bosoms I commit him
> But yet, alas, stood I within his grace,
> I would prefer him to a better place.
>
> (KL, I, 1, 269-74)

She believes her elder sisters are self-serving hypocrites and she believes that her father, now delivered into their hands will suffer under their care. She does not believe their easily professed love for Lear is real and presumably she has reason for this. Yet objectively, we, the audience would have no reason to suspect them of anything more than the wish to keep their unpredictable father happy.

They have lived with the old man long enough to know his foibles and they are accustomed to accommodating him. They know how to play his game. After Cordelia's departure, the remaining sisters discuss what has transpired and what they should do:

> GONERIL
> You see how full of changes his age is; the
> observation we have made of it hath not been
> little: he always loved our sister most; and
> with what poor judgment he hath now cast her off
> appears too grossly.
> REGAN
> 'Tis the infirmity of his age: yet he hath ever
> but slenderly known himself.
> GONERIL
> The best and soundest of his time hath been but
> rash; then must we look to receive from his age,
> not alone the imperfections of long-engraffed
> condition, but therewithal the unruly waywardness
> that infirm and choleric years bring with them.
>
> (KL, I, 1, 288-300)

They are legitimately concerned about the increasingly erratic behavior of the old king who even in the best of times was "rash." After this last display of "poor judgment" in banishing Cordelia and Kent they see signs of things to come, "the waywardness that infirm and choleric years bring with them." They are not overtly antagonistic to their father, but they do fear, based on history that Lear's behavior will not improve with age; that in fact, his behavior will turn in such a way that he will, in contemporary vernacular, become "a danger to self and others."

It isn't long before their fears come true. As a part of the "deal" cut at the division of the kingdom, Lear expressed his wish to live in his daughter's homes along with his retinue of 100 knights, rotating monthly between one and the other. Predictably, his presence throws the household into chaos. Goneril described her situation:

> By day and night he wrongs me; every hour
> He flashes into one gross crime or other,
> That sets us all at odds: I'll not endure it:

> *His knights grow riotous, and himself upbraids us*
> *On every trifle.*
>
> (*KL, I, 3, 3-7*)

So provoked, she resolves to bring the situation to a head. She tells her servant Oswald,

> *Put on what weary negligence you please,*
> *You and your fellows; I'll have it come to question:*
> *If he dislike it, let him to our sister,*
> *Whose mind and mine, I know, in that are one,*
> *Not to be over-ruled. Idle old man,*
> *That still would manage those authorities*
> *That he hath given away!*
>
> (*KL, I, 3, 12-8*)

She intends to put limits on her father, a man who for a lifetime has endured no limits. Is this an act of unkindness or the rational response to a situation clearly out of control? Is it to be expected that she should allow her father to set her home in an uproar? She reasons that because he is acting like a child, he must be treated as a child. "Now, by my life, / Old fools are babes again; and must be used/ With cheques as flatteries,--when they are seen abused." (*KL, I, 3, 18-20*)

When Lear returns from hunting, he finds himself treated without "that ceremonious affection as you were wont" and responds to the Oswald's insolence with blows. When Goneril enters the scene, she makes her case to Lear:

> *...your insolent retinue*
> *Do hourly carp and quarrel; breaking forth*
> *In rank and not-to-be endured riots. Sir,*
> *I had thought, by making this well-known unto you,*
> *To have found a safe redress; but now grow fearful,*
> *By what yourself too late have spoke and done.*
> *That you protect this course,*
>
> (*KL, I, 4, 202-8*)

She pleads:

> *I would you would make use of that good wisdom,*
> *Whereof I know you are fraught; and put away*

These dispositions, that of late transform you
From what you rightly are.

(KL, I, 4, 219-222)

In this plea, she strikes at the heart of the matter. Lear responds, "Doth any here know me?" (KL, I, 4, 226) There are two visions at conflict as to what he rightly is. Lear's vision is that he is still king; Goneril's that he is an out-of-control old man who needs to be reined in. Lear still clings to the power he has given away; Goneril exercises the power she has newly acquired. The world has changed and Lear finds himself in the nursery as he anticipated, but it is not one he imagined. Goneril explains his situation:

As you are old and reverend, you should be wise.
Here do you keep a hundred knights and squires;
Men so disorder'd, so debosh'd and bold,
That this our court, infected with their manners,
Shows like a riotous inn: epicurism and lust
Make it more like a tavern or a brothel
Than a graced palace. The shame itself doth speak
For instant remedy:

(KL, I, 4, 240-7)

That remedy is to reduce Lear's retinue by half which does not seem unreasonable given their behavior; nevertheless, Goneril is cast as the archetypal "Terrible Mother" who abuses and destroys her children. The "Terrible Mother" is a Jungian construct rooted in infancy. The infant, overwhelmed with unfulfilled needs, forms an image of the neglectful Terrible Mother that was the opposite or Shadow of the nurturing "Great Mother" who immediately gratifies the infant's needs. Jungian psychology posits that the image of the Terrible Mother recurs repeatedly throughout life when certain cues present themselves, that is, when a female figure fails to meet the needs of the individual the individual's emotional response is to cast that offending female figure as the Terrible Mother. Jungians believe that these are universal emotions connected with universal images that recur everywhere. This explains Lear's and by extension, the audience's negative response to Goneril's behavior. Lear responds violently. He calls her "degenerate bastard," "marble-hearted fiend," and "detested kite." He curses her before her husband, Albany:

Suspend thy purpose, if thou didst intend
To make this creature fruitful!

Into her womb convey sterility!
Dry up in her the organs of increase;
And from her derogate body never spring
A babe to honour her! If she must teem,
Create her child of spleen; that it may live,
And be a thwart disnatured torment to her!

(KL, I, 4, 276-83)

The audience is usually similarly repulsed by Goneril's behavior toward Lear because they also hard-wired to recognize and respond negatively to the Terrible Mother.

Lear, by his division of the kingdom, has voluntarily placed himself in the role of the dependent child, becoming "*L'Enfant terrible.*" The Fool explicitly makes the rather obvious point, saying, "...thou madest thy daughters thy/ mothers: for when thou gavest them/ the rod, and put'st down thine own breeches." (KL, I, 4, 172-4). He immediately goes to the image of the punishing mother, never considering the idea that Goneril and Regan could be anything but. Does he, like Cordelia, have knowledge about the sisters' nature that Lear either doesn't know or doesn't want to see? It is significant that Goneril and Regan are both motherless and childless. They seem to have no material role model or experience with childrearing and are now thrust into the unnatural role of "mothering" their father, a task they are singularly ill-prepared to deal with.

How the actress playing Goneril manages this scene is of critically importance to how the audience interprets her character. If she responds to Lear's barrage with an icy demeanor, the audience might infer that she is a cold-hearted and worthy of Lear's description, but it might also infer that this is not new behavior on the part of her father. If berating his daughters each time they disappoint him is his parental norm, these insults might roll off her back as so much water and she may see in Lear's dependency a means to take revenge on the old tyrant. If the actress reacts with a quivering lip and a single tear, we might infer that Lear's curses are uncharacteristic and deeply hurt his daughter, revealing that he is truly on his way to dementia. I believe the middle option is most consistent with the characters, but in any case, is it any wonder that Goneril hardens her position against Lear!

For his part, Lear still harbors hope, placing his faith in Regan:

yet have I left a daughter,
Who, I am sure, is kind and comfortable:
When she shall hear this of thee, with her nails
She'll flay thy wolvish visage. Thou shalt find

That I'll resume the shape which thou dost think
I have cast off for ever:

> (*KL, I, 4, 305-10*)

He gathers his companions and makes for Regan's protection.

Following Lear's departure, Goneril begins to see that Lear not only threatens the peace and tranquility of her home, but he may also threaten her position in the newly separated kingdom. With his 100 knights, he could well launch an attack on her to regain his kingdom by force, resulting in civil war. She tells her husband, "*He may enguard his dotage with their powers, / And hold our lives in mercy,*" and although Albany objects, that she "*fear[s] too far,*" Lear's behavior would suggest is fully capable of such action. For both emotional and practical reasons, it seems prudent that Goneril would wish to restrain her father.

Regan with her husband Cornwall is residing at the castle of the Duke of Gloucester, one of Lear's oldest friends. Gloucester is mired in his own family drama. His bastard son, Edmund has turned Gloucester against his natural son, Edgar, in order to usurp the family fortune. Regan, alerted by Goneril that Lear is on his way, has come to Gloucester's home in an attempt to avoid her father. When Lear arrives, he is first informed by Gloucester that Regan and Cornwall will not see him. When Regan finally does come to him and he makes his complaint against Goneril, he is shocked by Regan defense of her sister against him. Regan tells the old king,

I cannot think my sister in the least
Would fail her obligation: if, sir, perchance
She have restrain'd the riots of your followers,
'Tis on such ground, and to such wholesome end,
As clears her from all blame.

> (*KL, II, 4, 141-5*)

She adds insult to injury by saying out-loud what Goneril only implied:

... you are old.
Nature in you stands on the very verge
Of her confine: you should be ruled and led
By some discretion, that discerns your state
Better than you yourself.

> (*KL, II, 4, 147-51*)

She tells Lear to return to her sister and beg her forgiveness, and when Lear flies into a rage, hurling invectives at Goneril, Regan knowingly replies "so will you wish on me, / When the rash mood is on." (*KL*, II, 4, 169). At this point, Goneril arrives upon the scene and the sisters unite against their father. Regan tells Lear, "I pray you, father, being weak, seem so, (*KL*, II, 4, 201)" emphasizing his dependence and again directs him to return to Goneril with his reduced retinue. He responds: "Persuade me rather to be slave and sumpter/ To this detested groom" (*KL*, II, 4, 215-7) and, mistaking Regan's intention, he declares, "I can stay with Regan, / I and my hundred knights" to which she replies, "Not altogether so. (*KL*, II, 4, 230-2)" Regan asks why Lear needs even 50 knights, again leveling a logical explanation, "How, in one house, / Should many people, under two commands, / Hold amity? 'Tis hard; almost impossible." Objectively, she is correct, but Lear of course doesn't see it this way. She ups the offense, saying,

> *If you will come to me,--*
> *For now I spy a danger,--I entreat you*
> *To bring but five and twenty: to no more*
> *Will I give place or notice.*
>
> (*KL, II, 4, 245-8*)

Hearing this, Lear decides to return to Goneril because she will allow him 50 knights. Again he is wrong. Goneril now announces "What need you five and twenty, ten, or five, / To follow in a house where twice so many/ Have a command to tend you?" (*KL*, I, 4, 261-3). Slowly Lear is stripped of all his resources and finds himself completely dependent on his daughters. In a rage, Lear runs from the castle and into the approaching storm. The sisters reflect on what has transpired:

> REGAN
> *This house is little: the old man and his people*
> *Cannot be well bestow'd.*
> GONERIL
> *'Tis his own blame; hath put himself from rest,*
> *And must needs taste his folly.*
> REGAN
> *For his particular, I'll receive him gladly,*
> *But not one follower.*
>
> (*KL, II, 4, 290-2*)

It is interesting to note how fully Goneril is in the role of mother, saying that Lear must be allowed to endure the consequences of his actions. Regan, a bit more compassionate, is willing to take him in, but not one of his retainers. Nevertheless, the sisters are united against the king and Regan concludes the scene by saying "to wilful men, / The injuries that they themselves procure/ Must be their schoolmasters." (*KL*, I, 4, 303-5)

Are the sisters up to this point villainous? Are they unreasonable in their demands? Should they have just continued to indulge Lear's riotous behavior? When he runs off into the storm, should they have physically restrained him to protect him? The sisters, it seems to me, have no good options open to them. They do not seem to be acting so much out of malice, but out of frustration. In dealing with the childish Lear are they falling back on the parenting patterns they grew up with? Actions have consequences and they are content to have Lear learn the consequences of resisting his new dependency. They reason that the suffering he endures on the storm devastated hearth will bring him to his senses and to conformity with the expectations of his new world.

Meanwhile it is revealed that Albany and Cornwell are at odds and that, learning of this and of the treatment of Lear at the hands of his daughters, has moved France to muster forces at Dover to intervene on the king's behalf and restore his kingdom to him. Gloucester has learned of this and shares this intelligence with Edmund who promptly betrays him to the Duke. Although expressly forbidden by Cornwall to aid Lear, he ventures out into the storm after his friend, to bring his fire and food. He finds the king quite mad at this point, and informs Kent (who has earlier re-entered the service of the king in disguise) that he has "o'erheard a plot of death upon [the King]." He doesn't reveal where the plot originated, whether it is with Cornwall, Regan, and/or Goneril, all together or any one separately. Of the three, I believe Cornwall alone is the plotter as he has been shown to be the most overtly ruthless of the trio. The sisters have shown at this point no inclination to see Lear dead, only humbled and restrained. Cornwall, on the other hand, would see Lear as a threat to his power and having no familial bond to the king, would most likely want to see him quietly eliminated. Gloucester, knowing of the French forces waiting at Dover, instructs Kent to take Lear there for his safety.

When Gloucester returns to his castle, he is greeted by the angry Duke of Cornwall and Regan, and in one of Shakespeare's most brutal scene, tortured by having his eyes plucked out. During the scene, after Cornwall has gouged out one eye, one of Cornwall's servants is so appalled by the treatment of the old man that he attacks Cornwall and administers a fatal blow before he himself is killed by Regan, striking from behind. Throughout the scene, Regan is shown in her anger to be as brutal and sadistic as her husband, and for the first time, her villainy shows itself in full. Gloucester is thrown out of his own castle and told to "sniff his way to Dover."

While this is going on, Goneril has returned to her palace, escorted by Edmund with whom she has become infatuated. Her servant Oswald, who had gone on ahead, meets her and informs her that her husband has been informed of the impending French invasion and of Edmund's betrayal of his father into the hands of Cornwall and Regan. Albany seems to actually welcome the news of the coming of the French and is enraged at Edmund's actions. Learning this, Goneril sends Edmund back to Regan and confronts her husband who greets her, saying "Goneril. You are not worth the dust which the rude wind/ Blows in your face." (*KL*, IV, 2, 29-31). He explains his meaning:

> *What have you done?*
> *Tigers, not daughters, what have you perform'd?*
> *A father, and a gracious aged man,*
> *Whose reverence even the head-lugg'd bear would lick,*
> *Most barbarous, most degenerate! have you madded.*
>
> (KL, IV, 2, 39-43)

Without hearing her side or giving her the benefit of doubt, he upbraids her and her sister as monsters and she-fiends. Goneril counters, calling Albany a "Milk-liver'd man" and demanding to know why he is not preparing his forces to repulse the French. As they argue a messenger arrives and reveals Gloucester fate and Cornwall's demise. Albany vows to thank old Gloucester for his kindness to the King and to avenge his torture. Goneril is more concerned that the newly widowed Regan will rival her for Edmund's affection.

As Goneril fears, Regan has always undertaken the seduction of Edmund, and Regan believes she has won his heart. Goneril and Albany are advancing with their army and Goneril sends a message ahead to Edmund, professing her love and proposing the murder of her husband. The message is however intercepted and falls into the hands of the Edgar, Gloucester's maligned son. Lear, mad and ill, has arrived at Dover and is taken under the care of Cordelia who has arrived with the French invasion force. The French are alerted the English forces are approaching and they prepare for battle. Events have now progressed beyond domestic drama into the realm of power politics.

Christina Leon Alfar in her chapter" Looking for Goneril and Regan" in *Fantasies of Female Evil* (2003), argues that *King Lear* is a play consciously created as an indictment of the absolute power potential in the patriarchal monarchial system. She suggests that by having "Goneril and Regan respond to their role as leaders of the state in a traditional masculine manner" that their behavior is defined by the audience as "unnatural."[5] This is because the sisters represent two competing assumptions: the first assuming a feminine model of behavior associated with a natural inclination toward mercy and obedience and the second assuming a ruthless model of action more natural for masculinity. [6] When the sisters act ruthlessly and out of self-interest, they are taking on the unnatural mantle of the usually male monarch. She goes on to argue that "[r]ather then denouncing the women for their masculine performance of power, the play asks us to reject the tyranny of absolute monarchy.'[7]

Alfar's conclusion is consistent with that of "New Historicism," a relatively new school of literary criticism "unhappy with the exclusion of social and political circumstances (commonly known as the "context") from the interpretation of literary works... the central task of the New Historicism is the same as that of Marxist criticism: first to call into question the traditional view of literature as an autonomous realm of discourse with its own problems, forms, principles, activities, and then to dissolve the literary text into the social and political context from which it issued."[8] The problem with New Historicism is that in following the methods of post-structuralism where a literary works means any number of things to any number of readers, the critic may be tempted to ascribe the ideology he "finds" in a text and its historical/cultural moment is in fact there and "is not simply his own political sympathy which has been injected into the work and then ''located'' there by means of an ingenious selection of the evidence."[35] This question occurs "spontaneously to anyone who reads very widely in New Historicist writing, so much of which expresses a politically au courant sympathy for exploited peoples, powerless women, workers, slaves, and peasants." [9]

While I think that Alfar is correct that the play can be read as a condemnation of absolute monarchy, I believe it is only the misuse of the absolute monarchy that Shakespeare is indicting. It is Lear's model of monarchy that is opposed. Alfar makes the jump that "kingship signifies ruthlessness" in the same way that the rubric "absolute power corrupts absolutely" condemns absolute power. She rejects out of hand the possibility of a benign or beneficent monarchy and argues that this is Shakespeare's position in King Lear. I don't think we can make the jump that Shakespeare's condemnation of Lear's monarchy can imply a condemnation of all monarchy. While Shakespeare does show human vulnerability and weaknesses in all his kings and rulers, it is generally agreed that Shakespeare valued order above all else. King Lear, more than any other of Shakespeare's tragedies, represents the specter of an uncertain and crumbling throne, and the chaos that arises under such conditions. In this instance the breakdown of the family results in the breakdown of the state and ultimately war. We are again reminded of the legend of the Fisher King whose personal illness results in a withering of his lands. The land can only be restored when the King is restored. Alfar even admits the possibility of a benevolent kingship in Shakespeare, remembering that *The Winter's Tale* ends not with the destruction of monarchy, but with the restoration of a "benevolent" kingship.

Setting aside Alfar's indictment of all absolute monarchy, there is no "feminine" way to exercise power in this system. There is only power wielded in self-interest; even Queen Elizabeth acted ruthlessly when it served her purposes. Nevertheless, the play does condemn Goneril and Regan for their ruthlessness even though their ruthlessness grows as a legitimate response to the increasing unruliness of their father and then the threat of a foreign invasion. They behave no differently than we would expect any ruler to act, but because they act in normally masculine ways; they have disrupted the natural order of things that Shakespeare most values. John J. McLaughlin correctly summarizes:

> *Much of the behavior of Goneril and Regan can be explained by what [Alfred] Adler called the "masculine protest," a refusal by women to accept the weakness of the feminine role. Where the masculine protest is in evidence, women construct a wide variety of strategies for reversing their subordinate feminine roles. The way Goneril and Regan treat, not only their father, but also their husbands, shows that they are determined to master the men in their lives and reduce them to inferiors. Their infatuation for Edmund is also a symptom of the masculine protest. They both abandon the passive feminine sexual role—Cordelia's role—and become masculine aggressors, competing for sexual favors from the man whose open drive for power they emulate and hope to surmount.*[10]

Once again as in the *Henry VI* trilogy, Shakespeare's audience is confronted with the uncomfortable image of a woman in armor at the head of an army and, just as Joan La Pucelle and Queen Margaret have to be destroyed for their "unnatural" behavior, so too do Goneril and Regan.

The British army is successful against the French invaders and once the sisters feel secure in their power, they immediately fall out over their lust for Edmund. Regan has the most legitimate claim on him, being widowed, but Goneril has conspired with him to murder her husband. To remove Regan from the competition, Goneril uses the very Machiavellian (and feminine) tool of poison to eliminate her rival sister. Up until this act, we may have been able to excuse Goneril's action as necessary for the preservation of her household and her kingdom. Even her wish to murder her husband, a man who clearly holds her in contempt, is understandable, if not excusable. The murder of her sister, however, is another matter entirely. It is an inexcusable act of sheer villainy carried out by the most villainous method. Even while the poison is working on Regan and

Edmund lies dying following a duel with his half-brother, Edgar, Albany confronts Goneril with her letter to Edmund and accusing her of high treason. She all but laughs in his face and replies: "Say, if I do, the laws are mine, not thine. / Who can arraign me for't?" (*KL*, V, 3, 159). She denies her husband's authority and reserves for herself alone the absolute power of monarchy. Like Lear, she considers herself above the law. Her final words as she exits the stage echo Iago's: "Ask me not what I know." (*KL*, V, 3, 261). Moments later, a gentleman returns with a bloody dagger in his hands and informs all present that Goneril has committed suicide. She who has already dispatched her sister with a woman's weapon, poison, significantly takes her own life with a masculine weapon, a knife. Suicide is her ultimate rejection of an inferior feminine role.[11]

Notes

1. McLaughlin, John J. "The Dynamics of Power in King Lear: An Adlerian Interpretation." *Shakespeare Quarterly*, Vol. 29, No. 1 (Winter, 1978), p. 38

2. Allgaier, Johannes." Is King Lear an Antiauthoritarian Play?" *PMLA*, Vol. 88, No. 5 (Oct., 1973), pp. 1035.

3. Ibid

4. Alfar, Christina Leon," Looking for Goneril and Regan" in *Fantasies of Female Evil* (2003),

5. Ibid 43.

6. Ibid, 85.

7. D. G. Myers, *The New Historicism in Literary Study.* Originally published in Academic Questions 2 (Winter 1988-89): 27-36. Accessed at http://dgmyers.blogspot.com/p/new-historicism-in-literary-study.html

8. Ibid

9. McLaughlin, 41.

10. Ibid, 42.

11. Lee, Adam. "That Monstrous Regiment." *Daylight Atheism* (blog), March 8, 2006. http://www.patheos.com/blogs/daylightatheism/2006/03/that-monstrous-regiment/

SOMETHING WICKED THIS WAY COMES: SECOND WITCH: MACBETH

In 1558, John Knox, an influential figure behind the Protestant Reformation in Scotland, published *The First Blast of the Trumpet Against the Monstrous Regiment of Women*. Reacting specifically to the regency of Mary of Guise during the minority of her daughter, Mary, Queen of Scots and to the Catholic rule of Queen Mary I of England, Knox penned his polemic against the rule of women while exiled from both Scotland and England for his participation in the Protestant reformation. In 1547 Knox was arrested in Scotland for his Protestant activism. After serving a term as a galley slave to the French from 1547-49, he was released to exile in England. Knox found in the England of Edward VI a more congenial environment to spread his Protestant faith and was employed by the Church of England as preacher, and was subsequently appointed as one of the six royal chaplains serving the King. Things went well until the premature death of Edward resulted in the elevation of his Catholic half-sister Mary to the throne. The new Queen's commitment to restoring the Catholic faith in England placed Knox in an untenable position and he was forced to flee to the Continent in early 1554.

No doubt stung by the need to flee before the power of two Queens, Knox published ... *the Monstrous Regiment of Women* while exiled in Geneva. Knox explicitly states that the purpose of the pamphlet was to demonstrate "how abominable before God is the Empire or Rule of a wicked woman, yea, of a traiteresse and bastard." He originally published it anonymously and in England, the pamphlet was predictably and officially condemned by royal proclamation. In the same year, Elizabeth Tudor became Queen of England after the death of Mary and, although Knox had not targeted Elizabeth, she was deeply offended by the pamphlet and never forgave him.

Often cited as one of the most misogynistic documents produced by the western world, Knox was not far from the mainstream of thought that dominated Christianity throughout Europe. His opening paragraph leaves no doubt about his thesis:

> *To promote a woman to bear rule, superiority, dominion, or empire above any realm, nation, or city, is repugnant to nature; contumely to God, a thing most contrary to his revealed will and approved ordinance; and finally, it is the subversion of good order, of all equity and justice.*[1]

Knox calls the reign of women "monstrous", "abominable, odious, and detestable", "repugnant to nature", "a thing most odious in the presence of God", a sin "more heinous than can be expressed by words" and "treason and conspiracy committed against God". It strikes at the very order of the universe, at the concept of the Great Chain of Being where man is always superior to woman just as King is always superior to subjects. "First," he continues, "I say that woman in her greatest perfection was made to serve and obey man, not to rule and command him... woman in her greatest perfection should have known that man was lord above her; and therefore that she should never have pretended any kind of superiority above him, no more than do the angels above God the Creator, or above Christ their head." [2]

Women, Knox preaches, are "weak, frail, impatient, feeble, and foolish; and experience has declared them to be inconstant, variable, cruel, lacking the spirit of counsel and regiment." He grounds his assertions in Christian scripture and tradition. 1 Corinthians 11:8-9 says "For the man is not of the woman: but the woman of the man. Neither was the man created for the woman; but the woman for the man." Even more to the point, he turns to Ephesians 5:22-24: "Wives, submit yourselves unto your own husbands, as unto the Lord. For the husband is the head of the wife, even as Christ is the head of the church: and he is the saviour [sic] of the body. Therefore, as the church is subject unto Christ, so let the wives be to their own husbands in everything." And finally, to 1 Timothy 2:12 that says "...suffer not a woman to teach, nor to usurp authority over the man, but to be in silence." The church fathers provided Knox with further support. Tertullian (ca. 150-225) said to women "You are the port and gate of the devil. You are the first transgressor of God's law". Augustine (354–430 C.E.) warned that women who seek power should be "repressed and bridled". Jerome (c.347 – 420) wrote "Adam was deceived by Eve, and not Eve by Adam, and therefore it is just, that woman receive and acknowledge him for governor whom she called to sin, lest that again she slide and fall by womanly facility" And Ambrose (c. 340 – 397), said that "Woman ought not only to have simple arrayment, but all authority is to be denied unto her. For she must be in subjection to man...as well in habit as in service"[3]

Shortly following the publication of this tirade, Knox returned to his native Scotland as the Queen regency of Mary of Guise was drawing to a close. On 24 October, 1559, the Scottish nobility formally deposed Mary. It took two years for her daughter, Mary, Queen of Scots to arrive in her Kingdom, coming from France, but it only took two weeks for Knox to alienate her by railing against her reign from the pulpit. When she accused him of inciting a rebellion against her mother and of writing a book against her own authority, Knox answered that as long as her subjects found her rule convenient, he was willing to accept her governance, but came short of denouncing his position on the rule of women. By then, his position in Scotland made him immune from a full scale attack, so the two settled into a kind of "cold war" that persisted throughout her short reign. Forced to abdicate in 1566, Mary was succeeded by her son James VI on July 1567. Knox preached the coronation sermon for the 13-month old monarch. On 24 March 1603, James succeeded another Queen, Elizabeth I, to become King of England and Ireland as James I. What James thought of his mother's adversary, John Knox, is not known; Knox died in 1572 when James was only six years old.

Did James share Knox's view about the role of women in politics and in society? Although he never directly commented on *The First Blast of the Trumpet Against the Monstrous Regiment of Women* in his prolific writings, James' dislike of women was common knowledge in both Scotland and England at that time. His misogyny was in part manifested in a demonstrable obsession with witchcraft that resulted in one of his most famous publications, *Daemonologie*, in 1597. James, while still James VI of Scotland, James VI directly participated in the notorious North Berwick witchcraft trials of 1590. The trials developed as a response to storms that delayed James' return to Scotland from Denmark where he had gone to collect his future bride, Princess Anne. James came to believe that the storms were the result of witchcraft, and upon safely reaching the shore of home, he launched the investigation that resulted in the arrest of over 100 "witches" suspected of plotting against his life. Historians have suggested that the trials were politically motivated, giving James the opportunity to attack his enemies. Strangely, the North Berwick plot involved women and men who were not leaders of his political enemies but midwives, wives of merchants or burghers, and laborers. These were people with no real power. Francis Bothwell, the Earl of Bothwell and an enemy of the King, was the only noble caught up in the trials and was forced to flee the Country. Under torture, sometimes supervised by the King himself, many confessed to having met with the Devil in the church at night, and devoted themselves to doing evil, including poisoning the King and other members of his household, and attempting to sink the King's ship. The trials ran for two years and implicated 70 people. The final number executed was not recorded.

While the North Berwick witchcraft trials may have been politically motivated, it is noteworthy that the vast majority of those caught up in the trial's net were female. Traditionally, historians have suggested that while witchcraft trials added fuel to the misogyny of the age, they were not a direct result of it. On the other hand, modern feminist writers have argued that witchcraft and infanticide were two crimes created specifically to persecute and control women. Anne Barstow, Marianne Hester and Carol Karlsen insist that witchcraft must be seen as sexual violence against women within the context of male domination. It was an ideological practice that controlled women's lives and maintained male supremacy. According to Hester, the definition of a witch relied on an "eroticized construct of female behavior" that perceived women as threatening and uncontrolled. The witch was ruled by an overly active and insatiable sexuality that could only be satisfied by perverse practices with the devil. Witch trials were an attempt to contain that sexuality. In King James' words:

> as that sexe is frailer than man is, so it is easier to be intrapped in these grosse snares of the Devell, as was over well proved to be true, by the Serpents deceiving of Eva at the beginning, which makes him the homelier with that sexe sensine.

Women who were unassimilated into patriarchal society were particularly vulnerable to witchcraft accusations. These outcast women included the unmarried, widows, midwives, and women who were economically productive. Karlsen theorizes that such women were victimized because they were seen as stepping beyond the role and position assigned to them in a masculine social structure.

Within a year of assuming the monarchy James replaced the Elizabethan conjuration act with a statute of his own, stiffening the penalties for lesser instances of bewitching and adding specific crimes. His 1604 Act, *An Act against Conjuration, Witchcraft and dealing with evil and wicked spirits,* made it made it a felony to "consult, covenant with, entertain, employ, feed, or reward any evil and wicked spirit to or for any intent or purpose." First-time offenses became punishable by death and between the enactment of this statute and 1606 there were at least 35 recorded executions.

James's obsession with witchcraft went beyond his general misogyny for he believed himself the particular object of attacks by witches. Witchcraft was linked in his mind and in the minds of many of his contemporaries with regicide and attacks on the Government. The North Berwick affair was only the first satanic attack on James. All subsequent plots against the King and his Government in some manner were shown to have diabolic elements. In 1600, John Ruthven, 3rd Earl of Gowrie and his brother plotted the murder of the King as revenge for the execution of their father 16 years earlier. When the King and his retinue managed to foil the plot by slaying the two brothers, at least one was said to be carrying "magical incantations," thus making the crime of attempted regicide all the more repugnant for its link to Satanic forces. The more famous Gunpowder Plot of 1605 which sought to detonate barrels of gunpowder under the House of Lords during the State Opening of Parliament. If the plot had been successful, it would likely have killed the King , many of his nearest relatives, members of the Privy Council, senior judges of the English legal system, most of the Protestant aristocracy, the bishops of the Church of England and members of both the House of Lords and the House of Commons, It was the equivalent of blowing up the American Congress building during a State of the Union address and the plot sent horror through the Kingdom as intense as that experience by American's following the events of 9/11/2001. The plot's long range goal was to loosen the Protestant hold on religion in England and reestablish religious tolerance for English Catholicism. In the aftermath of the plot's discovery, the participants were rounded up and warrants were issued for three Jesuit priests: Father Garnet, Father Gerard, and Father Greenway. Although these men were probably on the periphery of the plot, the King's Attorney-General Sir Edward Coke insisted that the Father Garnet, the only priest caught, was the chief instigator of the plot and had bound the conspirators with rituals involved Black Masses and sacrilegious oaths.[43] Placing Garnet at the center of the plot wove a tapestry of intrigue linking the attempted regicide with the diabolical Jesuits who in turn were linked to the black arts. Again the King was cast as the intended victim of witchcraft, painting the conspirators not only of treason but of trafficking with the Prince of Darkness.

Considering these important influences and interests on the part of King James, it is little wonder that these elements, i.e. the proper role of woman and the evils of witchcraft would feature prominently when Shakespeare penned his "Scottish play." Written probably in 1606-7, *Macbeth* was intended to honor James, who at the time was patron of Shakespeare's acting company and is one of Shakespeare's darkest works. It is the story of a brave and noble Scottish Lord who falls victim to temptation and murders his sovereign so that he might seize the throne. The play follows Macbeth's short reign and recounts his steady decent into ever increasing evil until his countrymen are forced to put him down like the rabid dog he has become. As one of Shakespeare's most internal characters, Macbeth is something of an open book. With his numerous soliloquies, the audience has a window into tyrant's mind and can follow his descent into the realm of the damned. His motives, doubts and fears are on open display. Not so with one of Shakespeare's most famous, most maligned and most opaque characters: Lady Macbeth.

Lady Macbeth is one of Shakespeare's most iconic female characters. Along with Juliet, her name is readily identified as a Shakespearean character even by those who have never read or seen a Shakespeare play. Her famous exclamation, "Out, damned spot!" has entered the popular lexicon and has been used repeatedly to sell laundry detergent. When asked to identify the evillest woman in Shakespeare's canon, most people will respond Lady Macbeth. Type "Most Evil Women in Literature" into any search engine and Lady Macbeth will appear in every "Top 10 List." There is little doubt that Lady Macbeth would surely have figured prominently on King James's Top Ten List of Evil Women. She is constructed with three strikes against here: 1st she is a woman: "daughter of Eve" and all that; 2nd she pushes her husband around, driving him into his crime, and 3rd she demonstrates characteristics associated with witches, the sworn enemies of God and God's representative on Earth, James I of England.

In her first appearance on stage, Lady Macbeth, learning of the witches' prophesies for her husband, immediately launches into an invocation to the dark forces.

> Come, you spirits
> That tend on mortal thoughts, unsex me here,
> And fill me from the crown to the toe top-full
> Of direst cruelty! make thick my blood;
> Stop up the access and passage to remorse,
> That no compunctious visitings of nature
> Shake my fell purpose, nor keep peace between
> The effect and it!
>
> (M, I, 5, 40-47)

The spirits she calls upon are those who "tend on mortal thoughts," that is, on thoughts of this world instead of those of the immortal world to come. The term "mortal" recalls not only temporal thoughts, but also thoughts of mortality, of matters of life and death. In the next line, she makes this explicit calling them "murdering ministers" who "wait on nature's mischief." Recalling the tradition of the witch's familiar feeding at the witch's teat, she calls upon them to "Come to [her] woman's breasts, And take [her] milk for gall." (M, I, 5, 47-48). She goes on to invoke "thick night," the realm of Hecate, goddess of the moon and queen of witches, to be bound up in the "smoke of hell," so that her deeds might be hidden even from the eye of Heaven. (M, I, 5, 50-3).

Is Lady Macbeth a witch or only a witch "wannabe?" Is she evil or an instrument of evil? The traditional view is that Lady Macbeth's "willed submission to demonic power..." at the very least, leaves her "open to the invasion of witchcraft."[44] Productions often associate her visually with the weird sisters in her physical appearance and dress and a few productions that include the Hecate scene in Act IV, scene 1 have the actress playing Lady Macbeth double in the role of Hecate. Lady Macbeth's first speech is certainly full of "witch-talk," but Garry Wills suggests that while she "tries to become an intimate of evil," she technically does not achieve it. He notes that she never "in fact enters into supernatural dealings with devils or their agents. There is no reciprocal activity of the sort Macbeth engages in. She is a witch of velleity and gestures, while he is one in fact."[4]

If Lady Macbeth is not a witch, she is certainly aligned with them. The witches are sexually ambiguous. When Macbeth and Banquo first encounter the witches, Banquo cries out "you should be women, /And yet your beards forbid me to interpret/That you are so." (*M*, I, 3, 45-47). Lady Macbeth seeks the same ambiguity, not so much in appearance as in character. Lady Macbeth seeks to be unsexed so as to shed the stereotypical softness and compassion associated with feminine nature. She wishes for the murderous ambition that she equates with masculinity, but ironically, her chief masculine role model she believes "too full o' the milk of human kindness/To catch the nearest way." (*M*, I, 5, 16-18). The very ruthlessness she admires as masculine, she finds lacking in Macbeth. It is also, I think, noteworthy that she asks to be unsexed, not to be endowed with the masculine traits she believes necessary to murder a king and seize a throne. As it turns out, it could be argued that she achieves her wish. She loses the feminine traits of passivity and compassion, but does not gain the force of will necessary to murder Duncan in his sleep when she had the opportunity. She excuses her failure to act, saying "Had he not resembled/My father as he slept, I had done't." (*M*, II, 2, 12-3). She is unsexed in that she loses the positive attributes of a woman without gaining what she defines as the positive aspects of a man.

If Lady Macbeth loses the positive attributes of a woman, she certainly retains those negative aspects of womanhood railed against by the pamphleteers. As we have noted elsewhere, the role of the wife in the household was to be one of service, of obedience to her husband. Recall that St. Paul in his letter to Timothy wrote:

> For I do not allow woman to teach, or to exercise authority over men; but she is to keep silent. For Adam was formed first, then Eve. And Adam was not deceived, but the woman was deceived and became a transgressor.
> (1 Timothy 2:12-14, KJV)

Similarly, in Ephesians 5:22-24, he wrote:

> "Wives, submit yourselves unto your own husbands, as unto the Lord. For the husband is the head of the wife, even as Christ is the head of the church: and he is the savior of the body. Therefore as the church is subject unto Christ, so let the wives be to their own husbands in everything."

It was the man's burden to control the wild impulses of women. Macbeth fails in his responsibility. Like Adam, he is led by his wife into damnation. It was also incumbent upon the wife to serve as helpmate to her husband, and some have argued that Lady Macbeth was fulfilling this obligation by pushing him to pursue that which he most desires: the throne. However, the wife's most important duty, preached from the pulpit, was to assist her husband against all assaults of the devil and to dissuade her partner from the courses of evil, persuading him into the ways of righteousness.[5] Lady Macbeth, of course, acts opposite this duty as she presses her husband along the pathway to Hell. These twin evils of feminine domination and masculine submission were so great that even Francis Quarles was forced to admit that he could not determine which was "more ungodly."[6]

The inversion of authority in the Macbeth household would be as ominous to Shakespeare's audience as Lady Macbeth's invocation to her dark spirits. The political and theological discourses of the Early Modern period identified unruly wives, scolds or shrews explicitly with witches. To a "culture that accepted the patriarchal household as both the source and analogical representation of good government," the post-Reformation rebellious wife embodied a "demonic tyranny [that] was an affront to all well-governed commonwealths but also to every state of moral equipoise."[7] Martin Luther, for example, explicitly explored the analogy between witches and forward wives who rebelled against the God-given order within the family. In the secular realm represented by Elizabethan court proceedings, the crimes of witchcraft and scolding were at times explicitly connected and cucking stools were, according to Jean E. Howard, "used to discipline scolds, shrews, and witches" alike. A vividly horrific symbol of this coalescence is a seventeenth-century metal "brank" or gag for punishing shrews, called the "Witches Bridle." In her scolding shrew-like manipulation of her husband, Lady Macbeth falls clearly into the camp the witches.

But Lady Macbeth is not a comic shrew like Katharina. Katharina, unlike Lady Macbeth, wields no real power over the men who surround her. She is mock-dangerous in that she may be loud and disruptive, she may bluster and rant like a spoiled child, she may even break a lute over the head of Hortensio, but she never really exercises any control over her own life or seriously threatens the patriarchy in any significant way. Lady Macbeth, on the other hand, exercises real power over her husband, being far more influential on his actions that the Weird Sisters ever do. Indeed, her tactics can scarcely be better described than by referring to the official Elizabethan *Homilies'* condemnation of ambitious wives who "see their husbands in such rooms, to be made underlings and who 'upbraidth them with cumbersome talk, and call them fools, dastards, and cowards so as to goad them into ambitious and aggressive action."[49] When news arrives of the witches' prophesy, Lady Macbeth accepts it as a foregone conclusion. Her only concern is that Macbeth is "is too full o' the milk of human kindness/To catch the nearest way." (*M*, I, 5, 16-18). She sees in Macbeth ambition, saying "thou wouldst be great; /Art not without ambition, but without/The illness should attend it." (*M*, I, 5, 18-20). She believes that ambition without the will to win by any means necessary is weakness. She never pauses to consider the morality of "*play*[ing] *false*" to achieve ones goal. Her plan is to "pour my spirits in thine ear; /And chastise with the valour of my tongue/All that impedes thee from the golden round," (*M*, I, 5, 25-8). Significantly, she will not persuade or encourage, but *chastise* her husband. The Free Dictionary defines *chastise* as 1) to punish, as by beating, 2) to criticize severely; rebuke, and 3) to purify. Lady Macbeth is going to literally use her tongue to whip her husband into shape by severely criticizing him. We don't get to see this, but two scenes later, it is obvious that her plan to assassinate Duncan has been put in place and that her husband, at least up to this point, on board. But now Macbeth is having second thoughts. Unlike his wife, Macbeth does have moral scruples:

> First, as I am his kinsman and his subject,
> Strong both against the deed; then, as his host,
> Who should against his murderer shut the door,
> Not bear the knife myself. Besides, this Duncan
> Hath borne his faculties so meek, hath been
> So clear in his great office, that his virtues
> Will plead like angels, trumpet-tongued, against
> The deep damnation of his taking-off;
> And pity, like a naked new-born babe,
> Striding the blast, or heaven's cherubim, horsed
> Upon the sightless couriers of the air,
> Shall blow the horrid deed in every eye,
> That tears shall drown the wind
>
> (*M*, I, 7, 13-25)

Thus wracked with guilt, when his wife approaches him during the banquet for Duncan, he abruptly tells her, "We will proceed no further in this business" (*M*, I, 7, 32). She explodes. Here she displays that "direst cruelty" that she prayed for earlier in Act I. She attacks her husband displaying stereotypical tactics: he doesn't love her, he is too cowardly to take what he wants, he is less than a man. The stage tradition of this scene, at least from the seventeenth century stage if David Garrick (1717-1779), is to have the actress rant out disappointment in a bombastic tirade of verbal abuse. The standard was set by Hannah Pritchard (1711-1759) who was lauded as the best Lady Macbeth of her age. Playing opposite the diminutive David Garrick, Pritchard dominated his Macbeth, both physically and verbally. The effect of her performance was to reduce the culpability of Macbeth in the murder of Duncan and thereby heighten his role as a tragic hero. It is not his ambition that is his fatal flaw, but the ambition of his wife and his inability to resist her domineering assaults. Pritchard was succeeded by Sara Siddons (1755-1831) and brought to the English stage an even more dominating and demonic Lady Macbeth. This characterization of husband and wife continues to the present day with few exceptions. Even taller and more imposing than Pritchard, Siddons initially tried to infuse her interpretation of Lady Macbeth with "all the charms and graces of personnel beauty," but quickly found the audience unwilling to accept the softer view. Instead she embraced the dark side of the Lady. Reviewing her performance, commentator Charles Hazlitt wrote "[t]ill then...a figure so terrible had never bent over the pit of the theatre." She drove her husband with "horrible purpose...fixed posture, determined eye and full deep voice of fixed resolve," and celebrated his deadly deed with "the ghastly horrid smile of a 'triumphant fiend.' "[8] Siddons was, however, able to successfully an element of pathos into the sleepwalking scene, wanting the audience to accept Lady Macbeth, fierce as she is, is also capable of remorse and is suffering in a hell of her own making.

This pattern of performance continued through to the middle of the nineteenth century, but in the last decades of the eighteenth century a new pattern was introduced in Germany when Rosalie Nouseul (1750-1801) set aside the stereotypical monster queen and acted Lady Macbeth as an affectionate wife who partners with her husband, coxing and cajoling him toward his crime instead of badgering and bullying him. German critics generally deplored this innovation, but Nouseul's performance let the proverbial genie out of the bottle and subsequent Lady Macbeths began to slowly move toward a more human, multidimensional character.[9] In mid nineteenth century England, Helena Faucit (1817-1898) conveyed a Lady Macbeth full of wifely devotion to her husband. The English critics, like those in Germany, were also critical of this "new" Lady Macbeth. They found her lacking in the fierceness of Sarah Siddons; Lady Macbeth, wrote one of the critics in the Lady's Newspaper "is odious as well a criminal woman, who could hardly be personated by the most feminine and delicate of our actresses, and the effort to throw tenderness into the part seems absurd."[10] Although considered one of the finest actors of her day, Lady Macbeth was considered one of Faucit's few failures. The fearsome Lady continued to dominate the stage.

Faucit was succeeded as the premier Shakespearian actress on the English stage by Ellen Terry (1847-1928). The fair-haired Terry carried on and intensified the feminization of Lady Macbeth that Siddons dreamed of and Faucit attempted without success. When she took on the role in 1888, Terry followed Faucit's example, portraying Lady Macbeth, not as the leader of the deadly enterprise, but as a loving partner of her husband in the crime. She guides Macbeth on his path with gentle and tender caresses except when she is compelled to stiffen his resolve.

The twentieth century introduced Shakespeare to the emerging technology of the cinema. We no longer have to rely on written descriptions of performances, but now have the opportunity to repeatedly view and review performances. By looking at the Lady Macbeths on film, we are able to see how the two dominant patterns of the portrayal represented by the Pritchard/Siddons model and the Faucit/Terry mode. The domineering shrew-like pattern can be seen by reviewing the 1983 BBC production of Macbeth (available at http://www.youtube.com/watch?v=EzSJtX33yz8) staring Nicol Williamson as Macbeth and Jane Lapotaire as Lady Macbeth. When Lady Macbeth is introduced (at 18:31 on the link above) she is clearly aligned with the dark forces. Lapotaire's Lady Macbeth is clearly thrilled by the prophesy of the Weird Sisters. She invokes her "murdering ministers" as she writhes upon her bed in near sexual ecstasy, gasping out her lines as if in the grip of orgasm. When her husband arrives, she virtually leaps upon him and the kiss passionately. His voice is hoarse as he whispers "My dearest love" into her ear. He clearly has affection for his wife, but he is wary of her ambition which he seems to know well. She is clearly in command, seductively advising him in the art of deception and telling him to "leave the rest to me." The plans are laid, but when doubts plague Macbeth, Lapotaire's Lady Macbeth shows (at 29:41) her shrew-like anger, tongue-lashing her faltering husband with assaults on his courage and masculinity until he submits. After the murder of Duncan (40:16), Macbeth emerges unhinged by the deed and Lady Macbeth attempts to soothe him until she notices that he has brought the bloody daggers with him from the scene of the crime. Her anger again flairs and she contemptuously wrests the daggers from his hands and places them by the sleeping grooms. After Macbeth is crowned, there is a noticeable shift in the relationship between husband and wife. She now is fearful; he is aloof and resolute (1:06:48). When she attempts to embrace her husband, he stops her and moves away. In his agitation, Macbeth grasps his wife by the throat and makes to choke her, while he is lost in rambling madness. It is obvious that Lady Macbeth is afraid of her husband, realizing that what she has created, she is now unable to control. For his part, Macbeth no longer appears to love his wife as he did in Act I, scene 5 and seems to resent her for what she drove him to do. They are increasing estranged as the play move forward. By the time of her final scene (1:57:14), guilt over her crime has turned Lady Macbeth into a raving somnambulist, forced to relieve her crimes in sleep. The key challenge of the scene is to understand our response to it. Do we feel satisfied that the Lady is justly punished or do we pity her distress? The response to the question probably says more about the viewer than the character; however, the response may be guided by the actress. Lapotaire plays the scene with an intensity equal to and reminiscent of her earlier scenes. She graphically reminds the audience of her guilt by replaying her participation in Macbeth's murders and by doing so, she blunts any sympathy we might feel for her. She is wandering in a nightmare of her own making that is only a preview of the hell to come. When the end comes, we like Macbeth, are neither surprised nor distressed. He and we are so alienated from Lady Macbeth that we can only shake our collective heads and then move on.

The more human Faucit/Terry model is probably best exemplified by the performance of Francesca Annis in Roman Polanski's 1971 adaptation of the play. Polanski's Lady Macbeth is both young and beautiful. While she reads Macbeth's letter in Act I, scene 5, she gently caresses the dogs that surround her. She exhibits "all the charms and graces of personnel beauty" that Siddons originally wanted to pour into her Lady Macbeth. When her husband arrives (available at https://www.youtube.com/watch?v=GMdAGCqM2Ok&list=PL225F2124CCD5043E) Lady Macbeth runs to greet him, obviously elated to see him. He sweeps her up in his arms and carries her immediately to their bedroom where she playfully hints at her plans for Duncan. Her demonic invocation is moved from following the reading of the letter to a voice-over meditation as Lady Macbeth watches Duncan approach her castle (available at https://www.youtube.com/watch?v=Jrjyek0OlKw). It has none of the passion of Lapotaire delivery. Annis delivers the lines less like an invocation and more like a meditation. With Lapotaire's performance, the audience can believe that Lady Macbeth is serious about calling upon the dark forces. In the case of Annis, Lady Macbeth seems to be speaking metaphorically, summoning up her inner darkness to steel herself for the night to come. When it comes to Act I, scene 7, the scene where the reluctant Macbeth is rebuked by his wife, Annis takes a tact far different from Lapotaire's scold. Instead of raging at her husband, Annis sulks like a teenage girl told she cannot go to the prom. She is both bitterly disappointed and furious that Macbeth would back out of his promise. Instead of placing the emphasis on emasculating her husband, Annis' Lady Macbeth emphasizes her feelings of betrayal. Tears roll down her cheeks and she literally shames him into giving her what she wants. The assassination of Duncan now has less to do with Macbeth's ambition and proving he is a man than his wish to reaffirm his love and commitment to his wife. After the assassination, Polanski's Macbeth is more regretful than deranged (available at https://video.search.yahoo.com/video/play;_ylt=A2KIo9edqylTx1IAbkD7w8QF;_yl u=X3oDMTEwODBhaW80BHNlYwNzcgRzbGsDdmlkBHZ0aWQDVjExNgRncG9zAzQ z?p=polanski+macbeth&vid=dc38cee2168c7be5207b7d6fc3e5da73&l=5%3A24&turl =http%3A%2F%2Fts4.mm.bing.net%2Fth%3Fid%3DVN.608032743446154419%26 pid%3D15.1&rurl=http%3A%2F%2Fwww.youtube.com%2Fwatch%3Fv%3DHy0U8d

mcxZs&tit=Macbeth+di+Polanski&c=12&sigr=11a16sk20&sigt=10j8p7vli&age=0&b= 31&fr=yfp-t-316-s&tt=b). When he approaches his wife and tells her "I have done the deed," his expression and inflection are those of a husband resentful of having to something unpleasant at the prodding of his wife. He may as well have gotten up from his easy chair to take out the trash. As in the BBC version, Lady Macbeth is still controlling the situation, but Polanski's Macbeth is more self-controlled and there is a coldness now evident toward his wife than we have seen before. That coldness persists throughout the remainder of the film and Lady Macbeth is more and more isolated from her husband. Meanwhile, Lady Macbeth is troubled with sleepwalking. Polanski famously had Annis perform this scene (available at https://www.youtube.com/watch?v=0GZ4HJ8Lb-o) in the nude and although considered gratuitous by many, the scene does, I believe, heighten sympathy for the Lady by emphasizing her vulnerability. Annis is more subdued than Lapotaire and shows more remorse than madness. Her sobs and groans are more heartfelt and hopeless. Is her performance enough to that we pity her? Certainly more than we pity Lapotaire, but she like Lapotaire cannot rise to the level of tragic heroine. Like Macbeth, we have seen too much of her ruthless ambition and may likely find it impossible to forgive.

In the final analysis the play is not entitled *The Tragedy of Macbeth and Lady Macbeth*. Lady Macbeth, along with the witches, is intended as the villainous prime mover in the downfall of Macbeth. She is to Macbeth what Iago is to Othello. She is aligned with demonic forces, is bare-faced in her ambition, she is an emasculating scold. Even when she is softened and humanized as in Polanski's film, she is ultimately a villain. Whether a literal witch, a witch wanna-be, or a devout wife only trying to serve her husband's best interests, one thing is obvious: Macbeth would never have murdered Duncan were it not for his wife's prodding. Try as we may to rehabilitate her, Lady Macbeth is a villain of the first order.

Notes

1. Wills, Gary. *Witches and Jesuits: Shakespeare's Macbeth*. New York: Oxford University Press, 1995, 51.

2. Muir, Kenneth and Philip Edwards, Ed's. *Aspects of Macbeth*. Cambridge University Press, 1977.

3. Wills, 83.

4. Clark, Stuart. "King James's Daemonologie: Witchcraft and Kingship." *In The Damned Art: Essays in the Literature of Witchcraft*, edited by Sydney Anglo, 156-81. London: Routledge, 1977.

5. Wilkinson, Robert. *The Merchant Royall: A Sermon Preached at White-Hall*, 1607. ed. Stanley Pargellis (Herrin, I ll. 1945), p. 32.

6. Francis Quarles. *Hadassa or the History of Queene Ester* (London, 1 621).

7. "Certain Sermons or Homilies Appointed to be Read in Churches" (Oxford, 1822), p.469, qtd in Roland Mushat Frye, "Macbeth's Usurping Wife." *Renaissance News*, Vol. 8, No. 2 (Summer, 1955), pp. 102-105.

8. Rosenberg, Marvin. "Macbeth and Lady Macbeth in the eighteenth and nineteenth centuries" in Brown, John Russell, ed. *Focus on Macbeth*. London: Routledge & Kegan Paul, 1982, 77.

9. Ibid, 79.

10. Ibid, 81

MISCELLANEOUS MISCREANTS AND MINIONS, MOBS AND MONSTERS

MISCREANTS: "LORD ANGELO IS PRECISE" : MEASURE FOR MEASURE: DUKE VINCENTIO

      Because *Measure for Measure* is one of Shakespeare's lesser known plays, a brief synopsis of the principle action is in order. Duke Vincentio of Venice is displeased by the lawlessness of his State that has resulted from his leniency in enforcing the law. He resolves to leave town and place the city in the hands of the strict judge, Angelo, to restore order. The first thing Angelo does is condemn one Claudio to death for the "crime" of getting his betrothed, Julia, pregnant prior to their marriage. Claudio's sister Isabella, a novice, comes to beg for her brother's life, but the strict Angelo refuses her initial request. He is, however, suddenly overtaken with a passion for the lady and offers to exchange her brother's life for her chastity. Outranged by his lascivious advance, Isabella threatens to expose Angelo, but realizes that Angelo's reputation is so impeccable that she will not be believed. She goes to the prison to bid her brother goodbye, and there meets the Duke who has not left Venice, but has instead taken on the guise of a friar to observe how Angelo performs in his place. When he hears of Isabel's predicament, the Duke/Friar Lodowick proposes a plan. The Duke tells Isabella to agree to Angelo's demand, but on the stipulation that the act will be performed in utter darkness. Angelo, we learn, had been betrothed to a Mariana, but had put her aside when her dowry was lost at sea. The Duke will substitute Mariana for Isabella and it will be Mariana whom Angelo deflowers. Mariana, who is still in love with Angelo, agrees, the deed is done, but to everyone's surprise, Angelo sends an order to the prison that Claudio be executed straight away. By a fortunate coincidence, a pirate resembling Claudio has died and it is his head, not Claudio's that is sent to Angelo. Strangely, the Duke allows Isabella to believe that her brother has been executed. The Duke sends out word that he is returning and tells Isabella to denounce Angelo publicly before the Duke at the city gate. This she does and the Duke pretends disbelief. Mariana then comes forward to support Isabella's story and the Duke feigns outrage, asking them who goaded them into the slander of Angelo. He is told Friar Lodowick is involved and sends for him. The Duke then leaves the assembly, leaving it to Angelo and fellow judge Escalus to sort out the truth. The Duke returns in the guise of Friar Lodowick and just as he is judged to be a co-conspirator in the slander of the State, he reveals himself and doles out justice. Angelo he condemns to first marry Mariana and then to be executed. Mariana begs for the life of Angelo and persuades Isabel to join her in pleading for Angelo's life even though Isabella still believes Angelo is responsible for her brother's death. The Duke relents and then produces Claudio to his relieved sister. Claudio is also pardoned and ordered to marry his betrothed forthwith. Finally, the Duke turns to Isabella and unexpectantly proposes marriage to her.

Measure for Measure is one of the so called "problem plays" and one of the most criticized of any of Shakespeare's canon. Classified as a "comedy" in the First Folio, because it ends with marriages instead of funerals, *Measure* plays like a tragedy until the final scene when the dark elements of the play are all reversed in a "happy" endings that feels both contrived and unsatisfying. John Dryden a poet and playwright in the 17th Century wrote that *Measure* was a play "either grounded on impossibilities, or at least, so meanly written that the comedy neither caus'd you mirth, nor the serious parts your concernment."[1] Charlotte Lennox, an author, poet and critic writing a century later, said of *Measure* that Shakespeare "tortured it into a Comedy" as is evident in "the low Contrivance, absurd Intrigue, and improbable Incidents, he was obliged to introduce, in order to bring about three or four weddings, instead of one good Beheading, which was the Consequence naturally expected.[2] In the 19th century, Samuel Taylor Coleridge called *Measure for Measure*, "The most painful . . . part of his [Shakespeare's] genuine works. The comic and tragic parts equally border on [hateful], the one disgusting, the other horrible; and the pardon and marriage of Angelo . . . baffles the strong indignant claim for justice."[3] In the 20th Century, *Measure* has found greater acceptance as modern critics have come to appreciate the play's lofty ambition of exploring the concepts of justice and mercy. Critics have explored the play within the historical, social and political climate of its time and have uncovered influences and topical allusions that both interesting and compelling.

Thomas Fulton, for example, has examined *Measure for Measure* in the context of the medieval morality tradition where the characters represent abstract concepts like greed, lust, justice and mercy. He argues that *Measure* is a meditation on "how to balance justice and mercy in both temporal and divine applications," a topic particularly relevant in light of the "cultural anxiety over forms of legalism and fundamentalism that reemerged with the uncertainties surrounding the religious settlement at the accession of James."[4] This "legalism and fundamentalism," is most associated with the rising Puritan influence in early 17th Century England. It was these reformers that pushed for a Mosaic legal system to govern all of England. *Measure for Measure*, Fulton suggests, "engages an increasing trend of biblical fundamentalism, in which legislative proposals for the death penalty for adultery — shot down in Parliament in 1584 and 1604 — were only part of a larger movement that has been described as 'the rise of Protestant legalism.'"[5] By describing Angelo as "precise," (*MM*, I, 3, 50) Shakespeare signals the audience that he represents this particular form of legalism and serves as argument against Puritan justice. In describing his conception of the law, Angelo tells Isabella, "Your brother is a forfeit of the law" and then, "*It is the law, not I condemn your brother:/Were he my kinsman, brother, or my son, /It should be thus with him: he must die.*" (*MM*, II, 2, xxx). As the law is written, it must be enforced without human accountability or regret. In this instance, Puritan legalism as embodied by Angelo comes off rather badly.

Maurice Hunt, agreeing with Futon, suggests that the play offers two alternatives to legalism in the administration of secular justice. First, Shakespeare give us Escalus, the older judge, who represents the concept of equity in the law. The principle of equity allows for mitigation of a prescribed penalty as a result of considering the circumstances surrounding the crime and the character of the criminal. Through the exercise of reason and conscience, the administrator of equity makes an exception to the universal application of positive law because the existential circumstances of the accused suggest that to do so would be fairer. Escalus, as the embodiment of equity, is less interested in carrying out the exact letter of the law than in using the law to achieve desirable effects.[6] He explains his position to Angelo as he argues for Claudio's life: "Let us be keen, and rather cut a little,/ Than fall, and bruise to death." (*MM*, II, 1, 6-7).

The Duke offers a third approach to secular justice in his concluding application of Christian mercy to the fallen Angelo. In the strict application of the law, Angelo is owed the same sentence that he applied to Claudio in that they are both guilty of carnal relations with women not their wives. In equity, there would be nothing in the circumstances of the crime (sexual extortion) or the character of

Angelo (a hypocritical prig) to excuse him. Only in Christian mercy, advocated by Mariana and Isabella, can he be forgiven and freed from dying the death he justly deserves. "The major problem," according to M. W. Rowe, "... is that the ending seems so flagrantly unjust; far from receiving a well-deserved comeuppance, Angelo is made to honour his plight to Mariana but is otherwise let off completely."[7] How can this be reconciled? Some have suggested that the Duke is a Christ figure or a model for the ideal Christian ruler, but each of these raise significant problems. How, for example, could a Christ-like Duke participate in and advocate for the immoral "bed-trick" that allows Isabella to maintain her virginity by sacrificing the virginity of Mariana? Similarly, is the Duke's extension of mercy to Angelo something the ideal Christian ruler would do? The entire thrust of the plot was to restore order to decadent Venice. By extending mercy to Angelo, the Duke is right back to where he began, winking at crimes. The act of forgiveness will again show a weakness in the enforcement of the laws of the State and this will in turn encourage the very lawlessness that the Duke wished to suppress. On the other hand, the Duke's resort to marriage to deal with the crimes of sexual license echoes St. Paul's exhortation to the Corinthians: "I say therefore to the unmarried and widows, It is good for them if they abide even as I [i.e., chaste].But if they cannot contain, let them marry: for it is better to marry than to burn."[8]

Rowe proposes a novel explanation of the Duke's action by putting forth that the action of the play is Duke directed from beginning to end; an attempt to "find out whether the new puritan conception of morals can withstand the demands of power as well or better than the old regime [represented by the Duke's policy of lenience] has withstood it for at least the last fourteen years." Angelo fails the test miserably and then is forgiven "because he was set up: the Duke both wanted and expected him to fail."[9] The Duke's experiment, as put forth by Rowe, is problematic because it explores the corruptibility of the strict judge, but does not address the problem of lawless Venice. One would have expected the experiment to weigh the effectiveness of the new system against that of the old, but this is never seriously evaluated.

Other critics have explored *Measure for Measure* in the context of the ascension of James I to the throne of England in 1603. Rowe, for example, comments that James I was "a very considerable scholar" as was the Duke (*MM*, III, 2, 148) and was profoundly interested in the relationship between justice and mercy at a practical as well as theoretical level. James also had a low opinion of Puritans, and was much struck by the idea of using dissimulation to find out what his people and courtiers were doing.[10] Since Shakespeare and his company had recently gained the new King's patronage, it would behoove him to draw a central character with whom James could identify with. In *Basilicon Doron*, a treatise on government written by James in 1599, he warned against the very mistake made by the Duke in *Measure for Measure*. If "ye kyth your clemencie at the first, the offences would soone come to such heapes, and the contempt of you grow so great, that when ye would fall to punish, the number of them to be punished, would exceed the innocent . . . I confesse, where I thought . . . to win all mens hearts to louing and willing obedience, I by the contrary found the disorder of the country and the losse of my thanks to be all my reward."[11] In addition to presaging the Duke's dilemma, The *Basilicon Doron* also criticizes both Roman Catholics and Puritans, showing James preference for the middle way represented by the Anglican Church.

While these allegorical explanations are interesting, a play rises and falls on its text and its characters and *Measure for Measure*, irrespective of the improbabilities of plot elements, does present us with a villain that we can truly loathe. And loath him I do. Of all Shakespeare's villains, Angelo affects me at the most visceral level. I recoil from this character like I recoil from a spider. He is certainly not Shakespeare's most evil character. In fact, the results of his evil acts are all thwarted: no one is physically harmed by him. He is "small potatoes" when compared with the monumental evil of an Aaron, Iago, Richard or Macbeth. His crimes are to attempt to extort sexual favors from Isabella and then to renege on his promise to pardon Claudio. He ends up guilty of an abuse of power, of extortion for sexual favor, and of lying to cover it up. In this, he seems almost mundane, but no less repulsive in the context of 21st Century social reality. Bosses and politicians execute quid pro quo employee harassment; police officers exchange leniency for sex; priests, pastors, and teachers use their positions of trust to exploit the innocent: all of these occur with sufficient frequency that they have become an entertainment trope fueling everything from TV sit-coms to criminal justice dramas. Why than does Angelo disgust me more than Shakespeare's other, more criminal, villains?

Perhaps it is because he is a poster child for the stereotypical Puritan, with all the negativity that label implies in contemporary society. Although recent scholarship has called into question the validity of the stereotype, it has also confirmed the traditional view that Puritans were marked by "a distinctive preciseness or scrupulosity about their own and other people's moral conduct."[12] "Less radical early modem Protestants," according to Maurice Hunt, "often ridiculed more godly Protestants — Puritans — for a hypocritical presumption that they could virtually perfect their morals and manners in accordance with Old Testament directives."[13] The Puritans of Shakespeare's era were principally concerned with reforming the Anglican Church to a simpler and less Catholic rituals and hierarchy. With the accession of King James I of England, they brought forth the Millenary Petition, a Puritan manifesto of 1603 for reform of the English church, but James wanted a new religious settlement along different lines. At the Hampton Court Conference in 1604, James agreed to hear the views of four prominent Puritan leaders, but he rejected their demands for reform. While the Petition focused almost entirely on the Church alone, Puritans believed that the church **and the government** should be operated according to the Bible. During the 1600's, the Puritans increasingly opposed the religious and political policies of the Stuart rulers, King James I and his son, King Charles I leading ultimately to the overthrow of the monarchy in 1642.

The Puritan are, however, best remembered for their strict moral code. Their core belief that lives should be ordered according to the word of God made manifest in the Bible resulted initially in efforts to purify their individual lives along Biblical guidelines. In this, the Puritan were not attempting to win Heaven by good works. Martin Luther and his Protestant followers had roundly rejected that Catholic precept. Luther proposed that man was granted eternal life through faith in the saving sacrifice of Jesus Christ. The Puritan view articulated by John Calvin added a peculiar spin on this by introducing the idea that who was "saved" and who was "lost" was predetermined from the beginning of the world. If you had been predestined for Heaven, there you went. For the Puritans the question then was "Am I one of the elect?" In 1620, Robert Burton commented on a mental disturbance of religious melancholy observed in "devolt and precise" Englishmen the propensity to "torture and crucify" themselves to uncover "signs and tokens" they were truly God's elect.[14] As a result, the Puritan became obsessed determining their relationship with God and soon adopted the idea that assurance fell on the "fruits of faith in a highly regulated life."[15] In their minds, if they were able to live the Godly life prescribed by the scriptures, it proved to them that they were among the "elect." The next logical step for them was to look at the behavior of others to determine if they were also under the grace of God. Bad behavior would indicate that the observed "other" was not of the elect and, therefore, in the grip of Satan. Oddly enough, this did not mean that there were not good men who performed good deeds who were not among the elect. On this point, they seemed to believe that such things were part of the impenetrable mysteries of God.

The Puritan life in keeping true to the divine law did everything in moderation. While they did dress in their social classes and drank alcoholic beverages, they condemned those who would take these things to excess. Richard Baxter, a highly regarded Puritan is quoted as saying, "Overdoing is the most ordinary way to undoing." Undoing meaning your condemnation to hell.[16] Again we see the paradox: while this sounds like "overdoing" can un-elect the elect", the Puritan actual belief would be "that your behavior of overdoing would be a sign that you were not among the elect" and that the elect should condemn your behavior and shun you from their community. The fear was not that you would in some way "un-elect the elect," but that the elect should only interact with the other elect according to their Biblical interpretation. This principle went to the extreme in Puritan New England where community leaders made strenuous efforts to exclude the "unsanctified" from the colony. Thus, in 1636 the town of Boston outlawed any person's entertaining strangers for more than two weeks, without obtaining permission from the town government.[17]

While the early Puritans at the beginning of James I's reign were more inwardly than outward concerned about behaviors, they did take exception to a number of activities. Sports, for example were attacked by the Puritan not because they brought joy to people, but because they played on the Sabbath and took people away from a productive and consecrated use of the body. In 1617, they managed to apply enough pressure on the king for a ruling on the propriety of Sunday sports. In response King James issued the *Book of Sports*, a declaration declaring that it was lawful to play some sports on Sundays, but not others. Criticizing the opinions of "puritans and precise people", the Book listed archery, dancing, "leaping, vaulting, or any other such harmless recreation" as permissible sports for Sundays. It forbade bear-baiting, bull-baiting, "interludes" and bowling.

Similarly, the Puritans distained the theater. Considerable literature upon this subject has come down to us from the sixteenth century, the most famous example being Stubbs's *Anatomie of Abuses*. Since Puritanism was largely a revolt against medievalism, medieval practices and observances, folk festivals and such like, often innocent enough in themselves, frequently sparked rioting and wantonness. By the time of Shakespeare, the theatre was the main channel through which these "saturnalian" elements of medieval life carried over into the 16th Century. Additionally, since the Renaissance theater was the successor of medieval miracle-play which were half liturgy and half folk-play, the theater was twice damned because, like the folk-play, it was heathen, and, like the mass, popish. Lacking authority in scripture, Puritans concluded that the theater should not be permitted in any Christian community.[18]

The objection to the secular theater was hardy an exclusively Puritan concern. The city merchant also hated the players. The customary processions through the streets, before playing, interfered with traffic. Public performances were a possible source of disturbance. And, as for the actor himself, he and his like, as the Lord Mayor informed the Privy Council upon one occasion, were "a very superfluous sort of men." He lived for and by pleasure alone, grew rich by beguiling the simple poor of their money and, hereupon, aped the manners and habits of gentlefolk, swaggering about the city in dress so extravagant and costly as to be positively offensive to the eye. In short, his profession, as it seemed to the civic mind, represented a definite and constant drain on the national resources. Even one of the most erudite humanists of the 16th century, Michel de Montaigne grouped "enterlude-players" with "harlots and curtizans," and described them as "vagabond objects." [19]

In spite of these objections, the theater had a strong supporter in Queen Elizabeth I and the popularity of the theater increased during her reign. After Elizabeth's death, the right of noblemen to patronize players was virtually withdrawn by the repeal of the previous statutes exempting the members of their companies from the penalties of vagrancy. Instead the company of actors became a kind of department of the Revels' office with direct subordination to the Court. By entering into this close relation with the Court the reputation for respectability which the actors had slowly acquired during Elizabeth's last years was finally established. Given the animosity of the Puritans for the stage, it is little wonder that Shakespeare would paint his Puritan characters in a dark light.

Returning to Angelo who is an overt stand-in for the Puritan mentality, the Duke tells Escalus:

> we have with special soul
> Elected him our absence to supply,
> Lent him our terror, dress'd him with our love,
> And given his deputation all the organs
> Of our own power
>
> (MM, 1, 1, 17-20)

From the first, the Duke calls attention to Angelo's Puritan identity through his "election" as the Duke's deputy. Like his Puritan brothers already described, Angelo is obsessed with leading the Godly life of the "elect." He does not, however, profess that his election or that his behavior is founded in religion.

The Duke later tells Friar Thomas that

> Lord Angelo is precise.
> Stands at a guard with envy, scarce confesses
> That his blood flows or that his appetite
> Is more to bread than stone.
>
> (MM, 1, 3, 48-52)

He is seen by others and by himself as totally in control of his mind and body. He seems totally disinterested in the state of anyone's soul, other than his own. He is only concerned with behaviors, with actions and consequences. In the same conversion, the Duke reveals to Friar Thomas his purpose in appointing Angelo as chief judge in Vienna. During the Duke's reign, the laws of the State have been laxly enforced and as a result, crime has risen and morality declined. Rather than personally correcting the problem his own leniency has created, the Duke empowers Angelo to administer justice in Vienna as he sees fit while the Duke, who is supposed to be on a mission to Poland, remains hidden in the city to observe what happens. He does not direct Angelo to enforce the laws rigorously, but allows him to execute them at his own discretion: "*your scope is as mine own/ So to enforce or qualify the laws/ As to your soul seems good.*" (*MM*, 1, 1, 64-6). However, given that the Duke knows Angelo to be "precise," it would surely seem likely that he would expect his deputy to enforce the law to the letter, while allowing the Duke to stand apart from the dirty work. Additionally, the Duke seems interested in testing the effect of power on his "precise" deputy. He says to Friar Thomas, "*Hence shall we see. If power change purpose, what our seemers* be." (*MM*, I, 3, 53-4)

The first laws Angelo enforces in his new role are those related to loose sexuality. He has arrested, tried and condemned to death, in strict accordance with Vienna's laws, Claudio, a man of good family, who has impregnated his betrothed, Julia. It matters not that the sex was consensual or that the couple were soon to be married. The law seems outrageously harsh, but it should be remembered that the Puritans tried twice (once in 1584 and again in 1604) to enact a similar law in England, It is, however, important to recall that Angelo did not enact this law, but only enforces it to the letter. He repeatedly emphasizes this point. To Isabella he says,

> *It is the law, not I condemn your brother:*
> *Were he my kinsman, brother, or my son,*
> *It should be thus with him:*
>
> (*MM, II, 2, 80-82*)

And later he explains:

> *I show it most of all when I show justice;*
> *For then I pity those I do not know,*
> *Which a dismiss'd offence would after gall;*
> *And do him right that, answering one foul wrong,*
> *Lives not to act another.*
> (*MM, II, 2, 100-104*)

Angelo's explanation, although harsh, is rationale and is consistent with the Duke's stated goal in having Angelo serve in his place. Considering that it was within the Duke's power to revoke the law or emend its penalty, we must assume that he was in agreement with it. That Angelo would enforce it against a man of good standing is in fact proper because he is demonstrating that no one is above the law.

When Escalus asks Angelo to empathize with Claudio and consider

> *Whether you had not sometime in your life*
> *Err'd in this point which now you censure him,*
> *And pull'd the law upon you.*
>
> *(MM, II, 1, 14-16)*

Angelo replies:

> *You may not so extenuate his offence*
> *For I have had such faults; but rather tell me,*
> *When I, that censure him, do so offend,*
> *Let mine own judgment pattern out my death,*
> *And nothing come in partial.*
>
> *(MM, II, 1, 27-31)*

He will not exempt even himself from the law.

Overall, Angelo's "preciseness" in the application of the laws, when examined, may not be to my liking, but it is neither immoral nor villainous. He never verbalizes on the immorality of the action for which Claudio is condemned. He is only doing Duke Vincentio's dirty work and is doing it with mechanical efficiency. He takes no joy in his actions and does not seem regretful nor proud of it.

If I can't fault Angelo for his Puritanical adherence to the letter of the law, I can perhaps fault him for his hypocrisy. Hypocrisy is a term thrown about so cavalierly, particularly in political discourse, that it warrants definition before applying it to Angelo. Hypocrisy is "a pretense of having a virtuous character, moral or religious beliefs or principles, etc., that one does not really possess."[20] Hypocrisy is evident in the politician who professes to care about global warming while flying from place to place in a private jet to encourage others to reduce their consumption of fossil fuels. Hypocrisy is evident in the priest or pastor who condemns homosexuality from the pulpit and is, himself, a serial child molester. Hypocrisy is evident in the man who wants a petty thief locked up for life while he steals thousands of dollars cheating on his income tax. Audiences have a strong emotional response to characters who exhibit hypocrisy. It may provoke anger at the hypocrite or empathy for the victim, but in either case, it is a sure way to instantly generate a reaction. Angelo is a double hypocrite: not only has he has asked Isabel to commit fornication with him, which stands in opposition to his condemnation of Claudio, but he has also offered to circumvent the law, which is directly opposed to his earlier statements about rigid enforcement.

In the first instance, when Angelo propositions Isabella, is his action really hypocritical? Hypocrisy implies that the guilty party believes one way, but acts another. It suggests that the hypocrite is sufficiently self-aware to know that his public face is at odds with his inner character. In the case of Angelo, I'm not sure that this is a case. Prior to his encounter with Isabella, there is nothing in his life, even his casual rejection of Marianna that would suggest he could be so overcome with lust that he would fall so monumentally. When asked to empathize with the condemned Claudio, Angelo is unable to do so. He responds "Tis one thing to be tempted, Escalus, another thing to fall," (*MM*, II, 1, 17-18), suggesting that he is unable to envision a temptation sufficient to make him fall. W. M. T. Dodds writes that "Angelo has no way of coming to terms with his own sexuality; it is ... incompatible with his concept of himself as a morally responsible individual. Angelo [is] incapable of accepting sexual desire as an integral part of his identity."[23] When he is overcome by it, he is totally at the mercy of a newly liberated libido that he has previously repressed to such a degree that he could almost deny its existence. That he succumbs to it is a sign of moral weakness, but not, I think hypocrisy; no man is guaranteed against a sudden fall from grace. As Dodd notes, "the case for branding Angelo dissembler [hypocrite] rests on the supposition that nothing but a long course of covert sinning could have fitted him to make his bed in hell with such rapidity."[24] There is no internal evidence that this is the case. No one is more shocked at his weakness than Angelo himself:

> *What's this, what's this? Is this her fault or mine?*
> *The tempter or the tempted, who sins most?*
> *Ha!*
> *Not she: nor doth she tempt: but it is I*
> *That, lying by the violet in the sun,*
> *Do as the carrion does, not as the flower,*
> *Corrupt with virtuous season. Can it be*
> *That modesty may more betray our sense*
> *Than woman's lightness? Having waste ground enough,*
> *Shall we desire to raze the sanctuary*
> *And pitch our evils there? O, fie, fie, fie!*
> *What dost thou, or what art thou, Angelo?*
>
> *(MM, II, 2, 161-172)*

His soliloquy shows a man appalled by his own feelings and, more to the point, a man having an identity crisis. He asks "What art thou, Angelo?" because for the first time he is confronted with illicit feelings he cannot control, feeling so alien to him that he does not recognize himself. Is he the man he believed himself to be, and if so, how is it possible that he, one of God's elect, could be so snared by lust? On the other hand, has he been self-deluded all this time; is he not one of the elect and subject to the same evil nature of other, lesser men? Like his spiritual brother, Macbeth, Angelo is a man struggling in a moral dilemma: to continue as the good if strict, man of the law or to join the human race by embracing man's propensity to sin. His is the state of a man in hell. Perhaps only Macbeth ever endured such spiritual agony as Angelo before the commission of a crime. In his soliloquy, the extreme of anguish is reached, for in it the will to God and the will to evil do not so much struggle as co-exist in mutual loathing, while Angelo experiences the external antipathy of these adversaries.[25] I would suggest we have more sympathy for Macbeth because he waivers between renouncing his ambition and embracing it. Angelo, on the other hand, experiences a sudden, intense experience and then, almost instantaneously, he throws himself wholly into scratching his itch. It takes him only a night of "chewing" on the name of Heaven to decide irrevocably on his path. After propositioning Isabella, the next morning, he tells her:

> I have begun,
> And now I give my sensual race the rein:
> Fit thy consent to my sharp appetite;
> Lay by all nicety and prolixious blushes,
> That banish what they sue for; redeem thy brother
> By yielding up thy body to my will;
> Or else he must not only die the death,
> But thy unkindness shall his death draw out
> To lingering sufferance.
>
> (MM, II, 4, 159-167)

Consistent with his personality, once Angelo embraces his path he commits to it absolutely. Unlike the ordinary characters of comedy who are brought to self-awareness by the action of the play, Angelo has the capacity for suffering usually seen on Shakespeare's tragic characters. Although his suffering is never as deep or its consequences never as severe because he finds himself in a Comedy, Angelo's suffering is real and the weakness that overcomes him is completely unexpected. Since he was unable to envision the weakness, he wrongly assumed he was invulnerable to it and so when he succumbs to it, he is not being hypocritical, he is merely another fallen man.

In the second instance, the willingness to trade Claudio's life for sexual advantage, is more difficult to excuse. That Angelo would compromise his professed reverence for the law to gain Isabella's sexual favor is beyond hypocritical. While one can argue that nothing in his previous experience had prepared him for Isabella, it is inconceivable that Angelo had never encountered situations where he could have gained in some fashion by "winking" at an offense. His entire career is based on his strict application of the law. As he explains to Escalus, Angelo believes the strict application of the law deters future offences. His fall, ironically, undermines his belief. His own behavior does not deter him from committing the same offense that he has just condemned Claudio for. This does not however make Angelo a hypocrite, only mistaken. By making Angelo the first person to solicit sex after he sentences Claudio to death for a similar offense, Shakespeare is making the point that deterrence, especially for that kind of offense, does not work.[26]

More to do with his hypocrisy is his offer to pardon Claudio in exchange for Isabella's sexual favors. In his first soliloquy, Angelo says,

> O, let her brother live!
> Thieves for their robbery have authority
> When judges steal themselves.
>
> (MM, II, 2, 174-176)

His new position is in direct opposition to what he has professed to Escalus earlier:

> I not deny,
> The jury, passing on the prisoner's life,
> May in the sworn twelve have a thief or two
> Guiltier than him they try. What's open made to justice,
> That justice seizes: what know the laws
> That thieves do pass on thieves?
>
> (MM, II, 1, 18-23)

Angelo is now suggesting that it is appropriate for the law to show leniency when the judges of the law are guilty of the same offense being tried. The law is no longer for him an abstract thing which condemns the offender, but a kind of "guideline" to be applied at the discretion of the judge. Unfortunately, the lesson Angelo learns is not the accepted one. He is not interested in excusing Claudio because the penalty for Claudio's crime is out of proportion to the offense or because there are mitigating circumstances that should soften the grip of the law. Instead, Angelo is willing to now excuse Claudio because he is about to commit an even worse offense. Here again we see the gross hypocrisy of Angelo. In his discussion with Escalus he said:

> You may not so extenuate his offence
> For I have had such faults; but rather tell me,
> When I, that censure him, do so offend,
> Let mine own judgment pattern out my death,
> And nothing come in partial.
>
> (MM, II, 1, 27-31)

Now he seeks to set aside the penalty of the law for his own protection. It is only when he is undeniably caught in his crime that Angelo reverts to kind and begs the Duke to extend to him the same justice that he had extended to Claudio.

While Angelo's hypocrisy is despicable, it pales in relation to his abuse of power. Since the late 1960's in America, there has been a general distrust of political and judicial corruption that has been increasingly uncovered by an aggressive press. Official abuses of power have heightened the sensitivity of the public and increased public ire at its perpetrators. When Angelo offers to exchange Claudio's life for Isabella's sexual favors, he crosses a line beyond contempt and when, after Isabella threatens to reveal him, he threatens to have Claudio tortured to death. He assures her that his reputation and position will protect him from her complaints. When the Duke contrives the "bed-trick," having Marianna, Angelo's deserted fiancé, substitute for Isabella, his expectation is that Angelo will make good on his promise and pardon the unfortunate Claudio, but this is not to be. Fearing that Claudio, after learning of the terms of his release, will seek revenge, Angelo immediately after sating his lust, orders Claudio executed. It is only through the intervention of the Duke and the jailer that Claudio keeps his head. Strangely enough, as appalled as I am by Angelo's corruption of office, Martha Widmayer in her article "To Sin In Loving Virtue" casually writes, "...as he well knows, none of Angelo's offenses is criminal, including his failed attempt to extort sexual favors from Isabella. Thus, though his wrongdoing may be far more grievous than that of Claudio and Juliet, the deputy cannot be prosecuted under the law. He can, however, be subjected to the kind of punishment he seems to fear most." I admit I was shocked by her contention, but apparently at the time Shakespeare was writing Measure for Measure, malfeasance in office and judicial extortion where not criminal offenses, punishable by law. The worst the malefactor could expect was dismissal from office. Widmayer explains that "[j]ustices of Shakespeare's age had virtually no legal discretion;

statutes were to be enforced as written. Personal conduct regulations, however, offered an exception to the rule. This discretion was a major concern of John Bond, a lawyer and outspoken opponent of the discretionary power over personal conduct given justices. "'Who are not grieved at the luxuriant authority of Justices of the Peace?' he asked his fellow members of the commons. 'For magistrates are men, and men have always attending on them two ministers, libido and iracundia. Men of this nature do subjugate the free subject.'"[21] When magistrates abused their discretionary powers, the method of discipline was public humiliation, designed both to punish the official and hold him up as an example to others.[22] This is precisely what the Duke inflicts on Angelo and, although to our 21st Century eyes an appallingly lenient penalty for Angelo's abuse of power, we cannot condemn it in the context of the times.

But wait, the Duke condemned Angelo to death! Yes, but that was in response to Angelo's fornication, to the same crime that Claudio was convicted of. Although Angelo's intent was to essentially rape Isabella, what he ends up doing is engaging in sexual congress with the willing Marianna. His behavior is identical to Claudio's and the punishment he receives is identical to the punishment he meted out to Claudio. When his crime is publicly uncovered, Angelo is at least consistent, insisting on death. In an earlier discussion with Escalus, when Escalus was arguing that Angelo should empathize with Claudio's weakness, Angelo rejects his pleas, saying,

> When I, that censure him, do so offend,
> Let mine own judgment pattern out my death,
> And nothing come in partial.
>
> (MM, I, 4, 29-31)

When his crime is uncovered by the Duke, Angelo immediately confesses and begs for justice:

> ...good prince,
> No longer session hold upon my shame,
> But let my trial be mine own confession:
> Immediate sentence then and sequent death
> Is all the grace I beg.
>
> (MM, V, 1, 370-74)

Supporting Widmayer's contention, Angelo's words indicate that he is more afraid of public shaming than he is of death. The Duke issues Angelo's sentence and explains to Isabella:

> *...but as he adjudged your brother,--*
> *Being criminal, in double violation*
> *Of sacred chastity and of promise-breach*
> *Thereon dependent, for your brother's life,--*
> *The very mercy of the law cries out*
> *Most audible, even from his proper tongue,*
> *'An Angelo for Claudio, death for death!'*
> *Haste still pays haste, and leisure answers leisure;*
> *Like doth quit like, and MEASURE still FOR MEASURE.*
> *Then, Angelo, thy faults thus manifested;*
> *Which, though thou wouldst deny, denies thee vantage.*
> *We do condemn thee to the very block*
> *Where Claudio stoop'd to death, and with like haste.*
>
> (MM, V, 1, 403-415)

The Duke is now testing Isabella's mettle: will she that pleaded for the pardon of her brother, now plead for the man she believes is responsible for his death? Marianna, still inexplicably in love with Angelo, begs the Duke for Angelo's life, When the Duke refuses, Marianna implores Isabella to speak for mercy. Even though she is unaware that her brother still lives, Isabella joins Marianna in asking for mercy for Angelo's offense of fornication. She is consistent in being willing to beg for the same quality of mercy for Angelo as she pleaded for her brother, Claudio:

> *Look, if it please you, on this man condemn'd,*
> *As if my brother lived: I partly think*
> *A due sincerity govern'd his deeds,*
> *Till he did look on me: since it is so,*
> *Let him not die. My brother had but justice,*
> *In that he did the thing for which he died:*
> *For Angelo,*
> *His act did not o'ertake his bad intent,*
> *And must be buried but as an intent*
> *That perish'd by the way: thoughts are no subjects;*
> *Intents but merely thoughts.*
>
> (MM, V, 1, 444-53)

Strangely, Isabella states that her "*My brother had but justice, /In that he did the thing for which he died,*" but she says Angelo's "*act did not o'ertake his bad intent,*

/And must be buried but as an intent/That perish'd by the way." Is she suggesting here that since Angelo was unsuccessful in bedding her that he is not guilty of fornication even though he bedded her surrogate, the willing Marianna? How is this "intent" only when the act was consummated? Her argument is ludicrous on its face! For his final trick, the Duke presents the living Claudio, forgives Angelo his crime, and then meets out punishment to "one…I cannot pardon," Lucio. Lucio is a secondary character who slanders the Duke repeatedly throughout the play. For this, he is forced to marry the abandoned mother of his child and then is to be "Whipt first…and hanged after." On reflection, the Duke's "justice" is even more out of proportion than that meted out to Claudio by Angelo.

  Measure for Measure is a play that ultimately raises more questions than it can answer about crime, justice, punishment, and mercy. All of its characters, with the possible exception of Escalus, are deeply flawed individuals. The Duke is cowardly, manipulative, and vindictive. Isabella is cold and inflexible. Lucio is a slanderer. No one except the drunken Barnardine and the incompetent Elbow is particularly likable. And the most unlikable is of course Angelo whose paradox is he is a humorless villain in a comic play. We cannot laugh with or at Angelo as we can with Richard III, or Iago, or Aaron. We can, at least, admire, to some degree, the cleverness of Richard, or the improvisational brilliance of Iago or the downright malignant glee of Aaron. We cannot pity Angelo because he is remorseless until he is caught. Even Macbeth and Edmund showed remorse for their crimes. What can we admire in Angelo? He is arrogant, self-righteous, and humorless. He is impatient and inflexible, cowardly and corrupt. He is a liar and a lecher. And worst of all, I think, he is totally believable. Few of us have met someone like Richard III, Iago, or Aaron, but unfortunately, most of us have encountered an Angelo. We can convince ourselves that Richard, Iago and Aaron are exaggerations, bogeymen created to frighten us for our entertainment like Michael in the *Halloween* film series. Angelo is our worst imagining of political abuse of power, and we are predisposed to accept that his behavior is not as farfetched as other Shakespeare villains. When Gallup asked in 2010 "Do you think that quite a few of the people running the government are crooked, not very many are, or do you think hardly any of them are crooked?", 55% of those answered "quite a few." A 2009 study published in the *Yale Law Journal* estimated "over one million bribes are paid in the U.S. judicial system each year."[27] Given our general distrust of officialdom and significant evidence to support our distrust, it is easy to see why we are so quick to dislike Angelo.

Notes

1. Wheeler, Richard P. "Introduction" in *Critical Essays on Shakespeare's Measure for Measure.* (New York: G. K. Hall and Co., 1999), 2
2. Ibid, 1–2

3. Coleridge, Samuel Taylor, *Shakespearean Criticism*, ed. Thomas Middleton Raysor, 2nd ed. (New York, 1960), I, 102.

4. Fulton, Thomas. "Shakespeare's Everyman: Measure for Measure and English Fundamentalism." *Journal of Medieval and Early Modern Studies* 40:1, Winter 2010, 120.

5. Ibid, 120.

6. Hunt, Maurice. "Being Precise in Measure for Measure." *Renascence*, 243 (4) Summer 2006, 261.

7. Rowe, M. W. "The Dissolution of Goodness: Measure for Measure and Classical Ethics." *International Journal of the Classical Tradition* /Summer 1998, 42.

8. King James Bible, I Corinthians, 7. 8-9.

9. Rowe, 43

10. Ibid, 33-4.

11. Higgins, John C. "Justice, Mercy, and Dialectical Genres in *Measure for Measure* and *Promos and Cassandra*." *English Literary Renaissance*. Oxford, UK: Blackwell Publishing. Ltd, 2012, 262.

12. Hunt, 243.

13. Ibid.

14. Bozeman, Theodore Dwight. *The Precisianist Strain: Disciplinary Religion & Antinomian Backlash in Puritanism until 1638*. Chapel Hill: The University of North Carolina Press, 2004, 128.

15. Ibid, 133.

16. Koernig, Bob. *The Puritan Beliefs* at http://www3.gettysburg.edu/~tshannon/hist106web/site15/BOBS/puritan beliefpage11.htm

17. Rothbard, Murray N. "The Puritans "Purify": Theocracy in Massachusetts." In *Conceived in Liberty, Volume 1* (Mises Institute, 1999 [1975], pp. 174-181. http://mises.org/page/1427

18. "Volume VI. The Drama to 1642, Part Two XIV. The Puritan Attack upon the Stage. § 2. Theological and moral objections." *The Cambridge History of English and American Literature in 18 Volumes* (1907–21). http://bartleby.com/216/1402.html

19. "Volume VI. The Drama to 1642XIV. The Puritan Attack upon the Stage. § 1. The attitude of the Reformers towards the Stage." The Cambridge History of English and American Literature in 18 Volumes (1907–21). http://bartleby.com/216/1401.html

20. Dictionary.com. http://dictionary.reference.com/browse/hypocrisy

21. Widmayer, Martha. "'To Sin In Loving Virtue': Angelo of Measure for Measure." *Texas Studies in Literature and Language,* Summer 2007, 49(2), 155-80.

22. Samaha, Joel. *Law and Order in Historical Perspective: The Case of Elizabethan Essex.* (New York: Academic Press, 1974), 99.

23. Dodds, W. M. T. "The Character of Angelo in 'Measure for Measure'" *The Modern Language Review,* 41 (3), Jul, 1946, 246-255. http://www.jstor.org/stable/3717058.

24. Ibid.

25. _____. "Iago and Angelo as the Hypocrites of Shakespeare's Othello." *123HelpMe.com.* 24 Jul 2014. http://www.123HelpMe.com/view.asp?id=7510.

26. Time, Victoria M. *Shakespeare's Criminals: Criminology, Fiction, and Drama.* (Westport, Connecticut: Greenwood Press, 1999), 127.

27. Stratos Pahis. Corruption in Our Courts: What It Looks Like and Where It Is Hidden. *The Yale Law Journal,* 118:1900, 2009. http://judicial-discipline-reform.org/docs/Corruption_in_courts-SPahis_YaleLJ_09.pdf

"THE WORSE TO HER, THE BETTER LOVED OF ME." TITUS ANDRONICUS: TAMORA (TO HER SONS)

If we are repulsed by the oily reality of Angelo's abuse of trust and power, I would suggest that the animalistic behavior of the barbarian brothers, Chiron and Demetrius in *Titus Andronicus*, chills us because we have heard them following us through the park at dusk or we have heard them whispering from the dark alley we just passed. They represent a more primal evil then the sophisticated banal evil of petty bureaucrats; they are the street thugs who haunt our newspaper headlines and urban nightmares. Brutal random violence perpetrated by alienated and aimless young people is a feature of both urban legends and urban reality. One of the most recent examples is apparent in attacks that the media has dubbed the "knockout game." These are assaults where one or more assailants attempt to knock out an unsuspecting victim, often with a single sucker punch, all for the amusement of the attacker(s) and their accomplice(s). Commenting on the attacks, former FBI profiler Clint Van Zandt said "It appears these are just random acts of violence. There's no robbery, there's no rhyme or reason; it's just simply youths making a decision they're going to punch somebody out — sometimes as simple as $5 bet between themselves." The perpetrators, according to clinical psychologist, Jeff Gardere "are young people who have dead-end lives, who have no real goals, who have no educational objectives." In other words, they are fueled by aimless anger and boredom. "They're doing this to get a thrill," Most tellingly, Gardere notes that the kind of violence they have been used to seeing in the media and in video games just isn't doing it for them anymore — in fact, they're "desensitized" now and need a bigger and better fix, as if it were a drug.[1]

The "knockout game" is only the most recent of urban panics involving out of control youths. In 1989, an incident in New York's

Central Park captured the attention of the nation when a group of youthful offenders attacked a young Manhattan investment banker who was out jogging. A loosely organized gang of 32 schoolboys, whose random, motiveless assaults terrorized at least eight other people over nearly two hours, raped and savagely beat the young woman, igniting a firestorm of fear throughout the City. Several of the young people involved in the incident intimated that this was not an isolated event but the product of a youthful past time called "wilding," the street term for beating, robbing, and torturing complete strangers for fun. Gardere's observations could be applied as easily to these perpetrators as to those applied to the young people playing the "knockout game."

When Julie Taymor directed *Titus*, the big screen release of Shakespeare's *Titus Andronicus*, one might wonder if she had images of "wildings" in her head as she filmed the attack of Bassianus and Lavinia in that "lonely part of the forest." It would certainly seem so given her stated goal "to create connections between a world of fiction and the real world."[2] In this heart-rending scene, Act II, scene 3, Bassianus and Lavinia stumble upon Arron and the vengeful Tamora in an isolated part of the forest where a royal hunt is taking place. Aaron has been laying a trap for the Andronici and Tamora has been showing her gratitude with amorous advances. Arron tells his Queen,

> *This is the day of doom for Bassianus:*
> *His Philomel must lose her tongue to-day,*
> *Thy sons make pillage of her chastity*
> *And wash their hands in Bassianus' blood.*
>
> *(TA, II, 3, 42-5)*

On cue, Bassianus and Lavinia discover them in a passionate embrace and threaten to report them to the Emperor. Chiron and Demetrius enter the scene, obviously planted nearby by the clever Aaron, and rush to their mother's defense, stabbing to death the defenseless Bassianus. Tamora asks for a dagger so she can personally exact her revenge on Lavinia, but is stopped by Demetrius who tells her *"Stay, madam; here is more belongs to* her; / *First thrash the corn, then after burn the straw.*" (*TA*, II, 3, 122-3). The brothers intend to "*Drag hence her husband to some secret hole, /And make his dead trunk pillow to our lust.*" (*TA*, II, 3, 129-30). Tamora sends them off with this encouragement:

> *Remember, boys, I pour'd forth tears in vain,*
> *To save your brother from the sacrifice;*
> *But fierce Andronicus would not relent;*
> *Therefore, away with her, and use her as you will,*
> *The worse to her, the better loved of me.*
>
> (*TA, II, 3, 163-67*)

The two brothers rape and mutilate poor Lavinia, cutting off her hands and tongue so she cannot reveal the identity of her assailants. In one of the most horrific scenes written by Shakespeare, Act II, scene 4, Demetrius and Chiron lead the ravished Lavinia onto the stage and taunt her before leaving her to be discovered by her uncle, Marcus.

These scenes, during nineteenth-century productions, were often expurgated from the play or performed without the rape or mutilations.[3] Taymor's film production does none of these things; she plays the scenes pretty much as Shakespeare wrote them. "The real challenge for both the play and the film," according to Taymor, "is to show audiences that it is not so much about violence as it is about how audiences promote and encourage and demand violence. The film does not simply display violence, it also asks audiences to think about their role in promoting that violence."[4] By showing Lavinia's rape and mutilation, the audience is, hopefully, driven to compassion for Lavinia. Similarly, by showing the sadism and brutality of Chiron and Demetrius, Taymor demonizes the brothers and denounces their casual violence.

She dresses them appropriately in modern punk-Goth garb and features them most prominently in a modern game room featuring assorted video games and a pool table. They "rock out" to heavy metal music and gesticulate like coked-out druggies. They are both engaged in playing violent video games as the scene opens and through their hyper-stimulated state, Taymor shows that video games produce a type of masculinity that is hyper- violent. Indeed, Tamora's sons are portrayed as surrounded by culturally mediated images of masculinity which reach them through video-games, television advertisements, and music videos, and which mix the titillation of violence with that of sex, producing a type of masculinity intimately connected with dominance, which ends up with the dispossession of Lavinia.[5] The brothers are hedonistic man-children, willing to try to kill each other over Lavinia in Act II, scene 1, and then only laugh at her and mock her after they are done raping and torturing her. Coupling the game room scene with the rape scene where the brothers kill Bassianus and ravage Lavinia, the viewer may also be reminded of Alex and his psychopathic "droogs" in Stanley Kubrick's 1971 classic meditation on purposeless, sadistic violence, *A Clockwork Orange*. In other words, they look like the stereotype of every (white) street thug we have been conditioned to fear. The final effect is to make Chiron and Demetrius as frightening and repulsive as possible, literally young barbarians from whom we expect and receive the worst.

The barbarian brothers, although principally monsters, do serve other functions in the play. It should be remembered that their violence is not strictly purposeless as the knockout games and wildings appeared to be. The brothers are tools of their mother's revenge against the Andronici. That Lavinia fits into the plan is a fortunate coincidence that allows the brothers to expend their sadistic lust on Titus' daughter. Their action serves to heighten the villainy of Tamora. Similarly, when they are featured in Act IV, scene 2 where the nurse presents Aaron with his and Tamora's love child, Chiron and Demetrius want to immediately kill the child to protect their mother. Aaron has other plans: he kills the nurse to silence her. The brothers are shocked by the casual murder. That they can be shocked by Aaron's action serves to magnify his villainy (that he is evil beyond their monstrous understanding) just as Tamora's cruelty toward Lavinia magnifies hers. There is, however, more going on in this scene than showing Aaron off as a superior monster. Aaron defends the infant against Chiron and Demetrius. He killed the nurse to defend his son and threatens to do the same to the brothers if they attempt to kill the child.

Stay, murderous villains! will you kill your brother?
Now, by the burning tapers of the sky,
That shone so brightly when this boy was got,
He dies upon my scimitar's sharp point
That touches this my first-born son and heir!

(TA, IV, 2, 88-92)

After Aaron kills the nurse, Demetrius, shocked, asks "wherefore didst thou this?" and Aaron explains "Shall she live to betray this guilt of ours, / A long-tongued babbling gossip? no, lords, no." He instructs the brothers to send the midwife to him (the only other person to have seen the black baby) so he can assure her silence in the same way he assured the nurse's. Chiron wryly comments, "I see thou wilt not trust the air/ With secrets." This episode further highlights the distorted family values found in Rome. The play opens with Saturninus and Bassianus ready to kill one another for the throne. Act II, scene 1 shows Chiron and Demetrius ready to kill one another over their lust for Lavinia. We have seen Titus killing his own son for the crime of "blocking [his] way in Rome." Tamora sends Aaron's baby to him to be killed. The message is that in Rome, families kill one another for pride and advantage. Only the arch villain, Aaron is willing to kill and be killed to protect his own.

Notes

1. CNN Newsroom interview with Jeff Gardere. "Is the 'knockout game' a cheap thrill?" November 21, 2013. http://www.cnn.com/video/data/2.0/video/us/2013/11/21/nr-live-gardere-knockout-game-cheap-thrill.cnn.html
2. Lindroth, Mary. "'Some device of further misery': Taymor's Titus brings Shakespeare to film audiences with a twist." *Literature/Film Quarterly* 29.2 (2001): 107-115.
3. Ibid, 110.
4. Ibid, 111.

5. Robinson, Bryan (March 18, 2004). "What drives thrill killings". *ABC News* http://abcnews.go.com/US/story?id=96770&page=1

"HENCEFORWARD ALL THINGS SHALL BE IN COMMON." HENRY VI, PART II: JACK CADE

Virtually the entire 4th Act of *Henry VI, part II* is dominated by a character and a series of events that are marginal to the plot of the play. The character is the historical Jack Cade and the events surround his popular revolt of 1450. Beginning in May and lasting through the beginning of July, a "ragged multitude of hinds and peasants" numbering over 5,000 marched on London under the leadership of Jack Cade for the redress of grievances that included high taxes, corrupt local officials, and the recent loss of Normandy. Composed primarily of rural peasants, artisans, and tradesmen from the towns of Kent, the rebels were, at least initially, well organized and disciplined. Assembling at Blackheath, about five miles southeast of London Bridge, the rebels issued a written set of demands which they sent to King Henry articulating fifteen articles or "complaints." Hoping to nip the rebellion in the bud, Henry dispatched a small force led by Sir Humphrey and William Stafford to disperse the rebels. The royal forces were ambushed and the two Stafford brothers were killed. Gaining confidence from their victory, the rebels advanced to the southern end of London Bridge in late June and set up their headquarters. On July 3rd, the rebels entered London proper and immediately set up a series of tribunals dedicated to seeking out and convicting those accused of corruption. James Fiennes, 1st Baron Saye, the Lord High Treasurer was brought in for a sham trial, found guilty of treason and beheaded along with his son-in-law William Crowmer. The heads of the two men were put on pikes and paraded through the streets of London while their bearers pushed them together so that they appeared to kiss. While initially orderly, the rebels soon began to engage in looting and riotous behavior that outraged the citizens of London who had been sympathetic to the rebels' complaints. When on the night of July 7th the rebel army returned to its headquarters on the south side of the Thames, the citizens of London gathered at

London Bridge to block their return to the City. The next evening, the rebels attempted to reenter London but were blocked by the citizens in a pitched battle for the bridge. After the battle on London Bridge the momentum of the rebellion ebbed, King Henry, through his Lord Chancellor persuaded Cade's followers to abandon the cause by issuing official pardons and promising to fulfill the rebel's demands. Shortly after calm was restored, Henry voided the pardons and placed a price on the head of Jack Cade, who was tracked down by one Alexander Iden and slain on July 12th.

The Cade rebellion supplies Shakespeare with opportunity to introduce some action and humor into the otherwise slow paced and highly political second play of his Henry VI tetralogy. *Henry VI, Part II* sets the scene for his depiction of the War of the Roses in the succeeding plays, *Henry VI, Part III* and *Richard III*. Act 4, the Cade story, is a series of short scenes with masses of actors moving around the stage, crisp dialogue, and enough banter and violence to stir up the groundlings. The dizzying feeling that accompanies Act 4 also reflects the dismemberment of the body politic that overshadows the entire tetralogy. The concomitant chaos with its attendant violence creates an intoxicating energy as anarchy and festivity intermingle.

At the center of all this mayhem is the character of Jack Cade, a combination of stage vice and stage clown, and the absurd spokesperson for the grievances of the common folk. Cade is introduced well before he is seen. In Act III, scene I, the Duke of York upon being dispatched by the King to Ireland to put down a rebellion, confides to the audience that "Whiles I in Ireland nourish a mighty band, / I will stir up in England some black storm/ Shall blow ten thousand souls to heaven or hell." (*HVI, II*, III, 1, 348-50). To stir up the storm, he has chosen "a headstrong Kentishman, John Cade of Ashford, / To make commotion, as full well he can, / Under the title of John Mortimer." (*HVI, II*, III, 1, 358-9). York paints Cade as something of a fierce and madcap warrior, saying:

In Ireland have I seen this stubborn Cade
Oppose himself against a troop of kerns,
And fought so long, till that his thighs with darts
Were almost like a sharp-quill'd porpentine;

And, in the end being rescued, I have seen
Him caper upright like a wild Morisco,
Shaking the bloody darts as he his bells.

(HVI, II, III, 1,360-366)

The description shows Cade as a warrior tenacious in battle and impervious to pain. After a battle where he endured numerous leg wounds and had "darts" still logged in his legs, Cade is described as "capering like a wild Morisco shaking the bloody darts as his bells." York's choice of words alludes to the "Morris dance" The Morris (or Moorish) dances were a quite common feature of the seasonal rejoicings in the villages of England. Its origin is unknown, but in the 15th Century, the dances were widespread as entertainment for the "country folk." Standard features of the Morris dances include particularly frantic dance movements and costumes that included bells worn on the legs of the dancers. Traditionally performed as a group dance, by the time of Shakespeare, it was also performed by a solo dancer, sometimes at the conclusion of a theatrical performance. Shakespeare's great clown, Will Kempe, was known for performing particularly frenzied Morris dances for appreciative crowds.

The association of the Morris dance with the rural seasonal festivals normally celebrated at Christmas, May Day, and Whitsuntide (the Christian festival of Pentecost, the seventh Sunday after Easter). These festival were week-long events during which the common folk in rural communities were freed from service on their lord's demesne for the week. This uncommon freedom came to be identified as a period of licensed misrule and featured the selection of a mock (or summer) king in order to celebrate disorder, irreverence and rebellion.[1] The tradition of the Lord of Misrule is rooted in the Roman festival of Saturnalia, which fell during December. During this festival, there was a reversal of traditional roles, with slaves wearing fine garments and sitting at the head of the table while they were waited upon by their masters. The Lord of Misrule presided over the festival proceedings, comically leading excesses of the celebration, but then, in a dark turn at the end of the festival the Lord was killed, a symbolic scapegoat taking on and extinguishing the sins of his fellows and signaling a return to normalcy.[2]

By the 15th Century, the Lord of Misrule served as master of the revels was a clownish figure of fun. He was no longer executed at the end of the festival and his presence had expanded beyond the Christmas festival to include May Day and Whitsuntide.

York goes on to say of Cade:

> *This devil here shall be my substitute;*
> *For that John Mortimer, which now is dead,*
> *In face, in gait, in speech, he doth resemble:*
> *By this I shall perceive the commons' mind,*
> *How they affect the house and claim of York.*
>
> (HVI, II, III, 1, 371-5)

His referencing Cade as a "devil" may only be an epithet, but it also recalls that comedic-evil character of the stage: the Vice. Like the clown and the Lord of Misrule, the Vice was a comedic character, but one with a dark purpose. As the Devil's emissary, he is sent to lure "Everyman" into sin and trap souls for his master. He is a minor devil who on occasion may take on the identity of his superior and is often berated and beaten for his presumption. Cade assumes a similar role when he echoes the suggestions of his master York and puts on the role of mock king by claiming to be John Mortimer, the missing (and fictitious!) son of Edmund Mortimer, the 5th Earl of March, who after the deposition of Richard II, was imprisoned by Henry IV because of his superior claim to the throne. Descendants of the Mortimer line (including Richard, Duke of York) were thereafter the focus of plots against Lancastrians. By assuming the name John Mortimer, Jack Cade identified himself with the family of Henry VI's rival, the duke of York and indirectly reminds the populace of York's legitimate claim to the throne. Thus, in a few short lines, Shakespeare through York outlines the character and the role that Cade will portray in Act 4: clown, Lord of Misrule and Vice.

At the opening of Act IV, the audience again hears about Jack Cade before they see him. Two rebels discussing Cade identify him as a "clothier" set to redress the commonwealth that has gone "threadbare" under the rule of the squabbling nobility. The analogy is not meant to identify Cade as a literal clothier, but as one of the working class who are oppressed by the "gentlemen" of England. When Cade arrives on stage at the head of a large body of men, he is announcing his right to the throne by claiming his "father was a Mortimer" and his "mother a Plantagenet." He is suggesting that his father was Edmund the 3rd Earl of March who was married to Philippa, 5th Countess of Ulster, the daughter of Lionel, 1st Duke of Clarence who was the third son of King Edward III. Remember that the year is 1450. Edmund died in 1381 and Philippa in 1382. If Cade had, in fact, been their offspring, he would have been at least 68 years of age! The validity of his claim is patently false and is even recognized as nonsense by his followers who in asides, ridicule his every assertion, making him an object of fun, i.e., a clown. Nevertheless, the rebels follow him because he speaks for their legitimate grievances and makes fantastical promises that "when I am king, as king I will be..."

> There shall be in England seven
> halfpenny loaves sold for a penny: the three-hooped
> pot; shall have ten hoops and I will make it felony
> to drink small beer: all the realm shall be in
> common; and in Cheapside shall my palfrey go to
> grass
>
> (HVI, II, IV, 2, 65-70)

Like a pre-Marxist radical, he is preaching the violent eradication of privilege and class differences, a leveling of society and a redistribution of property. Cade tells his followers there "shall be no money" and that he will "apparel ... all in one livery," expressing ideas taken directly from Sir Thomas More's *Utopia*. Like the traditional Lord of Misrule, his intention is to invert the order of society, raising up the lowly and casting down the powerful. And like the traditional figure of the clown or fool, he refuses to recognize class differences. Before he is confronted by Sir Humprey, he insists upon investing himself as a knight so he can confront Sir Humprey as an equal. Such a presumption on his part would be certain to offend the nobility. And while he is at once calling for a leveling of society, he does not question the idea of kingship, setting himself up as the rightful heir to the throne and saying that all the people will "agree like brothers and **worship me their lord**." (*HVI, II,* IV, 1, 75). He also shows what kind of king he will be when the Clerk of Chatham is brought before him, absurdly charged with the ability to read and write. The Clerk naively confesses to these skills and Cate cruelty orders him hanged "with his pen and ink-horn about his neck."

When confronted by the first challengers to his revolt, Sir Humprey and William Stafford, Cade rallies his followers, saying:

> *And you that love the commons, follow me.*
> *Now show yourselves men; 'tis for liberty.*
> *We will not leave one lord, one gentleman:*
> *Spare none*
>
> (*HVI, II, IV, 2, 181-85*)

The mob is ordered to disband, but Cade counters with two demands. First, he offers to allow the King to continue as king, but under the "protectorship" of Cade thereby reminding all that Henry has, in fact, been under the protectorship of others for nearly his entire reign. Second, Cade and his followers demand the head of Lord Say "for selling the dukedom of Maine" and for speaking French which Cade insists makes him a traitor. When it becomes obvious that Cade is implacable, Humprey and Stafford attack the mob. The King's men are routed by the rebels and Humprey and Stafford are killed and their bodies are desecrated by the rebels as they advance on London. King Henry and his court flee the city in advance of the mob, but Lord Say bravely remains, fearing that his presence with the King will further inflame the crowd.

Cade and his rebels succeed in taking London Bridge and entering the city. Cade proceeds to London-stone where, striking the Stone with his staff, he declares himself "Mortimer lord of this city." One would assume there is some significance to this ceremony, but in fact there is no historical ceremonial significance to the Stone. It has, however, been associated with the stone from which King Arthur pulled the sword to reveal that he was rightful king.[3] Whether this was in Shakespeare's mind in writing this scene is unknown, but it seems Cade intends to institute the Stone as new ceremonial site to commemorate the establishing of his new kingdom in the same way that he created himself a knight before his encounter with Humprey and Stafford. Cade in this second instance of self-elevation tells his followers "henceforward it shall be treason for any that calls me other than Lord Mortimer." (*HVI, II, IV*, 6, 5-6). This is immediately followed by a darkly comic scene:

> Enter a Soldier, running
> **Soldier**
> Jack Cade! Jack Cade!
> **Cade**
> Knock him down there.
> They kill him
>
> (*HVI, II, IV*, 6, 7-8).

The rebels continue on in an orgy of looting, burning and violence. Advancing to Smithfield in northwest London, they pause as Cade issues another proclamation where he next assumes the role of Parliament unto himself: "Burn all the records of the realm: my mouth shall be the parliament of England." (*HVI, II, IV*, 7, 14-15). His follower's response is now more tempered. Where earlier they responded to Cade's grandiosity with good humored sarcasm, their asides now take on a more cynical tone. Holland for example responds to Cade's most recent proclamation saying "Then we are like to have biting statutes, unless his teeth be pulled out," indicating his fear that Cade may be a solution more dangerous than their current situation under King Henry. (*HVI, II, IV*, 7, 18). The intoxicating energy of anarchy and festivity previously balanced and intermingled is growing ominous as Cade's megalomania overshadows the legitimate goals of the rebellion.

The climax of the rebellion comes when Lord Say falls into the hands of the mob and is brought before Cade for judgment. Mixing both the legitimate and the absurd, Cade charges Say with losing Normandy to the dauphin of France and "of most traitorously corrupt[ing] the youth of the realm in erecting a grammar school" where the children are taught to write and tally, skills he claims are used to repress the unlettered masses. Further, Say is charged with building a paper mill and of surrounding himself with men who "usually talk of a noun and a verb, and such abominable words as no Christian ear can endure to hear." Finally, Say is accused of appointing "justices of peace, to call poor men before them/about matters they were not able to answer. / Moreover, thou hast put them in prison; and because/ they could not read, thou hast hanged them." (*HVI, II, IV,* 7, 38-44). Say denies the charges and emphasizing the essential split between the commoners and himself, says "ignorance is the curse of God, / Knowledge the wing wherewith we fly to heaven." This alone is sufficient to condemn him. Cade wants to roll back time to the idyllic state of Eden where he envisioned a society leveled in its ignorance. For Cade, knowledge is the greater divider that separates man into classes and makes some rich and others poor. By uniting mankind in common ignorance he insists all men will be happily equal under the semi-divine rule of King Cade. Say is of course condemned to beheading and along with him his son-in-law, Sir James Cromer. In a spectacle of the grotesque, Cade orders their heads placed on spikes and paraded through then city, stopping them and having them kiss at every corner. Now with his seething madness on full display, Cade announces that "The proudest peer in the realm shall not wear a head/ on his shoulders, unless he pay me tribute."

Here enters the king's ambassadors, Buckingham and Clifford, announcing the king will pardon the rebels if they give up their rebellion and go home.

> Who loves the king and will embrace his pardon,
> Fling up his cap, and say 'God save his majesty!'
> Who hateth him and honours not his father,
> Henry the Fifth, that made all France to quake,
> Shake he his weapon at us and pass by.
>
> (*HVI, II, IV,* 8, 14-8)

The rebels cry out, "God save the king! God save the king!" and begin to disband. Cade, shocked and betrayed, cries out:

> you are all recreants and dastards,
> and delight to live in slavery to the nobility. Let
> them break your backs with burthens, take your
> houses over your heads, ravish your wives and

daughters before your faces: for me, I will make
shift for one; and so, God's curse light upon you
all!

(HVI, II, IV, 8, 27-32)

The fickle rebels cry out again, this time saying "We'll follow Cade, we'll follow Cade!"

Clifford responds by invoking the revered name of King Henry V and England's gloried past victories in France. He warns that as civil war rages in Henry's England, France is busy preparing to invade England while she is in a weakened state. Is Cade, he says, the man to repulse the hated French? Not likely! Using the age old unifying trick of the politician, he calls upon the people to launch a preemptive attack against France and regain their lost possessions.

The crowd now cries out "A Clifford! a Clifford! we'll follow the king and Clifford." Cade knows he has lost.

Was ever feather so lightly blown to and fro as this
multitude? The name of Henry the Fifth hales them
to an hundred mischiefs, and makes them leave me
desolate.

(HVI, II, IV, 8, 55-8)

He flees the scene with a price on his head and Buckingham and Clifford take the good news to King Henry. Henry's joy at the news is short-lived as a messenger brings news that the Duke of York is newly come from Ireland at the head of an army. York's stated objective is to see the Duke of Somerset, his chief rival and Henry's ally, imprisoned for treason. Henry again dispatches Buckingham as his ambassador to tell York he will accede to his demand and hold Somerset for trial.

Meanwhile, the action returns to Cade who is now reduced to a man on the run. For five days he has alluded capture, but now hunger forces him into the open. He climbs a wall and enters the garden of farmer Alexander Idem, an esquire of Kent. Idem, coming upon him, is aggressively confronted by Cade, and even though Idem is willing to see Cade fed and let him pass in peace, Cade cannot temper his manner and provokes Idem into a fight. Idem easily defeats the famished Cade and so ends his reign of terror.

Notes

1. Laroque, François. "The Jack Cade Scenes Reconsidered: Popular Rebellion, Utopia, or Carnival?" *Shakespeare and Cultural Traditions: The Selected Proceedings of the International Shakespeare Association World Congress*, Tokyo, 1991. Ed. Tetsuo Kishi, Stanley Wells, and Roger Pringle. Newark: University of Delaware Press, 1994. P.76-89.
2. Barber, C. L. (1990). *Shakespeare's Festive Comedy; A Study of Dramatic Form and its Relation to Social Custom*, Princeton, NJ: Princeton University Press. http://rauldesaldanha.blogspot.com/2010/08/c-l-barber-shakespeares-festive-comedy.html
3. "The London Stone" (2002). *The Hitchhikers Guide to the Galaxy: Earth Edition.* http://h2g2.com/edited_entry/A863309

MINIONS

No one would deny that Shakespeare created great characters, many of whom have been discussed in great detail throughout this book. Major characters, like Hamlet, Othello, Lear and Macbeth have enjoyed a long history of study as have many of Shakespeare's minor characters: Mercutio in *Romeo and Juliet*, Kent and the Fool in *King Lear*, the Weird Sisters in *Macbeth*, Polonius in *Hamlet*, etc. A group of characters who have not received a great deal of attention are the often ignored and certainly underappreciated bit parts that flesh out the plays. Often dismissed as simply scenery or props, the bit players usually appear in a single scene, many times identified only by their function: Messenger, Servant, Porter, or Murderer. On average, Shakespeare featured eighteen roles in his comedies, twenty-seven in his tragedies, and thirty-five in his histories. *Othello* with thirteen characters excluding messengers and attendants, etc. has the fewest number of characters, but if all characters that have one line of speech or more are included, there are twenty-six actors needed. *Richard III* calls for more than forty characters so it is remarkable that his theater company only consisted of twenty-six principle actors. This means that some actors would be called upon to play multiple roles in plays featuring a large cast. Although this was a common practice on the English stage, it does raise the question why Shakespeare and his contemporaries would include so many bit parts when they were limited in the number of available players.

No matter how small, it should be assumed that every bit player has some dramatic purpose in the overall performance. There are of course numerous silent characters on-stage in court scenes, battlefield scenes, and tavern scenes who simply flesh out the scene, thus making the action more believable. The Prologue in *Henry V* invites the audience to "Piece out our imperfections with your thoughts; / Into a thousand parts divide one man." Nevertheless, several men will be needed on stage to stand in for thousands in our imagination. When Henry V delivers his

St Crispin's Day speech it should be before a gathering of men, not just the few named characters in the scene (Gloucester, Bedford, Exeter, Erpingham, Salisbury and Westmoreland), so the stage directions include "Erpingham's host" to swell the on-stage presence. Crowd scenes like the scene where Antony addresses the citizens of Rome following the murder of Caesar would not be particularly effective if only two or three actors are seen on stage. Similarly, scenes of battle like the storming of Orleans in *Henry VI, Part I* lack the desired dramatic impact if only the speaking roles are present on the stage. A silent part might also be used to advance the action of a scene. A king calls for his armor and attendants arrive with it and help him prepare for battle. Cleopatra calls for wine to drink a toast to Anthony and a servant arrives with the cup. Without the servant the Queen would be left to serve herself, an action that would be grossly inconsistent with her status. Such characters appear throughout Shakespeare's plays, either to heighten the dramatic effect of a scene or to reveal or confirm something about the principle actors with whom they share the stage.

The smallest speaking part in all of Shakespeare's is assigned to Second Senator in *Cymbeline* who has just one brief line: "Ay." in Act 3, Scene 7. Many more are similarly brief. In Act 4, Scene 6, the rebel leader, Jack Cade announces "henceforward it shall be treason for any that calls me other than Lord Mortimer." At that moment, a Soldier runs onto the stage calling "Jack Cade! Jack Cade!" and is immediately killed by Cade's followers. While the role of Soldier is painfully brief, his function in this darkly comic scene if to relieve some of the tension of the preceding scenes of murder while heightening the audience's horror at Cade's increasing lunacy. A slightly larger, but far more important role is that of Friar John in Act 5, Scene 2 of *Romeo and Juliet*. Friar John has been sent by Friar Lawrence to Romeo in Mantua to deliver a letter describing the conspiracy that he and Juliet have contrived to reunite the young lovers. When Friar John returns, Friar Lawrence anxiously asks about Romeo's response to his letter and is told that the letter was not delivered because an "infectious pestilence" in a town on the way to Mantua prevented its delivery:

I could not send it,--here it is again,--

Nor get a messenger to bring it thee,
So fearful were they of infection.

(R&J, V, 2, 14-6)

Friar John appears in just this single short scene and speaks a total of 13 lines, but his impact on the outcome of the tragedy exceeds that of others who enjoy larger parts.

Unlike the Second Senator or the Soldier, Friar John is a named as well as a speaking character. This might lead one to think that named and speaking characters have more importance than the unnamed or silent ones, but this is not the case. Two of Shakespeare's most studied and discussed bit payers are *Hamlet*'s Gravedigger. The Gravediggers appear in the penultimate scene of *Hamlet*, adding a touch of humor to an otherwise melancholy scene featuring the burial of Ophelia. They are representative of a class of roles frequently used by Shakespeare for comic effect, clever peasants or clowns who use their wit when interacting with their social superior. Like Lear's Fool or the Gardeners in *Richard II*, they often throw light and comment on the central themes of the play. The Gravedigger's begin the scene with a mock legal argument about the propriety of offering Christian burial to one who has committed suicide. Here is another take on the "To be, or not to be" reflection on suicide made by Hamlet earlier in the play, but instead of philosophically pondering the consequence of suicide, the Gravediggers define the act, conclude that Ophelia committed the act, but that being of noble birth, the "crowner" (King) has chosen to deny the act, rule the suicide not a suicide and thus assure the maid a Christian burial. The King's command violates the accepted traditions of the church and arouses the indignation of the grave-diggers. Their speech is more a condemnation of the capriciousness of the nobility to rule against reality than a condemnation of the suicide itself. Even the lowly gravediggers are aware that there is "something rotten in Denmark." The Second Gravedigger leaves the scene to "fetch... a stoup of liquor" when Hamlet and Horatio enter it. The First Gravedigger continues to dig the grave while singing a morbid little song, lamenting mortality. The song and the casual tossing of a skull from the ground he is digging prompts Hamlet to also meditate on mortality as the great leveler of humanity. The skull, he observes, may have belonged to a great lawyer or landowner, but now is knocked about with "this rude knave's" dirty shovel. It is often the case that that Shakespeare's bit players will provide the principle actors with occasion to ponder life's complexities. When Hamlet engages to Gravedigger, he is greeted with the same straightforward and irreverent tone that the Gravedigger had used with his companion. Using wit instead of violence, the Gravedigger like Jack Cade, narrows the social divide between the ruling and peasant classes. His leveling speech combines with his casual handling of the skeletal remains to underscore the common humanity of princes and beggars.

Shakespeare uses nameless bit parts to flesh out the action of his plays and one-character group that is prominent are the nameless villains in the service of great men. Some such characters barely appear on stage. For example, in Act IV, scene 2 of *Macbeth*, the usurping king sends his minions to kill MacDuff and all his family. An unspecified number of Murderers enters the scene and finding Lady MacDuff and her young son, the "First Murderer" accuses MacDuff of being a traitor and when the son protests, the First Murderer commits one of the most shocking acts portrayed any of Shakespeare's plays: he stabs the child. The reflexive brutality of the murder of the child exhibits the depth of the inhumanity of the killer and, by extension, his employer. The murderers in this scene are probably the same men employed earlier by Macbeth in Act III, scene1 to assassinate Banquo and Fleance. Macbeth has persuaded the two murderers that Banquo is their energy and the author of their misfortunes. When he meets with them, he asks:

> Do you find
> Your patience so predominant in your nature
> That you can let this go? Are you so gospell'd
> To pray for this good man and for his issue,
> Whose heavy hand hath bow'd you to the grave
> And beggar'd yours for ever?
>
> (M, III, 1, 85-9)

To this, the First Murderer replies, "We are men, my liege," as if that answer was sufficient in and of itself. The response suggests that as men they are neither patient nor "gospell'd to pray" for their enemy. The First Murderer clearly believes in the most degraded nature of man and is unable to imagine a "man" who is capable of such goodness. However, Macbeth having personally pondered what heights and depths a "man" is capable of demands a less ambiguous answer. The catalogue of "man," he informers the murderers, is rich in variety like the catalogue of "dog". Some are fleet, others are loyal, and still others are vicious. Macbeth continues, pressing them:

> if you have a station in the file,
> Not i' the worst rank of manhood, say 't;
> And I will put that business in your bosoms,
> Whose execution takes your enemy off,
>
> (M, III, 1, 101-4)

They respond:

> **Second Murderer**
> I am one, my liege,
> Whom the vile blows and buffets of the world
> Have so incensed that I am reckless what
> I do to spite the world.
> **First Murderer**
> And I another
> So weary with disasters, tugg'd with fortune,
> That I would set my lie on any chance,
> To mend it, or be rid on't.
>
> (M, III, 1, 108-12)

Their responses are telling. Unlike the villains who have populated this text and who have murdered to achieve revenge or power or just to satisfy a perverse pleasure derived from the misery of others, these villains are the product of circumstances so desperate that they care little for their own lives and nothing for the lives of others. Although they have been led to believe Banquo is the immediate cause of their grief, the revenge they seek is incidental to their violence. What they are really striking out at is the world and circumstances in which they exist. Banquo is only the most accessible target available. Of all the villains in the canon, these two desperate men are the most likely to be understood by the groundlings standing in the pit. Oppression and the feeling of victimization has long been associated with criminality.

Similarly, the two murderers of Clarence in *Richard III* are hired killers, but there is no reason to think they have any animus toward their victim. Richard warns them to refrain from conversation with Clarence lest they pity their victim. The First Murderer dismisses his concern:

> *Fear not, my lord, we will not stand to prate;*
> *Talkers are no good doers: be assured*
> *We come to use our hands and not our tongues.*
>
> *(RIII, I, 3, 349-51)*

This stern response is, however, undermined when they actually encounter the sleeping Clarence in the Tower. A comic exchange takes play between the two killers as they debate whether to awake Clarence before killing him. Doubt begins to creep into the mind of the Second Murderer, who suddenly is concerned he may "be damned for killing him" (*RIII*, I, 4, 111). When his companion tells him to return and tell this to Richard, the following comic dialogue ensues to reduce the intensity of the murder that is to be done:

> **Second Murderer**
> *I pray thee, stay a while: I hope my holy humour*
> *will change; 'twas wont to hold me but while one*
> *would tell twenty.*
> **First Murderer**
> *How dost thou feel thyself now?*
> **Second Murderer**
> *'Faith, some certain dregs of conscience are yet*
> *within me.*
> **First Murderer**
> *Remember our reward, when the deed is done.*
> **Second Murderer**
> *'Zounds, he dies: I had forgot the reward.*
> **First Murderer**

Where is thy conscience now?
Second Murderer
In the Duke of Gloucester's purse.
First Murderer
So when he opens his purse to give us our reward,
thy conscience flies out

(RIII, I, 4, 117-30)

As soon as the resolve of the Second Murderer is restored, the conscience of the First Murderer becomes clouded and it now falls to companion to prop him up. This prattle wakes Clarence and the scene turns serious, almost philosophical, as Clarence and the Murderers argues conflicting demands between temporal and celestial powers. The murders argue that they have authority under the power of the King to lawfully execute Clarence with a clear conscience. Clarence argues God's "law commanded/ That thou shalt do no murder: and wilt thou, then, / Spurn at his edict and fulfil a man's?" (RIII, I, 4, 196-8). In Clarence's reading, his death will be a murder rather than a lawful execution, will be an affront to law in that he has had no trial, and no evidence has been brought against him for capital crimes. The murderers counter that Clarence has, during the War, murdered others, specifically the son of Henry VI, and still felt justified in taking the sacraments. How then can he argue that their acts are any different than his? Clarence explains that he acted on behalf of his brother and the Murderers ironically reply that they also act on behalf of his brother and reveal that it is Richard who placed Clarence in their hands. Clarence falls to pleading for his life and detects "some pity in th[eir] looks," but the First Murderer, at last, strikes and stabs him to death. The Second Murderer does not strike and is immediately appalled by his role in the killing. He refused to help the First Murderer hide the body and refuses to return to Richard for payment.

It is reasonable to question why, following the chilling brilliance of Clarence's famous "Dream" monologue, that Shakespeare would complete the scene with the drawn out killing of Clarence by two relatively inarticulate murderers. As mentioned earlier, one reason is to lighten the mood between Clarence's ominous dream and his murder.

Their discussion of conscience reminds the audience of the psychomachia of the medieval morality play that Richard's drama is rooted.[1] Their prose dialogue identifies them as simple practical men doing a job and the speech of the Second Murderer anticipates Falstaff's brilliant discourse on honor in *Henry IV, Part I*.

> *I'll not meddle with it. It is a dangerous thing. It makes a man a*
> *coward: a man cannot steal, but it accuseth him; a man cannot swear,*
> *but it checks him; a man cannot lie with his neighbour's wife, but it*
> *detects him. 'Tis a blushing shamefast spirit, that mutinies in a man's*
> *bosom. It fills one full of obstacles. It made me once restore a purse of*
> *gold that I found: it beggars any man that keeps it. It is turn'd out of*
> *towns and cities for a dangerous thing, and every man that means to*
> *live well, endeavors to trust to himself, and live without it."*
>
> (RIII, I, 4,126-135)

The Second Murderer view agues eloquently that conscience is a luxury, like honor, that can be enjoyed by the rich and powerful, but is one that the lower classes can ill-afford.[2] One Clarence awakens, the Murderers speech pattern significantly changes from prose to verse; this results in the elevation of the characters signifying that they now represent more than themselves. If we subscribe to Tillyard's thesis that Richard, in facts, acts as a scourge of God to the evil men controlling England, the murderers become his instruments. They are elevated to Clarence's level and they engage Clarence in conversation so Clarence understands why he must die.[3]

Clarence's death is the only murder done on stage in *Richard III* and has a whole harrowing scene devoted to it. Much shorter, but equally harrowing is the reported murder of the young princes in the Tower. Its report by Tyrrel occupies just over half of Scene 3 in Act IV. Sir James Tyrrel, the chief assassin, is hired to oversee the murders and has hired, in turn two "flesh'd villains, bloody dogs," Dighton and Forrest, to commit the act. It is interesting that the names of these hired killers are a part of the text unlike the nameless killers of Clarence. The obvious reason is that these two men are identified by history, specifically in a confession supposedly given by Tyrrel in 1503. The confession, reported in Sir Thomas More's *History of King Richard III*, identifies John Dighton and Miles Forrest as the actual killers of the young princes, but the confession itself has never been found, and its actual existence is in doubt. Nevertheless, it is a history Shakespeare had access to and for the purpose of historical "accuracy" he includes the names in his drama. The nameless murders in the Clarence scene, as discussed above, are in some ways larger than their physical being. They are allegorical agents for divine justice and instruments of Richard's evil. In this case, their names are no more relevant than the specific style of weapon used to stab Clarence. The murderers of the princes are no more than men who live by villainous deeds; they receive no larger meaning because when all the killings in Richard III are considered, the murder of the princes is the only one where the victims are wholly without guilt. The description of the murders is intended to communicate the horror of the deed, one so evil that even the hearts of these "bloody dogs" are softened. Like the murderers of Clarence, Dighton and Forest are plagued by conscience and remorse; they commit the deed, but when they report back to Tyrrell, they "Wept like two children."

Two more nameless murderers show up after they kill the Duke of Gloucester on his sick bed in Act III, Scene 2 of *Henry VI, Part II.* Unlike the murderers of Clarence, they only have four lines, but in those lines they foreshadow the killers in Richard III. Like the killers of Clarence in *Richard III*, they are hired killers in the employ of the Duke of Suffolk and like the killers of Clarence, they come to regret their action:

> First Murderer
> Run to my Lord of Suffolk; let him know
> We have dispatch'd the duke, as he commanded.
> Second Murderer
> O that it were to do! What have we done?
> Didst ever hear a man so penitent?
>
> (HVI, II, III, 2, 1-4)

Most of the featured hired killers in Shakespeare's canon show regret and remorse. The only conscienceless killers are found in *Macbeth* and they are revengers, not mercenaries. It is interesting to note that the killers of Banquo are in the employ of Shakespeare's most guilt-ridden villain as if Macbeth absorbs all the guilt of the killings he initiates. The others killers who feel guilt are in the employ of the two of Shakespeare's most conscienceless villains, Richard III and the Duke of Suffolk. The chief difference between the murderers in *Macbeth* and all the others is that they are personally as well as financially invested in killing Banquo. They have been convinced that Banquo is the author of their misery; the fact that they will be financially rewarded for killing him is a happy coincidence. Shakespeare's other killers have no relationship with their victims. Like modern "hitmen," they do not select their victims; they act on orders. Shakespeare develops these killers as different from the psychopathic, i.e., conscienceless, men who employ them. None of them would fit the characteristics of the professional hitman we experience today. The professional hitman is untroubled by his actions; he has chosen a profession and has found ways to rationalize it, to accommodate his moral feelings. In his study of professional killers, Alfred Blumstein, Ph.D., president of the American Society of Criminology and Dean of the Heinz School of Public Policy and Management at Carnegie-Mellon University in Pittsburgh, reports that a "rush of exhilaration is often experienced by criminals and is associated with risk-taking."[4] Otherwise, the professional killer looks at his work as just another job, at times unpleasant but a financial necessity. Shakespeare's "little killers" are not professionals irrespective of how they are described by their employers. They are troubled by conscience, not so much as a result of killing, but as a result of who they are killing. Like soldiers, they kill on orders and without fear of punishment, but also like soldiers they retain a morality that differentiates between the enemy and the innocent. Unlike the banal evil of the SS guards in the Concentration Camps who were able to blur the distinction between enemy and innocent, Shakespeare's little killers, although committing terrible deeds, retain that core humanity that indict them and perhaps lead them to future mercy and salvation.

Notes

1. Gürle, F. Meltem. "Reasoning with the Murderer: The killing of

Clarence in Richard III," *Journal of the Wooden O*, Volume 11, Southern Utah UP, 2011, 56. https://www.academia.edu/3319057/Reasoning_with_the_Murderer_The_Killing_of_Clarence_in_Richard_III

2. Ibid, 58.

3. Ibid, 57.

4. Montefiore, Simon Sebag. "The Thrill of the Kill: Inside the head of a Russian hit man. Mysterious thrills or doing God's will?" *Psychology Today*: published on January 1, 1993 - last reviewed on June 20, 2012. Accessed at https://www.psychologytoday.com/articles/200910/the-thrill-the-kill.

MOBS

Mob action in the form of riot and rebellion was a constant concern of England's ruling and merchant classes. During Shakespeare's time there was a steady stream of propaganda that flowed from the pulpit and the pamphleteers cautioning the populace against being deluded by charismatic and self-interested rabble-rousers and joining in violent uprising against authority. In the 1587 "authorized homily on rebellion, designed to be read regularly 'unto the people, that thereby they both learn their duty towards God, their Prince, and their neighbors,' it is asserted that the multitude is the backbone of insurrection" and charges the multitude to reject the support of the "restless ambitious."[1] In 1607, Robert Wilkinson published his *Sermon Preached at North-Hampton...upon occasion of the late Rebellion and Riots in those parts committed.* The rebellion referred to is the violent eruption, referred to as the Newton Rebellion, resulting from the enclosure of lands, a practice by landholders to restrict the general populace from the use of previously common land for farming and grazing. Roughly 1000 participated in the protest, knocking down hedges and filling in trenches until the gentry reinforced by Royal forces suppressed the rebellion, killing between 40 and 50 people and executing their leaders. Wilkinson acknowledge that the riot occurred as a result of the "excessive covetousness of some (the gentry) and the extreme want of others (the commoners). He cautioned against both the "oppression of the mighty, and rebellion of the many," noting that such "mischief" has resulted in the miscarriage of "many flourishing kingdoms and countries."[2] In 1586, a pamphlet entitled The *English Myrror*, George Whetstone likened the multitude to "a barrel that is ready to receive every liquor" and easy prey to the manipulation of "the envious man."[3] While the 21th century reader will perhaps recall the revolts of Jack Straw or Wat Tyler or Jack Cade and, perhaps remember them in colorful or fanciful ways, the common man in England experienced the reality of civil disorder in quite a different way. The fact is that London alone, according to Roger B. Manning, endured thirty-five general outbreaks of disorder between 1581 and 1602. The country as a whole saw hundreds of riots specifically "protesting enclosures of commons and wastes, drainage of fens and disafforestation" between 1530 and 1640.[4] Violent riots were a fact of life and a particular nightmare for the country's gentry and rising middle class. The rioters tended to represent the lower sort, cottage artisans and common wage laborers, who were being squeezed economically by the changing socio-economic climate.

As pervasive as the sermons and pamphlets were, such generalized injunctions against insurrection that appeared throughout the reigns of Elizabeth and James were probably less impactful than the propaganda from the London stage which had the greater opportunity to influence the common masses. Riots and their consequences were familiar to the man in the theater's pit. Shakespeare took up the subject of mobs in three of his plays and, unsurprisingly, the mobs didn't come off very well. I say unsurprisingly because it was well understood that drama would either speak to the Regime's interests or it would be denied a stage. But it is a little known fact that Shakespeare was also very much of the rising middle class, one of the Stratford's commodity traders in corn. He, therefore, had an economic as well as a "patriotic" interest in suppressing mob actions and presenting mobs in his plays in an unfavorable light. His imaging of the crowd took on the characteristics of a distinct character: a "the blunt monster with uncounted heads" and a "still-discordant wavering multitude" as they are called in *Henry VI, Part 2*. (Induction, 17-18). Martius calls the mob a "beast with many heads." (C, 4, 1, 1-2). The images are referential to the many-headed monsters of mythology: Cerberus, the Chimaera, and the Hydra.

Chimera

Cerberus

Hydra

Images from Wilki-Commons

In myth-psychology, the Hydra in particular is associated with "the lust that devours the soul" so Shakespeare may be suggesting that the mob's lust for "stuff" as seen in *Henry VI, Part 2* and *Coriolanus* destroys their reason and humanity.[5] The Hydra in mythology was also a particularly dangerous monster and Shakespeare in selecting its image to characterize the crowd emphasized the crowds violent and uncontrollable nature. Additionally, it takes a great hero to suppress or destroy the multi-headed monsters: it takes Hercules to suppress Cerberus and to destroy the Hydra; Bellerophon mounted on Pegasus is required to kill the Chimera. In Shakespeare's *Julius Caesar*, the great rhetorician, Brutus, is unable to soothe the mob and in *Coriolanus*, Martius, the greatest warrior in Rome, is unable to defeat the mob. Only the name of the great English King, Henry V, is capable of putting down Cade's rebels in *Henry VI, Part II*.

The crowds in Shakespeare come in three forms: protestors in *Coriolanus*, rioters in *Julius Caesar*, and rebels in *Henry VI, Part II*. The protestors in *Coriolanus* are leaderless, but they are heavily influenced even manipulated by their governmental representatives, the tribunes, Sicinius and Brutus. The play opens with the angry, nameless Citizens coming on stage "with staves, clubs, and other weapons," obviously prepared for violence. The first speaker is the anonymous First Citizen is not so much a leader as choral master for the crowd. "You are all resolved rather to die than to famish?" he asks. "Resolved. Resolved," the crowd responds. "you know Caius Marcius is chief enemy to the people," he says. "We know't, we know't," they reply. Then the First Citizen concludes, "Let us kill him, and we'll have corn at our own price. Is't a verdict?" and the crowd call out, "let it be done! (C, I, 1, 3-9). A Second Citizen speaks up for Caius Marcius, reminding all of his good service to Rome, but the First Citizen, though conceding this, is unwilling to forgive his haughty treatment of the common people. They are interrupted by the entrance of the patrician, Menenius Agrippa, who tries to calm the crowd. The First Citizen again serves as spokesperson, reasonably listing the grievances of the plebeians:

> They ne'er cared for us
> yet: suffer us to famish, and their store-houses
> crammed with grain; make edicts for usury, to
> support usurers; repeal daily any wholesome act
> established against the rich, and provide more
> piercing statutes daily, to chain up and restrain
> the poor. If the wars eat us not up, they will; and
> there's all the love they bear us.
>
> (C, I, 1, 66-73)

As Menenius reasons with the crowd, Caius Marcius comes upon the scene and with discourteous fury rejects their grievances and voices his desire to kill them all. Marcius, however, also brings news that soothes the anger of the crowd: they are to have five tribunes to represent their interests with the Senate. That, along with the fact that they are, at heart according to Menenius, "passing cowardly" disbands the mob and quells the protest.

Later, after Marcius' great victory at Corioli and his return to Rome, the tribunes plot his downfall, knowing he will never yield in any fashion to the needs of the plebeians. When Marcius, now renamed Coriolanus, comes up for consulship, he is required to win the support of the multitude he despises. Grudgingly, he summits to their questions and grudgingly, they lend him their support until, provoked publicly by Sicinius at the end of Act III. When reminded of his past injuries to the people and responding to his rage at their tribunes, the mob turns in an instant upon Coriolanus, first calling for his death, but then settling for his banishment from Rome. When Coriolanus turns traitor and threatens Rome, the multitude, fearing his wrath, turns again, denying they had ill will toward him.

> First Citizen
> For mine own part,
> When I said, banish him, I said 'twas pity.
> Second Citizen
> And so did I.
> Third Citizen
> And so did I; and, to say the truth, so did very
> many of us: that we did, we did for the best; and
> though we willingly consented to his banishment, yet
> it was against our will.
>
> (C, IV, 6, 139-45)

Cominius, Rome's chief consul, contemptuously responds, "Ye re goodly things, you voices!" His comment shows the protesters for what they are: all words without action. The mob in Coriolanus is appropriately anonymous because the individual members have subsumed their individuality in the herd mentality. They have no individual opinions so their voices raised in collective assent is no more than parroting the voices of one another. They have no courage so they take no action; they speak collective so they avoid any personal accountability. They show themselves in Act IV to be worthy of the contempt Coriolanus shows for them in Act I.

The mob in Julius Caesar is ready to act. They represent the kind of mob we are most familiar from the 21st century riots that seem to occur with frightening regularity. The behavior of the mob in Julius Caesar has been extensively studied in the 20th century by sociologists led by the work of Gustave le Bon and is remarkably consistent with those of contemporary rioters. Unlike a rebellion which we will consider shortly, the riot is a relatively self-contained and time-limited event. It has no clear leader, but the riot is precipitated by an emotionally charged event that brings people together in one place and can be sparked inflammatory rhetoric or acts. Because the rioting mob is leaderless, it is also goalless, beyond venting its anger and frustration. It achieves this catharsis through acts of vandalism, theft, and violence. Being both leaderless and goalless, the rioters often splinter off into small units that act independent of one another, based on group suggestion and the availability of suitable targets. These smaller units, however, never become small enough to weaken the deindividuation that is essential to mob action. During deindividuation, the member of the mob yields his or her individual values and norms and conforms to the behavior exhibited by others in the group. While an individual might never consider breaking someone's window in the normal course of events, if caught in the frenzy of a herd mentality, that same individual will gleefully break the window because they feel no individual responsibility for the act.

The citizen's riot in Julius Caesar demonstrated all of these dynamics. The crowd first gathered at the Forum in Act I, scene 2. The assassins, led by Brutus, determine to go before the multitude, who are "beside themselves with fear" (JC, III, 1, 180) to "appease" them by explaining their action against Caesar. Brutus speaks first to the assembled crowd and succeeds in winning the crowds support. Antony then enters with Caesar's body for the express purpose of delivering a eulogy, but instead he cleverly turns the multitude from approval of Caesar's assassination to anger against the assassins. As in Coriolanus, the crowd is shown to be fickle and easily persuaded, given more to appeals to emotion than to reason. Whipped into a frenzy by Antony's inciting rhetoric, the crowd cries out against the conspirators, "Revenge! About! Seek! Burn! Fire! Kill! Slay! / Let not a traitor live!" (JC, III, 2, 204-5). Similar to the protestors in Coriolanus, the mob in Julius Caesar does not follow a single leader, but is instead influenced by a self-serving and ambitious man to act in violent and destructive ways. Antony does not tell the mob to do this or go there; instead he is the spark to ignite crowd anger and once ignited, the crowd moves and acts independent of Antony. As the enraged mob moves out into the city, he says, "Now let it work. Mischief, thou art afoot, / Take thou what course thou wilt!" (JC,

III, 2, 260). As in Coriolanus, individual members of the mob are never identified; they are only First Citizen, Second Citizen, etc. thus reminding the audience that they are unimportant except as a collective entity. They have achieved deindividuation. Initially, they have a specific target: "fire the traitors' houses," but this quickly degenerates into madness as Shakespeare takes pains to show in the following scene. The mob encounters Cinna the Poet in the street, surround him, and badger him with questions. When he reveals his name, which is the same name as one of the conspirators, the First Citizen calls out, "Tear him to pieces; he's a conspirator." Cinna protests, "I am Cinna the poet, I am Cinna the poet." And the Fourth Citizen, showing the madness of the mob now caught up in the intoxication of destruction, responds, "Tear him for his bad verses, tear him for his bad verses." (JC, III, 3, 28-31).

The final mob type seen in Shakespeare is the rebellious mob that is found in *Henry VI, Part 2*, Act 4 under the leadership of Jack Cade. The rebellious mob shares aspects of both the protest and the riot. Like the protestors, the rebels are more homogenous, sharing particular grievances and goals. In *Coriolanus*, the protestors are seeking bread. In *Henry VI*, they are seeking to eliminate the current regimen they believe oppresses them and is responsible for the unequal distribution of wealth that disadvantages them. The protestors in Coriolanus are leaderless and undifferentiated like the rioters in *Julius Caesar*. In *Henry VI*, the rebels have a leader in the person of Jack Cade and are to a degree, individualized in that Shakespeare assigns them proper names. We meet George Bevis, John Holland, Dick the butcher, and Smith the weaver. Bevis and Holland in Scene 2 explain the people's perception of the cause of the rebellion:

> BEVIS
> *I tell thee, Jack Cade the clothier means to dress*
> *the commonwealth, and turn it, and set a new nap upon it.*
> HOLLAND
> *So he had need, for 'tis threadbare. Well, I say it*
> *was never merry world in England since gentlemen came up.*
> BEVIS
> *O miserable age! virtue is not regarded in handicrafts-men.*

HOLLAND
The nobility think scorn to go in leather aprons.
BEVIS
Nay, more, the king's council are no good workmen.
HOLLAND
True; and yet it is said, labour in thy vocation;
which is as much to say as, let the magistrates be
labouring men; and therefore should we be
magistrates.

(Henry VI, Part II, IV, 2, 5-18)

Dick the butcher and Smith the weaver offer different information. They know Cade for the madcap that he is, but they follow him, not so much because they have specific grievances against the government as expressed by Bevis and Holland, but for sheer hell-raising. While Cade is making outrageous promises to the rebels, Dick's first thought is "let's kill all the lawyers." (*Henry VI, Part II*, IV, 2, 76). Immediately on the heels of this declaration, a rebel group hustles the Clerk of Chatham and in a scene similar to the murder of Cinna the poet in *Julius Caesar*, the poor man is condemned for being able to write his name and hanged "with his pen and ink-horn about his neck." (*Henry VI, Part II*, IV, 2, 109-10). This is followed by the repulse of the King's forces led by Sir Humphrey and William Stafford. In the wake of their victory, the rebels move on to London Bridge, burning and looting along the way. While the citizens "fly and forsake their houses, / The rascal people, thirsting after prey, / Join with the traitor, and they jointly swear / To spoil the city." (*Henry VI, Part II*, IV, 4, 50-3). With their victory of the King's men, the rebels are emboldened and Cade's madness blossoms. He declares "henceforward it shall be treason for any that calls / me other than Lord Mortimer." than has one of his soldiers killed for unwittingly calling him Jack Cade. When Lord Say, a particular target of the rebels, is captured, Cade and the crowd torment the man and not satisfied to simply kill him, they display their increasing savagery by parading his head through the streets on a spike. Now at the peak of its fury, the mob is confronted by the Duke of Buckingham and Lord Clifford who, acting as emissaries of the King, offer pardon to those rebels who break off the rebellion and return to their homes. Suddenly and inexplicably the crowd turns, crying out "God save the king! God save the king!" Cade, appalled by the sudden turn of the crowd, rebukes them:

> *I thought ye would never have given out*
> *these arms till you had recovered your ancient*
> *freedom: but you are all recreants and dastards,*
> *and delight to live in slavery to the nobility. Let*
> *them break your backs with burthens, take your*
> *houses over your heads, ravish your wives and*
> *daughters before your faces: for me, I will make*
> *shift for one; and so, God's curse light upon you*
> *all!*
>
> *(Henry VI, Part II, IV, 8, 25-32)*

The crowd showing the same fickleness seen in the protestors of *Coriolanus* and the rioters in *Julius Caesar*, the crowd responds "We'll follow Cade, we'll follow Cade!" (*Henry VI, Part II*, IV, 8, 33) Then Clifford, using the argument that this civil strife invites French aggression and threatens the safety of all England, turns the crowd again: "A Clifford! a Clifford! we'll follow the king and Clifford." Cade, now aware that all is lost, bitterly comments:

> *Was ever feather so lightly blown to and fro as this*
> *multitude? The name of Henry the Fifth hales them*
> *to an hundred mischiefs, and makes them leave me*
> *desolate.*
>
> *(Henry VI, Part II, IV, 8, 55-8)*

The three plays that feature crowds of commoners all show them in an unfavorable light and, along with the generally mocking or comedic portrayal of commoners in Shakespeare's other plays, have led several critics to decide that the playwright was generally anti-democratic and contemptuous of what Philostrate calls "hard-handed men ... which never labour'd in their minds," in *A Midsummer Night's Dream*. Walt Whitman, for example, wrote the Shakespeare's plays were "poisonous to the idea of the pride and dignity of the common people." Ernest Crosby similarly opines that "having a poor opinion of the lower classes taken man by man, Shakespeare thinks, if anything still worse of them taken *en masse.*" Leo Tolstoy and George Bernard Shaw shared similar positions.[6] Shakespeare, however, is not without his defenders. Such notables as Samuel Coleridge and A.C. Bradley argue that Shakespeare's "poor and humble are, almost without exception sound and sweet, faithful and pitiful."[7] The middle position is, as suggested by Brents Stirling, that "Shakespeare's plebeians in the mass are anarchic and dangerous, but that as individuals they are often lovable."[8] Stirling, I think, is most correct in his assessment that Shakespeare's mobs reflect the general fear of collective action evident throughout the reigns of Elizabeth and James, a fear not exclusive to the aristocrats of the time, but one shared by the theater going public. Recognizing how easily mobs can be manipulated by charismatic demagogues like Cade and Antony, Shakespeare does seem to subscribe to the opinion of Secretary Robert Cecil who warned against "libelous railers" who "move the common sort to sedition":

> I have no fear of men of worth; when has England felt any harm by soldiers or gentleman or men of worth? The State has ever found them truest. Some Jack Cade or Jack Straw and such rascals are those who endanger the kingdom.[9]

In evaluating Shakespeare's portrayal of mobs and rebellion, one may also want to consider the response of officialdom to historian John Hayward's *The First Part of the Life and Raigne of King Henrie IIII* depicting the reign of Richard II. Placed in the Tower for sedition in 1601, Hayward was asked "Might [you] think that this history would not be very dangerous to come upon the common people?"[10] Shakespeare had covered similar ground without repercussion in 1595, but the failed Essex rebellion of 1601 made the nobles sufficiently nervous that they considered Hayward's history seditious and accused the work as "cunningly insinuating that the same abuses being now in the realm were in the days of Richard II the like course might be taken for redress."[11] Considering that Shakespeare's company was hired to perform a special staging of his *Richard II* on the eve of the Essex rebellion, it was perhaps Shakespeare's tradition of denouncing rebellious mobs in his dramas that allowed him to avoid the same fate as Hayward. Because political security may have contributed to his negative portrayal of mobs, it is perhaps unfair to denounce Shakespeare as anti-democratic.

It can also be argued that Shakespeare was influenced by both the dictates of his source materials and by the demands of the dramatic form. Stirling observes that it is wrong to assume that when Shakespeare lifts a scene from the source material, that it is done without reference to political significance or Shakespeare's political disposition. As an example, Stirling points to the scene in *Julius Caesar* involving the murder of Cinna the Poet by the mob. Stirling notes that this scene is just one from Plutarch that could have been chosen to demonstrate the chaos that followed the assassination of Caesar. But in Stirling's words, "Choice itself can be emphasis; Shakespeare could have omitted the scene entirely."[12] By selecting and embellishing the Cinna scene from Plutarch, Shakespeare highlights the mindless brutality of the mob and by association, condemns the indifference of Antony to the wellbeing of Rome and its citizens when he incites the mob to vengeance.

It is obvious to the objective reader that the mobs in *Henry VI, Part 2* and *Julius Caesar* are more "colorful and alive" than they appear in Holinshed or North. Cade and his rebels are more buffoonish in Shakespeare than in Holinshed and the Plebeians in *Coriolanus* are more ascorbic than in Plutarch. Are these portrayals drawn from Shakespeare's contempt for the commons or only for the dramatic impact resulting from such portrayals? Stirling suggests the latter. Returning to the case of Cinna the Poet, his murder by the mob is surely a condemnation of the mob, but more importantly, it heightens the drama by personalizing the object of the violence. Descriptions of burning buildings and of beatings in the street have less dramatic impact on an audience than the witnessing of the murder of an innocent man.

Similarly, it is noteworthy that after Cade, Shakespeare's earliest mob, the members of the mobs remain nameless. By robbing them of their names, I would suggest that Shakespeare intends to depersonalize the mob. Cade and his mob invites a degree of ambiguity: they have names, they can be funny, but they are also brutal and fickle. By taking away the mob's individuality in *Julius Caesar* and *Coriolanus*, the members are less identifiable as commons, becoming less ambiguous and sympathetic. The mob, in the final analysis becomes, as suggested at the beginning of this chapter, a character independent of its individual members. As an independent character, the mob is classless and, to a large degree, apolitical. For the mob, everything becomes personnel: in *Henry VI, Part II* they are driven by a desire for more stuff; in *Julius Caesar*, a desire for revenge; and in *Coriolanus*, their hatred on one man. I would suggest that Shakespeare, by deliberately discarding individualization of the mob members, is consciously disassociating the commons for whom he has a degree of (condescending?) affection from the mob, releasing the individual mob members from responsibly by fusing them into a single monstrous entity.

Notes

1. Stirling, Brents. "Shakespeare's Mob Scenes: A Reinterpretation," *Huntington Library Quarterly*, Vol. 8, No. 3 (May, 1945), 214.

2. Ibid, 224.

3. Ibid, 214.

4. Manning, Robert B. *Village Revolts: Social Protest and Popular Disturbances in England, 1509-1640*. New York: Oxford University Press, 1988,

5. Glaveanu, Vlad Petre. "From Mythology to Psychology – an essay on the Archaic Psychology in Greek Myths." *European Journal of Psychology*, Vol 1, No (2005). Accessed on-line at http://ejop.psychopen.eu/article/view/351/html .

6. Stirling, Brents. "Anti-democracy in Shakespeare: A Re-survey." *Modern Language Quarterly*, 1941, 487-8.

7. Ibid, 489.

8. Ibid.

9. Ibid, 496.

10. Ibid.

11. Ibid, 497.

12. Ibid, 500.

...AND A MONSTER

Throughout his literary career, Shakespeare introduced the theater-going public to an array of monsters in human form from consciousless killers like Richard III and Aaron to the malignancy of Edmund and Iago and on to the sympathetic, if malevolent, Macbeth and Shylock. In the early modern period, the pejorative "monster" was applied to the large and mythical inhuman creatures represented by dragons and sea serpents, but was also associated with genetically and developmentally disabled or deformed people who were often pressed into popular entertainment venues such as "monster spectacles." The term "monster" is sprinkled throughout Shakespeare. In a few instances it is used in conjunction with the idea of a sea serpent. More often it is used as a metaphor for death (*Cymbeline*, 5.3.70-72), jealousy (*Othello*, 3.3.165-67), envy (*Pericles*, 4.Cho.11-13), ingratitude (*King Lear*, 1.5.40 and *Coriolanus*, 2.3.9-13), and the multitude (2 *Henry IV*, Ind.15-20). In Shakespeare's final independent drama, The *Tempest*, he gives us one of his two literal "monsters" the first being Bottom's transformation to man-ass hybrid and the island dweller, Caliban. In Caliban, Shakespeare anticipates the later expansion of the monster definition to include all inhuman creatures, even otherwise human beings who commit heinous deeds that go beyond normal human limits on cruelty or evil doings.[1] Using this expanded definition, many if not most of the characters covered in this book qualify for this label. Nevertheless, Caliban is the only character explicitly labeled a monster, and as such, he merits special consideration.

In the dramatis personæ of *The Tempest*, Caliban is identified as "a savage and deformed slave." The audience learns of him before he appears on stage when Prospero describes him as "A freckled whelp hag-born--not honour'd with/ A human shape." (*T*, I, 2, 336-7). When Prospero calls him forth, he terms Caliban his slave and the audience must surely have been on the edge of their seats to see what this creature would look like. Unfortunately, there is little to guide the actor as to the actual physical appearance of the character. Late in the play, Prospero says of Caliban, "He is as disproportion'd in his manners/ As in his shape." (*T*, I, 2, 286-6). This comment and the former suggest deformity and a not quite human shape, but what exactly this means is open to imagination. He is the offspring, says Prospero, of an Algerian witch named Sycorax and a devil. On the stage he has been portrayed a wild man, a deformed man (should we think of Richard III?), a man-beast, and a mix of fish and man. Caliban's physical appearance on stage is most likely guided by the director and/or actor based on their interpretation of the character and the play as a whole. Caliban can be played for laughs or for pathos; he can be foolish or malicious.

Images of Caliban:

    1. *William Hogarth, 1736.*

    2. *A charcoal drawing by Charles Buchel of Herbert Beerbohm Tree as Caliban in a 1904 production of Shakespeare's The Tempest.*

    3. *Frank Benson playing Caliban in The Tempest at the Shakespeare Memorial Theatre in the early 1900s.*

    4. *Fyodor Paramonov as Caliban, Maly Theatre (Moscow), 1905*

    5. *Caliban, 2010 Stratford Shakespeare Festival.*

    6. *Corey Jones as Caliban in the Utah Shakespeare Festival's 2013 production of The Tempest*

Constance Jordan has suggested that Caliban's role highlights the contradiction between the natural and civil worlds. Derived from Aristotelian theory, the "natural, bestial man" serves as the baseline against which civilized man is evaluated. Driven by instinct, the natural man "was incapable of rational, deliberative choice and was therefore... a figure outside and prior to law and morality but necessary for their implementation."[2] Caliban's history is one of isolation from civilization until Prospero appears on his island. Prior to Prospero, Caliban's only contact with humanity is in the person of his mother, who dies sometime before Prospero's arrival. Caliban, when discovered by Prospero, is benign. He describes their meeting:

> When thou cam'st first,
> Thou strok'st me and made much of me, wouldst give me
> Water with berries in 't, and teach me how
> To name the bigger light and how the less,
> That burn by day and night. And then I loved thee,
> And showed thee all the qualities o' th' isle,
> The fresh springs, brine pits, barren place and fertile.
>
> (T, I, 2, 397-405)

He was without language, considered a cardinal sign of the civilized. Miranda, Prospero's young daughter, says to Caliban:

> I pitied thee,
> Took pains to make thee speak, taught thee each hour
> One thing or other. When thou didst not, savage,
> Know thine own meaning, but wouldst gabble like
> A thing most brutish, I endowed thy purposes
> With words that made them known. But thy vile race,
> Though thou didst learn, had that in't which good natures
> Could not abide to be with.
>
> (T, I, 2, 424-34)

All this harmony came to a sudden end when Caliban, according to Prospero "didst seek to violate/The honor of my child." (*T*, I, 2, 416–17).

In exchange for his proffered friendship of his island's invaders, Caliban is "adopted" into Prospero's little family with Prospero setting himself up as a father figure and Miranda as precocious sister to the "pathetic" island dweller. Up to the point of the attempted rape, he is accepted as a part of the family, but I would argue, more as a pet than as a child or sibling. Prospero ignores or discounts Caliban's masculinity and the instinctual call of sexuality, so he never takes the trouble to attempt to indoctrinate him to normal social conventions. Prospero suggests Caliban had the property to learn, but that his basic nature would override any nurture. In his arrogance, Caliban has learned the language of the Europeans, but knows nothing of morality. Is this Prospero's failure for neglecting to teach Caliban right from wrong or is the "natural man" incapable of overruling or subordinating his instinctual drives? Either way, the assault on Miranda introduces gendered relations into Prospero's little family unit and transforms the natural world into a primitive version of civil society. What had previously been a benign patriarchy turns suddenly into an oppressive tyranny. Prospero accepts no responsibility for his failure in nurturing (socializing) Caliban. The civilized man is compelled to subordinate the natural man for his own safety.

In a way, Shakespeare's Caliban anticipates the philosophical argument to come between Thomas Hobbes and Jean-Jacques Rousseau concerning the nature of man found in primitive or natural state. In his most famous work, *Leviathan* (1660), Hobbes painted man in the primitive state and selfish, violent and brutal whose life is destined to be "solitary, poor, nasty, brutish, and short." Although Hobbes frames his conclusion through logic, it is consistent with the Christian thinking found in 1 *Corinthians* 2 where St. Paul uses the word natural to refer to someone still in his original (sinful) state. They are led by instinct rather than by the spirit of God and instinctually choose sin. Hobbes used his view of natural man as the justification for strong, authoritarian government and the value of education and progress in improving the human condition. Rousseau, on the other hand, took an opposite opinion on natural man. Writing in *Discourse on the Origin of Inequality* (1754), Rousseau posited that "... [N]othing is so gentle as man in his primitive state, when placed by nature at an equal distance from the stupidity of brutes and the fatal enlightenment of civil man."[3] Rousseau believed that man has instinctive disinclination to witness suffering which counters the instinctive drive toward self-interest. Thus, he argued instinct and emotion, when not distorted by the unnatural limitations of civilization, would balance each other making man both free and good in the state of nature. Rousseau focuses on natural man's aggression and acquisitiveness, but does not touch on natural man's instinctive sexual drive. Applying his argument that empathy counters selfishness in the natural man, can we extrapolate that a female's rejection of a male's advances would be received by the male with a shrug because he would be disinclined to witness, let alone cause, the female discomfort? Or does Rousseau believe that in nature, the female would have the same sexual instinct of the male and would be disinclined to reject any male's advance? Is, in his opinion, sexual morality or regulation or choice simply a social construct that artificially creates a conflict between natural inclination and acceptable behavior?

Shakespeare's Caliban, at first glance, conforms to the Hobbesian view of natural man. He has attempted to molest Miranda. He constantly curses Prospero. He draws Trinculo and Stephano into a plot to murder Prospero. I would posit, however, he is a monster more sinned against than sinning. In his assault on Miranda, one is left to wonder if he had any idea that his advances would be met with rejection and recriminations. Prospero and Miranda took pains to teach Caliban language, but there is no indication of moral teaching. This is to be expected because they never viewed Caliban as anything higher than an animal (or monster) capable of learning tricks of language and a few simple concepts such as the difference between the sun and moon. Prospero and Miranda rejection of Caliban's humanity is, however, called into question when Miranda, seeing Ferdinand for the first time, exclaims "This is the third man that e'er I saw, the first that e'er I sigh'd for" (*T*, I, 2, 445-447). Since she says Ferdinand is the third man, her father and Caliban have to be the other two, but later she tells Ferdinand that she has only seen two men, her father and him (*T*, III, 1, 50-52) and thus excludes Caliban. In any case, Caliban's humanity is confirmed by his maternity. He is the offspring of a human mother and even if his father is, as Prospero contends, "a devil," he is at worst a human-devil hybrid who would have at least the human potential for goodness, even if his devil-side gave him a propensity for evil. This raises again the nature/nurture agreement already discussed in considering the character of Richard III.

Richard, of course, was fully human, if deformed. In the Medieval tradition, Richard's external deformity would have been taken as an external sign of his internal moral deformity. By the time of Shakespeare, this tradition was in decline. Richard's deformity could, instead, be seen as a cause of his evil behavior as the physical deformity would set him apart from all others and making him the object of distain and derision. Caliban's case is different: he is unaware that he is deformed, has never felt the rejection of others, has been able to live his life according to his own dictates. He has a sensuous appreciation of natural beauty, telling Trinculo and Stephano:

> *"Sometimes a thousand twangling instruments*
> *Will hum about mine ears; and sometime voices,*
> *That if I then had waked after long sleep,*
> *Will make me sleep again, and then in dreaming*
> *The clouds methought would open and show riches*
> *Ready to drop upon me, that when I waked*
> *I cried to dream again."*
>
> *(T, III, 2, 135-144)*

If fact, his early life seems to support Rousseau's thesis regarding natural man. Then comes Prospero.

Caliban accepts him and his daughter warmly. It is only after his failed assault on Miranda that he grows malicious. Prospero, using his magical superiority, converts Caliban from family pet to slave. Solicitous paternity is followed by brutal tyranny. Understandably, the previously free and happy Caliban is rebellious and resentful. From Caliban's perspective, he is "subject to a tyrant, a/ sorcerer, that by his cunning hath cheated [him] of the island." (*T*, III, 2, 42-44). Prospero's condescension toward and contempt for Caliban is founded in the European attitude toward primitive (that is, non-European) man. Post-colonial theorists have suggested that Caliban's experience reflects that of the indigenous inhabitants of the New World, many of whom were welcoming to the strange European explorers who were arriving on their shores with increasing frequency during the 16th century. The English experience in the New World progressed slower and less aggressively than that of the Portuguese and Spanish. Although their interests were focused on maritime expansion, the English did feel an obligation to civilize and Christianize the native populations. Their hope was to achieve these goals without coercion or violence, but their Anglo-centric worldview compelled them, in the end, to see the native population as savage subaltern "others" who had to be compelled if not persuaded to adopt the superior civilized social order. As was the case with Prospero and Caliban, the English first adopted a paternalistic role relative to their neighbors, but quickly established authoritarian tyranny when the native populations failed to meet the English standards of behavior.[4]

Finally, in a play rife with mirror images, Caliban can be read as a mirror image of Prospero himself. Prospero has been overthrown and exiled by his brother. Prospero in turn overthrows Caliban as ruler of the island and enslaves him. Both Prospero and Caliban seek revenge for the wrong done to them and to have restored what was taken from them. Prospero being the civilized man, ultimately rejects taking revenge on his enemies and Caliban, being the simple natural man fails because he places his trust foolishly in the basest of allies. In a psychological reading, Caliban has been associated with Prospero's id, the magician's baser nature, and Arial with his superego. This interpretation is played out in one of the strangest adaptations of a Shakespeare play, the 1956 science fiction classic, *Forbidden Planet*.

In this rendering, a Starship is dispatched to a distant planet, Altair IV, to determine the fate of a 20-year-old expedition. When the ship arrives, the crew discovers that there is only one survivor of the original expeditionary team, Dr. Edward Morbius and his daughter, Altaira. Morbius informs the new arrivals that an unknown "planetary force" killed nearly everyone and finally vaporized their starship, the Bellerophon, as the last survivors tried to return to Earth. Only Morbius, his wife (who later died of natural causes) and their daughter Altaira were somehow immune. Morbius further assures his would-be rescuers that he is safe and comfortable, serviced by a robot (the Arial analogue) he "tinkered" together, and has no desire to return to Earth. The Starship commander, John Adams, is under orders to return with any Bellerophon survivors and plans to take Morbius back, with or without his consent. Morbius warns/threatens that should Adams attempt to follow through with his plan, the Starship and its crew may call forth the same unknown "planetary force" that destroyed the Bellerophon. True to the prediction, first the Starship and then its crew are attacked by an invisible force that destroys equipment and tears crewmembers "limb from limb."

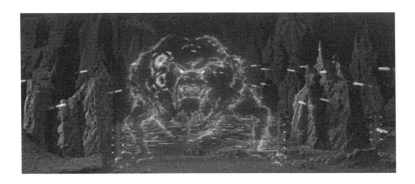

The invisible id monster illuminated during an attack on the Starship,
Forbidden Planet (MGM), 1954

In the wake of the attacks, Morbius is compelled to reveal to the history of the planet. 200,000 years before, the planet was occupied by a highly advanced race, the Krell, who mysteriously died out suddenly in a single night. In a Krell laboratory Morbius shows Adams and the Starship's Medical Officer the "plastic educator", a device capable of measuring and enhancing intellectual capacity. It was this device that permanently doubled Morbius's intellect, enabled him to build Robby and the other "technological marvels" of his home with information obtained from a Krell library. It is only later, when the Doctor uses the plastic educator on himself that the real fate of the Krell and the origin of the planet's lethal invisible force is uncovered. The Krell advanced to the point where they were able to materialize thought; that is, they were able to create a material object by thinking it into being. Morbius, also has acquired this power. What the Krell and Morbius failed to consider was the unconscious operation of the mind, the Freudian id, where the baser emotions and desires reside. When they slept, the Krell ids produced monsters that literally destroyed their entire civilization in a single night. Similarly, when he sleeps, Morbius liberates his inner monster, his Caliban, to destroy those who oppose his will. His mind materialized the monster that attacks Adam's ship and, comes to destroy Adams and Altaira, who defies her father by falling in love with the Commander. Because the monster lives in Morbius's unconscious, he is unable to control it until he acknowledges it. Like Prospero, he must first say, "this thing of darkness I/ Acknowledge mine." (T, V, 1, 275-6). Once he recognizes responsibility for his monster, he is able to banish it although the effort costs him his life.

In the end, both Morbius and Prospero defeat their Calibans. Morbius destroys and is destroyed by his Caliban. Prospero defeats and punishes his Caliban, but then what? Prospero determines to return to Malian along with his daughter. He frees Arial, he forgives his old enemies, he casts away his staff and his book of magic, but what does he do with Caliban? As with so much about Caliban, the playgoer is left to fill in the blanks. And if the interpretation reflected in the *Forbidden Planet* is accurate, it is fully consistent that the fate and future of Caliban, the natural man, the base nature of man, the raw uncontrollable id is left to the unknowable unconscious.

Notes

1. Asma, Stephen T. (2009-09-16). *On Monsters: An Unnatural History of Our Worst Fears*. Oxford University Press. Kindle Edition, p. 6.
2. Jordan, Constance. *Shakespeare's Monarchies: Ruler and Subject in the Romances*. Cornell University Press, 1999, p. 171.

3. Rousseau, Jean-Jacques (1754), "Discourse on the Origin of Inequality, part two", The Basic Political Writings, Hackett, p. 64.
4. Oberg, M. L. (1999). Dominion and civility: English imperialism and Native America, 1585-1685. Cornell University Press, pp. 16-17.

Bibliography

Abbott, Mary. *Family Ties: English Families 1540-1920*. Routledge, 1993.

Alfar, Christina Leon," Looking for Goneril and Regan" in Fantasies of Female Evil (2003).

Allgaier, Johannes. "Is King Lear an Antiauthoritarian Play?" *PMLA*, Vol. 88, No. 5 (Oct., 1973), pp. 1035.

Aristotle. *History of Animals*, Book IX, part 1. [Online]. http://classics.mit.edu/Aristotle/history_anim.9.ix.html.

Asimov, Isaac. *Asimov's Guide to Shakespeare*. Avenel Books, 1970.

Asma, Stephen T. (2009-09-16). *On Monsters: An Unnatural History of Our Worst Fears*. Oxford University Press. Kindle Edition.

Bacon, Francis. *On Revenge*. http://people.brandeis.edu/~teuber/bacon.html .

Barber, C. L. *Shakespeare's Festive Comedy; A Study of Dramatic Form and its Relation to Social Custom*. Princeton University Press, 1990. http://rauldesaldanha.blogspot.com/2010/08/c-l-barber-shakespeares-festive-comedy.html

Barnet, Sylvan. "Coleridge on Shakespeare's Villains." *Shakespeare Quarterly* 7:1 (1956), 16.

Barnet, Sylvan, "*Titus Andronicus* on Stage and Screen" in *Shakespeare: The Tragedy of Titus Andronicus*, ed., Sylvan Barnet. Signet Classics, 2005).

Barr, Jane. "The Influence of Saint Jerome on Medieval Attitudes to Women [Online]." First published as Ch. 6, in *After Eve*, edited by Janet Martin Soskice, 1990. http://www.womenpriests.org/theology/barr.asp.

Bloom, Harold. *Shakespeare: The Invention of the Human*. Penguin 1998.

Boose, Lynda E. "Scolding Brides and Bridling Scolds: Taming the Women's Unruly Member." *Shakespeare Quarterly*. 42.2 (1991): 181.

Bowers, Fredson. *Elizabethan Revenge Tragedy*. Princeton University Press, 1940.

Bozeman, Theodore Dwight. *The Precisianist Strain: Disciplinary Religion & Antinomian Backlash in Puritanism until 1638*. The University of North Carolina Press, 2004.

Bradbrook, Muriel C. *Themes and Conventions of Elizabethan Tragedy*. Cambridge University Press, 1935.

Bradley, A. C. *Shakespearean Tragedy*. McMillian, 1981.

Brooke, Tucker. *The Romantic Iago*.
http://www.theatrehistory.com/british/iago001.html.

Bruster, Douglas, and Robert Weimann. *Prologues to Shakespeare's Theatre*. Routledge, 2004.

Burton, Robert. *The Anatomy of Melancholy*. Ed. Holbrook Jackson. New York Review Books, 2001.

Calvin, John. "A Sermon of Maister. Iohn Caluine, vpon the first Epistle of Paul, to Timothie, published for the benefite and edifying of the Churche of God [Online]." http://www.truecovenanter.com/calvin/calvin_19_on_Timothy.html.

Carlson, Eric Josef. *Marriage and the English Reformation*. Blackwell, 1994.

Clark, Stuart. "King James's Daemonologie: Witchcraft and Kingship." In *The Damned Art: Essays in the Literature of Witchcraft*, edited by Sydney Anglo, 156– 81. Routledge, 1977.

"Certain Sermons or Homilies Appointed to be Read in Churches" (Oxford, 1822), p.469, qtd in Roland Mushat Frye, "Macbeth's Usurping Wife." *Renaissance News*, Vol. 8, No. 2 (summer, 1955), pp. 102-105.

Coe, Charles Norton. *Demi-Devil: The Character of Shakespeare's Villains*. Bookman Associates 1963.

Coleridge, Samuel Taylor, *Shakespearean Criticism*, ed. Thomas Middleton Raysor, 2nd ed. (New York, 1960).

"The Creation, in *The Towneley Plays*," ed. Martin Stevens and A. C. Cawley. Published for the Early English Text Society by the Oxford University Press, 1994, vol. 1, ll. 132-36, 7.

Dash, Irene G. *Wooing, Wedding, and Power: Women in Shakespeare's Plays*. Columbia University Press, 1981.

Delgado deTorres, Olivia. "Reflections of Patriarchy and Rebellion of Daughters in Shakespeare's Merchant of Venice and Othello." *Interpretation: A Journal of Political Philosophy.* 21:3 (1994), 333-351.

Detmer, Emily. "Civilizing Subordination: Domestic Violence and The Taming of the Shrew." *Shakespeare Quarterly.* 48.3 (1997): 278.

DiLorenzo, Thomas James. "Abraham Lincoln, U.S. Authoritarianism and Manipulated History." Exclusive interview, Sunday, May 16, 2010, *The Daily Bell.* http://www.thedailybell.com/1053/Thomas-DiLorenzo-Abraham-Lincoln-US-Authoritarianism-Free-Market-History.html.

Dodds, W. M. T. "The Character of Angelo in 'Measure for Measure'" *The Modern Language Review,* 41 (3), Jul, 1946, 246-255. http://www.jstor.org/stable/3717058.

Dreher, Diane E. *Domination and Defiance: Fathers and Daughters in Shakespeare.* University of Kentucky Press, 1986.

Dusinberre, Juliet. *Shakespeare and the Nature of Women, 3rd Ed.* Amazon Kindle Edition, 2003, location 783.

El-Hai, Jack. "Black and White and Red" *American Heritage.* http:www.americanheritage.com/articles/magazine/ah/1991/3/1991.

Elizabeth I's *Speech to the Troops at Tilbury*, 1588. http://www.nationalcenter.org/ElizabethITilbury.html.

Evans, G. B., ed. *The Riverside Shakespeare.* Houghton Mifflin Co., 1974.

Ferguson, Wallace K. *The Renaissance in Historical Thought.* University of Toronto Press, 2006.

Fiedler, Leslie A. *The Stranger in* Shakespeare. Barnes and Noble, 1972.

Fremouw, William, Ragatz, Laurie., Schwartz, Rebecca., Anderson, Ryan., Schenk, Allison and Kania, Kristina. "Criminal Thinking, Aggression, and Psychopathy in Late High School Bully-Victims -poster" Westin Bayshore Hotel, Vancouver, BC, Canada, Mar 17, 2010 <Not Available>. 2011-06-05. http://www.allacademic.com/meta/p406323_index.html.

Frey, Charles. "Shakespeare's Imperiled and Chastening Daughters of Romance." *South Atlantic Bulletin* 43.4 (Nov. 1978): p125-140.

Fulton, Thomas. "Shakespeare's Everyman: Measure for Measure and English Fundamentalism." *Journal of Medieval and Early Modern Studies* 40:1, Winter 2010, 120.

Galton, Francis. *English Men of Science: Their Nature and Nurture.* Macmillan and Co., 1874.

Garber, Marjorie. *Shakespeare After All.* Anchor Books 2004.

Glaveanu, Vlad Petre. "From Mythology to Psychology - an essay on the Archaic Psychology in Greek Myths." *European Journal of Psychology*, Vol 1, No (2005). Accessed on-line at http://ejop.psychopen.eu/article/view/351/html.

Goddard, Harold. *The Meaning of Shakespeare, Volume 1.* University of Chicago Press, 1960.

Goldberg, Carl. "Iago's Malevolence" in *Jihad and Sacred Vengeance*, Ed. Jerry S. Piven and Chris Boyd (iUniverse), 2002.

Granville-Barker, Henry. *Prefaces to Shakespeare.* Hill and Wang, 1970.

Gunther, G. D. *Shakespeare as Traditional Artist.* Johansen Printing and Publishing, 1994.

Gürle, F. Meltem. "Reasoning with the Murderer: The killing of Clarence in Richard III," *Journal of the Wooden O*, Volume 11, Southern Utah UP, 2011, 56. https://www.academia.edu/3319057/Reasoning_with_the_Murderer_The_Killing _of_Clarence_in_Richard_III

Hankey, Julie. "Victorian Portias: Shakespeare's Borderline Heroine." *Shakespeare Quarterly*; Winter 1994; 45, 4.

Hare, R. *PCL-R 20-item checklist.*
http://www.angelfire.com/zine2/narcissism/psychopathy_checklist.htm

Heldriss of Cornwall. *Silence.* Roche-Mahdi, Sarah (ed. and trans... Colleagues Press Ltd, 1992.

Higgins, John C. "Justice, Mercy, and Dialectical Genres in Measure for Measure and Promos and Cassandra." *English Literary Renaissance.* Oxford, UK: Blackwell Publishing. Ltd, 2012, 262.

Hooker, Richard, "Early Christianity," 1996
http://www.wsu.edu/~dee/CHRIST/AUG.HTM.

Hunt, Maurice. "Being Precise in Measure for Measure." *Renascence,* 243 (4) Summer 2006, 261.

Katz, Steven. *The Holocaust in Historical Context, Vol. I.* Oxford University Press, 1994.

Kaul, Mythili "Background" in *Othello: New Essays* by Black Writers, Ed. Mythili Kaul. Howard University Press, 1997.

Kantovitz, Ernst H. *The King's Two Bodies: A Study in Medieval Political Theology.* (Princeton. Princeton University Press, 1959.

Keane, Marie-Henry. "Woman seen as a 'problem' and as 'solution' in the theological anthropology of the Early Fathers: Considering the Consequences [Online]." Paper presented to *Catholic Theological Society of South Africa,* October 1987. http://www.catherinecollegelibrary.net/theology/keane1.asp.

Kehler, Dorothea. "Echoes of the Induction in The Taming of the Shrew." *Renaissance Papers* 1986.

King James I. *Works* (1592).
http://www.wwnorton.com/college/history/ralph/workbook/ralprs20.htm.

King, Stephen. The Dead Zone. New American Library, 1979.

Knowlton, E. C. "The Genius of Spencer," *Studies in Philology,* XXV (1928)

Knox, John. "First Blast of the Trumpet Against the Monstrous Regiment of Women (1558) [Online]." http://www.gutenberg.org/files/9660/9660-h/9660-h.htm.

Koernig, Bob. "The Puritan Beliefs" at http://www3.gettysburg.edu/~tshannon/hist106web/site15/BOBS/puritanbeliefpage11.htm.

Kolb, James J. "The Taming of the Shrew: Study Guide." Hofstra University, Department of Drama and Dance, 1996, 10-12.

Johnston, Joni E. "Children Who are Cruel to Animals: When to Worry." *Psychology Today*. April 27, 2011. http://www.psychologytoday.com/blog/the-human-equation/201104/children-who-are-cruel-animals-when-worry.

Jones, Eldred D. *The Elizabethan Image of Africa*. Univ. Press of Virginia, 1971

Jordan, Constance. *Shakespeare's Monarchies: Ruler and Subject in the Romances*. Cornell University Press, 1999.

Jorgensen, Paul A. "Shakespeare's Coriolanus: Elizabethan Soldier." *PMLA*, Vol. 64, No. 1 (Mar., 1949).

Laroque, François. "The Jack Cade Scenes Reconsidered: Popular Rebellion, Utopia, or Carnival?" *Shakespeare and Cultural Traditions: The Selected Proceedings of the International Shakespeare Association World Congress*, Tokyo, 1991. Ed. Tetsuo Kishi,

Stanley Wells, and Roger Pringle. University of Delaware Press, 1994.

Laslett, Peter, Karla Oosterveen and Richard M. Smith (eds.), *Bastardy and its Comparative History*. Arnold, 1980.

"Last Diary Entry of John Wilkes Booth." http://law2.umkc.edu/faculty/projects/ftrials/lincolnconspiracy/boothdiary.html.

Lee, Adam. "That Monstrous Regiment." *Daylight Atheism* (blog), March 8, 2006. http://www.patheos.com/blogs/daylightatheism/2006/03/that-monstrous-regiment/.

Lindroth, Mary. "'Some device of further misery': Taymor's Titus brings Shakespeare to film audiences with a twist." *Literature/Film Quarterly* 29.2 (2001): 107-115.

"The London Stone" (2002). *The Hitchhikers Guide to the Galaxy: Earth Edition.* http://h2g2.com/edited_entry/A863309.

Lowell, Francis C. *Maid of Heaven*, Chapter 5 http://www.maidofheaven.com/joanofarc_gower_imprisonment_trial.asp.

Manning, Robert B. *Village Revolts: Social Protest and Popular Disturbances in England, 1509-1640.* Oxford University Press, 1988.

Marlowe, Christopher. *The Complete Plays*, Steane, J. B., ed. Penguin, 1969. "Macbeth's Curse: Link between Sleeplessness and Paranoia Identified." http://www.sciencedaily.com/releases/2009/01/090108150857.htm.

Maslin, Janet. *Soft! What Light? It's Flash, Romeo."* New York Times, (Nov 1, 1996).

McLaughlin, John J. "The Dynamics of Power in King Lear: An Adlerian Interpretation." *Shakespeare Quarterly*, Vol. 29, No. 1 (Winter, 1978), p. 38

Montefiore, Simon Sebag. "The Thrill of the Kill: Inside the head of a Russian hit man. Mysterious thrills or doing God's will?" *Psychology Today*: published on January 1, 1993 - last reviewed on June 20, 2012. Accessed at https://www.psychologytoday.com/articles/200910/the-thrill-the-kill.

More, Thomas. *The history of King Richard the thirde.* http://www.luminarium.org/renascence-editions/r3.html.

Muir, Kenneth and Philip Edwards, Ed's. *Aspects of Macbeth.* Cambridge University Press, 1977.

Myers, D. G. "The New Historicism in Literary Study." Originally published in *Academic Questions* 2 (Winter 1988-89): 27-36. Accessed at http://dgmyers.blogspot.com/p/new-historicism-in-literary-study.html.

Neale, J. E. *Queen Elizabeth I: A Biography.* London: Jonathan Cape, 1954.

Newman, Karen. "Renaissance Family Politics and Shakespeare's The Taming of the Shrew." *English Literals/ Renaissance*. 16:1 (1986):90.

"Nuns: Origins and history." *New Advent Catholic Encyclopedia* [Online]. http://www.newadvent.org/cathen/11164a.htm.

Oberg, M. L. (1999). *Dominion and civility: English imperialism and Native America, 1585-1685.* Cornell University Press.

"Prefaces to Shakespeare," ed. Muriel St. Clare Byrne (1946; rpt., Princeton Univ. Press, 1963.

Prosser, Eleanor. *Hamlet and Revenge, 2nd ed.* Stanford University Press, 1971.

Richardson, William. "On Shakespeare's Imitation of Female Characters (addressed to a friend)." 1788. http://www.shakespearean.org.uk/fem1-ric.htm.

Robinson, Bryan (March 18, 2004). "What drives thrill killings". *ABC News.* http://abcnews.go.com/US/story?id=96770&page=1.

Rousseau, Jean-Jacques (1754), "Discourse on the Origin of Inequality, part two", *The Basic Political Writings*, Hackett.

Rosenberg, Marvin. "Macbeth and Lady Macbeth in the eighteenth and nineteenth centuries" in Brown, John Russell, ed. *Focus on Macbeth.* London: Routledge & Kegan Paul, 1982.

Rosenberg, Marvin. *The Masks of Othello.* University of California Press, 1961.

Rosenthal, Daniel. *Shakespeare on Screen.* Octopus Publishing Group, 2000.

Rothbard, Murray N. "The Puritans 'Purify': Theocracy in Massachusetts." In *Conceived in Liberty, Volume 1* (Mises Institute, 1999 [1975]). http://mises.org/page/1427.

Rowe, M. W. "The Dissolution of Goodness: Measure for Measure and Classical Ethics." *International Journal of the Classical Tradition* /Summer 1998, 42.

Russell, Jeffrey Burton. *The Prince of Darkness.* Cornell University Press, 1988.

Samaha, Joel. *Law and Order in Historical Perspective: The Case of Elizabethan Essex.*
Academic Press, 1974.

Sears, L. C. *Shakespeare's Philosophy of Evil.* The Christopher Publishing House,
1974.

Shakespeare's Moor: The Sources and Representations.
,http://www.geocities.com/Wellesley/7261/gripes5.html?20084 .

Siebert, Charles. "The Animal-Cruelty Syndrome." *The New York Times*, June 11,
2010.
http://www.nytimes.com/2010/06/13/magazine/13dogfightingt.html?pagewanted=
all&_r=0.

Spencer, Charles. "The Taming of the Shrew at the Novello Theatre," (review).
The Telegraph: 6 Feb 2009.
http://www.telegraph.co.uk/culture/culturecritics/charlesspencer/4687431/The-
aming-of-the-Shrew-at-the-Novello-Theatre-review.html.

Stratos Pahis. Corruption in Our Courts: What It Looks Like and Where It Is
Hidden. *The Yale Law Journal*, 118:1900, 2009. http://judicial-discipline-
reform.org/docs/Corruption_in_courts-SPahis_YaleLJ_09.pdf.

Stirling, Brents. "Anti-democracy in Shakespeare: A Re-survey." *Modern Language
Quarterly*, 1941, 487-8.

Stirling, Brents. "Shakespeare's Mob Scenes: A Reinterpretation," *Huntington
Library Quarterly*, Vol. 8, No. 3 (May, 1945), 214.

Spivack, Bernard. *Shakespeare and the Allegory of Evil.* Columbia University Press,
1958.

Tillyard, E. M. W. *The Elizabethan World Picture.* Vintage Books, 1942.

Time, Victoria M. *Shakespeare's Criminals: Criminology, Fiction, and Drama.*
Greenwood Press, 1999.

"The Trial of Joan of Arc, Being the verbatim report of the proceedings from the
Orleans Manuscript," translated by W.S. Scott, 1956, Associated Book Sellers.
http://smu.edu/ijas/1431trial.html.

Vergil, Polydore. *Anglica Historia*, Chapter XXV (1534).
http://www.philological.bham.ac.uk/polverg/25eng.html

"Volume VI. The Drama to 1642, Part Two XIV. The Puritan Attack upon the Stage. § 2. Theological and moral objections." *The Cambridge History of English and American Literature in 18 Volumes* (1907–21). http://bartleby.com/216/1402.html.

Warner, Maria. *Joan of Arc: The Image of Female Heroism*. The University of California Press, 2000.

Weinraub, Bernard. "Audiences in Love with the Doomed Lovers." *New York Times*, (Nov 1, 1996).

Wheeler, Richard P. "Introduction" in *Critical Essays on Shakespeare's Measure for Measure*. G. K. Hall and Co., 1999.

Widmayer, Martha. "'To Sin In Loving Virtue': Angelo of Measure for Measure." *Texas Studies in Literature and Language*, Summer 2007, 49(2), 155-80.

Wilkinson, Robert. "The Merchant Royall: A Sermon Preached at White-Hall, 1607." ed. Stanley Pargellis (Herrin, I ll. 1945)

Wills, Gary. *Witches and Jesuits: Shakespeare's Macbeth*. Oxford University Press, 1995.

Printed in Great Britain
by Amazon